PHILOSOPHY IN THE 20TH CENTURY: CATHOLIC AND CHRISTIAN

PHILOSOPHY IN THE 20TH CENTURY:
CATHOLIC AND CHRISTIAN

Volume I:

AN ANNOTATED BIBLIOGRAPHY OF PHILOSOPHY IN CATHOLIC THOUGHT 1900-1964

Edited by George F. McLean, O.M.I.

FREDERICK UNGAR PUBLISHING CO.
NEW YORK

PREFACE

This comprehensive and annotated bibliography of works on philosophy in Catholic thought has been compiled as an aid to the professor, student, and general reader.[1]

Works have been included which are for the most part formally philosophical in character, include some extended philosophic content, or make extensive comparisons of the nonphilosophic with the philosophic approaches. The term "Catholic thought" is understood as extending to works in or about the tradition of St. Augustine, St. Thomas Aquinas and other Scholastics, as well as to works by or about Catholics of the more recent existential, personalist, or phenomenological orientations. The bibliography does not include works in the history of philosophy, unless they are intended to clarify the relation of various historical positions to the above-mentioned philosophy or are evaluated in the light of that philosophy.

The books in Part I of the bibliography are divided into thirteen chapters, corresponding to the accustomed subject division of philosophy courses. Part II, consisting of chapters XIV-XVII, is concerned with different schools of Christian philosophy: Augustinian, Thomistic, Franciscan, and personalist-existentialist-

---

[1] Earlier bibliographies in this field: (A) Vernon J. Bourke, *Thomistic Bibliography, 1920-1940, Modern Schoolman, XXI* (1945). This includes books and articles and also covers theological topics, but is without annotations. (B) Thomas R. Leigh, "An Annotated Bibliography of Books for Seminarians," *The Catholic Library World,* III (1959), 273-84. This list contains 162 books. (C) Donald Smythe, *Focus, an Annotated Bibliography of Catholic Reading* (Washington, D. C.: National Newman Club Federation, 1962). The philosophy section of *Focus* is more limited than the list by Thomas Leigh. (D) Sr. M. Regis (ed.), *The Catholic Bookman's Guide* (New York: Hawthorn, 1962). On philosophy this contains only a survey of the history of philosophy and a chapter on the philosophy of science. However, it can serve as a perfect complement to the present bibliography.

phenomenological. While the individual studies in Part I generally reflect the thought of one of these schools, Part II groups together the works concerning these currents of thought as such. To accomplish this, it has been necessary to include many works of an historical nature on the key figures and their schools. Cross references are provided between Parts I and II and between particular chapters.

Within each chapter the books are arranged alphabetically by author. For each work the following information is supplied, wherever possible: author, title, number of volumes, translator, original title, most recent edition and revision, series and number, city, publisher, year of most recent cloth publication, year of first appearance in any language (in parentheses), number of pages, bibliography, and index. Because of the particular usefulness of paper editions to students, the fact of such editions is noted within parentheses simply by the word "paper" or by the name and number of the paper edition if this differs from the previously noted information.

In addition to the basic data of publication, a brief annotation is given for each book. These annotations generally include an indication of the nature of the work where this is not clear from the title. This is followed by a statement of the contents or mode of approach, and by any critical notes. To this is appended a letter indicating the level of readership for which the work might be of service. The key to this classification is the following:

A   Those readers without a formal introduction to the study of philosophy;

B   Students enrolled in formal courses of introduction to philosophy as a whole or to that major division in which the book falls;

C   Undergraduate students doing special research in the area treated by the book; particularly capable students in introductory courses in the major areas of philosophy; or students in more advanced (graduate) courses;

D   Scholars.

These divisions should also enable those who are not students to gauge the relevance of the books to their own reading interests.

These annotations reflect the judgment of over one hundred philosophy professors who met in The Catholic University of America Philosophy Workshop, "Teaching Thomism Today," in June, 1962, the evaluations of a number of specialists in the various areas, and of many of the more important reviews. Ultimately, however, they must be the responsibility of this author.

Finally, there is appended to the annotation a selection of the major reviews, indicating the reviewer and the journal, its volume number, year, and pages.

The works themselves were culled on the basis of an exhaustive review of the shelves and shelf lists of the magnificent research library of the Ecclesiastical Research Center, Sedes Sapientiae, the University of Ottawa; of the Mullen Memorial Library, The Catholic University of America; of the library of the Jesuit Fathers' Scholasticate, Weston College; and of the library of the Oblate Fathers' Scholasticate, Oblate College, Washington, D. C. This has been complemented by research at the Library of Congress, the Widener Library, and other libraries of the Washington, Boston, and Montreal areas. To all of these, for their generous hospitality, and to the many who have aided in various ways in carrying this work to completion, the author expresses his sincere appreciation.

G.F.M.

ABBREVIATIONS

A	America
AAS	Acta Apostolicae Sedis
ABR	American Benedictine Review
ACHR	American Catholic Historical Society Records
ACPA	American Catholic Philosophical Association Proceedings
ACSR	American Catholic Sociological Review
AER	American Ecclesiastical Review
AM	Ave Maria
An	Angelicum
AQ	Anthropological Quarterly
Bl	Blackfriars (now, New Blackfriars)
BR	Benedictine Review
C	Commonweal
CAQ	Catholic Art Quarterly
CB	Classical Bulletin
CBER	Catholic Business Education Review
CBQ	Catholic Biblical Quarterly
CC	Cross Currents
CCr	Cross & Crown
CD	Catholic Documents
CE	Catholic Educator
CER	Catholic Educational Review
CHR	Catholic Historical Review
CJ	Catholic Journalist
CL	Catholic Lawyer
CLa	Catholic Layman
CLM	Clergy Monthly
CM	Catholic Mind
Cn	Continuum
CR	Clergy Review
Cr	Critic
CSJ	Catholic School Journal

CTS	Catholic Theological Society of America Proceedings
CUL	Catholic University Law Review
CW	Catholic World
D	Dominicana
DC	Doctor Communis
DmC	Documentation Catholique
DR	Downside Review
DS	Dominican Studies
DuR	Dublin Review (now, Wiseman Review)
EC	Ephemerides Carmeliticae
ECQ	Eastern Church Quarterly (now, One in Christ)
ED	Euntes Docete
EM	Ephemerides Mariologicae
ER	Ecclesiastical Review
Et	Etudes
F	Furrow
FL	Fordham Law Review
FS	Franciscan Studies
G	Gregorianum
GCP	Guild of Catholic Psychiatrist Bulletin
GLR	Georgetown Law Review
HB	Historical Bulletin
HJ	Heythrop Journal
HC	Herder Correspondence (originally, Herder Korrespondenz)
HPR	Homiletic and Pastoral Review
I	Information (now, Catholic Layman)
IER	Irish Ecclesiastical Record
IJE	International Journal of Ethics
IM	Irish Monthly
IPQ	International Philosophical Quarterly
IR	Interracial Review
ITQ	Irish Theological Quarterly
J	Jubilee
JRI	Journal of Religious Instruction
Ju	Jurist
LA	Liturgical Arts
LLR	Loyola Law Review
LQ	Linacre Quarterly
LV	Lumière et Vie

LVt	Lumen Vitae
MD	Maison Dieu
MeS	Medieval Studies
MF	Miscellanea Franciscana
Mo	Month
MS	Modern Schoolman
Ms	Manuscripta
NA	Nuntius Aulae
NCEA	National Catholic Educational Association Bulletin
NDL	Notre Dame Lawyer
NLF	Natural Law Forum
NRT	Nouvelle Revue Théologique
NS	New Scholasticism
OC	One in Christ
P	Priest
PL	Pastoral Life
PrS	Priestly Studies
PS	Philosophical Studies
Ps	Perspectives
PSp	Pope Speaks
PT	Philosophy Today
R	Relations
RE	Religious Education
RF	Razon y Fe
RN	Revue Nouvelle
RP	Review of Politics
RPL	Revue Philosophique de Louvain
RR	Review for Religious
RSE	Review of Social Economy
RU	Review of the University of Ottawa
S	Sign
Sa	Sapientia
SFB	Sister Formation Bulletin
SJLR	St. John's Law Review
SJR	Social Justice Review
SM	St. Meinrad Essays
SO	Social Order (no longer published)
St	Studies
T	Thought

Ta	Tablet
TD	Theology Digest
Tm	Thomist
To	Torch
TR	Traditio
TS	Theological Studies
U	Unitas
VI	Vie Intellectuelle
VS	Vie Spirituelle
W	Work
WJ	World Justice
Wo	Worship
WR	Wiseman Review

CONTENTS

PART I *Subject Areas of Christian Philosophy: 1900-1964*

    I   Research Instruments 3

    II   Introduction and Survey of Philosophy 8

    III   Logic 38

    IV   Epistemology 53

    V   Cosmology: Philosophy of Physical Nature, Philosophy of Science 67

    VI   Psychology 84

    VII   Metaphysics 113

    VIII   Theodicy—Natural Theology 145

    IX   General Ethics 172

    X   Special Ethics 206
- A. Legal Ethics 208
- B. Medical Ethics 210
- C. Sociological Ethics 216
- D. Domestic Ethics 218
- E. Political Ethics 221
- F. Economic Ethics 227
- G. Industrial Ethics 230
- H. Marxian Ethics 234
- I. International Ethics 239

    XI   Esthetics: Philosophy of Art 244

    XII   Philosophy of Education 252

    XIII   Philosophy of History 262

PART II   *Schools of Christian Philosophy: 1900-1964*

XIV   Augustinian Philosophy   269
XV   Saint Thomas Aquinas   282
XVI   Franciscan Philosophy   308
XVII Personalist-Existential-Phenomenological
      Philosophy   319

INDEX   337

PART I

Subject Areas of
Christian Philosophy: 1900-1964

CHAPTER I

Research Instruments

This chapter contains a list of general source materials, such as dictionaries, lexicons, bibliographies, and periodicals, useful in research and teaching in the area of Christian philosophy. Periodic general information concerning these materials can be found in the quarterly "Chronicle of Philosophy" by the present author, appearing in *The New Scholasticism*. Lists of general source materials in all languages appear in *The Catholic Bookman's Guide* and in the *Introduction to Philosophy* by L. De Raeymaeker, both of which are mentioned in greater detail later in this chapter.

AMERICAN CATHOLIC PHILOSOPHICAL ASSOCIATION PROCEEDINGS. Annual. Washington, D.C.: The American Catholic Philosophical Association, 1926—

I-VI   Miscellaneous Subjects
VII   *Political Philosophy*
VIII   *Current British and American Realism*
IX   *Philosophy of Society*
X   *Philosophy of Religion*
XI   *Philosophy of the Sciences*
XII   *Christian Philosophy and the Social Sciences*
XIII   *Philosophy of Education*
XIV   *Causality in Current Philosophy*
XV   *Philosophy of the State*
XVI   *The Problem of Liberty*
XVII   *Philosophy and Order*
XVIII   *Truth in the Contemporary Crisis*
XIX   *Philosophy and Reconstruction*
XX   *Philosophy of Democracy*
XXI   *Philosophy of Being*
XXII   *The Absolute and the Relative*
XXIII   *Philosophy and Finality*
XXIV   *The Natural Law and International Relations*
XXV   *The Nature of Man*
XXVI   *Philosophy and the Experimental Sciences*
XXVII   *Philosophy and Unity*
XXVIII   *The Existence and Nature of God*
XXIX   *Knowledge and Expression*
XXX   *Role of Philosophy in the Catholic Liberal College*
XXXI   *Ethics and Other Knowledge*
XXXII   *The Role of the Christian Philosopher*
XXXIII   *Contemporary American Philosophy*
XXXIV   *Analytic Philosophy*
XXXV   *Philosophy and Psychiatry*
XXXVI   *Justice*
XXXVII   *Philosophy in a Pluralistic Society*
XXXVIII   *The History and Philosophy of Science*
XXXIX   *Philosophy and the Arts*
Index of THE PROCEEDINGS OF THE AMERICAN CATHOLIC PHILOSOPHICAL ASSOCIATION, *Vols. I—XXXIX (1926-1965)*.

BOURKE, Vernon J. *Thomistic Bibliography, 1920-1940.* Supplement to *The Modern Schoolman,* XXI (1945) . viii, 312 pp. Indices. (Paper)

A selected listing of both books and articles, without annotation. The work is divided into sections on the life, works, philosophy, theology, and historical relations of St. Thomas Aquinas. Each area of philosophy has its distinct subdivision. B-D

> *See:* D 30 (1945) 142-43; FS 26 (1945) 462; MS 23 (1945) 48-49; RUO 15 (1945) 248; T 20 (1945) 563-64; Tm 8 (1945) 411; TS 6 (1945) 435-37.

CATHOLIC BOOKLIST. Chicago, Ill.: Rosary College, 1942.

An annual prepared for the National Catholic Book Week, under the auspices of the Catholic Library Association. It includes books of interest to philosophers, published during the preceding year. There are brief but effective annotations. B-D

DEFERRARI, Roy J. *A Latin-English Dictionary of St. Thomas Aquinas, Based on the* SUMMA THEOLOGICA *and Selected Passages of His Other Works.* Boston: St. Paul, 1960. 1115 pp.

An abridged edition of the 1948-1955 *Lexicon of St. Thomas Aquinas.* It contains all the words and meanings given in the *Lexicon* and most of the research value, but the omission of examples more easily allows a choice of a wrong meaning from among the many definitions given. B-C

———, and BARRY, Sr. Mary I. *A Complete Index of the* SUMMA THEOLOGICA *of St. Thomas Aquinas.* Washington, D.C.: The Catholic University of America Press, 1956. 386 pp.

A listing of terms of philosophical or theological import and places in which they appear in the *Summa theologica.* While not the originally projected complete concordance, it is very useful for research. C-D

> *See:* IER 90 (58) 50; J. Jelinek, MS 35 (1958) 145; B. Wuellner, NS 31 (1957) 425; W. Clarke, T 32 (1957) 630; C. Whelan, TS 18 (1957) 123.

———. *A Lexicon of St. Thomas Aquinas Based on the* SUMMA THEOLOGICA *and Selected Passages of His Other Works.* 5 vols. Washington, D.C.: The Catholic University of America Press, 1948-1953.

A listing of terms, their meaning, examples of their use, and, where possible, a definition in the words of St. Thomas Aquinas. Though not all the philosophical implications of each term are detailed, it is an invaluable research instrument. C-D

See: J. Fenton, 120 (1949) 154-55; Bl 30 (1949) 133-34; J. O'Donnell, CHR 35 (1950) 486-87; T. James CLW 21 (1950) 246; D 34 (1949) 44-45; A. Wolter, FS 9 (1949) 457-58; J. Berkmyre, HPR 50 (1949) 90; E. Roelker, J 10 (1950) 113.

GALLAGHER, Donald A., and GALLAGHER, Idella. *The Achievement of Jacques and Raissa Maritain, a Bibliography, 1906-1961*. Garden City, N.Y.: Doubleday, 1962. 256 pp.

A chronological list, without annotation, of all editions and translations. C-D

See: CLW 32 (1961) 281-93; J. Evans, NS 37 (1964) 381-83; RR 22 (1963) 487.

INAGAKI, Bernard R. *Scholastic Bibliography in Japan*. Nagoya, Japan: Catholic University of Nagoya, 1957. 49 pp.

Works on scholastic philosophy published in Japan, with some non-Japanese titles added. The work reflects some initial integration of the philosophies of East and West. C-D

PETERSON, Gilbert C., and Sr. MELANIA GRACE. *Books for Catholic Colleges: A Supplement to Shaw's* LIST OF BOOKS FOR COLLEGE LIBRARIES. Chicago, Ill.: Catholic Library Association, 1948-1955.

The philosophy section, pp. 56-64, includes titles and data for cataloguing, without annotations. B-C

REYNOLDS, Sr. Mary Regis. (ed.) *The Catholic Bookman's Guide: A Critical Evaluation of Catholic Literature*. New York: Hawthorn, 1962. 638 pp. Index.

Of special interest, in addition to chapters on general bibliographical sources, are the chapters on the history of philosophy by V. Bourke and J. Collins, and on the philosophy of science by J. Weisheiple. Unfortunately, most major philosophical areas, such as the philosophy of man, metaphysics and ethics, have been entirely omitted. B-C

See: RF 168 (1963) 280; RR 22 (1963) 607.

SMYTHE, Donald. *Focus: An Annotated Bibliography of Catholic Reading.* Washington, D.C.: National Newman Club Federation, 1962. 134 pp.

The selection of works in philosophy is limited to but one section of this brief work. Nevertheless, its choice of works is apt and current, and its annotations are clear and helpful. A-B

WUELLNER, Bernard. *Dictionary of Scholastic Philosophy.* Milwaukee: Bruce, 1956. xvi, 138 pp. Bibliography.

A vocabulary of technical terms in philosophy. The clarification and distinction of meanings of individual terms are sometimes inadequate because of the excessive brevity unfortunately so common in dictionaries. A-B

See: CR 41 (1956) 765; V. Bourke, NS 31 (1957) 266; PS 6 (1956) 239; TS 17 (1956) 447.

————. *Summary of Scholastic Principles.* Chicago, Ill.: Loyola University, 1956. 164 pp.

A unique catalogue of the initial and distinct philosophical insights from which flow the reasoning which constitutes the various areas of Scholastic philosophy. The index and teaching aids help to make it useful as a reference work. B-C

See: NS 32 (1958) 145.

CHAPTER II

Introduction and Survey of Philosophy

This chapter is devoted to materials on Christian philosophy which are introductory or general in character. Here, the term "introductory" is meant to designate not only those works explicitly planned as a first book on philosophy, but also more profound works on the general nature of philosophy. The chapter does not include works on the history of philosophy, though a good case can be made for the historical approach as an introduction to philosophy.[1]

The reader is referred to Chapters I, V, VI, and VIII of *A Bibliography of Christian Philosophy and Contemporary Issues* by the same editor.

Since many introductions are written as surveys of the content of philosophy, general works on Christian philosophy also are included in this chapter. Such works range from complete surveys of the whole field of philosophy in multi-volume sets to partial surveys concentrating on a variety of subjects or key philosophic problems. This chapter also includes collections of philosophic essays not restricted to any particular branch of philosophy or school of thought; those works which are thus restricted will be included in the appropriate subsequent chapter. Finally, there are evaluations of modern thought from the viewpoint of Christian philosophy and surveys of Christian philosophy in relation to contemporary trends.

---

[1] See Etienne Gilson's general introduction in Armand Maurer, *Medieval Philosophy*, Vol. II of *A History of Philosophy*, ed. Etienne Gilson (New York: Random House, 1962), pp. vii-xiii.

ARMSTRONG, Arthur H., and MARKUS, R. A. *Christian Faith and Greek Philosophy*. New York: Sheed and Ward, 1964 (1960). ix, 162 pp. Index.

A study of the development of the classical understanding of man and reality under the impetus of the Christian vision. The first part, by A. H. Armstrong, surveys the structure of reality: God, man, and the material universe. The second section, by R. A. Markus, treats such problems as knowledge, love, and faith. B-C

See: CR 46 (1961) 499; DR 79 (1961) 63; IER 96 (1961) 329; R. Walker, Ta 215 (1961) 14.

BANDAS, Rudolph G. *Contemporary Philosophy and Thomistic Principles*. Milwaukee: Bruce, 1932. 350 pp.

A survey of the ways in which Thomism can contribute to work on problems in modern thought. The section on religious experi-ence points to the contribution of theology to the understanding of some authentically philosophical positions. Apologetic in ap-proach. B

See: IER 40 (1932) 424-27.

BASCHAB, Charles R. *A Manual of Neo-Scholastic Philosophy*. 3d ed. revised. St. Louis: Herder, 1930 (1924). xviii, 460 pp.

A survey of most areas of Scholastic philosophy, with individual sections on cosmology, psychology, metaphysics, and theodicy. The material is presented in essay, rather than in thesis, form. B

See: C 1 (1924) 52; CW 118 (1924) 869.

BOCHENSKI, Innocentius (J.) M. *Philosophy: An Introduction*. Trans. by W. Newell from *Weg zum philosophischen Den-ken*. Dordrecht: Reidel, 1963 (1958). 112 pp.

A series of radio talks delivered in Bavaria as an introduction to modern, especially twentieth century, philosophy. Particular emphasis is placed on the special characteristics of this philosophy in the English-speaking world. A-B

BRAUER, Theodore, *et al. Thomistic Principles in a Catholic School*. St. Louis: Herder, 1949 (1943). x, 321 pp. Index.

Essays by professors at the College of St. Thomas. After a general statement on the nature of the curriculum and the place of religion, it traces the contribution of Thomism to theology, economics, and the modern social and physical sciences. C

See: CER 43 (1960) 59; D 28 (1943) 207-208; FS 25 (1944) 107-109; HPR 43 (1943) 1138; MS 21 (1943) 54-55; NS 17 (1943) 384; S 23 (1943) 123; TS 4 (1943) 464-65.

BREMOND, André. *Philosophy in the Making: A Study in Wonder and Order.* New York: Benziger, 1939. viii, 222 pp.

An historically-oriented introduction to philosophy written in a light, literary vein. Considerable attention is given to the ancient philosophers and to Descartes. A-B

See: A 61 (1939) 406; AM 50 (1939) 187; C 30 (1939) 223; T 14 (1939) 493.

BRENNAN, Robert E. (ed.) *Essays in Thomism.* New York: Sheed and Ward, 1942. ix, 427 pp. Bibliography, index.

The essays gravitate toward metaphysics, epistemology, and ethics. They are the products of some of the most fertile minds in Scholastic circles at the time. C

See: C 38 (1943) 53-55; CW 157 (1943) 98-99; D 28 (1943) 130-31; HPR 43 (1943) 958; MS 21 (1944) 186.

BRUCKMANN, William D. *Keystones and Theories of Philosophy: A Handbook to Aid in the Study of Philosophy.* New York: Benziger, 1946. viii, 230 pp.

A presentation of philosophical terms and problems in dictionary form. There is a general explanation of theories, a glossary of technical terms, and a brief historical conspectus accompanied by a chart. Its definitions can be of particular use to beginners. Frequently in conflict with usual Thomistic positions, like most works of this type, it tends toward labeling and oversimplification. A-B

See: AM 64 (1946) 539; CER 45 (1947) 381; CSJ 46 (1946) 32A; CW 164 (1947) 475-76; D 31 (1946) 292; ER 115 (1946) 314-15; MS 24 (1946) 58; S 26 (1946) 59; Tm 10 (1947) 130-31.

BRUNI, Gerardo. *Progressive Scholasticism.* Trans. by J. Zybura from *Riflessioni sulla scolastica*. St. Louis: Herder, 1929 (1927). xxxviii, 185 pp.

A study of the special problems implied in Scholasticism's confrontation with modern trends. The relation of faith and reason is reviewed in the modern context, and the developmental and historical character of truth is related to systems of truth, in particular to those of Aristotle and St. Thomas. The issues treated have taken on a renewed and special interest since the Second World War. C

See: A 42 (1929) 117; C 9 (1929) 574; C 11 (1929) 142; CW 130 (1929) 241.

BRUNNER, August. *Fundamental Questions of Philosophy*. Trans. by S. Raemers from *Die Grundfragen der Philosophie; ein systematischer Aufbau*. St. Louis: Herder, 1937 (1933). 350 pp.

An introduction to many areas of Scholastic philosophy. It is weak in its criticisms of modern philosophy, and clarity has suffered in the attempt to cover too much. Collateral reading. A-B

See: AM 46 (1937) 378; C 26 (1937) 444; DR 56 (1938) 214; IER 51 (1938) 108.

CANFIELD, Francis X. (ed.) *Philosophy and the Modern Mind* (Edward Cardinal Mooney Lecture Series, 1960-1961.) Detroit: Sacred Heart Seminary, 1961. 65 pp. (Paper)

Lectures by three outstanding American Catholic philosophers: V. Smith, "Modern Physics and Thomistic Philosophy"; J. Collins, "The Religious Theme in Existentialism"; and A. Pegis, "St. Thomas and the Origin of Creation." B-C

See: MS 39 (1962) 301.

COLLINS, William B. *Metaphysics and Man*. Dubuque, Iowa: Loras College, 1959. 332 pp.

A clearly written text covering most areas of rational psychology, metaphysics, and natural theology. The format's different type sizes underline effectively the order of presentation and argumentation. B

————. *Speculative Philosophy: A Survey for Beginners.* Dubuque, Iowa: Loras College, 1947. 477 pp. Appendix, index.

A general over-view, omitting formal logic and ethics. Effectively presented in essay rather than outline form, it contains an appendix on the historical positions on the theory of knowledge. B

CONNOLLY, Frederick. *Science Versus Philosophy.* New York: Philosophical Library, 1957. 90 pp.

A general introduction to the relations between the various intellectual virtues and between science, art, philosophy, and theology. The degrees of abstraction are treated only later in the work. A-B

See: D 42 (1957) 376; CER 56 (1958) 210; CSJ 59 (1959) 63; NS 32 (1958) 396; RUO 28 (1958) 404; PS 8 (1958) 247; Tm 21 (1958) 235; TS 18 (1957) 634.

CONWAY, Pierre H., and ASHLEY, Benedict. *The Liberal Arts in St. Thomas.* Washington, D.C.: Thomist, 1959. 74 pp.

The division of the liberal arts in the thought of St. Thomas as differing from modern and less realist divisions of knowledge. The place of philosophy is given special attention, as is the problem of the integration of knowledge. B-C

See: CER 59 (1961) 275; D 45 (1960) 186; IER 96 (1961) 261.

COTTER, Anthony C. *The A B C of Scholastic Philosophy.* Weston: Weston College, 1947. vii, 428 pp. Bibliography, index.

An expansion of the author's *Logic and Epistemology* to include both an introduction to philosophy and ontology. The book is clearly divided, following the thesis method, with an intensive development of definitions and the addition of a series of objections and their answers. B

CROONENBURG, Engelbert J. Van. *Gateway to Reality: An Introduction.* Pittsburgh: Duquesne University Press, 1963. x, 155 pp.

Written with a strong phenomenological emphasis, it treats the nature of philosophical experience and illustrates this experience by a discussion of authentic being and man, his fulfillment, and his meeting with the Absolute as person. A fine introduction to the phenomenological method. B-C

D'ARCY, Martin D. *Of God and Man.* Wilkes Barre, Pa.: Dimension, 1964. ix, 173 pp.

A series of brief reflections on points of key philosophical and theological interest. The passages are approximately a page and a half in length, and of the broadest range, but they present the nucleus of many insights by this important thinker. A-B

DONDEYNE, Albert. *Contemporary European Thought and Christian Faith.* See VIII.

————. *Faith and the World.* See VIII.

DOOLAN, Aegidius. *Philosophy for the Layman.* 2d. ed. revised. Dublin: Dominican, 1954. 246 pp.

A collection of essays and radio talks on most key philosophical issues. The manner is both informal and informative. A-B

See: CR 40 (1955) 58; IER 83 (1955) 78.

————. *Revival of Thomism.* Dublin: Clonmore and Reynolds, 1951. 54 pp.

A brief survey of the nature of Thomism and of the renewal of Thomistic studies, with notes on Vincent McNabb and Jacques Maritain. Essentially a declaration of the need for Thomism today. A-B

See: D 37 (1952) 237; HPR 52 (1952) 1129.

DRENNAN, Donald A. (ed.) *A Modern Introduction to Metaphysics.* See VII.

DUBARLE, Dominique. *Scientific Humanism and Christian Thought.* Trans. by R. Trevett from *Humanisme scientifique et raison chrétienne.* New York: Philosophical Library, 1956 (1953). viii, 119 pp.

A series of essays stressing the human import of recent advances in technology. The discussion of the relation between philosophy and science generates a statement of the opportunities for progress in philosophic thought and of the challenges resulting from technological progress. A-C

See: ABR (1957) 87; Bl 38 (1957) 277; CBQ 19 (1957) 162; CR 42 (1957) 571; D 41 (1956) 364; IER 87 (1957) 78; J 4 (1956) 53; NS 31 (1957) 586; R 14 (1954) 267.

DUBRAY, Charles. *Introductory Philosophy: A Textbook for Colleges and High Schools.* Revised ed. New York: Longmans, Green, 1923 (1912). xxiv, 689 pp.

A clear, concise, and comprehensive treatment of the problems of empirical psychology, and of the systematics and history of philosophy. B

DULLES, Avery R., DEMSKE, James M., and O'CONNELL, Robert J. *Introductory Metaphysics: A Course Combining Matter Treated in Ontology, Cosmology, and Natural Theology.* New York: Sheed and Ward, 1958 (1955). ix, 345 pp. Bibliography.

Beginning with the problem of change and multiplicity, it proceeds to the existence and nature of God, and then returns to limited beings in terms of finality and providence. The problems are clearly stated, compared to alternate positions, and then analyzed. Readings are suggested for each section. A-B

EASBY-SMITH, Mildred. *The Scholastic Synthesis According to the Mind of St. Thomas of Aquin.* Philadelphia: Dolphin Press, 1932. 129 pp.

The survey concentrates on the historical background and on the life and works of St. Thomas as the context for the synthesis, which is summarized in thirty pages. The subsequent struggles and successes of this synthesis are also traced. B

FARRELL, Walter. *A Companion to the* SUMMA. 4 vols. New York: Sheed and Ward, 1938-1942.

A lively, popular summary of the thought of St. Thomas' *Summa Theologica.* The presentation is arresting. The numerous timely illustrations make the ideas more clear but, at times, impede philosophical precision. Each chapter is schematically outlined; the volumes are separately indexed. A-B

See: VOLUME ONE: A 67 (1942) 77; AM (1942) 26; C 35 (1942) 275; D 26 (1941) 247-48; ER 106 (1942) 393; HPR 42 (1942) 692; MS 19 (1942) 77; S 21 (1941) 312; T 18 (1943) 161-62; Tm 4 (1942) 355-56.

VOLUME TWO: C 30 (1939) 55; CR 16 (1939) 56-57; CW 149 (1939) 255; ER 130 (1940) 103; HPR 139 (1939) 433-35; MS 16 (1939) 43; NS 13 (1939) 182-83; S 18 (1939) 379; Ta 173 (1939) 350; Ta 173 (1939) 350-52, 427-29, 461-62; T 14 (1939) 337-38.

VOLUME THREE: A 63 (1940) 358; AM 52 (1940) 250; CW 152 (1940) 248; C 32 (1940) 215; D 25 (1940) 123-25; HPR 41 (1941) 556; NS 14 (1940) 417-18; S 20 (1940) 123; T 15 (1940) 548-50; Tm 3 (1941) 380-84.

VOLUME FOUR: A 68 (1948) 412; AM 57 (1943) 506; CW 156 (1943) 766; D 27 (1942) 271-72; ER 107 (1942) 470; HPR 43 (1943) 859-60; MS 20 (1943) 105; S 22 (1943) 377; TS 4 (1943) 311-13; T 18 (1943) 161-62; Tm 6 (1943) 119-21.

FLEMING, Thomas V. *Foundations of Philosophy.* London: Shakespeare Head, 1951. 210 pp.

Special attention is given to Scholastic principles relevant to the problems of modern philosophy. The main part of the work is epistemological, treating various systems of knowledge, especially the British empiricists. To this are added some problems from cosmology, such as causality, space, and time; and from rational psychology, such as life, the spirituality of the soul, and free will. Penetrating in insight, it is directed especially to the well educated person without philosophical training. B

See: T 27 (1952) 472.

From an Abundant Spring: The Walter Farrell Memorial Volume of the Thomist. Ed. by the staff of *The Thomist.* New York: Kenedy, 1952. 555 pp.

Essays on philosophical and theological themes. Of particular philosophical interest are: R. Nogar, "Cosmology without a Cosmos"; W. O'Connor, "Freedom and Beatitude"; G. Phelan, "Being and the Metaphysicians"; and J. Maritain, "The Cultural Impact of Empiricism." B-C

GARRIGOU-LAGRANGE, Reginald. *Reality: A Synthesis of*

Thomistic Thought. Trans. by P. Cummins from *La synthèse thomiste* and the *Dictionnaire de Théologie Catholique*. St. Louis: Herder, 1950 (1946). xii, 419 pp.

A classical and dependable presentation of modern Thomistic thought as a single philosophical-theological synthesis. It reflects both the work of the major commentators and the intellectualist concerns of the first part of this century. The description of Scotistic and Suarezian positions is disappointing. B-C

See: E. Duff, A 81 (1959) 232; A. Schlitzer, AM 69 (1949) 762; Bl 31 (1950) 563; D 34 (1949) 46; J. Mullaney, T 24 (1949) 745.

GERRITY, Benignus. *Nature, Knowledge, and God: An Introduction to Thomistic Philosophy*. Milwaukee: Bruce, 1947. xii, 662 pp. Bibliography, index, readings.

A clear, simple, systematic presentation of Thomistic philosophy, except logic and ethics. At times too simplified, there are weaknesses in its views on history, both medieval and modern. B

See: A 79 (1948) 33; S 27 (1948) 71; TS 9 (1948) 337-38.

GILSON, Etienne. *Being and Some Philosophers*. See VII.

————. *Christianity and Philosophy*. Trans. by R. MacDonald from *Christianisme et philosophie*. New York: Sheed and Ward, 1939 (1936). xxvi, 134 pp.

An analysis of the special character of philosophy, developed within a Christian culture and theology which emphasizes the superiority of divine revelation over the human intellect, without minimizing the latter. Predominantly non-philosophical, it is an excellent clarification of the pressing problem of the use of natural reason within the context of revelation. C

See: A 62 (1939) 331; C 31 (1939) 100; CW 150 (1940) 626; HB 18 (1940) 44; HPR 40 (1940) 924; MS 17 (1940) 38; S 19 (1939) 315; T 15 (1940) 129-33.

————. *Elements of Christian Philosophy*. See XV.

————. *History of Philosophy and Philosophical Education* (The Aquinas Lecture, 1947). Milwaukee: Marquette University Press, 1948. xvi, 49 pp.

History is shown as vitalizing the genuine philosophic quest for truth and providing a laboratory for testing various positions. B-C

See: CHR 34 (1948) 221; D 33 (1948) 242; NS 23 (1949) 115-16; J. Mullaney, T 23 (1948) 738; J. Anderson, T 7 (1948) 17; Tm 11 (1948) 533-35.

———. *The Philosopher and Theology.* Trans. by C. Gilson from *La philosophie et la théologie.* New York: Random House, 1962 (1960). 236 pp.

A personal account of the struggle to integrate the whole of human knowledge by means of theology and of the part played in this endeavor by a Christian philosophy. Of special philosophical interest are the chapters on Bergson, Christian philosophy and its future, and being a Thomist. B-C

See: CER 61 (1963) 205; CW 195 (1962) 246; IPQ 1 (1961) 697-713; MS 38 (1961) 334; MS 40 (1963) 331; A. Thiry, NRT 84 (1962) 337-64; RR 22 (1963) 311; VS 104 (1961) 221.

———. *Reason and Revelation in the Middle Ages.* See VIII.

———. *The Unity of Philosophical Experience.* New York: Scribner's 1937. xii, 331 pp.

A study of the main directions of modern philosophic thought, exemplifying its coherence. Philosophy is traced from the late medieval, through the Cartesian, to the Kantian period. Lesser thinkers are studied in their subordinate relation to the key philosophers in each age, and the varied approaches to being are woven into an ordered pattern. It concludes with a reflection on the unity of development in the history of philosophy. B-C

See: C 27 (1938) 444; CR 16 (1939) 243-46; CW 146 (1938) 759; DuR 205 (1939) 187; Bl 20 (1939) 305.

GLENN, Paul J. *An Introduction to Philosophy.* St. Louis: Herder, 1944. viii, 408 pp. Index.

The work first surveys the history of philosophy, then outlines the contents of the usual systematic courses. A

See: A 71 (1944) 582; AM 60 (1944) 269; CER 43 (1945) 377-78; ER 113 (1945) 157-58; JRI 15 (1945) 882; NS 19 (1945) 180-81; RR 3 (1944) 355-56; SJR 37 (1946) 63; T 19 (1944) 733-35.

GRENIER, Henri. *Thomistic Philosophy*. 4 vols. Trans. by J. O'Hanley from *Cursus philosophiae*. Charlottetown, Canada: St. Dunstans, 1948-1950 (1944).

A systematic course for the seminarian, presenting the principle tenets of Thomistic philosophy in the succinct thesis-proof format. Many ideas presented and their relevancy are inadequately explained, and at times the translation is too literal. A source of quick reference for the basic distinctions, terms, and arguments developed in Scholasticism through the ages. B

> *See:* D 34 (1949) 57-58 (Vol. I), 170 (Vol. II), 249 (Vol. III); T 9 (1946) 465-67.

GRYST, Edward. *Talk Sense! A Pilgrimage through Philosophy*. New York: Macmillan, 1961. ix, 111 pp.

An entertaining, but oversimplified presentation of philosophy in the form of conversations between a philosophy professor and one not yet introduced to the field. The basic principles of a first course in Scholastic philosophy are gradually introduced. A

> *See:* CE 32 (1962) 467; St 52 (1963) 436.

HART, Charles A. (ed.) *Aspects of the New Scholastic Philosophy*. New York: Benziger, 1932. 311 pp.

Essays in honor of Msgr. Edward A. Pace. Some articles review the development of Scholastic thought in America in relation to science, humanism, society, and religion; others are on psychology and education. C

> *See:* A 48 (1932) 217; C 16 (1932) 375; CW 136 (1933) 500; T 7 (1933) 668-71.

HARVEY, Rudolph. *It Stands to Reason: An Invitation to Philosophy*. New York: Wagner, 1960. 287 pp.

A general reflection upon man and his world. The brisk, light style and the absence of technical terminology make the work attractive for those unacquainted with philosophy; but it occasionally sacrifices accuracy for cleverness of expression. A

> *See:* AER 145 (1961) 358; CER 32 (1961) 110; CR 47 (1962) 433; HPR 61 (1961) 497; IER 96 (1961) 407; S 40 (1961) 61.

HAWKINS, Denis J. *Approach to Philosophy*. Albany, N.Y.: Magi, 1964 (1938). 116 pp.

A clear, terse survey of philosophy, with a general phenomenological approach. Beginning with a careful descriptive analysis of experience, it traces various problems within philosophy seen as a unified whole and identifies the structure of man's conception of reality. B

See: Bl 20 (1939) 234; CR 16 (1939) 247-48; IER 53 (1939) 104-105; St 28 (1939) 532; Ta 172 (1938) 464.

————. *Crucial Problems of Modern Philosophy*. New York: Sheed and Ward, 1957. 150 pp. (Notre Dame)

A study of the development of modern philosophy discussed in relation to the problems of Humian empiricism and Kantian phenomenalism. While intending to be positive, the emphasis in the evaluation of modern philosophers is rather negative, possibly as a result of stating the problems of modern thought in Aristotelian terms instead of focusing on subsequent ontological insights. A-B

See: A 98 (1958) 755; ACSR 19 (1958) 263; AER 139 (1958) 283; CER 56 (1958) 351; CW 187 (1958) 236; D 43 (1958) 205; ECQ 13 (1959) 93; IER 89 (1958) 467; ITQ 25 (1958) 88; PS 7 (1957) 366; T 33 (1958) 299; Ta 210 (1957) 366; TS 19 (1958) 469; S 48 (1959) 241.

HILDEBRAND, Dietrich Von. *What Is Philosophy?* Milwaukee: Bruce, 1960. viii, 242 pp.

A well-informed description, not only of philosophy, but of the work of contemporary philosophers. In sympathy with Husserl's earlier philosophical position, the work contains excellent insights into many philosophical concepts, particularly the nature of philosophical knowledge, the meaning of the phenomenological method, and its relation to philosophy. B-C

See: A 104 (1961) 542; W. Marra, A 104 (1961) 542; MS 39 (1961) 74; NS 36 (1962) 241; PS 11 (1961) 329; S 40 (1961) 58; T 36 (1961) 300; Tm 25 (1961) 188.

KANE, William H. *Approach to Philosophy; Elements of Thomism: A Collection of Essays*. Washington, D.C.: Thomist Press, 1962. 179 pp. (Paper)

A collection of essays which originally appeared in *The Thomist* and which reflect the spirit of the founder of the Albertus Magnus Lyceum. They begin with an introduction to philosophy, proceed through questions concerning the structure of the philosophy of nature and its principles, and conclude at the threshold of metaphysics on being as being. The order of the sciences and the contribution of the philosophy of nature to metaphysics are stressed. B-C

See: D 47 (1962) 310.

KILEY, W. Paul. *Human Possibilities: A Dialectic in Contemporary Thinking*. New York: Philosophical Library, 1963. vii, 94 pp.

An assessment of the tensions in modern and contemporary thought. Acknowledging the danger in seeking clear answers, the author indicates that the relational character of the self, and of subjectivity to objectivity is a more adequate frame of reference. He stresses, however, that the other to which the self is opened must also be a self and not merely the world. A-B

KLOCKER, Harry R. *Thomism and Modern Thought*. New York: Appleton-Century-Crofts, 1962. xiv, 320 pp. Bibliography.

A college text intended to supplement the study of Thomism with an understanding of modern, non-Thomistic systems. These are studied in their origins and compared with the philosophy of St. Thomas Aquinas. Kant is taken as a starting point, and his limitation of the human intellect is contrasted with the triumph of the mind in idealism. This is followed by studies of pragmatism, naturalism, positivism, and existentialism. About thirty percent of these sections, each of which contains a bibliography, is reserved for readings from the philosophers themselves. The last section consists of readings from Gilson, Maritain, and Sertillanges, on the problem of knowledge and the destiny of man. More emphasis might have been placed on phenomenology and nonpositivistic analytic philosophy. B

LATTEY, Cuthbert. (ed.) *St. Thomas Aquinas* (Papers from the

Cambridge, England, Summer School of Catholic Studies, 1924). London: Herder, 1925. ix, 311 pp.

While these essays are mostly theological, also included are studies of the relation of philosophy to theology and to modern thought, especially in the field of moral and political questions. C

See: A 33 (1925) 429; CW 122 (1925) 134; T 1 (1926) 373.

LINEHAN, James A. *Harmony, in Catholic Universities and Schools, Between the Teaching of Modern Science, Catholic Philosophy and Theology.* Eagle Bay, New York: 1962. xvii, 196 pp. (Paper)

A survey of the problem of integrating the curriculum of the Catholic college. Special attention is given to philosophical issues. The work is loosely organized. A

LITTLE, Arthur. *Philosophy without Tears.* Buffalo, N.Y.: Desmond and Stapleton, 1947. viii, 128 pp.

A concise study of Scholasticism vis-à-vis such current philosophical problems as knowledge, time, providence, freedom, and immortality. It is cast in the form of a dialogue between a professor and his adversaries. B

See: AM 67 (1948) 378; D 33 (1948) 62; IM 74 (1946) 406-409; St 36 (1947) 123-24.

LORD, Daniel. *Armchair Philosophy.* New York: America Press, 1932 (1918). 128 pp. (Paper)

A simple, interesting introduction to the meaning of philosophy, its purpose and its utility. It deals in a sprightly fashion with such subjects as skepticism, free will, personal responsibility, immortality, and morality. A

See: A 20 (1918) 299.

LYNCH, William F. *The Integrating Mind.* New York: Sheed and Ward, 1962. vi, 181 pp.

A discussion of the need to appreciate the complementary character of all facets of reality in order to be able to avoid self defeating choices between imagined contradictories. The contributions to this theme, of analogy and of the gift of sensibility and awareness, are discussed. B-C

See: ACSR 23 (1962) 177; C 76 (1962) 380; HPR 62 (1962) 921; J 10 (1962) 45; Ps 7 (1962) 121; SJR 55 (1962) 102; J. Lawler, TS 23 (1962) 501; T 37 (1962) 472.

McCORMICK, John F. *St. Thomas and the Life of Learning* (The Aquinas Lecture, 1937). Milwaukee: Marquette University Press, 1937. 25 pp.

A discussion on the scholarly inspiration of St. Thomas Aquinas, traced to his considerations on the nature of knowledge, and on the object of knowledge and wisdom. Emphasis is placed on the personal qualities of the thinker as exemplified in St. Thomas. A

See: MS 15 (1937) 22.

McGANNON, J. Barry, COOKE, Bernard J., and KLUBERTANZ, George P. *Christian Wisdom and Christian Formation.* New York: Sheed and Ward, 1964. 306 pp. Appendix, index.

A collection of articles on the elements included in college and seminary formation, derived from a study carried out by the combined Jesuit Provinces of the United States. The articles center on theology, philosophy, and moral, religious, and spiritual formation. The nature and teaching of philosophy, both as an academic discipline and in relation to undergraduate education, is discussed in a number of articles. C

McLEAN, George F. (ed.) *Philosophy and the Integration of Contemporary Catholic Education.* See XII.

———. *Philosophy in a Technological Culture.* See IX.

———. *Teaching Thomism Today.* Washington, D.C.: The Catholic University of America Press, 1963. xii, 394 pp. (Paper)

A positive and creative study of the confrontation of the tradition of Christian philosophy with contemporary philosophies. The collection of papers by leading philosophers treats, first, the relation of the main bodies of scholastic thought, then the major contemporary trends, and finally the challenges and opportunities of uniting the two in teaching courses in the main divisions of philosophy. B-C

McMORROW, George J. *A Preface to Catholic Philosophy.* Nazareth, Mich.: Nazareth College (Ann Arbor: Edwards Lithoprint), 1946. 135 pp. Bibliography.

A loosely organized introduction to philosophy by way of comparison to other areas of thought. After being defined, philosophy is related to science, oriental religions, the Catholic faith, and education. B

McNABB, Vincent J. *The Catholic Church and Philosophy* ("The Calvert Series"). New York: Macmillan, 1927. xviii, 124 pp.

A study of the contributions of the Church to philosophy. While the early and modern periods are treated, the greatest stress is given to the articulation of Christian philosophy in such various branches as logic, ethics, and metaphysics during the Middle Ages. A-B

See: A 37 (1927) 21; T 2 (1927) 332.

McWILLIAMS, James A. *Philosophy for the Millions.* New York: Macmillan, 1963 (1942). x, 206 pp.

This book begins with a description of the human person, and then broadens the perspective to social, spiritual, and historical dimensions. A particularly clear work without oversimplifying, it is one of the best general introductions. A

See: A 67 (1942) 721; AM 57 (1943) 90; CHR 29 (1943) 138-39; CW 156 (1943) 638; D 27 (1942) 272; ER 107 (1942) 399; HPR 107 (1943) 379; MS 20 (1942) 54; S 22 (1943) 378; T 18 (1943) 348.

————. *Progress in Philosophy: Philosophical Studies in Honor of Rev. Dr. Charles A. Hart.* Milwaukee: Bruce, 1955. vi, 216 pp.

A collection of outstanding essays on metaphysics: J. Maritain—substance, E. Salmon—unity, W. Clark—the real; on the philosophy of nature: I. Brady—substance; A. Pegis—unity; and on ethics: G. Phelan—law. B-C

See: NS 31 (1957) 120.

MARITAIN, Jacques. *An Essay on Christian Philosophy.* Trans. by E. Flannery from *De la philosophie chrétienne.* New York: Philosophical Library, 1955 (1933). xi, 116 pp. Index, glossary.

A study of the nature of philosophy, and of the objective and subjective contributions of Christianity to philosophy. Also reviewed is the relation of theology to philosophy and to natural ethics. C

See: ABR 7 (1956) 329; C. Hart, CER 53 (1953) 206; D 40 (1955) 213; RP 17 (1955) 548; TS 16 (1955) 325; L. Dewart, Tm 19 (1956) 523-25; L. Duvait, Tm 19 (1956) 523.

————. *Freedom of the Intellect, and Other Conversations with Theonas.* Trans. by F. Sheed from *Théonas, ou les entretiens d'un sage et de deux philosophes sur diverses matières inégalement actuelles.* New York: Sheed and Ward, 1935 (1921). 208 pp.

A more popular presentation of the themes scientifically elaborated in the author's *Degrees of Knowledge,* and originally published as *Theonas, Conversations of a Sage.* The place of the intellect and heart in Christian humanism is studied, and the nature of true progress in philosophy is seen as that which reconciles metaphysics and the natural sciences by loving movement while holding stability in honor. B-C

See: A 51 (1934) 354; CW 51 (1933) 636.

————. *Introduction to Philosophy.* Trans. by E. Watkin from *Eléments de philosophie.* New York: Sheed and Ward, 1947 (1921). 272 pp.

A study of the nature and divisions of philosophy from the Aristotelian-Thomistic point of view, and a judgment of modern philosophical systems in this light. The presentation of the teachings of ancient philosophy leads to a definition of philosophy, which is viewed in comparison with the special sciences, theology, and

common sense knowledge. The character and interrelation of the
main branches of philosophy are also studied. B

    See: A 43 (1930) 409; CW 132 (1931) 500.

————. *On the Use of Philosophy.* New York: Atheneum, 1965
(1961) . 71 pp. (Paper)

Three studies of the practice of philosophy. While remaining a
liberal knowledge, philosophy, by providing knowledge of the
nature and goals of man, indispensable to social efforts, is seen to
have a practical value. The mode of cooperation in this task is
considered to be by the guidance contributed by individual philosophers, rather than by the working of abstract systems. C

    See: AM 95 (1962) 25; D 47 (1962) 216; MS 39 (1962) 299; NS 36 (1962)
    413; Ta 216 (1962) 379.

————. *Science and Wisdom.* Trans. by B. Wall from *Science et
sagesse.* New York: Scribner's, 1940. x, 241 pp.

A collection of essays on the philosophy of nature, Christian philosophy, moral philosophy, and science and wisdom. Christian
philosophy is treated as a complex of rational habits in a given
historical state. B-C

    See: A 63 (1940) 441-42; Bl 21 (1940) 336-37; CSJ 40 (1940) 245; D 25
    (1940) 252; DuR 207 (1940) 120; ER 103 (1940) 202-204; Ta 175 (1940)
    631-32; Tm 3 (1941) 172.

MARTIN, William O. *The Order and Integration of Knowledge.*
Ann Arbor, Mich.: University of Michigan Press, 1957. ix,
355 pp.

The various areas of mathematical and historical, practical and
speculative, philosophical and theological knowledge are reviewed, with special attention to the problems of their proper
characteristics and interrelation. The context is basically that of
traditional philosophy, enriched by many insights of recent American realism. C-D

    See: NS 33 (1959) 395; PS 9 (1959) 223.

MERCIER, Désiré J. *A Manual of Modern Scholastic Philosophy.*
2 vols. Trans. by T. Parker and S. Parker from *Cours de*

philosophie. 3d English ed. London: Kegan Paul, 1949 (1894).

An abbreviation of the *Cours de philosophie,* the joint work of several professors at the University of Louvain. Although rightly considered a classic of its time, the physical science it discusses in cosmology, and the educational psychology are out of date in many places, and its epistemology has been much disputed. B

See: A 19 (1918) 559; CW 105 (1917) 251-54; CW 107 (1918) 389-91.

MOREUX, Theophile. *Modern Science and the Truths Beyond: Being a Popular Outline of Philosophy in Relation to the Scientific Problems of To-day.* Trans. by M. Fitzsimons from *Pour comprendre la philosophie.* New York: Benziger, 1931 (1926). xxi, 240 pp.

A survey of all parts of philosophy, except ethics, by one who is himself a scientist. Inevitably, the science is now dated. A

See: A 47 (1932) 312.

MORRIS, Hilaire. *Philosophy for Beginners.* Westminster, Md.: Newman, 1960. xi, 247 pp. Bibliography, index, vocabulary.

An excellent manual of Scholastic philosophy, written with clarity and simplicity. It contains formal logic, metaphysics, cosmology, and psychology. A

See: CR 46 (1961) 496; IER 96 (1961) 127.

MORRISON, Bakewell and RUEVE, Stephen J. *Think and Live* ("Science and Culture Series"). Milwaukee: Bruce, 1947. 183 pp.

A brief philosophical survey. Using the principle of causality as a link, the authors proceed step by step from epistemological topics to sufficient reason, man, and God. The concluding chapter relates this perspective to the full dimensions of life. B

See: W. Stokes, A 103 (1960) 379; AM 92 (1960) 24; CSJ 60 (1960) 40; DR 79 (1961) 6; IER 94 (1960) 330.

MUNIER, André. *A Manual of Philosophy.* Trans. by T. Connolly from *Manuel de philosophie.* New York: Desclée, 1964. Vol. I. 580 pp.

A section of a general philosophy text integrating the subject centered insights into the traditional philosophic pattern. The areas included in this first volume are cosmology and philosophical psychology. B

NEDONCELLE, Maurice. *Is There a Christian Philosophy?* (*Twentieth Century Encyclopedia of Catholicism,* Vol. 10). Trans. by I. Trethowan from *Existe-t-il une philosophie chrétienne?* New York: Hawthorn, 1960 (1956). 154 pp.
A general survey of the problem of Christian philosophy. After presenting the positions of the past and the debate of 1931, subsequent progress toward synthesis is charted. While no single generally acceptable concept of Christian philosophy is discovered, the author develops the view that it relates itself to Christianity as to a different and superior order. B-C

NEILL, Thomas P. *Makers of the Modern Mind.* Milwaukee: Bruce, 1963 (1949). xii, 420 pp. Index.
A study of eleven influential thinkers from Luther to Freud. They are seen as weakening the common estimation of human reason and its powers, with consequent lethal social effects. While the selection of authors is limited and tends toward an oversimplification of the thesis, the exposition is succint and lucid. B
See: J. Long, AM 70 (1949) 314; H. Edwards, Bl 30 (1949) 553; C 50 (1949) 634; J. McSorley, CW 170 (1949) 76; D 34 (1949) 162; E. Ryan, T 24 (1949) 695.

NICHOLL, Donald. *Recent Thought in Focus.* London: Sheed and Ward, 1952. 250 pp.
A meditative and skillful study of recent methods in philosophy, science, and psychology. Emphasis is given to problems concerning the nature and destiny of man, ultimate values, and religious truths. B
See: A 88 (1953) 654-55; ABR 4 (1953) 280; AER 129 (1953) 142; DR 70 (1953) 93-95; IER 79 (1953) 326; Ta 200 (1952) 398.

OLGIATI, Francesco. *The Key to the Study of St. Thomas.* Trans. by J. Zybura from *L'anima di san Tommaso.* 2d ed. revised. St. Louis: Herder, 1929 (1923). vii, 176 pp.

An introductory study of the unity and originality of the thought of St. Thomas Aquinas, as founded on his concept of being. The contributions of his predecessors are tested and criticized in the light of his metaphysical conception; the systems of Kant, Descartes, and Berkeley are also evaluated. The author provides many references to primary sources. C

See: A 34 (1926) 432; C 4 (1926) 25; CW 122 (1926) 857-58; T 1 (1926) 561.

O'MAHONY, James E. *Christian Philosophy.* London: Burns, Oates, and Washbourne, 1939. viii, 184 pp.

A presentation of the notion of Christian philosophy, drawing heavily on the riches of the Franciscan tradition. The philosophical problems and their related solutions are treated, with special attention to the position of St. Bonavenutre. Also discussed are the relevant implications for morality, the person, wisdom, and life's ultimate end. A-B

See: CR 18 (1940) 59-60; IER 54 (1939) 544-45; St 29 (1940) 172-73.

————. *Reform or Revolution.* Cork: Cork University Press, 1944. 59 pp.

A series of essays on philosophy at a time of political turmoil. The relation of philosophy to modern life is considered, with special attention to the inferences to be drawn by the democratic institutions of today.

See: CR 18 (1940) 150; IM 67 (1939) 441.

O'NEIL, Charles J. (ed.) *An Etienne Gilson Tribute.* Milwaukee: Marquette University Press, 1959. x, 347 pp.

This diverse and valuable collection of essays by the North American students of Etienne Gilson is an impressive testimony to the intellectual vigor of their teacher, the founder of the Pontifical Institute of Mediaeval Studies, Toronto. Reflecting their master in a broad sense, the authors have chosen topics related to history and metaphysics, with some epistemological studies. C

See: MS 37 (1960) 321-25; NS 35 (1961) 231; PS 11 (1961) 281.

PEGIS, Anton C. *Christian Philosophy and Intellectual Freedom*

(Gabriel Richard Lecture, 1955) . Milwaukee: Bruce, 1960.
89 pp.

A penetrating, personal reflection on philosophers and philosophy in the Catholic intellectual milieu. It discusses the order and integration of the college curriculum, the necessity of accepting absolute truths, and the honesty of Catholics in intellectual life, particularly in regard to the relation of creative intelligence to authoritative structure. B-C

See: CER 59 (1961) 417; IER 95 (1961) 424; J 9 (1961) 46; P 18 (1962) 343; RR 21 (1962) 74; St 50 (1961) 456.

———. (ed.) *Essays in Modern Scholasticism*. Westminster, Md.: Newman, 1944. 295 pp. Bibliography.

A collection of essays, by a group of prominent American philosophers, written in honor of John F. McCormick. The essays fall generally into the areas of logic, psychology, metaphysics, and history. A bibliography of the writings of J. McCormick is also included. C

See: D 30 (1945) 46; AER 113 (1945) 239; FS 26 (1945) 338-39; MS 23 (1945) 52-53; T 20 (1945) 68-72.

———. (ed.) *A Gilson Reader: Selected Writings of Etienne Gilson*. Garden City, N.Y.: Hanover, 1957. 358 pp. Bibliography. (Image: D 55)

An excellent selection of passages from the works of Etienne Gilson. The divisions reflect the main themes and subjects to which he has so richly contributed: the intellect, the history of medieval philosophy, Christian philosophy, St. Thomas Aquinas, wisdom, and the Catholic teacher. The material is well-ordered and there is a valuable bibliography of Gilson's publications. B-C

See: P. Scharper, C 67 (1958) 390; R. Ostermann, CW 186 (1958) 392; D 43 (1958) 176.

———. *The Middle Ages and Philosophy: Some Reflections on the Ambivalence of Modern Scholasticism* (James Roosevelt Bayley Lecture, Seton Hall University, No. 1) . Chicago: Regnery, 1963. xiv, 102 pp.

An elucidation of the problem of modern scholasticism in finding its philosophical identity. This problem is traced to St. Thomas, by whom philosophy was considered to be a rational tool employed by theology. From this derives the difficulty of arriving at his personal positions in philosophy itself. C-D

PERRIER, Joseph L. *The Revival of Scholastic Philosophy in the Nineteenth Century.* New York: Columbia University Press, 1909. 344 pp. Bibliography, index.

A survey of early Neo-Scholastic thought. In the first half of the work the main content of this philosophy is presented. The second half outlines the history of its renewal in the nineteenth century. B

See: A 1 (1909) 187; CW 89 (1909) 678.

PETERS, J. (ed.) *The Present Situation of Philosophy Among the Catholics in Various Countries.* Brussels: Spectrum, 1948. 68 pp.

A survey of Catholic activity in the field of philosophy, composed for an international philosophical meeting. The work being done in each country is indicated briefly, with annotations concerning various Catholic institutes and organizations. Particularly weak, it nonetheless is of some historical value. A

PHILLIPS, Richard P. *Modern Thomistic Philosophy: An Explanation for Students.* 2 vols. London: Burns, Oates, and Washbourne, 1962 (1934). Bibliography, index.

A clear, intelligible, and generally quite reliable interpretation of the Thomistic system, covering all its branches except logic and ethics. The work contains excellent examples and a sufficient indication of the classical philosophical disputes, both within and outside Thomism. B

See: CW 14 (1947) 4; VOLUME ONE: Bl 16 (1935) 67; CW 144 (1936) 253; DR 53 (1935) 250; Ta 165 (1935) 169.
VOLUME TWO: Bl 17 (1936) 64; DR 54 (1936) 256; IER 47 (1936) 446; MS 14 (1937) 42-43; T 11 (1936) 139; Ta 167 (1936) 169.

PHILOSOPHY IN A PLURALISTIC SOCIETY. See I.

PIEPER, Josef. *Leisure, the Basis of Culture and the Philosophical Act.* Trans. by A. Dru from *Musse und Kult* and *Was heisst Philosophieren.* New York: Pantheon, 1964 (1948). xxi, 138 pp. (MT 426)

An eloquent and enlightened statement of the contemporary relevance of the search for wisdom. The open character of the Thomistic synthesis is defended against its preconception as a closed system. The relationship of leisure and worship is well developed. This work is eminently readable and should be of considerable interest. A-B

See: ABR 4 (1953) 282; AM 76 (1952) 411; AM 79 (1954) 411; CR 37 (1952) 625; D 37 (1952) 211; DR 70 (1952) 342; NS 27 (1953) 237; SO 2 (1952) 147-54; T 28 (1953) 612; W 26 (1952) 378.

————. *The Silence of St. Thomas. See* XV.

RAEYMAEKER, Louis de. *An Introduction to Philosophy* ("Philosophical Series of the Higher Institute of Philosophy." University of Louvain). Trans. by H. McNeill from the 2d revised ed. of *Introduction à la philosophie.* New York: Wagner, 1948 (1938). 297 pp. Bibliography.

An initiation into the field of philosophy, which does not go beyond the threshold of philosophy to attempt a summary of its contents. This work treats, first, the nature of philosophy and its basic problems; second, the most significant contributions of ancient, medieval, modern, and contemporary philosophers; and third, the distinctive character of Thomism. The information on philosophic organizations is valuable. B-C

See: D 33 (1948) 146-47; HPR 48 (1948) 399; RUO 18 (1948) 137-38; R. O'Neill, T 23 (1948) 740; TS 9 (1948) 335-37.

REINHARDT, Kurt F. *A Realistic Philosophy: The Perennial Principles of Thought and Action in a Changing World.* New York: Frederick Ungar, 1962 (1944). xii, 272 pp. Bibliography, glossary, index.

A comprehensive introduction to the Aristotelian-Thomistic tradition. The work contains a survey of the nature, major divisions, and methods of philosophy, together with a bibliography and index. There is special material on modern developments in philosophy and science, and on Spanish American philosophy. C

See: A 72 (1945) 297; AM 62 (1945) 237; Bl 26 (1945) 317-18; CR 25 (1945) 267-68; FS 26 (1945) 83-84; HPR 45 (1945) 952; J 5 (1945) 310; MS 22 (1945) 173-74; NS 181 (1945) 266-68; RP 7 (1945) 382-84; RR 4 (1945) 64-65; SJR 39 (1947) 356; T 20 (1945) 564-66; TS 6 (1945) 127-29.

RICKABY, Joseph. *Scholasticism.* New York: Dodge, 1908. 121 pp.

A survey of the history and some of the principal contents of Scholasticism, tracing its origin and flowering in the thirteenth century, its subsequent decline, and its revival in modern times. The ethical and political doctrine is too briefly summarized to be of interest to the serious student of this subject. A

ROBERTS, James. *Faith and Reason.* See XVII.

ROBLES, Oswaldo. *The Main Problems of Philosophy: An Introduction to Philosophy.* Trans. by K. Reinhardt from *Propedeutica Filosofica.* Milwaukee: Bruce, 1946 (1943). 200 pp. Bibliography, index.

A brief description of the nature and work of philosophy. After some reflections on the distinctive characteristics of philosophy, its major divisions, and methods, the key problems arising in the various branches of philosophy are examined. The attempt to say too much in too brief a space has resulted in little more than a summary of philosophical purpose. A

See: CER 45 (1947) 188; FS 8 (1948) 84-86; HPR 48 (1947) 77-78; MS 25 (1947) 67; T 22 (1947) 542-43; Tm 11 (1948) 106-12.

ROLBIECKI, John J. *The Prospects of Philosophy.* New York: Benziger, 1939. 161 pp. Index.

A general survey of philosophy aimed at enticing students to a more complete study of the subject. The past acts as an introduction to an appraisal of the present problems and opportunities of philosophy as related to recent questions concerning the physical and social sciences, art, and religion. In conclusion, the book presents a hopeful view for the future of philosophy. A

See: AM 51 (1940) 698; C 31 (1940) 391; HPR 40 (1940) 1383; RP 4 (1942) 122; S 20 (1940) 125; T 15 (1940) 347; Tm 2 (1940) 308.

THE ROLE OF THE CHRISTIAN PHILOSOPHER. See I.

ROSE, Mary C. *Essays in Christian Philosophy.* Boston: Christopher Pub. House, 1963. 200 pp.

Twelve essays on such Christian themes as God, immortality, free will, and suffering. All sources of insight—the humanities, reason, and faith—are freely intermingled, with scant attention to evaluating the degree of certitude or the type of knowledge pertaining to each. A

See: MS 41 (1964) 299.

RYAN, James H. *An Introduction to Philosophy.* New York: Macmillan, 1924. xvi, 399 pp.

A well-conceived introduction to philosophy, with an historical approach. The key problems of philosophy, especially in the fields of rational psychology, metaphysics, and ethics, are surveyed. Reading lists are included. B

See: A 32 (1925) 405; C 1 (1925) 328; CW 32 (1924) 424.

RYAN, John K. *Basic Principles and Problems of Philosophy.* 2d ed. Westminster, Md.: Newman, 1954 (1944). xvii, 179 pp. (Paper)

A text for beginners in philosophy covering the areas of metaphysics and philosophical psychology. The presentation is schematic, simple, and clear. The work contains definitions and succinct statements, leaving to the professor the mode of exposition and proof. A-B

————. (ed.) *Philosophical Studies in Honor of the Very Reverend Ignatius Smith, O.P.* Westminster, Md.: Newman, 1952. x, 316 pp. Bibliography, index.

A collection of philosophical essays on various facets of Thomistic philosophy. The orientation of the papers is toward metaphysics and ethics. B-C

See: A 90 (1953) 272; AER 127 (1952) 472; D 38 (1953) 37-39; NS 28 (1954) 116; PS 3 (1953) 174; T 28 (1953) 472; Tm 16 (1953) 119-22.

————. (ed.) *Studies in Philosophy and the History of Philosophy*. Vols. I and II. Washington, D.C.: The Catholic University of America Press, 1961-1963.

A valuable collection of specialized studies in philosophy and philosophical history. Four essays are concerned with proof of the existence of God and reflect the work accomplished in this regard from the Middle Ages to the present day. Other essays provide a philosophical evaluation of certain physical and psychiatric theories. The remainder of the volume is devoted to historical and textual material. B-C

See: AER 148 (1963) 140; PS 12 (1963) 280.

SHALLO, Michael W. *Lessons in Scholastic Philosophy*. Philadelphia: Reilly, 1923 (1915). 423 pp.

A schematic text covering the various sections of philosophy. The essential features are given emphasis by means of bold type. Some observations on tendencies in science and research up to the time of writing are included. The manner of exposition is generally clear and simple, but the inexperienced student would need professional guidance. B

See: A 14 (1915) 137; A 30 (1924) 626; CW 119 (1924) 570.

SMITH, Vincent E. *Idea Men of Today*. Milwaukee: Bruce, 1951 (1950). x, 434 pp.

A collection of critical essays summarizing the thought of fifteen contemporary thinkers. Attention is given to John Dewey, Sigmund Freud, and the existentialists. The excellent introductory scrutiny of present-day philosophy draws some instructive conclusions concerning contemporary man and his search for truth. B

See: M. Sullivan, ABR (1950) 562; CER 49 (1951) 283; H. Hart, CW 174 (1951) 159; ER 134 (1951) 400; J. Collins, T 26 (1951) 146.

STAUNTON, John A. *Scholasticism: The Philosophy of Common Sense*. Notre Dame, Ind.: Notre Dame University Press, 1937. 70 pp.

A defense of Scholastic philosophy against the charge that it has been outmoded or refuted. The realistic dualism of the Aristotelian-Thomistic tradition is presented as the only solution to the contemporary dilemma. A-B

SULLIVAN, Daniel J. *An Introduction to Philosophy*. Milwaukee: Bruce, 1964 (1957). xvi, 328 pp. Bibliography, index.
A clear, thought-provoking introduction to philosophy, with particular emphasis on its pertinence to the current problems of modern society. Topics treated include the historical rise of philosophy, the meaning of man and his universe, and perennial philosophy, as related to common-sense knowledge, science, mathematics, and theology. A helpful list of selected readings accompanies each chapter. A-B
See: A 97 (1957) 386; D 42 (1957) 267; IR 30 (1957) 177; LA 26 (1957) 32; MS 36 (1959) 135; PS 7 (1957) 230; T 32 (1957) 619.

THOMAS AQUINAS, Saint. *Compendium of Theology*. See XV.

————. *The Division and Methods of the Sciences*. See XV.

————. *On the Truth of the Catholic Faith*. See XV.

————. *Summa Theologica*. See XV.

————. *The Teacher—The Mind*. See XV.

TRESMONTANT, Claude. *The Origins of Christian Philosophy*. See VIII.

TRETHOWAN, Illtyd. *An Essay in Christian Philosophy*. London: Longmans, Green, 1954. 186 pp.
An investigation into the nature of Christian philosophy and its foundations. After a general statement concerning Christian philosophy, the author turns to the problems of certitude, knowledge of God, morality, and reason and faith. In attempting to solve these problems in a way acceptable to the contemporary analytic philosopher, much of importance to traditional Christian philosophy becomes less apparent. C
See: Bl 35 (1954) 488; CR 40 (1955) 56; D 40 (1955) 317; DR 73 (1955) 93; Ta 204 (1954) 252.

VERSFELD, Martin. *The Mirror of Philosophers.* New York: Sheed and Ward, 1960. x, 301 pp.

A review, written in simple style, of the many agreements and disagreements between philosophers, especially in modern times. A-B

See: CR 46 (1961) 185; E. Crauzet, DR 79 (1961) 170; ITQ 28 (1961) 74; P. Mathews, MS 38 (1961) 354.

——. *The Perennial Order.* London: St. Paul Publications, 1953. 247 pp.

A general survey of the contributions of classical philosophies to an ordering of human knowledge. The nature of philosophy is presented from the viewpoint of the Scholastics and then from that of Bergson, Whitehead, and others. Viewed positively, the combined points of view provide a basis for assessments of the philosophy of science, morals, history, art, and culture. A-B

See: A 95 (1956) 144; W. Ardagh, Bl 36 (1955) 100; CER 54 (1956) 211; CR 40 (1955) 433; A. Armstrong, DR 73 (1955) 292; Ta 206 (1955) 134.

WALSHE, Thomas A. *The Quest of Reality: An Introduction to the Study of Philosophy.* St. Louis: Herder, 1933. xix, 594 pp.

An historical view of philosophy from the time of the ancient Greeks to that of contemporary thinkers. More a history of philosophy than an introduction to the study of philosophy, it is unified by the identification of the quest of reality with the search for truth, beauty, and goodness. It goes beyond philosophy when it concludes that divine revelation is a moral necessity so that truths which of themselves are accessible to human reason might be known with certitude by all men. B

See: A 50 (1933) 258; C 19 (1934) 584; CW 138 (1934) 507.

WUELLNER, Bernard. *A Christian Philosophy of Life.* Milwaukee: Bruce, 1957. ix, 278 pp. Index.

A handy synthesis of Thomistic thought. The work unifies and gives order to elements of philosophy which often remain unrelated. Better adapted than a formal textbook for the educated person who wishes a knowledge of Catholic philosophy. A

See: A 98 (1957) 351; CCr 10 (1958) 120; CW 187 (1958) 77; D 43 (1958) 201; MS 36 (1958) 75; NS 33 (1959) 124; NS 33 (1959) 360.

ZYBURA, John. (ed.) *Present-day Thinkers and the New Scholasticism: An International Symposium.* St. Louis: Herder, 1928. xviii, 543 pp. Bibliography.

A survey of American and European, Scholastic and nonscholastic, views concerning the renewal of Scholastic thought, its nature, spirit, and progress. It is an important, though not up-to-date, document on the history of the Neo-Scholastic revival. B

See: A 36 (1927) 603; CW 124 (1927) 561; T 1 (1927) 724-31.

CHAPTER III

Logic

This chapter is devoted to works on what is variously termed formal or minor logic, or dialectics.[1] The works included are those with some special relation to the Christian and Scholastic traditions, whether in subject matter or in point of view. Hence, works on the general history of logic have been omitted.[2] The few additional classical and contemporary works which complete the list of books on Aristotelian logic have been noted below.[3] Since logic is the closest approach to a neutral subject in the field of philosophy, philosophy programs in some institutions are restricted almost exclusively to this field.

The structure of texts on logic generally is quite uniform,

---

[1] For a discussion of the difficult distinctions between formal and material logic and between minor and major logic, see Yves Simon's introduction to *The Material Logic of John of St. Thomas* (Chicago: University of Chicago Press, 1955), pp. ix-xviii.

[2] E.g., Innocentius M. Bochénski, *Ancient Formal Logic* ("Studies in Logic and the Foundations of Mathematics"; Amsterdam: North Holland Pub., 1951); *A History of Formal Logic* (South Bend, Ind.: University of Notre Dame Press, 1961), the extensive bibliography of the history of logic, pp. 460-534; and *A Précis of Mathematical Logic*, trans. O. Bird (Dodrecht, Holland: Reidel, 1959). See also William and Martha Kneale, *The Development of Logic* (Oxford: At the Clarendon, 1962). On symbolic logic, see A. Church, *Journal of Symbolic Logic*, I (1936), for a bibliography extending from 1666 to 1935.

[3] Otto Bird, *Syllogistic and Its Extensions* (Englewood Cliffs, N.J.: Prentice-Hall, 1964); H. W. Joseph, *An Introduction to Logic* (Oxford: Clarendon, 1931); Jan Lukasiewicz, *Aristotle's Syllogistic from the Standpoint of Modern Formal Logic* (Oxford: Clarendon, 1951); Francis H. Parker and Henry B. Veatch, *Logic as a Human Instrument* (New York: Harper, 1959); Henry B. Veatch, *Intentional Logic: A Logic Based on Philosophical Realism* (New Haven: Yale University Press, 1952).

the material being divided according to the three acts of the mind —simple apprehension, judgment, and reasoning. Hence, most textbooks have the following order: first, definitions, then propositions, and finally argumentation or demonstration. This is the usual threefold division referred to in the following annotations.

It might be noted that in most logic texts these processes are studied only in the perspective of the demonstrative mode of human knowledge. If philosophy is to stand at the culmination of all facets of the arts and sciences, the study of this mode must be complemented by a view of the dialectical, rhetorical, and literary modes. Where this material is not introduced into the logic text or the course in literature, it could be added with profit from another source.[4]

The reader is referred to Chapter II of *A Bibliography of Christian Philosophy and Contemporary Issues* by the same editor.

---

[4] E.g. Benedict M. Ashley, *The Arts of Learning and Communication: A Handbook of the Liberal Arts* (Dubuque: Priory Press, 1958).

ADLER, Mortimer J. *Dialectic* (International Library of Psychology, Philosophy, and Scientific Method). New York: Harcourt, Brace, 1927. 265 pp.

A study of the diverse processes of discovery, description, and interpretation, aimed at sharpening one's grasp of truth. Controversy and discourse are studied as modes of discovery; the empirical, logical, and metaphysical modes of description are reviewed; and the characteristics proper to philosophical and scientific interpretation are distinguished. C

ASHLEY, Benedict M. *Aristotle's Sluggish Earth.* See V.

————. *The Arts of Learning and Communication: A Handbook of the Liberal Arts.* Dubuque: Priory Press, 1961 (1958). xvii, 622 pp.

A study of the various approaches of the mind to truth and its expression. The four types of logical discourse and the natural, formal, efficient, and final causes of the fine arts are discussed and exemplified, along with the nature of the science of numbers and magnitudes. This work can be very useful in broadening the scope of the usual logic course as the key to a philosophy which will be truly the culmination of the arts; it could also serve in high school English courses. A-B

See: R. Nordberg, CER 57 (1959) 417; CSJ 59 (1959) 52; D 44 (1959) 419.

BACHHUBER, Andrew H. *Introduction to Logic.* New York: Appleton-Century-Crofts, 1957. xiv, 332 pp.

A textbook in scholastic logic, proceeding inductively from examples to an understanding of general principles, and from the mechanics of logic to philosophical explanations. In some parts of the book, this puts a premium on memory rather than on reason. A distinction is drawn between intellective and rational induction. The treatment of modern mathematical logic is not adequate. B

See: MS 36 (1958) 75; NS 32 (1958) 274; T 33 (1958) 304.

BENNETT, Owen. *The Nature of Demonstrative Proof According to the Principles of Aristotle and St. Thomas Aquinas*

(The Catholic University of America. *Philosophical Studies,*
No. 75). Washington, D.C: The Catholic University of
America Press, 1943. 97 pp. Bibliography, index. (Paper)

A study of demonstration in the Thomistic tradition. Its origins
and metaphysical foundations are reviewed, but the main attention is given to its division, systematic explanation, and interpretation. C

> *See:* NS 16 (1942) 72.

BITTLE, Celestine N. *The Science of Correct Thinking: Logic,*
Revised ed. Milwaukee: Bruce, 1950 (1937). 419 pp.

A simple book following the usual threefold division, with the
addition of induction and the fallacies. Although wordy, it contains excellent chapter summaries and lists of suggested readings.
In the revised edition, exercises on the matter of each chapter are
included. A-B

> *See:* MS 13 (1935) 22; S 15 (1935) 127.

BODKIN, Richard C. *How to Reason: or, The A B C of Logic
Reduced to Practice in Analyzing Essays, Speeches, Books.*
4th ed. Dublin: Browne and Nolan, 1907 (1902). 231 pp.

A very clear text on logic, stressing the practical implementation
of logical analysis. After surveying the nature and rules for propositions and syllogisms, the author proceeds directly to the importance and methods of reducing sentences, paragraphs, and stories
to their component parts and subjecting each to close analysis.
An extended appendix contains a treatment of definition and fal-
lacy, along with passages from classical writings that can be of
service in exemplifying the logical procedures discussed. A-B

————. *Logic for All.* Chicago: Regnery, 1955. 91 pp. Appendix.
(Angelus Books; Divine Word)

A simple, almost pamphlet style, abbreviation of *How to Reason,*
describing the matter of logic. After a consideration of propositions and syllogisms, it proceeds to a section on logical analysis,
offering some practical advice on how to think precisely. An appendix contains some notions on fallacies and on definition. A

CLARK, Joseph T. *Conventional Logic and Modern Logic: A Prelude to Transition* (The American Catholic Philosophical Association. *Philosophical Studies*, Vol. 3). Woodstock: Woodstock College Press, 1952. x, 109 pp. Bibliography, indices.

A scholarly study of the relations between three different types of logic: Aristotelian, traditional, and Scholastic. The author presents evidence that ancient and Scholastic logic hold the seeds and inner requirements of modern symbolic techniques, especially those of propositional calculus. A preface by W. V. Quine is of special interest. C-D

See: D 6 (1953) 220; MS 31 (1953) 45.

CLARKE, Richard F. *Logic* ("Stonyhurst Philosophical Series"). London: Longmans, Green, 1926. 497 pp.

A thorough book in the Scholastic tradition. It is clearly written but goes more deeply than do most texts, tracing many positions in logic to their epistemological root in problems of modern philosophy. B-C

COFFEY, Peter. *The Science of Logic: An Inquiry into the Principles of Accurate Thought and Scientific Method.* 2 vols. New York: Smith, 1938 (1912).

The most comprehensive treatment of Scholastic logic existing in English. The first volume follows the usual threefold division, with a detailed statement of the nature of logic. The second volume follows the presuppositions and processes of the mind by which, through induction, hypothesis and demonstration, it arrives at certitude, probability, opinion or error. The author shows how the philosophy of Aristotle and the Schoolmen contains the basis for modern methods of scientific investigation, both inductive and deductive. C-D

See: A 7 (1912) 451; CW 96 (1912) 402.

COLLINS, William B. *Speculative Philosophy.* See II.

COTTER, Anthony C. *The A B C of Scholastic Philosophy.* See II.

————. *Logic and Epistemology*. Boston: Stratford, 1936. vii, 324 pp.

An elementary presentation of the fundamental principles of Scholastic philosophy in thesis form. Technical language is avoided. A-B

See: A 43 (1930) 409.

CRUMLEY, Thomas. *Logic: Deductive and Inductive*. New York: Macmillan, 1926. 442 pp.

A well-constructed work in which deductive logic is treated relatively briefly and according to the usual threefold division of terms, propositions, and syllogisms, with special attention being given to the role of hypothesis. B-C

See: A 35 (1926) 70.

DOPP, Joseph. *Formal Logic* (The Philosophical Series of the Higher Institute of Philosophy. University of Louvain). Trans. by J. Ramirez and R. Sweeney. New York: Wagner, 1960. xxvii, 191 pp.

This is only the first volume of the original French work, *Leçons de logique formelle*. Predicative propositions are presented along with a distinctive method for their analysis. Deduction is developed on the basis of the treatment of propositions. It contains lists of exercises. B-C

See: IER 96 (1961) 127; ITQ 28 (1961) 245; R. Connell, NS 37 (1964) 237-43.

DOUGHERTY, Kenneth. *Logic: An Introduction to Aristotelian Formal Logic*. 2d ed. revised. Peekskill, N.Y.: Graymoor Press, 1956 (1952). 158 pp. Bibliography, index.

According to the ordinary threefold division, the matter is grouped on the basis of its pertinence to concepts, judgments, or reasoning. There are many examples, and the whole work is marked by simplicity. A-B

See: AER 135 (1956) 278; O. Bennett, NS 30 (1956) 509.

GERRITY, Benignus. *Nature, Knowledge, and God*. See II.

GIANELLI, Arnold P. *Meaningful Logic.* Milwaukee: Bruce, 1962. x, 246 pp. (Paper)

A particularly effective, though simply written, basic logic text. After providing an initial insight into the significance of logic as a science, it studies the three levels of judgment and reasoning in a number of brief, clear chapters. These are followed by studies of the fallacies, induction, proof and hypothesis. A-B

See: PS 12 (1963) 323.

GILBY, Thomas. *Barbara Celarent: A Description of Scholastic Dialectic.* London: Longmans, Green, 1949. xiii, 303 pp.

A good exposition of Aristotelian-Thomistic logic, free of mnemonics other than the two words of the title. While obscure and highly technical words are replaced by more ordinary language, some background in philosophy would be required by the reader. It will reassure teachers of logic that their subject can be lively and even delightful. B-C

See: T. McGovern, A 81 (1949) 193; R. McCall, C 50 (1949) 440; J. Mullaney, CR 33 (1950) 235; G. McSorley, CW 171 (1950) 235; D 34 (1949) 160; J. Cameron, DR 67 (1949) 469; G. Klubertanz, MS 27 (1949) 62; E. Gannon, T 24 (1950) 739-40; J. O'Leary, T 8 (1949) 26; J. Hawkins, Ta 193 (1949) 286.

GLENN, Paul J. *Dialectics: A Class Manual in Formal Logic.* 4th ed. St. Louis: Herder, 1933 (1929). xxi, 187 pp.

A simple, yet comprehensive and well-organized Scholastic text designed for a one-semester undergraduate course. It contains useful outlines at the beginning of each chapter. However, its oversimplifications detract from its general clarity and scientific character. A-B

See: A 43 (1930) 409; CW 131 (1930) 253.

GLUTZ, Melvin. *The Manner of Demonstrating in Natural Philosophy.* See V.

GORMAN, Margaret. *General Semantics and Contemporary Thomism (The Educational Implications of the Theory of Meaning and Symbolism of General Semantics).* Lincoln,

Nebraska: University of Nebraska Press, 1962 (1958). xiii, 195 pp. Bibliography. (Bison: BB 146)

In this work, the historical background and central theories of symbolism and meaning proposed by the general semanticists are presented and compared with the positions of Thomistic philosophy. There is a critical study of the educational implications of these positions. B-C

See: ACSR 24 (1963) 93.

GRAJEWSKI, Maurice J. *The Formal Distinction of Duns Scotus.* See XVI.

GRENIER, Henri. *Thomistic Philosophy.* See II.

HARTMANN, Sylvester J. *Fundamentals of Logic.* St. Louis: Herder, 1949. vi, 271 pp. Bibliography, index.

An Aristotelian text that follows the order of the *Organon* and illustrates the topics under discussion. The section on scientific method contains examples and exercises drawn from other courses, thus encouraging students to integrate the whole program of instruction and immediately to apply what they learn. B

See: C. Miltner, AM 70 (1949) 250; C 50 (1949) 134; J. Ryan, CER 47 (1949) 569; CSJ 49 (1949) 18A; R. Smith, NS 23 (1949) 253-54; E. Gannon, T 24 (1949) 739; Th 12 (1949) 391-92.

————. *A Textbook of Logic: A Normative Analysis of Thought.* New York: American, 1936. xv, 448 pp.

This book develops the usual threefold division, according to concept, judgment, and inference, more amply than most textbooks. Consideration is also given to scientific method and to fallacies. There is an appendix on the psychological sources of error. Exercises and a synopsis conclude each chapter. B

See: A 56 (1937) 454; AM 45 (1937) 378; Bl 19 (1938) 157.

HOUDE, Roland, and FISCHER, Jerome J. *Handbook of Logic.* Dubuque: Brown, 1954. 156 pp.

A clear, concise, and adequate introductory text. It covers the three acts of the mind as in traditional Scholastic logic, and adds a consideration of contemporary problems pertinent to logic, such as mathematical logic, semantics, positivism, and propaganda. Exercises are available in a separate workbook. B

——. *Readings in Logic*. Dubuque: Brown, 1958. 316 pp. Bibliography.

A very well-organized, up-to-date collection of readings aimed at sharpening the critical faculties of the student. Parts I and II, on universals, statements, and arguments, are suitable for undergraduate use. Part III, on the history of logic, is planned for more advanced seminars. The exercises are effective. B-C

See: J. Mullally, NS 34 (1960) 120-24.

JOHN OF ST. THOMAS. *The Material Logic of John of St. Thomas*. See IV.

——. *Outlines of Formal Logic* (Medieval Philosophical Texts in Translation, No. 8). Trans. by F. Wade. Milwaukee: Marquette University Press, 1962 (1955). vi, 136 pp.

A work on formal logic divided according to the three operations of the mind. Continuing in the line of medieval Scholasticism, the detailed analysis of logical problems by John of St. Thomas represents the Scholastic culmination of the development of Aristotelian logic. C-D

See: G. Hollenhorst, NS 30 (1956) 490.

JOYCE, George H. *Principles of Logic*. 3d ed. ("Stonyhurst Philosophical Series"). London: Longmans, Green, 1956 (1908). 431 pp.

After treating comprehensively matters usually found in a logic text, the author discusses such questions of applied logic as experimentation, hypothesis, the elimination of chance, and classification. Some exercises are appended. The work is more thorough than most texts. B-C

See: CW 88 (1909) 830.

KNOWLEDGE AND EXPRESSION. See I.

KREYCHE, Robert J. *Logic for Undergraduates.* Revised ed. New York: Holt, Rinehart and Winston, 1961 (1954). xi, 356 pp. Bibliography.

A simple and practical Scholastic text. The usual divisions of a logic text are introduced, after which the author gives special attention to the categorical, argumentative, and hypothetical processes, together with symbolic correlations. The work contains many good illustrations, and has practical exercises at the end of each chapter. There is also a very helpful glossary. B

See: J. Madigan, CER 25 (1954) 262; J. Doyle, NS 29 (1955) 340.

McCALL, Raymond J. *Basic Logic.* 2d ed. revised. New York: Barnes and Noble, 1961 (1947). xxvi, 235 pp. (Paper)

A Scholastic text for undergraduates, based on Jacques Maritain's *An Introduction to Logic.* A digression on the value of Euler's circles as diagrams for explaining predication adds to the value of the book. However, material fallacies and relations to symbolic logic are not developed, and some minor terminological confusions may lead to difficulties for the student. B

See: Tm 10 (1947) 513-17.

McINERNY, Ralph. *The Logic of Analogy: An Interpretation of St. Thomas.* The Hague: Nijhoff, 1961. x, 184 pp. Bibliography.

A scholarly investigation of analogy identifying it particularly in terms of logic. After identifying the general problem, it is studied especially in relation to names. Then through the notions of cause and knowledge, the problem is extended to that of the divine names. D

See: D. Burrell, IPQ 2 (1962) 643-58; J. Ross, IPQ 2 (1962) 633-42, 658-62; MS 40 (1963) 198; J. Casaubon, Sa 18 (1963) 141.

McLAUGHLIN, Joseph A. *An Outline and Manual of Logic.* Revised ed. Milwaukee: Marquette University Press, 1938. xviii, 165 pp. Index.

A Scholastic text suitable only for a brief course. The essentials of minor logic are covered, with additional attention being given to classification and analogy. Effective examples illustrate the matter. B

See: A 48 (1938) 340.

MAHONY, Michael J. *Essentials in Formal Logic.* New York: Encyclopedia Press, 1918 (1917). 95 pp.

A textbook of logic following the traditional division according to simple apprehension, judgment, and reasoning. There are also some observations on method. The short, schematic chapters are too brief to provide more than the essentials, and are in need of explanation by the teacher. B

See: A 19 (1918) 194.

MARITAIN, Jacques. *Formal Logic* (*An introduction to Logic*). Trans. by I. Choquette from *Petite logique.* Revised ed. New York: Sheed and Ward, 1946 (1937). 300 pp.

In this well-planned general survey, the chapters are divided according to the three acts of the mind. There are appendices on logical algebra and pedagogical hints. B-C

See: A 59 (1938) 94; AM 47 (1938) 250; Bl 19 (1938) 155; C 27 (1938) 360; CW 147 (1938) 765; DR 56 (1938) 256; HPR 38 (1938) 782; IER 52 (1938) 101; MS 15 (1938) 68; S 17 (1938) 633; Ta 171 (1938) 142.

MERCIER, Désiré F. *Elements of Logic.* Partial trans. by E. Mac-Pherson of *Logique.* 3d ed. New York: Manhattanville Press, 1912 (1897). 77 pp.

A brief, simple, almost schematic presentation of the usual three sections of formal logic. There are also sections on scientific systematization, and on logic and truth. This work has many of the characteristics of the more comprehensive *Manual of Modern Scholastic Philosophy* by the same author. B

MOODY, Ernest. *The Logic of Ockham.* See XVI.

―――. *Truth and Consequences in Medieval Logic: Studies in Logic and the Foundations of Mathematics.* Amsterdam: North Holland, 1953. viii, 113 pp. Bibliography.

After surveying the development of medieval logic and such notions as signification and supposition, the author centers on the relation of the theories of truth conditions and consequence. D

See: J. Thomas, DS 7 (1954) 281.

MORRIS, Hilaire. *Philosophy for Beginners.* See II.

MOURANT, John A. *Formal Logic: An Introductory Textbook* ("Christian Wisdom Series"). New York: Macmillan, 1963. xvii, 421 pp. Bibliography, index.

In this general text on traditional and modern logic, the traditional threefold material logic is presented with a further study of fallacies. Some themes from modern logic, such as symbolic logic and calculation, are included, and there is a special section on induction. B

OESTERLE, John A. *Logic: The Art of Defining and Reasoning.* 2d ed. revised. Englewood Cliffs, N.J.: Prentice-Hall, 1963 (1952). vii, 279 pp. (Paper)

Clear and challenging, this text is one of the most highly praised for undergraduates. It is based on the *Organon* and on St. Thomas Aquinas. Both the formal and material logic of the act of reasoning are included, but the act of judgment by itself is not treated. The appendix contains an English translation of the first three lessons of St. Thomas' *Commentary on Aristotle's* DE INTER-PRETATIONE. A set of questions and one or two worksheets follow most of the chapters. B

See: D 38 (1953) 52-53; DS 6 (1953) 220; NS 27 (1953) 349; Tm 16 (1963) 296-97.

PEGIS, Anton. (ed.) *Essays in Modern Scholasticism.* See II.

POLAND, William. *The Laws of Thought, or Formal Logic: A Brief Comprehensive Treatise on the Laws and Methods of Correct Thinking.* Revised ed. Chicago: Loyola University Press, 1921 (1892). 110 pp.

Initially, this text follows the usual threefold division of matter according to ideas and terms, judgments and propositions, and reasoning and argument. Interesting material is added on the truth of premises and the scientific method. While somewhat dated, it is sufficiently divided to be clear without being schematic. B

See: A 6 (1911) 67.

RIEDL, John O. *Exercises in Logic.* Milwaukee: Marquette University Press, 1947. 55 pp.

A supplement to most textbooks, presenting practice materials. A summary of the fallacies and the rules of deduction are also included. B

SCHEU, Mary M. *The Categories of Being in Aristotle and St. Thomas.* See VII.

SIMMONS, Edward D. *The Scientific Art of Logic: An Introduction to the Principles of Formal and Material Logic.* ("Christian Culture and Philosophy Series"). Milwaukee: Bruce, 1961. xvi, 331 pp.

This attractive and challenging text is based mainly upon Aristotle's works in logic. Other sources include Porphyry, and the *Commentaries* of St. Thomas, St. Albert, Cajetan, and John of St. Thomas. The author is alert to the need of opening the perspective of logic to the full possibilities of dialectic and rhetoric in order to establish a relation of logic to other arts courses. This comprehensive and mature development of conventional logic leads to an adequate treatment of symbolic correlations. Included are many attractive and original exercises, with particular emphasis on syllogisms. B

See: CSJ 62 (1962) 17; MS 39 (1962) 410; J. Doyle, NS 37 (1964) 244-47; PS 11 (1961) 325.

SMITH, Vincent E. *The Elements of Logic.* Milwaukee: Bruce, 1957. xi, 298 pp.

In this Scholastic text the author, a philosopher of science, introduces several hundred quotations from eminent philosophers and scientists in order to exemplify both bad and good logic in discussions concerning the great issues. The philosophical foundations of logic are traced and emphasis is placed on modern applications of logic and its use in scientific methodology. It is more scientific than most texts. B-C

See: D 42 (1957) 268; ITQ 25 (1958) 206; MS 37 (1960) 143; PS 7 (1957) 240; Tm 21 (1958) 214-15.

SULLIVAN, Daniel J. *Fundamentals of Logic.* New York: Mc-Graw-Hill, 1963. xii, 288 pp. Bibliography, index, appendices.

The material of this general text is arranged according to the traditional threefold division, followed by a section on fallacies. Elements for a more penetrating course on the problem of universals, symbolic logic, and the theory of signs are placed in the appendices. The book is well-adapted for its stated purpose. B

THOMAS AQUINAS, Saint. *Demonstration.* See XV.

————. *Exposition of the Posterior Analytics.* See XV.

————. *On Interpretation.* See XV.

TOOHEY, John J. *An Elementary Handbook of Logic.* 3d ed. New York: Appleton-Century-Crofts, 1948 (1918). 194 pp. Bibliography, index.

A concise Scholastic text that gives the teacher an opportunity to introduce his students to Aristotle's own logical works and also to apply correct thinking to current problems. There is an interesting section on exceptions to the rules of the categorical syllogism. A-B

See: J. Ryan, CER 46 (1948) 685.

TURNER, William. *Lessons in Logic* (The Catholic University Series of Textbooks in Philosophy). Washington, D.C.: The Catholic Education Press, 1947. 302 pp.

A useful text that basically follows the usual division according to terms and definition, judgment and proposition, and syllogism and reasoning. There are also sections on induction and method. B

See: A 5 (1911) 546; CW 96 (1912) 254.

VARVELLO, Francesco. *Minor Logic*. Trans. and revised by A. Fearon from *Institutiones Philosophiae*. San Francisco, Calif.: University of San Francisco Press, 1942 (1931). 125 pp. (Paper)

The first section of this serviceable text is on perception and expression, but thereafter the author follows the conventional pattern of judgment followed by reasoning. There are very useful summaries of each chapter. B

VEATCH, Henry. *Realism and Nominalism Revisited* (The Aquinas Lecture, 1954). Milwaukee: Marquette University Press, 1954. vi, 82 pp.

In this lecture the problems of nominalism and realism are traced to the introduction of the mathematical conception of function and argument into logical analysis. These problems are identified in contemporary logic. The work will be of interest to those concerned with the nature of mathematical logic, provided they have some philosophical background. C

   See: D 40 (1955) 82; PS 5 (1955) 164.

WALSH, Joseph B. *Logic*. New York: Fordham University Press, 1940. 115 pp.

In this textbook the usual division according to the three acts of the mind is followed. There are ample examples and some exercises. B

WEBERING, Damascene. *Theory of Demonstration According to William of Ockham*. See XVI.

CHAPTER IV

Epistemology

The works in this chapter center on what is variously termed critics, criteriology, epistemology, material logic, or major logic.[1] They concern the variations in types of knowledge and concentrate on the truth value of each. As appropriate to the work of wisdom, this reflective process has classically been considered a part of metaphysics. Also included are works written from a Thomistic viewpoint that evaluate those contemporary philosophical systems, such as logical positivism or linguistic analysis, which concentrate on the truth value of knowledge. Works centering upon the type of knowledge proper to one or another of the other parts of philosophy have been placed within the respective chapters.

The reader is referred to Chapter II of *A Bibliography of Christian Philosophy and Contemporary Issues* by the same editor.

---

[1] For a discussion of the distinction between formal and material logic and between minor and major logic, see Yves Simon's introduction to *The Material Logic of John of St. Thomas* (Chicago: University of Chicago Press, 1955), pp. ix-xviii.

ADLER, Mortimer. *Problems for Thomists: The Problem of Species.* See VI.

ARDLEY, Gavin. *Aquinas and Kant: the Foundations of Modern Sciences.* See XV.

BARRON, Joseph T. *Elements of Epistemology.* New York: Macmillan, 1931. 225 pp.
A clearly written text on the problem of knowledge. Although brief, it is still sufficiently comprehensive for reference use and contains a creditable history of the problem of knowledge. B

BITTLE, Celestine N. *Reality and the Mind: Epistemology.* Milwaukee: Bruce, 1939 (1936). 390 pp. Bibliography, index.
This textbook provides a concise history of the problem of knowledge and a discussion on the inadequacy of modern theories. There are a glossary of definitions and diagrams which, however, would be of little value without professional direction. Although the vocabulary employed is simple enough, the author tends to be verbose, a fault that is partially remedied by brief chapter summaries. B
   See: AER 96 (1937) 219; HPR 37 (1937) 1005; IER 49 (1937) 215; MS 14 (1936) 19.

BRENNAN, Robert E. *Essays in Thomism.* See II.

CHARLESWORTH, Maxwell J. *Philosophy and Linguistic Analysis* (Duquesne Studies. "Philosophical Series, No. 9"). Pittsburgh: Duquesne University Press, 1959. xiii, 234 pp. (Paper)
An excellent introduction to analytic philosophy by a Thomist with prior training in linguistic analysis. The uniqueness of the activity rather than the doctrine of analytic philosophy is pointed out. The differences and similarities between the analysts are shown throughout the book, and especially in the concluding chapter, though the interpretation of Wittgenstein has been questioned. The ways in which Scholastic philosophy can be enriched by the analytic approach are underlined. Linguistic terms are

considered capable of expressing metaphysical issues, sometimes with special pertinence to the real issue. C-D

See: L. Barth, MS 38 (1960) 69; H. Nielsen, NS 34 (1960) 262; PS 9 (1959) 242; H. St.-Denis, RUO 29 (1959) 169*; Sa 15 (1960) 148; R. Smith, Tm 23 (1960) 306; W. Clarke, T 35 (1960) 416.

CHISHOLM, Roderick M. *Realism and the Background of Phenomenology.* See XVII.

COFFEY, Peter. *Epistemology; or the Theory of Knowledge: An Introduction to General Metaphysics.* 2 vols. Gloucester, Mass.: Smith, 1958 (1917).

A vast, comprehensive presentation of the usual epistemological questions along with what is actually a history of modern philosophy from the point of view of the problem of knowledge. Epistemology is viewed neither as an end in itself, nor as defensive metaphysics, but as a prolegomenon to that science. C

See: A 18 (1918) 501.

COPLESTON, Frederick. *Contemporary Philosophy: Studies of Logical Positivism and Existentialism.* Westminster, Md.: Newman, 1956. 230 pp.

A collection of essays dealing with empiricism, analytic philosophy, and existentialism. The personalist and existentialist philosophies are treated sympathetically, with special emphasis on the existentialist concern with human freedom, interpersonal communication, and the problem of God. A receptive approach is also manifested in treating the empiricist and analytic study of sense data. B-C

See: C. Boehm, AM 84 (1956) 23; Bl 37 (1956) 387; D 41 (1956) 367; J. Coulson, DR 74 (1956) 395; IER 86 (1956) 445; P. McKevitt, IEQ 23 (1956) 290; J. Collins, MS 35 (1957) 65; H. Veatch, NS 31 (1957) 422; PS 6 (1956) 199; T 32 (1957) 139; J. Cameron, Ta 207 (1956) 473; J. Mullaney, Th 20 (1957) 225.

COTTER, Anthony C. *The A B C of Scholastic Philosophy.* See II.

———. *Logic and Epistemology.* See III.

CUNNINGHAM, Walter F. *Notes on Epistemology.* Revised ed. New York: Fordham University Press, 1958 (1930). 179 pp. An extremely simple text in thesis form. After a consideration of certitude, doubt, and falsity, the validity of the various processes of knowledge is reviewed, and an attempt is made to ascertain a universal criterion of truth. A-B

DALOS, Patrick M. *The Critical Value of Concepts and Universal Ideas.* Romae: Officium Libri Catholici, 1959. 160 pp. (Paper)
A study of the history, nature, and value of universal ideas. After reviewing the history of universal ideas in ancient and modern philosophy, the author states their transcendent value in both the Kantian and realistic systems. Finally, the objective value of concepts, as presented in both moderate and critical realism, is defined. C

DAY, Sebastian J. *Intuitive Cognition.* See XVI.

DE KONINCK, Charles. *The Hollow Universe* (Whidden Lectures, 1959). New York: Oxford University Press, 1964 (1960). xii, 127 pp. (Paper)
An attempt to explain and prove that philosophy possesses a content distinct from that of modern science. As regards biology, the author challenges the view that scientific knowledge is of greater value than knowledge derived from all other sources. B-C
See: D 46 (1961) 78; NS 36 (1962) 554; PS 11 (1961) 259; T 36 (1961) 301.

DESAN, Wilfrid. *The Planetary Man.* See XVII.

ETHICS AND OTHER KNOWLEDGE. See I.

FLEMING, Thomas V. *Foundations of Philosophy.* See II.

FROM AN ABUNDANT SPRING. See II.

GALLAGHER, Kenneth T. *The Philosophy of Knowledge.* New York: Sheed and Ward, 1964. 305 pp. Index.

A general text on epistemology, with special emphasis on the problems and insights from contemporary existential thought. The modern problem of knowledge is traced from Descartes, and the point of departure for a study of knowledge is identified in the contemporary terms of being-in-the-world. The various acts of the mind are evaluated, and attention is centered on the problems of intersubjective knowledge and existential truth. B

GERRITY, Benignus. *Nature, Knowledge, and God.* See II.

GILBY, Thomas. *Phoenix and Turtle: The Unity of Knowing and Being.* New York: Longmans, Green, 1950. xi, 154 pp.

A Thomistic exposition of the unity of knowledge and being, achieved in an original and refreshing style. The subject is treated in the light of moderate realism in the Aristotelian tradition and there is an outline for the refutation of idealism. Anyone who considers philosophy dull will find here proof that the subject can be stimulating and pleasant. B-C

　　See: R. Pollock, A 83 (1950) 603; Bl 81 (195) 439; E. Littlejohn, C 52 (1950) 298; CW 171 (1950) 480; D 35 (1950) 193; E. Gannon, T 26 (1951) 475; T. Gregory, Ta 195 (1950) 360-61.

GLENN, Paul J. *Criteriology: A Class Manual in Major Logic.* St. Louis: Herder, 1937 (1933). xi, 261 pp.

A general survey of the field of epistemology. Special stress is laid on the problem of the reliability of rational knowledge as a basis for faith. A

　　See: A 50 (1934) 598; CW 138 (1934) 761.

GRENIER, Henri. *Thomistic Philosophy.* See II.

HASSETT, Joseph, MITCHELL, Robert A., and MONAN, James. *The Philosophy of Human Knowing: A Text for College Students.* Westminster, Md.: Newman, 1953. 173 pp.

A clear and uncluttered introductory textbook in which is analyzed the problem of knowledge. After exposing the positions of skepticism, idealism, and materialism, the authors aim to justify the truth-value of human knowledge. This they attempt by an

examination of the knowing process itself as it grasps reality. Selected readings are listed. A-B
See: CSJ 53 (1953) 37; T 29 (1954) 473.

HAUSMANN, Bernard A. *From an Ivory Tower.* See V.

HAWKINS, Denis J. *The Criticism of Experience.* London: Sheed and Ward, 1946 (1945). x, 124 pp. Bibliography, index.

A stimulating and original work, typical of the author's many writings. The problem of knowledge or criticism of experience in the seventeenth and eighteenth centuries is analyzed with both parsimony and relevance in order to achieve an effective historical clarification of the problem. His own theory of intuitive perception is inspired by Hamilton and Reid. C
See: Bl 27 (1946) 74-75; CR 26 (1946) 92-95; D 32 (1947) 213-15; DuR 218 (1946) 187-88; IER 68 (1946) 140; St 35 (1946) 137-38; Ta 186 (1945) 250.

HEALY, Emma T. *St. Bonaventure's* DE REDUCTIONE ARTIUM AD THEOLOGIAM. See XVI.

HOENEN, Peter. *Reality and Judgment According to St. Thomas* ("Library of Living Catholic Thought"). Trans. by H. Tiblier from *La théorie du jugement d'après St. Thomas d'Aquin.* Chicago: Regnery, 1952 (1946). xv, 344 pp. Appendix.

This work, an important contribution to contemporary Thomistic literature, affords an original theory of judgment, founded on reflection. While it heightens the attention given by St. Thomas to *esse,* the theory as stated can be ascribed to him only with reservation. There is a useful indexed collection of texts, both English and Latin, pertaining to judgment. The translation is excellent, but the notes are inconveniently placed at the end of the book. C-D
See: AER 130 (1954) 65; CER 51 (1953) 139; NS 28 (1953) 226; T 28 (1953) 287; Tm 16 (1953) 131.

HOUDE, Roland, and MULLALLY, Joseph. (eds.) *Philosophy of*

Knowledge: Selected Readings. Chicago: Lippincott, 1960. xiii, 427 pp. Bibliography.

An original and enterprising collection of papers, most of which were written by and for scholars, on the theory of knowledge, with a dominant Aristotelian-Thomistic strain. There is considerable diversity in the problems discussed and the positions defended through the twenty-four readings. C-D

See: M. Beardsley, NS 35 (1961) 221.

JOHN OF ST. THOMAS. *The Material Logic of John of St. Thomas: Basic Treatises.* Trans. by Y. Simon, G. Glanville, and D. Hollenhorst from *Ars logica.* Chicago: University of Chicago Press, 1955. 638 pp.

A timely translation of a classic in the field of logic. The book treats the object and nature of logic, the universal, antepredicamental inquiries, categories, signs and concepts, demonstration, and science, and demonstrates the integrative power of Aristotelian logic. C-D

See: D 40 (1955) 320; MS 34 (1957) 304; NS 30 (1956) 232; Tm 19 (1956) 409.

KEELER, Leo W. *The Problem of Error from Plato to Kant.* (Pontificia Universitas Gregoriana. *Analecta Gregoriana,* No. 6.) Romae: Pontificia Universitas Gregoriana, 1934. 281 pp.

A thought-provoking critical survey in which St. Thomas' theory, with its related doctrines, provides the key to the study and brings out the essential interdependence of metaphysics and epistemology. There are some bibliographical footnotes. C

See: T 11 (1936) 145-47.

KNOWLEDGE AND EXPRESSION. See I.

LONERGAN, Bernard J. *Insight: A Study of Human Understanding.* New York: Philosophical Library, 1957. xxx, 785 pp. Index.

A study of the various forms of knowledge. One of the classics of recent times, it leads to an appreciation of the act of understanding and thence to metaphysics and ethics. By building upon a considerable variety of literary and scientific experience and a profound study of St. Thomas, partially as interpreted by J. Marechal, it encompasses the whole of philosophy. The author seeks to reconcile philosophers among themselves and to scientists. C-D

See: A 97 (1957) 591; ACSR 19 (1958) 375; CC 109 (1958) 291-97; CB 43 (1958) 58; D 42 (1957) 263; DR 77 (1958) 72; AER 140 (1959) 279; G 39 (1958) 136; HPR 58 (1957) 216; ITQ 25 (1958) 195; MS 35 (1958) 236-44; RUO 29 (1959) 120; St 46 (1957) 494; T 210 (1957) 60; T 32 (1957) 445; Tm 21 (1958) 554-60; TS 18 (1957) 629.

MARITAIN, Jacques. *The Degrees of Knowledge.* Trans. under the supervision of G. Phelan from the 4th French ed. of *Distinguer pour unir: ou, Les degrés du savoir.* New York: Scribner's, 1959. xix, 476 pp. Index.

A comprehensive treatment of the method, scope, and limitations of the various types of knowledge. Both the complexity and the all-embracing unity of human knowing are underlined. This more recent translation is more correct than its predecessor and includes a valuable elucidation on subsistence. The work is a milestone in the development of contemporary Thomism and its assimilation of what is new. C-D

See: D 45 (1960) 165-69; NS 34 (1960) 370; T. Berry, S 39 (1959) 64; St 49 (1960) 106; R. Henle, TS 20 (1959) 662.

———. *Freedom of the Intellect.* See II.

———. *The Range of Reason.* Trans. by Mrs. P. Brodin from *Raison et raisons.* New York: Scribner's, 1952 (1947). xii, 227 pp. Index. (Paper)

A collection of ten essays divided into two sections, one on human knowledge and metaphysics, and the other on faith and the human community. It is a fair summary of Maritain's philosophical thought. B-C

See: Bl 34 (1953) 556; C 57 (1953) 386; CW 19 (1953) 4; I 7 (1953) 38; LA 31 (1953) 678; RP 15 (1953) 389-92.

MARTIN, William O. *The Order and Integration of Knowledge.* See II.

MILLER, Barry. *The Range of Intellect.* See VI.

MOREUX, Theophile. *Modern Science and the Truths Beyond.* See II.

MORRISON, Bakewell and RUEVE, Stephen. *Think and Live.* See II.

O'NEILL, Charles J. *An Etienne Gilson Tribute.* See II.

O'NEILL, Reginald. (ed.) *Readings in Epistemology.* Englewood Cliffs, N.J.: Prentice-Hall, 1962. xv, 240 pp. (Paper)
A well-chosen collection of texts from key authors in the ancient, medieval, and modern periods, with helpful notes. This work is specially planned to accompany the editor's *Theories of Knowledge.* B
See: MS 41 (1964) 304.

————. *Theories of Knowledge.* Englewood Cliffs, N.J.: Prentice-Hall, 1960. xiv, 242 pp. Index.
A serviceable textbook that presents the Scholastic realistic approach to knowledge. It contains an analysis of opposing theories from modern and contemporary philosophies, centering on a series of so-called pure positions which recur in various forms. Although some may find confusing the division of concepts employed in presenting the universal, this work in general successfully fulfills the need for a text which is clear and up-to-date. When used in conjunction with the companion volume, *Readings in Epistemology,* it makes for quite profitable study. B
See: NS 35 (1961) 385; T 35 (1960) 459.

PEGIS, Anton. (ed.) *A Gilson Reader.* See II.

PHILOSOPHY AND THE EXPERIMENTAL SCIENCES. See I.

POLAND, William. *The Truth of Thought; or, Material Logic: A Short Treatise on the Initial Philosophy, the Groundwork*

Necessary for the Consistent Pursuit of Knowledge. Chicago, Ill.: Loyola University Press, 1916 (1896) .

A defense of man's capacity for transsubjective knowledge. The author surveys the main modern objections to this capacity, and then defines and investigates the problem in relation to the intellect as well as to the internal and external senses. The nature of certitude and error and the criterion of truth are also studied. The material is well-divided and presented in an interesting essay style. B

See: CW 63 (1896) 836.

REGIS. Louis M. *Epistemology* ("Christian Wisdom Series") . Trans. by I. Byrne. New York: Macmillan, 1959. xii, 549 pp. Index.

A major contribution to contemporary Thomism, it treats the philosophical problem in general and the modern problem of knowledge by way of a long interpretative commentary on the epistemological texts of St. Thomas Aquinas. It does not, however, provide an epistemological evaluation of modern mathematical physics. The questions are carefully ordered, the expositions clearly divided, and the summaries frequent. C-D

See: D 45 (1960) 78-81; Montague, MS 37 (1960) 236-42; NS 34 (1960) 394-99; J. Weisheipl, Tm 23 (1960) 287-90.

————. *St. Thomas and Epistemology* (The Aquinas Lecture, 1946) . Milwaukee: Marquette University Press, 1946. vii, 95 pp. Bibliography.

A brief preview of the distinctive character of the epistemology of St. Thomas, that stresses the opposition of authentic neo-Thomism to idealism. Thomism is shown to be based on the evidence of being as being, the proper object of metaphysical knowledge, rather than on common sense, as is proposed by some neo-Thomists of a more Cartesian orientation. C

See: D 32 (1947) 215-16; MS 25 (1947) 68; St 36 (1947) 376; T 22 (1947) 739-40; Tm 11 (1948) 136-38.

RICKABY, John. *The First Principles of Knowledge* ("Stonyhurst Philosophical Series") . 4th ed. London: Longmans, Green, 1926 (1901) . xiii, 412 pp.

A text on epistemology from the point of view of material logic, in answer to nineteenth-century criticism. The nature of certitude, evidence, and truth is studied. It has served well many generations of philosophy students. B

RIET, Georges Van. *Thomistic Epistemology: Studies Concerning the Problem of Cognition in the Contemporary Thomistic School.* Trans. by G. Franks of *L'épistemologie Thomiste.* St. Louis: Herder, 1963-64 (1946). 2 vols.

The first half of the translation of one of the more outstanding works in epistemology. This volume traces the recent history of the subject, with special attention to the work of Noel, Gilson, and Husserl. It investigates such notions as abstraction, evidence, intuition, reflection, and truth, with special consideration of these in relation to moral thought and of the Thomistic response to contemporary idealism and phenomenology. C

ROTHER, Aloysius J. *Certitude: A Study in Philosophy.* St. Louis: Herder, 1924 (1911). 94 pp.

A simply written statement of the nature of certitude, in a general thesis format. The nature, requisites, and properties of certitude are explained rather than defended. While not attentive to the many disputes in this area, it is a positive presentation of the traditional position. B-C

———. *Truth and Error: A Study in Critical Logic.* Philadelphia: Reilly, 1924 (1914). 129 pp.

In this work, presented in a modified thesis form, the truth of simple apprehension and judgment and its degrees are studied. The problem of error is also examined, with special attention being given to the part played by the will and the necessity of error. B

See: A 10 (1914) 475; CW 99 (1914) 404.

ROUSSELOT, Pierre. *The Intellectualism of Saint Thomas.* Trans. by J. O'Mahony from *L'intellectualisme de Saint Thomas.* New York: Sheed and Ward, 1935 (1924). vii, 231 pp. (Paper)

This examination, from the original source, affirms the absolute value of the act of intelligence and links philosophy and theology in an indissoluble synthesis. Many difficulties raised in this early return to the Aristotelian sources of St. Thomas were real, but have been solved by the further research to which this work points. C

See: A 55 (1936) 283; CW 143 (1936) 366.

SMITH, Vincent E. (ed.) *The Logic of Science* (St. John's University Studies. Philosophical Series, Vol. 4). Jamaica, N.Y.: St. John's University Press, 1964. iii, 90 pp. Index. (Paper)

A collection of lectures on the method of scientific investigation. The general history of this approach is studied and exemplified in a particular study of physics and chemistry. Induction is analyzed for its logical structure, and questions beyond the sphere of the sciences are identified. C

STEENBERGHEN, Fernand Van. *Epistemology* ("The Philosophical Series of the Higher Institute of Philosophy." University of Louvain). Trans. by M. Flynn from the 2d revised and corrected ed. of *Epistémologie*. New York: Wagner, 1949 (1945). 324 pp.

The aim of this work, an effort to find the roots of Thomistic epistemology, is to examine knowledge philosophically and to obtain a deeper insight into its meaning. Epistemology is approached as a prolegomenon to all other philosophical questions. C

See: IER 67 (1946) 423.

TALBOT, Edward F. *Knowledge and Object* (The Catholic University of America. *Philosophical Studies*, No. 24). Washington, D.C.: The Catholic University of America Press, 1932. iii, 115 pp. (Paper)

A clear and effective treatment of the relation existing between the intellect and the external material world. After a study of the nature of the epistemological question and of immateriality as the basis of knowledge, the relativity and immediacy of knowledge are effectively treated. B-C

TRETHOWAN, Illtyd. *Certainty: Philosophical and Theological.* See VIII.

——. *An Essay in Christian Philosophy.* See II.

TRUTH IN THE CONTEMPORARY CRISIS. See I.

TYRRELL, Francis M. *The Role of Assent in Judgment: A Thomistic Study.* (The Catholic University of America. *Philosophical Studies,* No. 100). Washington, D.C.: The Catholic University of America Press, 1948. xiii, 184 pp. Bibliography, index. (Paper)

A study of judgment and assent in Scholastic philosophy. The history of the understanding of the act of judgment is traced from the time of St. Thomas Aquinas to the present day. In this context the role of assent in voluntary and non-voluntary judgments and in the metaphysics of knowledge is isolated and evaluated. C

See: D 34 (1949) 58.

VARVELLO, Francesco. *Major Logic (Epistemology).* Trans. by A. Fearon from *Institutiones Philosophiae.* San Francisco, Calif.: University of San Francisco Press, 1933 (1931). 157 pp. Index. (Paper)

In this general text the states of the intellect in relation to truth are discussed, along with the means and methods of acquiring truth. The thesis method is used, but subordinated to the continuous development of the themes. There are useful summaries. B

VEATCH, Henry. *Realism and Nominalism Revisited.* See III.

VIER, Peter C. *Evidence and Its Function According to John Duns Scotus.* See XVI.

WALKER, Leslie J. *Theories of Knowledge: Absolutism, Pragmatism, Realism* (Stonyhurst Philosophical Series). 2d ed. London: Longmans, Green, 1934 (1910). xxxix, 705 pp.

A competent exposition of knowledge and its systems. The presentation of absolutism and pragmatism is followed by a detailed study of knowledge in its psychological, metaphysical, and epistemological aspects.

WEIGEL, Gustave, and MADDEN, Arthur G. *Knowledge: Its Values and Limits.* Englewood Cliffs, N.J.: Prentice-Hall, 1961. viii, 118 pp. Bibliography, indices. (Spectrum: S 16)

A description and critical evaluation of the more commonly recognized forms of knowledge, based on lectures by Father Weigel on the theory of knowledge. It contains some historical material, and attends especially to the problems and new personal horizons of knowledge for the contemporary mind. B-C

See: CSJ 62 (1962) 38; RE 57 (1962) 230.

WILHELMSEN, Frederick D. *Man's Knowledge of Reality: An Introduction to Thomistic Epistemology.* Englewood Cliffs, N.J.: Prentice-Hall, 1956. xii, 215 pp. Bibliography, index.

This epistemological text offers profound insights into the problem of knowledge, centering on the position that man grasps concrete sensible reality in the existential judgment. Many would dispute this position unless it were to be otherwise complemented. Since, in general, undergraduates are insufficiently grounded in this subject to follow the debate, the book is generally not considered to be sufficiently clear as a text, though the chapters are brief and there are clear summaries of the content along the side of the text. C

See: E. Tyrrell, NS 31 (1957) 123; E. Simmons, Tm 21 (1958) 542-53.

CHAPTER V

Cosmology: Philosophy of Physical Nature, Philosophy of Science

This chapter is devoted to works on what is variously termed cosmology, the philosophy of physical nature or natural philosophy, and the philosophy of science. Leaving to the next section the philosophy of living reality, the attention here is directed to the philosophy of physical reality in general and of the non-living in particular. Hence, studies on the order of the sciences on the physical level and general works or collections on the confrontation of philosophy and the physical sciences are included. While the expansion of scientific data makes imperative a continual review of these problems, the authentic philosophical insights of earlier works remain valid. Also included in this section are investigations of the philosophy of technology—where these studies are not primarily ethical—and of the philosophy of mathematics.[1]

The reader is referred to Chapter III of *A Bibliography of Christian Philosophy and Contemporary Issues* by the same editor.

---

[1] The following bibliographies are of special interest to the area covered by this chapter: "Bibliographie de l'histoire des sciences," *Archive internationale d'histoire des sciences*, XXXII (1953), 395-419; "Critical Bibliography of the History and Philosophy of Science and of the History of Civilization," *Isis*, (1912—); "Répertoire bibliographique de la philosophie des sciences," Supplement to *Bulletin de l'académie internationale de philosophie des sciences*.

ARDLY, Gavin. *Aquinas and Kant.* See XV.

ASHLEY, Benedict M. *Aristotle's Sluggish Earth: The Problematics of* DE COELO. River Forest, Ill.: Albertus Magnus Lyceum, 1958. viii, 73 pp. Bibliography.

In this study, various approaches to problematics are detailed, from the common-sense approach to the specific and scientific, with additional attention to Aristotle's mechanics. The work also surveys the approaches to demonstration from the common-sense and mathematical to that of the science of physics. C

BASCHAB, Charles R. *A Manual of Neo-Scholastic Philosophy.* See II.

BITTLE, Celestine N. *From Aether to Cosmos: Cosmology.* Milwaukee: Bruce, 1941. x, 498 pp. Bibliography, index.

This text, now rapidly going out of use, departs from the traditional order of treating the subject and overemphasizes the dependence of cosmology on modern science. The scientific content is in need of revision. Included are excellent doctrinal summaries, specified reading lists, and a glossary of terms. A-B

See: MS 18 (1941) 79; Tm 40 (1942) 356-58.

CALLAHAN, John F. *Four Views on Time in Ancient Philosophy.* See XIV.

CAUSALITY IN CURRENT PHILOSOPHY. See I.

COLLIGAN, John J. *Cosmology: A Philosophical Study of the Corporeal World.* New York: McMullen, 1949. 95 pp.

This brief, schematic text follows closely the thesis method, with room for little more than definition and proof of the basic data. A-B

COLLINGWOOD, Francis J. *Philosophy of Nature.* Englewood Cliffs, N.J.: Prentice-Hall, 1961. xi, 306 pp.

This textbook traces admirably the development of physical theory among the Greek philosophers. The psychology of man's capacity to know physical reality, rather than the content of this knowledge, is accented. This has left the actual treatment of the science of nature open to the charge of being a priori. For this reason it might be used best for the philosophy of science or as collateral reading on special problems in the methodology of the sciences. B

See: MS 39 (1962) 281; M. Glutz, NS 37 (1963) 86-88; Sa 17 (1962) 212; Tm 25 (1962) 317.

COLLINS, William B. *Speculative Philosophy.* See II.

CONNOLLY, Frederick G. *Science Versus Philosophy.* See II.

DOUGHERTY, Kenneth F. *Cosmology: An Introduction to the Thomistic Philosophy of Nature.* 2d ed. revised. Peekskill: Graymoor Press, 1955 (1952). 192 pp. Bibliography, index.

A systematic treatment of the philosophy of the corporeal world, divided according to the four causes and attentive to the findings of science up to the time of publication. The Scholastic thesis method is used and should be complemented by use of the pertinent texts of Aristotle and St. Thomas Aquinas indicated at the end of each chapter. It contains a bibliography for each chapter along with review questions. B

DUBARLE, Dominique. *Scientific Humanism and Christian Thought.* See II.

DULLES, Avery, DEMSKE, James, and O'CONNELL, Robert. *Introductory Metaphysics.* See II.

EFFLER, Roy R. *John Duns Scotus and the Principle: Omne quod movetur ab alio movetur.* See XVI.

FLEMING, Thomas V. *Foundations of Philosophy.* See II.

FOLEY, Leo A. *Cosmology, Philosophical and Scientific* ("Christian Culture and Philosophy Series"). Milwaukee: Bruce, 1962. viii, 312 pp. Bibliography.

This up-to-date text stresses the unity of philosophical and scientific truth. In three sections it treats the philosophical principles of material reality, the general properties of bodies, and the main problems of scientific cosmology, such as the atomic and nuclear theories and the nature and philosophy of life. In each section there are extensive historical observations, with the accent gradually shifting from the ancient to the modern. B

FRIEDRICH, Lawrence W. (ed.) *The Nature of Physical Knowledge*. Milwaukee: Marquette University Press, 1960. 156 pp.

A symposium conducted under the auspices of the Council of the American Physical Society in search of ways to increase unity of thought and understanding among philosophers and physicists. It includes papers by competent physicists and philosophers, both Scholastic and non-Scholastic. C

   See: MS 39 (1962) 269; NS 36 (1962) 122; Tm 25 (1962) 318.

FROM AN ABUNDANT SPRING. See II.

GARDEIL, Henri D. *Cosmology.* Vol. II of *Introduction to the Philosophy of St. Thomas Aquinas.* Trans. by J. Otto from *Cosmologie.* St. Louis: Herder, 1958 (1952). xii, 218 pp. Index.

Half of this standard textbook consists of excerpts from St. Thomas' *Commentary on the* PHYSICS *of Aristotle* and a full translation of *On the Principles of Nature.* This does not leave room for an adequate explanation of the subject by the author. It contains a good index of both names and subject matter. B

   See: ABR 9 (1958) 247; AER 139 (1958) 357-58; Bl 34 (1953) 207; D 38 (1953) 360; NS 30 (1959) 371; PS 8 (1958) 232; Tm 22 (1959) 130.

GERRITY, Benignus. *Nature, Knowledge and God.* See II.

————. *The Relation between the Theory of Matter and Form and the Theory of Knowledge in the Philosophy of St. Thomas Aquinas.* (The Catholic University of America. *Philosophical Studies,* No. 40). Washington, D.C.: The

Catholic University of America Press, 1939. viii, 164 pp. (Paper)

Initially, this study concentrates on the matter-form complex. It then turns to knowledge, in its intellectual characteristics as abstracted from matter, and in its relation to the material world through the senses. B-C

GLENN, Paul J. *Cosmology: A Class Manual in the Philosophy of Bodily Beings*. St. Louis: Herder, 1949 (1939). 338 pp.

In this text consideration is given to the origin of bodies, to their quantitative and atomic characteristics, and to their end, with its implications of tendencies and laws. It is exceptional to find a consideration of creation in this context. A-B

See: AM 49 (1939) 571; CSJ 39 (1939) 102; CW 149 (1939) 254; D 24 (1939) 69-70; HPR 39 (1939) 990-91; IER 61 (1943) 142; MS 16 (1939) 93; ST 28 (1939) 533.

GLUTZ, Melvin A. *The Manner of Demonstrating in Natural Philosophy* (The Aquinas Library). River Forest, Ill.: College of St. Thomas, 1956. xii, 184 pp. Bibliography.

A penetrating study of Aristotelian methodology in natural philosophy, centering on a systematic exposition of the doctrine contained in the *Posterior Analytics* and *Physics*, II. C

See: MS 35 (1958) 144; NS 31 (1957) 559; Tm 20 (1957) 365-69.

GRENIER, Henri. *Thomistic Philosophy*. See II.

HART, Charles A. (ed.) *Aspects of the New Scholastic Philosophy*. See II.

HAUSMANN, Bernard A. *From an Ivory Tower: A Discussion of Philosophical Problems Originating in Modern Mathematics*. Milwaukee: Bruce, 1960. vii, 122 pp. Index.

A presentation of the genesis and nature of some modern philosophical problems connected with mathematics. The background for the discussion is laid by a description of Euclidean geometry and the origin of the non-Euclidean varieties. The problems of

numbers, infinite classes, and the Boole-Schroeder algebra are discussed. Nontechnical terminology is used as much as possible. B-C
See: MS 39 (1962) 179; NS 36 (1962) 116; T 25 (1962) 458.

THE HISTORY AND PHILOSOPHY OF SCIENCE. See I.

HOENEN, Peter. *The Philosophical Nature of Physical Bodies* (West Baden Readings in Philosophy and Theology). Trans. by D. Hassel from the 4th revised ed. of *Cosmologia*, IV-1 and 2. West Baden Springs, Ind.: West Baden College, 1955 (1931). 75 pp. (Paper)
An exceptionally capable exposition of the hylomorphic composition of physical bodies and an extended study of substantial form, its nature, origin, and unicity in a compound. Special emphasis is placed on the substantial unity of compounds and the virtual presence of elemental forms. Copious references to Aristotle and St. Thomas are included. B-C

————. *The Philosophy of Inorganic Compounds* (West Baden Readings in Philosophy and Theology). Trans. by P. Conen from the 5th revised ed. of *Cosmologia*, IV-3. West Baden Springs, Ind.: West Baden College, 1960 (1931). 123 pp. (Paper)
An excellent and detailed study of the atomic theory and of the nature of inorganic compounds in the light of the principles of the physics of Aristotle and St. Thomas. B-C

JUNKERSFELD, Mary J. *The Aristotelian-Thomistic Concept of Chance.* Notre Dame, Ind.: Notre Dame University (Ann Arbor: Edwards Lithoprint), 1945. 86 pp. (Paper)
After a direct study of the nature of chance, its relation to the notion of causality and to God is studied. B-C
See: T 21 (1946) 556-57.

KANE, William H. *Approach to Philosophy.* See II.

————, CORCORAN, John D., ASHLEY, Benedict M., and NOGAR, Raymond J. *Science in Synthesis: A Dialectical*

Approach to the Integration of the Physical and the Natural Sciences (The Aquinas Library. *Doctrinal Studies,* No. 5). River Forest, Ill.: College of St. Thomas, 1953. 289 pp.

A study of the unity of the sciences within a philosophical perspective. This is the proceedings of the 1952 summer session of the Albertus Magnus Lyceum of Natural Science. Discussions concerning physics, chemistry, biology, and psychology, and a tentative outline for a unified natural science are included. B-C

See: CER 52 (1954) 67; CCr 5 (1953) 483; D 38 (1953) 256; DS 6 (1953) 222; NS 27 (1953) 477; Th 17 (1954) 268.

KOCKELMANS, Joseph A. *Phenomenology and Physical Science.* Trans. from *Phaenomenologie en natuurwetenschap.* Pittsburgh: Duquesne University Press, 1964 (1962).

A study of the relation of philosophy and science as contributed to by phenomenology. The emphasis on man in the world as the point of initiation for intellectual inquiry is applied to the approaches of science. C-D.

KOCOUREK, Roman A. (ed.) *An Introduction to the Philosophy of Nature.* St. Paul: North Central, 1948. iv, 176 pp.

After an introductory twenty-five pages on the principles of nature, the main body of this useful work consists of St. Thomas' *Commentary on the* PHYSICS *of Aristotle,* I and II. Appended is an outline of the complete work and of the physical works of Aristotle. B

See: Th 12 (1949) 227-29.

KONINCK, Charles De. *The Hollow Universe.* See IV.

KOREN, Henry J. *An Introduction to the Philosophy of Nature.* Pittsburgh: Duquesne University Press, 1960. xii, 199 pp. Index. (Paper)

This helpful text should be supplemented by the author's *Readings in the Philosophy of Nature.* The author treats hylomorphism as the explanation of the nature of matter and reviews other systems; he then examines the properties of matter and efficient and final causality on this level. The book contains a useful listing of suggested readings and review questions. B

See: NS 35 (1961) 378; PS 10 (1960) 281.

―――. *Readings in the Philosophy of Nature* ("The College Reading Series," No. 2) . Westminster, Md.: Newman, 1958. xi, 401 pp. (Paper)

An anthology composed of selections from the works of scientists and philosophers, both Scholastic and non-Scholastic. As an adjunct to a textbook it is invaluable for acquainting students with key statements pertinent to the problems treated in an introductory course in the philosophy of nature. The juxtaposition of excerpts from authors whose opinions differ, such as on the problems of the division of the sciences or the proof of hylomorphism, is most effective. B

See: CR 43 (1958) 762; CSJ 59 (1959) 62.

LAER, Pierre H. Van. *Philosophico-Scientific Problems* (Duquesne Studies. "Philosophical Series," No. 3) . Trans. by H. Koren from the French and Dutch. Pittsburgh: Duquesne University Press, 1953. 168 pp. (Paper)

A simple, solid treatment of the relevance of philosophy to modern science. Some would consider the distinction between the philosophy of nature and natural science somewhat overemphasized. Though it may prove difficult reading for the nonscientist, the problems it treats are ones which everyone must face. B-C

See: FS 14 (1954) 448; MS 32 (1955) 369; RPL 53 (1955) 453; Th 17 (1954) 599; T 30 (1955) 97.

―――. *The Philosophy of Science* (Duquesne Studies. "Philosophical Series," Nos. 6 & 14) . 2 vols. Pittsburgh: Duquesne University Press, 1963 (I-1956 and II-1962) . Index. (Paper)

A study of the nature and division of the sciences. The first volume, entitled *Science in General,* is concerned with the notion of science as a system, its necessity, object, foundations, and methods. The second volume, *A Study of the Division and Nature of Various Group Sciences,* is an historical and speculative study of the criteria by which sciences are classified and an application of these criteria in distinguishing the physical, cultural, and ideal sciences of philosophy and theology. There is also a chapter on the unity of the sciences. B-C

See: Th 21 (1958) 114; T 23 (1957) 635.

McKEOUGH, Michael J. *The Meaning of the Rationes Seminales in St. Augustine.* See XIV.

McLEAN, George F. *Philosophy in a Technological Culture.* See IX.

McMAHON, George J. *The Order of Procedure in the Philosophy of Nature.* Quebec: Doyon, 1958. 225 pp.

An excellent exposition of the method of procedure in the physical sciences according to the mind of Aristotle. The work is really a commentary on the Proemium of Aristotle's *Physics.* First, science is seen to be concerned with principles, causes, and elements. Then the direction from general to specific causes is analyzed and defended at length. C

McMULLIN, Ernan. (ed.) *The Concept of Matter.* Notre Dame, Ind.: University of Notre Dame Press, 1963. xi, 624 pp. Index.

This important document consists of papers from a symposium on matter in which all types of scientific and philosophical approaches are represented. It includes reports of the discussions which followed the papers and manifests the state of the question of matter at the time of the discussions according to the most capable scientists and philosophers. C-D

McWILLIAMS, James A. *Cosmology: A Textbook for Colleges.* 2d ed. revised. New York: Macmillan, 1938 (1933). x, 232 pp. Bibliography, index.

This text follows the traditional thesis method. It was long considered the best neo-Scholastic treatise on cosmology on the undergraduate level. Controversy is avoided. As regards scientific material, it is now inevitably out-of-date. B

See: A 40 (1928) 21; A 51 (1934) 19; CW 129 (1929) 374; CW 149 (1939) 255; NS 13 (1939) 198.

MARGENAU, Henry. *Thomas and the Physics of 1958: A Confrontation* (The Aquinas Lecture, 1958). Milwaukee: Marquette University Press, 1958. vi, 68 pp.

This review is an extremely interesting attempt by a scientist to come to grips with philosophical problems. The work of reason is compared with that of the senses and the validity of the two is discussed. It should be noted that questions concerning the adequacy of its Thomistic perspectives have been raised by Pierre Conway in an extensive review article in *The Thomist*, XXII (1959), 68-118. B-C

See: PS 8 (1958) 248; RUO 29 (1959) 114; St 48 (1959) 118; Tm 22 (1959) 68-118.

MARITAIN, Jacques. *The Degrees of Knowledge.* See IV.

————. *Philosophy of Nature.* Trans. by I. Byrne from *La philosophie de la nature.* New York: Philosophical Library, 1951 (1935). x, 198 pp. Appendix, bibliography, index.

An excellent, brief historical and logical study of the division of the sciences. While not always easy reading, it is an indispensable vantage point for understandnig the American neo-Scholastic discussions on the relation of philosophy to the physical and mathematical sciences. An important appendix presents an article by Yves Simon, "Maritain's Philosophy of Science," *The Thomist*, V (1943), 85-102. B

See: AER 126 (1952) 481; D 36 (1951) 332-34; TS 12 (1952) 296; Tm 16 (1953) 127; T 10 (1951) 176; T 27 (1952) 108.

MARLING, Joseph. *The Order of Nature.* See VII.

MAZIARZ, Edward A. *The Philosophy of Mathematics.* New York: Philosophical Library, 1950. viii, 286 pp. Bibliography, index.

A study of the place of mathematics in the hierarchy of the sciences. The history of various views on the nature of philosophical abstraction is presented, but this work centers on the thought of St. Thomas Aquinas. The role of wisdom concerning the evaluation of the place of mathematics is stressed. C

See: Bl 31 (1950) 549; D 35 (1950) 271; CER 49 (1951) 497; RUO 21 (1951) 256*; T 27 (1952) 108.

MELSEN, Andrew G. Van. *From Atomos to Atom* (Duquesne Studies. "Philosophical Series," No. 1). Trans. by H. Koren from *Van atomos naar atoom*. Pittsburgh: Duquesne University Press, 1952 (1949). vii, 240 pp. Bibliography. (Harper: TB 517)

An excellent, though technical and difficult, study of the history of the concept of atom from its philosophical stage in Democritus and Aristotle to its use as a scientific term in quantum physics. The author attempts to relate modern scientific discoveries to the work done in the philosophy of nature. B-C

See: NS 27 (1953) 482; Tm 16 (1953) 151.

———. *The Philosophy of Nature.* (Duquesne Studies. "Philosophical Series," No. 2). 3d ed. Pittsburgh: Duquesne University Press, 1961. xi, 265 pp. Bibliography. (Paper)

This work centers more on the philosophy of science than on traditional cosmology. It is original in method, content, and approach. The treatment of problems related to modern science is effective and will appeal especially to those of a scientific background. B-C

See: FS 14 (1954) 448; MS 31 (1953) 52; NS 28 (1954) 357-60; PS 5 (1955) 127-38; Th 17 (1954) 412; T 30 (1955) 151.

———. *Science and Technology* (Duquesne Studies. "Philosophical Series," No. 13). Pittsburgh: Duquesne University Press, 1961. 373 pp. (Paper)

This is an extended and very creditable book on the nature of physical science and the implications of its practical application upon culture. The author first reviews the nonreflective, abstract, exact, and theoretical character of scientific knowledge, together with the basic philosophical structure of the physical world. He then studies the development of technology, with its dangers and opportunities, effectively remaining within the range of both the student of the sciences and the student of philosophy. It has an important message for the concerned and erudite general reader. B-C

See: D 47 (1962) 315; MS 40 (1962) 97; PS 11 (1961) 250; RUO 32 (1962) 182.

MORRIS, Hilaire. *Philosophy for Beginners.* See II.

MULLEN, Mary D. *Essence and Operation.* See VII.

NYS, Désiré. *Cosmology: The Philosophical Study of the Inorganic World.* 2 vols. Trans. by S. Raemers from the 4th revised ed. of *Cosmologie.* Milwaukee: Bruce, 1942 (1928). Index.

A most extensive, though early, study of the problem of the relation of philosophy and science. It includes a thorough exposition and appraisal of modern physical theories, along with the traditional hylomorphic explanation of the natural world. It has a good index, which makes it excellent for reference work. B-C

See: MS 20 (1943) 112-13; NS 17 (1943) 179-81; Tm 4 (1942) 543.

O'GRADY, Daniel C. *Cosmology, A Cross-Section: Footnotes on the Philosophy of Nature.* Ottawa: Graphic, 1932. 272 pp.

An assessment of the nature of material reality extending beyond the limits of the ordinary cosmology text. The author studies the origin of the universe, treats the nature of physical and living things, and concludes on the notions of purpose and evil. B

See: A 47 (1932) 23.

O'NEILL, John. *Cosmology: An Introduction to the Philosophy of Matter.* London: Longmans, Green, 1924. 308 pp.

This is the first of two projected volumes on cosmology, and it provides an historical survey of Aristotle's cosmological principles seen in the context of both pre-Socratic and Platonic thought and medieval Scholasticism. It contains an excellent history of the philosophy of matter from Thales to Suarez. C

See: CW 119 (1924) 710; C 1 (1924) 52; A 30 (1924) 576.

OSGNIACH, Augustine J. *Analysis of Objects.* See VII.

PHILLIPS, Richard P. *Modern Thomistic Philosophy.* See II.

PHILOSOPHY AND FINALITY. See I.

PHILOSOPHY AND THE EXPERIMENTAL SCIENCES. See I.

PHILOSOPHY AND THE SCIENCES. See I.

RABBITTE, Edwin. *Cosmology for All.* Cork: Mercier, 1963 (1956). 122 pp. (Paper)

A brief but solid exposition of the main themes of cosmology. Magnitude, change, activity, and essence are treated in relation to the physical sciences. B

RENOIRTE, Fernand. *Cosmology: Elements of a Critique of the Sciences and Cosmology* (The Philosophical Series of the Higher Institute of Philosophy, University of Louvain). Trans. by J. Coffey from the 2d revised ed. of *Eléments de critique des sciences et de cosmologie.* New York: Wagner, 1950 (1945). xv, 256 pp.

In this critique of modern science, the author accepts the scientist's views of law and theory and then attempts to establish the foundations of cosmology in the postulates of the physical sciences. The good analysis of the scientific method which it provides will be of special interest for courses emphasizing the philosophy of science. However, as a result, the presentation of the Thomistic philosophy of nature is rather inadequate. B-C

See: CSJ 52 (1952) 34; IER 68 (1946) 141-42; NS 26 (1952) 109-12; PS 2 (1952) 92; RUO 22 (1952) 71; TS 12 (1951) 608-13; Th 10 (1947) 385; Th 15 (1952) 501.

SHAPIRO, Herman. *The Notion of Time and Place According to William of Ockham.* See XVI.

SHEEN, Fulton J. *Philosophy of Science* (Science and Culture Series). Milwaukee: Bruce, 1934. xxv, 197 pp.

An historical sketch of the problem of the relationship between philosophy and modern science, together with the lines of a possible solution. A Scholastic evaluation of the scientific pronouncements of that day is presented, and the opinion that a sound philosophy can be based upon scientific conclusions alone is rejected. Some important points are treated too vaguely or briefly. B

See: A 51 (1934) 427; CW 140 (1934) 238; T 9 (1935) 696-702.

SMITH, Vincent E. *Footnotes for the Atom.* Milwaukee: Bruce, 1951. x, 208 pp.

A timely treatment of the points of conflict and contact between Scholastic philosophy and modern science. A major portion of the book is devoted to a lucid and penetrating analysis of scientific method. Written for those of scientific background, it does much to show the limitations of empirical methods and the necessity of other approaches to truths not restricted to the physical order. B-C

See: ABR 2 (1951) 253.

―――. *The General Science of Nature.* Milwaukee: Bruce, 1958. xiii, 400 pp. Bibliography, index.

An introductory textbook following the order of Aristotle's *Physics* with good chapter summaries and review questions. It contains a penetrating evaluation of the presuppositions of the modern sciences, with a view to putting these sciences in a context which will provide a basis for their conceptions of physical reality and open them to the subsequent work of metaphysics. It has been characterized as the best truly Thomistic textbook in any field. B

See: A 100 (1959) 435; CSJ 59 (1959) 57; D 44 (1959) 192; TS 20 (1959) 665; Tm 22 (1959) 434.

―――. *The Philosophical Frontiers of Physics* (The Catholic University of America. *Philosophical Studies,* No. 97). Washington, D.C.: The Catholic University of America Press, 1947. xii, 210 pp. Bibliography, index. (Paper)

A study of the philosophical issues raised in the methodology of modern physics. The functions of mathematics and of theory in this science are reviewed from a logical and epistemological point of view. Some attention is also given to atomism. B-C

————. *Philosophical Physics*. New York: Harper, 1950. 472 pp.

An eloquent exposition of the fundamental theses of the Aristotelian philosophy of nature, supplemented by a wealth of illustrations drawn from the empirical sciences. Part I is adapted to the general student; part II requires more scientific background. This division is useful in classes composed of students with varied academic orientations. B

See: CER 49 (1951) 428-30; CSJ 50 (1950) 34; D 35 (1950) 268; HPR 51 (1951) 664-66; MS 28 (1951) 310-12; Th 14 (1951) 277-79.

————. (ed.) *The Philosophy of Physics* (St. John's University Studies. "Philosophical Series," Vol. 2). Jamaica, N.Y.: St. John's University Press, 1961. 82 pp. (Paper)

A series of views on the relation between philosophy and physics presented by C. de Koninck, J. Maritain, K. Herzfeld, and B. Ashley at the St. John's University Philosophy of Science Institute. C

See: CSJ 61 (1961) 53; MS 39 (1962) 283; Tm 25 (1962) 318.

————. (ed.) *The Philosophy of Science* (St. John's University Studies. "Philosophical Series," Vol. 1). Jamaica, N.Y.: St. John's University Press, 1960. 164 pp. (Paper)

A valuable collection of the lectures delivered at the St. John's University Philosophy of Science Institute by C. Grindel, W. Carlo, W. Kane, V. Smith, A. Wolter, R. Allers, and W. McDonald. In these lectures the nature of the philosophy of science, organic and chemical substances, and the unconscious are examined. C

————. *St. Thomas on the Object of Geometry* (The Aquinas Lecture, 1953). Milwaukee: Marquette University Press, 1954. 99 pp.

A lecture on the place of mathematics in the Thomistic system of the sciences. The classical position of St. Thomas on the relation of mathematics to quantity is presented and compared to modern positions on this question. C

SULLIVAN, Sr. Helen. *An Introduction to the Philosophy of*

Natural and Mathematical Sciences. New York: Vantage, 1952. xxi, 188 pp.

A discussion text designed as an introduction to a Thomistic philosophy of science. It presents the various views, both within and outside Thomism, on the nature of physics and mathematics in relation to philosophy. Each chapter has a summary outline at the beginning, and a list of suggested readings. It is generally successful in attaining its aim. A-B

See: D 38 (1953) 147; MS 31 (1953) 52; NS 27 (1953) 347; Th 16 (1953) 297; T 28 (1953) 313.

THOMAS AQUINAS, Saint. *In libros Meterologicorum.* See XV.

―――. *In octo libros Physicorum* (I & II). See XV.

―――. *On Combining of the Elements.* See XV.

―――. *Physics and Philosophy.* See XV.

―――. *The Principles of Nature.* See XV.

VERSFELD, Martin. *The Perennial Order.* See II.

WALLACE, William A. *The Scientific Methodology of Theodoric of Freiberg: A Case Study of the Relationship Between Science and Philosophy.* (Studia Friburgensia: New Series, No. 26). Washington, D.C.: Thomist Press, 1962. xvii, 395 pp. (Paper)

An attempt to demonstrate the Albertus Magnus Lyceum position on natural science by way of an historical study, in the manner of the Harvard case studies in the experimental sciences. It contains newly edited texts and other matter of historical importance, but the author is mainly interested in their doctrinal significance. D

See: Ms 5 (1961) 97; NS 35 (1961) 397; RPL 61 (1963) 473; T 24 (1961) 113.

WEISHEIPL, James A. *The Development of Physical Theory in the Middle Ages.* New York: Sheed and Ward, 1959. 92 pp.

An historical survey of the roots of modern science in the Middle Ages. Its main interest to the reader is the author's exposition of the Aristotelian-Thomistic view of science and its relation to the mathematical-physical sciences. C-D

See: CSJ 61 (1961) 64; E. McMullen, IPQ 2 (1962) 483-89 & response, 629-32; NS 36 (1962) 409; PS 11 (1961) 315.

————. (ed.) *Dignity of Science: Studies in the Philosophy of Science Presented to William H. Kane, O.P.* Washington, D.C.: Thomist Press, 1961. xxxiii, 526 pp.

This book consists of twenty-two contributions by Catholic scholars to the modern problem of the relation between philosophy and science from the Thomistic viewpoint. Among the topics treated are scientific methodology, the history and philosophy of science, and special problems of science including its sociological aspects. It is generally an excellent statement of the position of the Albertus Magnus Lyceum on the unity of natural philosophy and natural science. C-D

See: D 47 (1962) 58-62; IER 96 (1961) 334; RUO 32 (1962) 124; Sa 17 (1962) 65; TS 23 (1962) 359.

WELLMUTH, John. *The Nature and Origins of Scientism* (The Aquinas Lecture, 1944) . Milwaukee: Marquette University Press, 1944. 60 pp.

An interpretation of the origin of the scientist orientations of modern times, which is traced back to the work of Ockham and Bacon. B

See: CW 161 (1945) 278-79; D 30 (1945) 46-47; FS 26 (1945) 309-16; MS 22 (1945) 232; RUO 15 (1945) 117-18; Th 8 (1945) 291; T 20 (1945) 372-73.

CHAPTER VI

Psychology

This section comprises general studies and texts on philosophical psychology, rational psychology, and the philosophy of man. It also includes works treating such special problems in these fields as evolution, man's spiritual dimension, and his freedom. Works of a more metaphysical nature are placed in subsequent sections. Historical and empirical materials [1] are not included unless they are explicitly related to philosophical issues.

The reader is referred to Chapters III, IV, and VII of *A Bibliography of Christian Philosophy and Contemporary Issues* by the same editor.

---

[1] Alexis Carrel, *Man the Unknown* (New York: Harper, 1939); Philip G. Fothergill, *Evolution and Christians* (London: Longmans, Green, 1961), and *Life, and Its Origins, a Discussion* ("Newman Philosophy of Science Series," No. 2 [London: Sheed and Ward, 1958]).

ADLER, Mortimer J. *Problems for Thomists: The Problem of Species*. New York: Sheed and Ward, 1940. 303 pp. Indices.

This work is a detailed statement of the problem of species. The author isolates two basic positions and institutes a dialectic to clarify the problem; he then proposes a tentative solution, and surveys the closely connected issues in modern moral and theological thought. C

> *See:* A 63 (1940) 471; C 32 (1940) 254-55; CR 19 (1940) 61; CW 154 (1941) 120-22; HP 41 (1941) 667-68; T 15 (1940) 710-12, Reply: 16 (1941) 200-204.

————. *What Man Has Made of Man: A Study of the Consequences of Platonism and Positivism in Psychology*. New York: Frederick Ungar, 1957 (1937) . 246 pp.

This book consists of four lectures which seek to orientate modern psychological thinking around the traditional Aristotelian-Thomistic systems. Controversial and provocative, its delineation and evaluation of the historical origins of modern psychology have received much unfavorable criticism from nonscholastics. The outline form and more than one hundred pages of explanatory notes make it more useful as a detailed guide than as general collateral reading. B

> *See:* A 58 (1937) 261; C 27 (1937) 53; CW 148 (1938) 120.

ANABLE, Raymond J. *Philosophical Psychology, with Related Readings: A Text for Undergraduates*. Revised ed. New York: McMullen, 1947. 361 pp.

The author achieves great clarity in this schematic presentation of rational psychology by explaining the real meaning of particular terms and by presenting the subject matter in syllogistic form. The list of related readings is essential. B

ARDLEY, Gavin. *Aquinas and Kant.* See XV.

AVELING, Francis. *The Immortality of the Soul* (Westminster Lectures) . St. Louis: Herder, 1905. 69 pp.

A brief discussion of the evidence and implications of the immortality of the soul. The clarity of the lecture is heightened by marginal notes and the appendix reporting on the discussion which followed the lecture. A-B

See: CW 82 (1906) 552.

BAKER, Richard R. *The Thomistic Theory of the Passions and Their Influence on the Will.* Notre Dame, Ind.: Notre Dame University Press, 1941. vii, 147 pp.

This study of the emotions and the appetite, especially in relation to the senses, is followed by an examination of passion and its relation to the will. B-C

BARRETT, James F. *Elements of Psychology.* Milwaukee: Bruce, 1931. 419 pp.

Although an early work, the text is still useful, and the examples practical and applicable. It contains useful summaries, true or false tests, review questions, and related readings at the end of each chapter. B

————. *This Creature, Man* ("Science and Culture Series"). Milwaukee: Bruce, 1937. xvi, 364 pp.

The author examines man in the light of experimental and rational psychology. The unity of the human composite is stressed, with attention to the relation of man's soul to his body. It offers good collateral reading for an integrated view of man. B

See: A 56 (1937) 574; CW 146 (1937) 125; S 17 (1937) 60.

BASCHAB, Charles R. *A Manual of Neo-Scholastic Philosophy.* See II.

BIOT, Rene. *What Is Life (Twentieth Century Encyclopedia of Catholicism,* Vol. 32). Trans. by E. Smith from *Poussière vivante.* New York: Hawthorn, 1959 (1957). 96 pp.

This study of the human composite emphasizes the physical aspect of man. The author considers man's material basis, his spiritual animation, and the meaning of both for human health and dignity. A-B

See: W. Donnelly, CR 45 (1960) 122; IER 92 (1959) 131.

BIRMINGHAM, William, and CUNNEEN, Joseph E. *Cross Currents of Psychology and Catholic Morality*. See X.

BITTLE, Celestine N. *The Whole Man: Psychology*. Milwaukee: Bruce, 1945. x, 687 pp. Bibliography, index, glossary.

The author achieves a limited success in his laudable attempt at an exposition of the full dimensions of man. A ponderous physiological treatment is included at the expense of a discussion of the rational level of man, and some explicitly intellectual functions are dismissed summarily. However, a lengthy bibliography, chapter summaries, an extensive index, and a glossary of terms give this book some lasting value. B

See: Bl 26 (1945) 318-19; FS 26 (1945) 464; MS 23 (1946) 103-104; NS 19 (1945) 281-82; T 20 (1945) 734-35.

BOELEN, Bernard J. (ed.) *Symposium on Evolution*. Pittsburgh: Duquesne University Press, 1959. 119 pp.

An important, contemporary statement of some of the problems posed by evolution in the fields of biology (F. Bawden), anthropology (G. Lang), philosophy (A. van Melsen), and theology (C. Vollert). Although complete data or an adequate survey of all possible solutions to the problems raised cannot be expected in this type of work, the philosophical section does compare various approaches of the past. Useful collateral reading. B-C

BOURKE, Vernon J. *Will in Western Thought: An Historico-Critical Survey*. New York: Sheed and Ward, 1964. vi, 247 pp. Index.

Originally presented as a lecture series at Boston College, this work first surveys the term "will," then treats its relation to the intellectual and rational orders; and finally studies freedom and the various meanings of will throughout history and in modern psychology in order to develop an adequate definition of will. C-D

See: R. Holzhauer, SL 10 (1964) 51.

BRENNAN, Robert E. *General Psychology: An Interpretation of the Science of the Mind Based on Thomas Aquinas*. Revised ed. New York: Macmillan, 1952 (1937) . xxxvii, 524 pp. Bibliography, indices.

A revision of a much used psychology textbook. It is divided into three books which treat, respectively, vegetative, sentient, and rational life, first on an empirical and then on a philosophical level. The author has had difficulty in keeping the empirical sections up-to-date. Some find the philosophical sections overly concise, although they are models of Thomistic clarity. B

See: AM 77 (1953) 25; CSJ 53 (1953) 26A; D 38 (1953) 39-40; IER 79 (1953) 484; NS 28 (1954) 245.

――――. *History of Psychology from the Standpoint of a Thomist.* New York: Macmillan, 1945. xvi, 277 pp. Bibliography, index.

A work which answers an obvious need on the part of both teachers and students, this history traces the development of psychology as a science and the establishment of its various schools. One chapter provides a Thomistic evaluation. The complexity of the material has left the book open to charges of omissions and misinterpretations. B-C

See: A 74 (1945) 243; CER 43 (1945) 312; D 30 (1945) 34-35; ER 113 (1945) 392-94; FS 26 (1945) 465; HPR 46 (1945) 76; MS 22 (1945) 230-32; R 6 (1946) 30; RUO 15 (1945) 117; Tm 8 (1945) 287-88; T 20 (1945) 566-67.

――――. *The Image of His Maker: A Study of the Nature of Man.* Milwaukee: Bruce, 1948. ix, 338 pp. Index.

Written to introduce the younger reader to the teaching of St. Thomas on the nature of man, this is an original, lucid, almost storybook presentation of the origin, powers, attributes, and destiny of the human soul. Both empirical and philosophic material are included, and the reader is encouraged to delve more deeply. A

See: AM 68 (1948) 506-507; CR 30 (1948) 215; D 33 (1948) 128; C. Burehl, HPR 49 (1948) 79-80; IER 71 (1949) 474; IM 77 (1949) 96; C. Curran, NS 23 (1949) 92-93; S 27 (1948) 55-56; St 38 (1949) 126; T 24 (1949) 167.

――――. *Thomistic Psychology: A Philosophic Analysis of the Na-*

ture of Man. New York: Macmillan, 1941. xxv, 401 pp. Bibliography, index.

This clearly written book is based upon Aristotle and Aquinas. The author refers to orientations in modern philosophy and (now dated) empirical psychology, but does not achieve a synthesis with that material. Each chapter is provided with a list of references. B

See: A 66 (1942) 383; AM 55 (1942) 122; Bl 23 (1942) 158; CSJ 41 (1941) 362; D 26 (1941) 248; AER 107 (1942) 233; HPR 42 (1942) 694-95; MS 19 (1941) 16; NS 16 (1942) 400-401; S 21 (1942) 509; Tm 4 (1942) 182-83; T 17 (1942) 149-51.

BRENNAN, Sr. M. Rose Emmanuella. *The Intellectual Virtues According to the Philosophy of St. Thomas* (The Catholic University of America, *Philosophical Studies,* No. 59). Washington, D.C.: The Catholic University of America Press, 1941. xii, 188 pp. (Paper)

A thorough study of the intellectual virtues and their implications. The author states the nature of virtues, distinguishes and compares the practical to the natural and supernatural virtues, and indicates their educational and social implications. Collateral reading in both psychology and ethics. B-C

CAMPBELL, Bertrand J. *The Problem of One or Plural Substantial Forms in Man as Found in the Works of St. Thomas Aquinas and John Duns Scotus.* Paterson, N.J.: St. Anthony Guild Press, 1940. vi, 131 pp. Bibliography, index.

In this study of the problem of the unity of man and one of its most fundamental principles, the doctrines of St. Thomas and Duns Scotus are presented and compared, and additional reflections drawn on the basis of subsequent biological data. C

See: T 15 (1940) 546-48.

CARUSO, Igor A. *Existential Psychology: From Analysis to Synthesis.* New York: Herder and Herder, 1964. 227 pp. Bibliography.

The influence of existential thought on the field of psychology is traced from the origin of the contemporary existential problem, through questions of method, to the resulting techniques in the field of psychology. Special attention is given to implications concerning symbols and to a methodological synthesis of philosophy and psychology. C

CLARK, Mary T. *Augustine: Philosopher of Freedom.* See XIV.

COADY, Mary A. *The Phantasm According To the Teaching of St. Thomas* (The Catholic University of America, *Philosophical Studies,* No. 23). Washington, D.C.: The Catholic University of America Press, 1932. 80 pp. (Paper)
The author reviews previous positions and then analyses the philosophy of St. Thomas Aquinas on the nature and necessity of the phantasm and its relation to abstraction. Collateral reading. B-C

COLLIN, Remy. *Evolution (Twentieth Century Encyclopedia of Catholicism,* Vol. 30). Trans. by J. Tester from *L'évolution: hypothése et problèmes.* New York: Hawthorn, 1959 (1958). 143 pp.
A brief and up-to-date presentation of the scientific data concerning evolution. The treatment of the philosophical aspects of evolution is perhaps too concise to be satisfying. Collateral reading. A-B
See: D 45 (1960) 279; IER 94 (1960) 127.

COLLINGWOOD, Francis J. *Man's Physical and Spiritual Nature.* New York: Holt, Rinehart and Winston, 1963. vii, 387 pp. Index.
This text on the philosophy of man emphasizes his unity by combining the empirical and philosophical approaches to the subject, and by juxtaposing the chapters on sense and intellectual knowledge, and those on the different levels of appetite. The method is very effective. B

COLLINS, William B. *Metaphysics and Man.* See II.

―――. *Speculative Philosophy.* See II.

CORTÉ, Nicholas (CHRISTIANI, Leon). *The Origins of Man (Twentieth Century Encyclopedia of Catholicism,* Vol. 29). Trans. by E. Smith from *Les origines de l'homme.* New York: Hawthorn, 1959 (1957). 144 pp.

A synthesis of the various theories concerning the origin of man. The concept is examined in the light of pre-philosophical presentations and ancient Greek and Oriental philosophies, and compared with the findings of modern science as well as biblical writings. A-B

See: IER 91 (1959) 247; D. Schlegel, Ta 213 (1959) 601.

COTTER, Anthony C. *Natural Species: An Essay in Definition and Classification.* Weston, Mass.: Weston College Press, 1947. vi, 274 pp. Bibliography, index.

An attempt to show how the interdependence of science, philosophy, and theology is necessary to the problem of the nature of species. The work is oriented toward the problem of evolution. C

See: CE 19 (1948) 193.

CRONAN, Edward P. *The Dignity of the Human Person.* New York: Philosophical Library, 1955. xvi, 207 pp.

A basic, almost popular presentation of the many dimensions of man. An evaluation of his unique position in the animal world and of his perfections provides a basis for a study of the dynamic possibilities of development in human interaction. A-B

See: CBQ 17 (1955) 674; CE 26 (1956) 530; CW 181 (1955) 397; CR 40 (1955) 562-63; D 40 (1955) 441; NS 30 (1956) 239; PS (1955) 142; H. St.-Denis, RUO 26 (1956) 246*.

DADY, Mary R. *The Theory of Knowledge of St. Bonaventure.* See XVI.

DAIM, Wilfried. *Depth Psychology and Salvation.* New York: Frederick Ungar, 1963. 315 pp. Bibliography, index.

A personal investigation of the emotional processes by which a crisis of nothingness can break the idols which restrict personal development. The need of this partial salvation is studied, as is its psychoanalytic implementation. This, in turn, is related to the work of total or cosmic salvation. C-D

D'ARCY, Martin. *The Mind and Heart of Love.* See VII.

DAY, Sebastian J. *Intuitive Cognition.* See XVI.

DEMPSEY, Peter J. *Psychology for All.* Techny, Ill.: Divine Word, 1964 (1952) . 128 pp. (Paper)

An elementary survey of psychology with special emphasis on empirical materials. The author reviews the key powers of sensation and intellection, as well as the soul. A

See: C. Miltner, AM 78 (1953) 25.

DONCEEL, Joseph F. *Philosophical Psychology.* 2d ed., revised and enlarged. New York: Sheed and Ward, 1961 (1955) . xiii, 497 pp. Bibliography.

A particularly successful and well-organized combination of the empirical and philosophic approaches to the nature of man. As a text, however, it presupposes metaphysics. Part V, entitled "Man as a Person," is especially effective. The book is clearly and concisely written and includes a list of pertinent works at the end of each chapter, and a lengthy final bibliography. B

See: A 97 (1957) 589; D. Wack, ABR 7 (1956) 171-73; A. Lambert, DR 76 (1958) 420; IER 89 (1958) 469; T. Crowley, ITQ 25 (1958) 89; R. Blackwell, MS 34 (1957) 217; L. Recktenwald, NS 30 (1956) 394; D. Corish, PS 7 (1957) 205.

DRISCOLL, John T. *Christian Philosophy: A Treatise on the Human Soul.* 2d ed. New York: Benziger, 1900 (1898) . xiii, 269 pp.

A study of the nature of the soul in the human composite. After reviewing other philosophical positions on the subject, the author considers problems concerning the relation of the soul to the brain, to thought, and to the body. A discussion of the substantiality, spirituality, and immortality of the soul constitutes the final part of the work. Although the book was written over sixty years ago, its basic positions are still pertinent. A

See: CW 67 (1898) 851.

FARAON, Michael J. *The Metaphysical and Psychological Principles of Love*. See VII.

FELL, Georg. *The Immortality of the Human Soul Philosophically Explained*. Trans. by L. Villing from *Die Unsterblichkeit der menschlichen Seele philosophisch beleuchtet*. St. Louis: Herder, 1906 (1892). 267 pp.

A rather lengthy defense of the immortality of the soul, founded upon its distinction from the body and its consequent spirituality. A-C

See: CW 85 (1907) 253.

FLEMING, Thomas V. *Foundations of Philosophy*. See II.

FRANZ, Edward Q. *The Thomistic Doctrine of the Possible Intellect* (The Catholic University of America, *Philosophical Studies*, No. 117). Washington, D.C.: The Catholic University of America Press, 1950. xii, 189 pp. (Paper)

A survey of the possible intellect in the philosophy of St. Thomas. After reviewing the historical context, the author presents a study of the nature, object, and functions of the possible intellect. Its relation to the internal senses is given special attention. Collateral reading. B

FUCHS, Oswald. *Psychology of Habit According to William of Ockham*. See XVI.

GAFFNEY, Mark A. *The Psychology of the Interior Senses*. St. Louis: Herder, 1942. iv, 260 pp. Bibliography, index.

In this more experimental than philosophical study of the internal senses, functions of common sense, imagination, memory, and instinct are reviewed. The book can be useful as an intermediate step in the rather swift progression from the study of external senses to the study of the intellect which most undergraduate rational psychology courses are forced to make. B

See: A 67 (1942) 50; AM 56 (1942) 26-27; CSJ 42 (1942) 200; D 27 (1942) 190-91; HPR 42 (1942) 886-87; JRI 12 (1942) 909-10; MS 21 (1943) 64-65; NS 16 (1942) 196-98; SJR 35 (1943) 390; T 17 (1942) 552-54.

GARDEIL, Henri. *Psychology* (Vol. III of *Introduction to the Philosophy of St. Thomas Aquinas*) . Trans. by J. Otto from *Initiation à la philosophie de S. Thomas d'Aquin*. St. Louis: Herder, 1966 (1952) . xiii, 303 pp. Index.

An undergraduate text patterned on the order of Aristotle's *De anima* and developed according to the thought of St. Thomas and his commentators. Although it includes relevant material from more recent philosophers, half the book consists of excerpts from the writings of St. Thomas. Scholastic terms are explained in modern terms but further subdivision and development of many points are necessary. Excellent collateral reading for texts such as those by G. Klubertanz or J. Royce. B

See: ABR 7 (1956) 173; AM 84 (1956) 24; RPL 53 (1955) 603.

GEIGER, James A. *The Origin of the Soul: An Augustinian Dilemma.* See XIV.

GERRITY, Benignus. *Nature, Knowledge, and God.* See II.

———. *The Relation between the Theory of Matter and Form and the Theory of Knowledge.* See V.

GLENN, Paul J. *Psychology: A Class Manual in the Philosophy of Organic and Rational Life.* St. Louis: Herder, 1936. viii, 391 pp. Index.

A clear, perhaps overly simple study of the nature and place of human life. The first section fixes life within the hierarchy of being; the second studies the place of man among the living. Without bibliography, footnotes, and references, it is no longer considered adequate as an undergraduate text. A

See: AER 97 (1937) 94; CSJ 37 (1937) 61; HPR 37 (1937) 1005.

GRENIER, Henri. *Thomistic Philosophy.* See II.

GRINDEL, Carl W. (ed.) *Concept of Freedom.* Chicago: Regnery, 1955. 512 pp. Bibliography, index.

This represents the combined efforts of several professors at St. John's University. The first part of the volume is concerned with the properly philosophical aspects of freedom and the nature of man, his knowledge, autonomy, and individual acts. The remainder of the volume is concerned with freedom in such diverse fields as art and ecomonics. B-C

See: ACSR 17 (1956) 260; AER 135 (1956) 213; CE 26 (1956) 587; D 41 (1956) 272; NS 30 (1956) 372; SO 6 (1956) 121-24.

GRUENDER, Hubert. *Free Will: The Greatest of the Seven World-Riddles.* 2d ed. St. Louis: Herder, 1916 (1911). 96 pp.

After stating the problem of free will, the author reviews the empirical and philosophical evidence of free will, tracing it to the nature of man. A

See: A 4 (1911) 547; CW 93 (1911) 257.

————. *Problems of Psychology: A Text for Undergraduates.* Milwaukee: Bruce, 1937. xi, 209 pp. Index.

A balanced employment of both speculative and empirical approaches in the study of man. Using, in part, material from the author's *Free Will* and *Psychology Without a Soul,* it treats the main topics of rational psychology: sensation, intellection, free will, personal identity, and the spirituality of the soul. B

See: A 59 (1938) 143; ER 99 (1938) 577; HPR 39 (1939) 888.

————. *Psychology without a Soul: A Criticism.* St. Louis: Herder, 1917 (1912). 245 pp.

A defense of the nature of the human soul against the position of materialism. Topics covered in this work are evolution, the soul's spirituality, freedom and personality. There is a useful glossary of terms. Due to the author's rather strongly empirical emphasis, much of what he says is now out of date. B

See: A 6 (1911) 282; CW 95 (1912) 395.

GUARDINI, Romano. *Freedom, Grace and Destiny.* See VII.

GUITTON, Jean. *An Essay on Human Love.* Trans. by M. Chaning-Pearce from *Essai sur l'amour humain.* New York: Philosophical Library, 1951 (1948). xi, 243 pp. Index.

A study of human love within the tradition of Christian philosophy. The mystery of love is explored, with attention to the conflict between flesh and spirit. The development of love is traced as far as oblation, in which context the significance of love and of sex is considered. B

See: D 37 (1952) 81-84; Tm 15 (1952) 509.

GURWITSCH, Aron. *The Field of Consciousness.* (Duquesne Studies, "Psychology Series"). Trans. from *Théorie du champ de la conscience.* Pittsburgh: Duquesne, 1964. xiv, 427 pp. Index.

In this phenomenological study, the author first describes the organization of the field of consciousness and then presents a theory of form, and a subsequent phenomenological interpretation of perception and its ontological implications. An important and useful book for both philosophy and phenomenology. C

GUSTAFSON, Gustaf J. *The Theory of Natural Appetency in the Philosophy of St. Thomas* (The Catholic University of America, *Philosophical Studies*, No. 84). Washington, D.C.: The Catholic University of America Press, 1944. xii, 125 pp. Bibliography, index. (Paper)

An assessment of the nature and extent of natural appetency in the philosophy of St. Thomas. The historical and speculative contexts are studied with special emphasis on the dynamic character of Thomistic teleology. In this setting the character of natural appetency and its implications are reviewed. C

GUZIE, Tad W. *The Analogy of Learning: An Essay Toward a Thomistic Psychology.* New York: Sheed and Ward, 1960. xiv, 241 pp.

A phenomenological approach to Thomistic psychology. The author, in what almost amounts to a philosophy of education, contrasts the results of philosophical and empirical psychology. B

See: D 46 (1961) 78-80; IPQ 1 (1961) 356; MS 39 (1961) 78; NS 36 (1962) 111; RP 24 (1962) 429; V. Smith, Tm 24 (1961) 664.

HARMON, Francis L. *Principles of Psychology.* 2d ed. revised.

Milwaukee: Bruce, 1951 (1936). xi, 656 pp. Bibliography, index.

The author treats psychology as a modern science, while recognizing that the ultimate nature of its crucial problems is philosophical. The presentation of the philosophical elements is better than the empirical data to which they are applied. Short summaries and well-selected references follow each chapter. B

See: T 14 (1939) 685.

HART, Charles. *Aspects of the New Scholastic Philosophy.* See II.

————. *The Thomistic Concept of Mental Faculty* (The Catholic University of America, *Philosophical Studies*, No. 20). Washington, D.C.: The Catholic University of America Press, 1930. 142 pp. Bibliography.

The author sees the theory of mental faculties as an advance by Aristotle over his predecessors. He examines and evaluates the medieval metaphysical and empirical foundations of the concept as well as its modern criticism. The work can be of value to graduate students if complemented by the more recent work on the active character of being. Collateral reading. C

HENRY, Paul. *Saint Augustine on Personality.* See XIV.

HILL, Owen A. *Psychology and Natural Theology.* New York: Macmillan, 1921. 351 pp. Index.

An undergraduate textbook for introductory courses in rational psychology and natural theology. The presentation is in thesis form and the statement of the question is effectively divided from the definition of terms and the proofs. Nevertheless the writer's style is sufficiently fluid to avoid the feeling of an outline. A-B

See: A 25 (1921) 188; CW 113 (1921) 536.

KLUBERTANZ, George P. *The Discursive Power: Sources and Doctrine of the "vis cogitativa" According to St. Thomas Aquinas.* St. Louis: Modern Schoolman, 1952. vii, 353 pp. Bibliography.

An extended treatment of the *vis cogitativa* in the philosophy of St. Thomas. After a lengthy study of the earlier history of the question, the author examines the various sectors of the works of St. Thomas and concludes with a synopsis of the doctrine. He adds a special note on the principle of individuation. This work is important for a full appreciation of the capacity of sense knowledge on which the human intellect so heavily depends. C-D

See: D 38 (1953) 151; FS 13 (1953) 13; MS 31 (1953) 50; J. Collins, T 28 (1953) 287.

――――. *The Philosophy of Human Nature.* New York: Appleton-Century-Crofts, 1953. 444 pp. Appendices.

This is an effectively organized and well-written undergraduate rational psychology text, in which philosophical psychology is developed with a full awareness of the significance of recent empirical data concerning man. The discussion of the interior senses is slightly reduced. Heavily footnoted, the book contains definitions, syllogistic proofs, and a list of reference works for each chapter. There are appendices on the philosophical systems and various related issues. It is among the best texts presently available in this field. B

See: Th 17 (1954) 272.

KOREN, Henry J. *An Introduction to the Philosophy of Animate Nature.* St. Louis: Herder, 1955. xiii, 341 pp. Bibliography, index.

Although he has written a quite simple exposition of the philosophical concept of man, the author presupposes that his readers have had a course in metaphysics. The book contains historical notes, a summary, and suggested readings at the end of each chapter. There are seventeen pages of review questions at the end of the book. B

See: HPR 56 (1956) 709; NS 31 (1957) 143; C. Hart, SJR 48 (1956) 364.

LeTROQUER, Rene. *What is Man?* (*Twentieth Century Encyclopedia of Catholicism,* Vol. 31). Trans. by E. Smith from *L'homme, qui suis-je?* New York: Hawthorn, 1961 (1957). 124 pp.

In this philosophical and theological work on the nature of man, the author covers philosophic material first, beginning with a review of man's composite nature. Then he concentrates on the soul and from a contemporary existential point of view examines man's nature as a person. A-B

See: CSJ 61 (1961) 53.

LINEHAN, James C. *The Rational Nature of Man with Particular Reference to the Effects of Morality on Intelligence According to Saint Thomas Aquinas: A Metaphysical Study* (The Catholic University of America, *Philosophical Studies,* No. 37). Washington, D.C.: The Catholic University of America Press, 1937. 127 pp. Bibliography. (Paper)

A study of the position of the intellect in the total human complex. The nature of the intellect and of knowledge are investigated not only in themselves but as realized in the human composite, where they are united to body, will, and emotions. There is a collection of pertinent texts from Saint Thomas. B

McKEOUGH, Michael J. *The Meaning of the "rationes seminales" in St. Augustine.* See XIV.

MacPARTLAND, John. *The March toward Matter: Descensus averno.* New York: Philosophical Library, 1952. 80 pp.

The trend towards the reduction of mind to matter in modern philosophy is traced from Descartes and is seen in terms of a descent into non-being. Although the author is quite often forced by his theme to be negative, his aim is ultimately positive. C

See: ABR 4 (1953) 284; AER 128 (1953) 315-16; Tm 15 (1952) 669-70.

MAHER, Michael. *Psychology: Empirical and Rational.* 9th ed. London: Longmans, Green, 1933 (1923). 603 pp. Index.

This is virtually an encyclopedic history of empirical and philosophical psychology with detailed discussion of 19th century psychological issues. Although the empirical sections are dated, it contains important material on the philosophy of the relation between soul and body. It is difficult reading, but would be helpful as a reference work. C

See: CW 72 (1901) 817-18.

MAINAGE, Theodore. *Immortality: Essays On the Problem of Life After Death*. Trans. by J. Lelen, from the 4th ed. of *Immortalité*. St. Louis: Herder, 1930 (1924). 273 pp.

A collection of evidence against the materialistic negation of the immortality of the soul. The testimony of the human consensus, religions, and the individual consciousness is traced to its philosophical roots in the nature of the soul. A-B

See: A 44 (1931) 439; C 11 (1930) 634.

MARCEL, Gabriel. *The Existential Background of Human Dignity*. See XVII.

————. *Man Against Mass Society*. See XVII.

MERCIER, Désiré F. *The Origins of Contemporary Psychology*. Trans. by W. Mitchell from *Les origines de la psychologie contemporaine*. London: Washbourne, 1918 (1897). xii, 351 pp.

The author surveys the philosophic perspectives of modern psychology in relation to Descartes and criticizes its idealistic, mechanistic, and positivistic characteristics. He concludes the work with the contributions which can be made to this field by a neo-Thomistic philosophy. The basic philosophical orientation of this work is still valuable. B-C

See: A 19 (1918) 559; CW 107 (1918) 389.

————. *The Relation of Experimental Psychology to Philosophy*. Trans. by E. Wirth. New York: Benziger, 1902. 62 pp.

The author emphasizes that experimental psychology and philosophy are complementary. The detailed work of the former will help the philosopher to grasp reality; the study of the unity of the human composite along Aristotelian and Thomistic lines provides the best foundation for the work of the psychophysiologist. A

See: CW 76 (1902) 258-59.

MILLER, Barry. *The Range of Intellect*. New York: Herder, 1963 (1961) . 251 pp. Bibliography, glossary, indices.

Intellectual knowledge, love, and knowledge by connaturality are all drawn into an ultimate synthesis, which has been disputed in its claim to Thomistic authenticity. C

> *See:* CR 47 (1962) 434; F 13 (1962) 244; G 43 (1962) 394; HJ 3 (1962) 197-98; IPQ 2 (1962) 341; ITQ 29 (1962) 332; PS 11 (1961) 290; J. McCormack, TS 24 (1963) 736.

MISIAK, Henry K., and STUDT, Virginia M. *Catholics in Psychology: A Historical Survey* (McGraw-Hill Series in Psychology) . New York: McGraw-Hill, 1954. 309 pp. Bibliography.

A survey of the contributions of Catholics to the empirical work of psychology in modern times. It may serve for reference and background use. A-C

> *See:* V. Herr, A 92 (1955) 456; AER 132 (1955) 426; AM 81 (1955) 23; F. Houlihan, CER 52 (1954) 633; CHR 41 (1955) 356; F. Harmon, SO 5 (1955) 236.

―――. *The Philosophical Roots of Scientific Psychology*. New York: Fordham University Press, 1961. xii, 135 pp. Index.

A study of the philosophical currents which have shaped the growth of modern psychology. The author shows the relation of psychology to philosophy and traces the influences of nineteenth century philosophy on psychology. He investigates the body-mind problem with its implications for empirical philosophy and associationism. There is a list of books for further reading. This book will be of considerable use to all who are majoring in psychology or interested in the nature of man. B-C

> *See:* E. Franz, NS 37 (1963) 533-35.

MONAHAN, William B. *Psychology of St. Thomas and Divine Revelation*. London: Baylis, 1935. 304 pp. Bibliography, index, appendices.

A study of the soul and its powers according to St. Thomas, including: an investigation of the soul's nature and relation to the body, a study of the faculties, especially knowledge and will, and, finally, some considerations of the implications of the above questions for moral philosophy. Throughout, the relevant theological problems are noted, especially those of the Incarnation. A-B

MORRIS, Hilaire. *Philosophy for Beginners.* See II.

MORRISON, Bakewell, and RUEVE, Stephen. *Think and Live.* See II.

MOUNIER, Emmanuel. *Be Not Afraid.* See XVII.

————. *The Character of Man.* See XVII.

————. *A Personalist Manifesto.* See XVII.

MOUROUX, Jean. *The Meaning of Man.* Trans. by A. Downes from *Sens chrétien de l'homme.* New York: Sheed and Ward, 1952 (1948). xiv, 304 pp. Bibliography. (Image: D 122)

The author examines the place of man within the divine perspective. He shows a deep appreciation of man's dignity as a composite of body and soul with a unique state which bridges the gap between spirit and matter in the pattern of creation. Despite the extensive footnotes, the author's use of metaphor and of theology prevents this work from being a simply scientific philosophical work. B

See: H. Gardiner, A 79 (1948) 599-600; J. Walsh, AM 69 (1949) 90; E. Quinn, Bl 30 (1949) 243-44; CR 32 (1949) 139-41; D 33 (1948) 244; DR 67 (1949) 230-31; IER 72 (1949) 369-71; M. Grajewski, NS 23 (1949) 437-39; W. Scanlon, S 28 (1948) 54; F. Copleston, Ta 193 (1949) 106; J. Hassett, T 24 (1949) 368-70.

MULLEN, Mary D. *Essence and Operation.* See VII.

THE NATURE OF MAN. See I.

NAUS, John E. *The Nature of the Practical Intellect.* See IX.

NICHOLL, Donald. *Recent Thought in Focus.* See II.

NOGAR, Raymond J. *Wisdom of Evolution.* New York: Double-
　　day, 1963. 408 pp. Index.
A philosophical evaluation of evolution. The biological and an-
thropogical facts of evolution are presented and evaluated, and
the limits of evolution and evolutionism are shown by the author.
He attempts to construct a synthesis of scientific evolution and a
philosophy of life which will agree with scientific fact and Judeo-
Christian philosophy, emphasizing the reality of cosmic order and
natural laws. B-C
　　See: J. Ewing, A 109 (1963) 745.

NUTTIN, Joseph. *Psychoanalysis and Personality.* Trans. from
　　Psychoanalyse en Spiritualische opvatting van de mens.
　　New York: Sheed and Ward, 1962. 310 pp. (Mentor: M 426)
An investigation of the philosophical context of psychoanalytic
efforts to integrate the human personality. After an introduction
concerning the place of these studies in a general philosophy of
culture, the author reviews the nature and work of psychoanalysis, and relates it to a dynamic theory of personality. In this context, he identifies the basic needs of personality and the work of
construction and integration which these needs require. This is
an important work illustrating the interdependence between the
two branches of science. B-C

O'BRIEN, Patrick. *Emotions and Morals.* See IX.

O'CONNOR, William. *The Concept of the Human Soul Accord-
　　ing to St. Augustine.* See XIV.

O'DONNELL, Clement. *The Psychology of St. Bonaventure and
　　St. Thomas Aquinas.* See XVI.

O'LEARY, Conrad. *The Substantial Composit of Man Accord-
　　ing to St. Bonaventure* (The Catholic University of Amer-
　　ica, *Philosophical Studies*, No. 22) . Washington, D.C.: The

Catholic University of America Press, 1931. 110 pp. (Paper)
The author first states the question of the unity of man and then
the relevant principles in the philosophy of St. Bonaventure:
form and matter, the eduction of form, and the *rationes seminales*. Finally, he focuses on the substantial union of the spiritual
and the corporeal in man. C

ONG, Walter J. (ed.) *Darwin's Vision and Christian Perspectives*. New York: Macmillan, 1960. xi, 154 pp. Index.

An important collection of papers on the evolutionary element in
modern thought. Of special interest are J. Collins' discussion of
the effect of Darwin on philosophy and W. Ong's review of the
implications of Darwin's work for a Christian view of history. C-D
    See: CER 59 (1961) 422; CW (1961) 314; HJ 3 (1962) 91; ITQ 28
    (1961) 161; NS 35 (1961) 549; Ps 6 (1961) 26; RP 24 (1962) 570; RR 21
    (1962) 74; D. Ehr, SJ 54 (1961) 66; J. Ewing, SO 11 (1961) 428; P.
    Scharper, T. 36 (1961) 291.

PEGIS, Anton C. *At the Origins of the Thomistic Notion of
Man*. New York: Macmillan, 1963. vii, 82 pp. Appendix.

A concentrated investigation of the origins of St. Thomas' appreciation of man. The ancient background is investigated and the
13th century setting is established. St. Thomas' insight into the
unity of man is clarified. C-D
    See: L. O. Donovan, TS 25 (1964) 140.

————. (ed.) *Essays in Modern Scholasticism*. See II.

————. *St. Thomas and the Problem of the Soul in the Thirteenth Century* (St. Michael's Mediaeval Studies) . Toronto:
St. Michael's College, 1934. 213 pp. Bibliography, index.

After reviewing the pertinent material in St. Bonaventure and
St. Albert the Great, the author turns to the metaphysical foundations for St. Thomas' theory of the soul and its articulation in
relation to the Platonic and Aristotelian traditions. There is a
final outline of the synthesis accomplished by St. Thomas in this
area. D
    See: T 10 (1935) 501.

PEIFER, John F. *The Concept in Thomism*. New York: Bookman, 1952. 225 pp. Bibliography.

A study of the nature and genesis of the concept. A general statement on the nature of knowledge is followed by a study of the genesis of the impressed species and its relation to the expressed species. C-D

See: R. Richard, NS 27 (1953) 489; J. Collins, T 28 (1953) 287.

PHILLIPS, Richard P. *Modern Thomistic Philosophy*. See II.

PHILOSOPHY AND PSYCHIATRY. See I.

PHILOSOPHY AND THE EXPERIMENTAL SCIENCES. See I.

PRENTICE, Robert P. *Psychology of Love According to St. Bonaventure*. See XVI.

THE PROBLEM OF LIBERTY. See I.

PYNE, John X. *The Mind*. New York: Benziger, 1926. 382 pp.

A study of the soul. After a discussion of the nature of psychology and its various approaches, there is an evaluation of various philosophies of the soul. Its nature and relation to the body are explained in considerably detailed propositions. The work does not constitute a complete text in rational psychology. C

See: A 35 (1926) 93; CW 124 (1926) 283; C 4 (1926) 509.

REGIS, Louis M. *Epistemology*. See IV.

RENARD, Henri. *The Philosophy of Man*. Revised ed. by M. Vaske. Milwaukee: Bruce, 1956 (1948). x, 313 pp.

An undergraduate philosophy text on man, making little direct use of empirical materials. It requires a prior knowledge of metaphysics, thus leaving some doubt as to the source of the knowledge of the immaterial, which it presupposes. There is a summary at the end of each chapter. B

See: NS 31 (1957) 278; T. Owens, T 24 (1949) 734.

RICKABY, John. *Studies on God and His Creatures*. See VIII.

RIETH, Herman R. *An Introduction to Philosophical Psychology*. Englewood Cliffs, N.J.: Prentice-Hall, 1956. 305 pp.

A manual built around copious passages from Aristotle and St. Thomas which together constitute the second half of the book, and which the author's text in the first half closely follows. The involvement of the total person in each human act is helpfully underlined. As a text, it would seem to require an above average undergraduate or professor particularly adept at introducing the students to an effective reading of classical texts; in which case, the second half might be used before the first. B-C

See: J. Otto, NS 30 (1956) 503.

ROYCE, James E. *Man and His Nature: A Philosophical Psychology*. New York: McGraw-Hill, 1960. 398 pp. Bibliography.

This is an effective text in which the author uses both the experimental and philosophical approaches, although some would desire a clearer distinction between the two types of materials. The book contains direct quotations, explanatory footnotes, many suggestions for further reading, and a lengthy list of review questions after each chapter. B

See: G 44 (1963) 419; MS 39 (1962) 175.

RUFFINI, Ernesto. *The Theory of Evolution Judged by Reason and Faith*. Trans. by F. O'Hanlon from *La teoria della evoluzione*. New York: Wagner, 1959 (1948). xii, 215 pp.

The author of this work presents a conservative viewpoint which rejects all but a highly limited process of evolution. The materialistic hypothesis that man's origin is entirely explained by evolution is rejected in the section which establishes the contrary position: the spirituality of the soul. Although this is an important work, some scientific observations need revision and further work on the scriptural exegesis would be desirable. B-C

See: T. Zubeck, HPR 59 (1959) 968; C. Vollert, TS 21 (1960) 332.

RYAN, Edmund J. *The Role of the "sensus communis" in the*

Psychology of St. Thomas Aquinas. Carthagena, Ohio: Messenger Press, 1951. x, 198 pp. Bibliography, index.

An introductory historical section surveys the theory of the interior senses according to Aristotle and the medieval philosophers. The nature of the *sensus communis* is isolated and its operations, organ, and relation to the other senses and to the intellect are examined. This work will be of assistance in appreciating the relation of the intellectual functions of man to his animal nature. B-C

See: D 36 (1951) 339-41.

RYAN, James F. *An Introduction to Philosophy.* See II.

RYAN, John K. *Basic Principles and Problems of Philosophy.* See II.

SAYRE, Kenneth, and CROSSEN, Frederick J. (eds.) *The Modeling of Mind: Computers and Intelligence.* Notre Dame, Ind.: University of Notre Dame Press, 1963. xi, 275 pp.

A collection of papers on the influence of technical developments upon the modeling of mental activity. The general nature of modeling is first investigated, followed by individual studies on the methods by which computers are programed according to mental and perceptual skills and decision-making. This work will be important for both philosophers and for scientists interested in the philosophical questions in their work. C-D

SCHUBERT-SOLDERN, Rainer. *Mechanism and Vitalism.* Ed. by P. G. Fothergill. Trans. by C. Robin from *Philosophie des Lebendigen.* Notre Dame, Ind.: University of Notre Dame Press, 1962. xviii, 244 pp.

The author, in attempting to draw mechanism and vitalism into an interdependent relationship, provides philosophers with much relevant biological data which is useful in treating questions on the epistemology of the sciences and on the forms and activities of living things. The book also illustrates the relevance of philosophy to biology. D

See: Bl 43 (1962) 443; CR 80 (1962) 276; PS 12 (1963) 255.

SHARPE, Alfred B. *The Freedom of the Will* (Westminster Lectures) . London: Sands, 1905. 53 pp.

An uncomplicated presentation of the freedom of the will. After rejecting materialism and determinism, the author attacks the problem of reconciling freedom with the will's need for motives. The pertinent theological perspective is noted. A-B

See: CW 82 (1905) 269.

SLAVIN, Robert J. *The Philosophical Basis for Individual Differences According to Saint Thomas Aquinas.* (The Catholic University of America, *Philosophical Studies,* No. 33) . Washington, D.C.: The Catholic University of America Press, 1936. 166 pp. (Paper)

After stating the problem, the author considers the nature of the soul and of the principle of individuation, and applies direct metaphysical and psychological arguments. The pertinent empirical data of the time is introduced. C

SMITH, Vincent E. (ed.) *Philosophy of Biology.* (St. John's University Studies. Philosophical Series, Vol. 3) . Jamaica, N.Y.: St. John's University Press, 1962. 95 pp. (Paper)

A collection of lectures on the relationship between philosophy and biology. There are special studies of method in biology, of evolution, and of the meaningfulness of the term "life." B-C

See: J. Sikora, MS 41 (1963) 84-85.

STAAB, Giles. *The Dignity of Man in Modern Papal Doctrine.* Washington, D.C.: The Catholic University of America Press, 1957. 154 pp. Bibliography.

A study of the understanding of man as expressed in modern Papal statements, this work surveys the nature of man in relation to his creator, the dynamic relations into which man enters, and the societies which result. This comprehensive study exemplifies the influences of a Christian philosophy. A-B

See: J. Newman, ITQ 25 (1958) 299.

STRAELEN, H. Van. *Man the Lonely.* See XVII.

STRASSER, Stephen. *Phenomenology of the Human Sciences: A Contribution to a New Scientific Ideal* (Duquesne Studies. "Psychological Series," No. 1). Pittsburgh: Duquesne University Press, 1963. xiii, 339 pp.

An attempt to develop and justify a phenomenological method for the sciences of man. After indicating the need for an approach which lies between the extremes of objectivism and subjectivism, the author searches for a type of objectivity which proceeds beyond that of common sense and science to join science and wisdom. This is then related to the empirical sciences of man in order to base them on a phenomenological approach. This work will be of great interest to both the philosopher and the scientist. C-D

See: R. Barry, T 38 (1963) 627.

———. *The Soul in Metaphysics and Empirical Psychology.* (Duquesne Studies. "Philosophical Series," No. 7). Trans. by M. Koren from *Het zielsbegrip in de metaphysische en in de empirische psychologie.* Pittsburgh: Duquesne Univ. Press, 1957 (1950). 275 pp. Bibliography, index. (Paper)

An attempt to find the difference between empirical and rational psychology through an investigation of the concept of soul. The author holds that the phenomenological method, which he uses throughout the book, is the only one which can show the relationship between empirical and rational psychology. He traces an historico-critical survey of some modern philosophical and psychological theories according to Thomistic-Aristotelian metaphysics and concludes with a constructive analysis. The translator has added a glossary. This work should be read by professional philosophers and psychologists. C-D

See: NS 32 (1958) 283; RUO 28 (1958) 403*; Tm 21 (1958) 116.

SULLIVAN, John E. *The Image of God: The Doctrine of Saint Augustine and Its Influence.* Dubuque: Priory Press, 1963. xvii, 356 pp. Index.

An excellent, detailed study of St. Augustine's contribution to the understanding of man in his relation to God. The development of the notion of image in Augustine leads to the presentation of his understanding of man as the image of God and of the Trinity. This doctrine is traced through the later Fathers and up to St. Thomas. D

See: J. Sullivan, D 48 (1963) 244.

SULLIVAN, Robert P. *Man's Thirst for the Good.* See IX.

TERRUWE, Anna A. *The Neurosis in the Light of Rational Psychology.* Ed. by Jordan Aumann. Trans. by C. Baars from *De Neurose in het Licht van der rationele Psychologie.* New York: Kenedy, 1960 (1954) . 200 pp.

A study of the sources and prevention of neurosis as seen against the background of an attempt to relate the Aristotelian-Thomistic to the modern dynamic psychology. The normal personality and the forces at work in personality development are considered, as is the origin, typology, and prevention of neurosis. The implications for free will are noted. B-C

THOMAS AQUINAS, Saint. *Aristotle's* De anima *with Commentary of St. Thomas Aquinas.* See XV.

————. *Law; Truth and Falsity; On Human Knowledge.* See XV.

————. *On Free Choice.* See XV.

————. *On the Truth of the Catholic Faith.* See XV.

————. *On the Virtues in General.* See XV.

————. *The Soul.* See XV.

————. *Summa theologica.* See XV.

————. *The Teacher; The Mind.* See XV.

————. *Treatise on Man.* See XV.

————. *The Trinity and The Unicity of the Intellect.* See XV.

————. *Truth.* See XV.

TOURNIER, Paul. *The Meaning of Persons.* See VII.

VAN EYKEN, Albert. *The Status of Man in the Universe.* London: Longmans, Green, 1956. vii, 128 pp.
A philosophic essay on the human situation, including reflections upon the dignity of man, the validity of sense experience, evolution, and free will. The problems of anthropomorphic religion are reviewed. A
> *See:* Bl 37 (1956) 135; IER 86 (1956) 138.

VANN, Gerald. *Awake in Heaven.* New York: Longmans, Green, 1948. 159 pp.
A loose collection of interesting addresses primarily concerning the meaning of man. The authentic dimensions of the person are traced and related to the divine as the source of ultimate fulfillment. A
> *See:* A. Schlitzer, AM 69 (1949) 378; CW 168 (1948) 251; D 33 (1948) 312; F. Ripley, HPR 49 (1949) 344; F. Frazer, S 28 (1948) 64; J. Mullaney, T 25 (1950) 186.

WALTERS, Sr. Annette, and O'HARA, Sr. Kevin. *Persons and Personality: An Introduction to Psychology* ("The Century Psychology Series"). New York: Appleton-Century-Crofts, 1953. 678 pp.
An approach to psychology centering on the development of human personality and its social implications. The clear exposition of Thomistic philosophy is coupled with a social psychology. Collateral reading. B
> *See:* R. Morris, ACSR 14 (1953) 136; F. Houlahan, CER 51 (1953) 283-84; A. Godin, T 29 (1954) 156.

WHITE, Victor. *God and the Unconscious.* See VIII.

ZAVALLONI, Roberto. *Self-determination: The Psychology of*

Personal Freedom. Trans. by V. Biasiol and C. Tageson of *La libertà personale nel quadro della psicologia della condotta umana.* Chicago: Franciscan Herald Press, 1963 (1956). xxiii, 341 pp. Bibliography, index.

An extensive study of the problem of freedom. The work opens with a survey of the historical development of freedom; proceeds to a phenomenological investigation; and then leads the reader to further considerations on the foundations, meaning, and nature of personal freedom, as well as its ethical and social consequences. C-D

See: GCP 10 (1963) 117.

CHAPTER VII

Metaphysics

This chapter comprises works in the field variously designated metaphysics, general metaphysics, ontology, or first philosophy. The material of special metaphysics, or natural theology, has been placed in Chapter VIII, while that of defensive metaphysics will be found in Chapter IV *(Epistemology)*. Works have been included in the present chapter when their predominant emphasis is on general metaphysics. Nevertheless, many, such as those on person, love, freedom, evil, value, and the order of the universe, also contain extensive material from other sections of philosophy. Studies of recent historical positions have been included where they are concerned with metaphysical questions and are evaluated from the viewpoint of a Christian philosophy.

The reader is referred to Chapters IV-VII of *A Bibliography of Christian Philosophy and Contemporary Issues* by the same editor.

ANDERSON, James F. *The Bond of Being: An Essay on Analogy and Existence*. St. Louis: Herder, 1949. xvi, 341 pp. Bibliography, index.

A careful, scholarly investigation of the analogies of inequality, attribution, metaphor, and proper proportionality. This essay considers the latter to be the sole true metaphysical analogy. Besides giving the Thomistic approach, it shows how, historically, misuse of analogy has led to philosophic error. Diversity in the act of existence is developed as the root of metaphysical analogy. C

See: D 34 (1949) 322; L. Kendzierski, T 25 (1950) 157; J. Croteau, RUO 21 (1951) 200*.

————. (ed.) *An Introduction to the Metaphysics of St. Thomas Aquinas*. Chicago: Regnery, 1953. 137 pp.

A selection of texts from the writings of St. Thomas Aquinas. The most extensive section is on the transcendental properties of being; but the nature, structure, and analogical character of being are also treated, as is the problem of knowledge of God. There are extensive notes on the selections. A source book. C

See: D 39 (1954) 197; Rowan, NS 28 (1954) 351.

BASCHAB, Charles R. *A Manual of Neo-Scholastic Philosophy*. See II.

BITTLE, Celestine N. *The Domain of Being: Ontology*. Milwaukee: Bruce, 1939. x, 401 pp. Bibliography, index.

A metaphysics textbook for beginners. In general it is overwritten and perhaps oversimplified even as an introduction; but it includes excellent summaries and reading selections at the end of each chapter. There is also a useful fourteen-page glossary of terms. A-B

See: ER 107 (1939) 449; HPR 40 (1940) 1276; MS 16 (1939) 70.

BRENNAN, Robert E. *Essays in Thomism*. See II.

BUCKLEY, George M. *The Nature and Unity of Metaphysics* (The Catholic University of America. *Philosophical Studies*,

No. 45). Washington, D.C.: The Catholic University of America Press, 1946. xvi, 261 pp. Bibliography, index. (Paper)

A study of the nature of the science of metaphysics. Isolating the subject of the science, its properties and principles, this book helps to clarify the distinctive and indispensable character of metaphysics. Much work has been done in this area since it was written, but it still can be of service on particular points. C

See: St 36 (1947) 125-26; BL 28 (1947) 281-82.

CASEY, Joseph T. *The Primacy of Metaphysics.* (The Catholic University of America. *Philosophical Studies,* No. 31). Washington, D.C.: The Catholic University of America Press, 1936. 108 pp. (Paper)

A study of the position of metaphysics in the hierarchy of the sciences. It reviews modern physical, mathematical, and experimental approaches to the problem of ultimate reality and, by criticizing them in the light of scholastic principles, establishes the primacy of metaphysics. Collateral reading. B

CASS, John A. *Quest of Certainty: A Modern Irenicon.* Paterson: St. Anthony Guild Press, 1950. 210 pp. Index.

An attempt to explore the certainties of life and the basic truths attainable by man, in order to find firm guidelines in a changing world. It concentrates on wisdom, God, man, and the problem of evil. Collateral reading. A-B

See: C. Miltner, AM 73 (1951) 826; D 36 (1951) 139.

CAUSALITY IN CURRENT PHILOSOPHY. See I.

CLARK, Mary T. *Augustine: Philosopher of Freedom.* See XIV.

COFFEY, Peter. *Ontology; or the Theory of Being: An Introduction to General Metaphysics.* New York: Smith, 1938 (1912). xii, 439 pp. Index.

An excellent and detailed survey in which the exposition of the problems of metaphysics is clear and thorough, with more detailed considerations in small print. It contains fine historical material but, since it is merely a reprint of the 1914 edition, it should be supplemented by texts containing more recent history and problems. C

See: A 12 (1914) 18; CW 10 (1915) 545.

COLEBURT, Russell. *The Search for Values.* New York: Sheed and Ward, 1960. 135 pp.

A timely work on the axiological queries of the modern mind. The relationship between science and philosophy is reviewed in order to provide the context of the problem. Sections are devoted to artistic, moral, and religious values, which are then placed within the perspective of sincerity in living. C

See: ACSR 21 (1960) 346; DR 79 (1961) 67; NS 35 (1961) 531; St 50 (1961) 107; Tm 24 (1961) 128.

COLLINS, James D. *The Lure of Wisdom* (The Aquinas Lecture, 1962) . Milwaukee: Marquette University Press, 1962. 160 pp.

An effective study of the presence of the problem of wisdom in modern times. This is traced from the skeptics and Stoics of the later renaissance through subsequent Cartesian orientations. Finally, the contemporary opportunities and demands for wisdom are surveyed, and ways to meet them effectively are suggested. C

See: D 47 (1962) 310; MS 40 (1963) 309; RR 22 (1963) 488; RUO 33 (1963) 78*.

COLLINS, William B. *Metaphysics and Man.* See II.

———. *Speculative Philosophy.* See II.

CONLEY, Kiernan. *A Theology of Wisdom.* See VIII.

COTTER, Anthony C. *The A B C of Scholastic Philosophy.* See II.

D'ARCY, Martin C. *The Meeting of Love and Knowledge: Perennial Wisdom* (World Perspectives, Vol. 15) . New York: Harper, 1957. xix, 167 pp.

A sympathetic, firm, and well-balanced contribution to the movement to unite East and West by finding the ultimate metaphysical wisdom behind the teachings of the great religions. The author admits a possibility of some agreement; but the crucial difference lies in the primacy of love in the Christian way of salvation which aims, not at absorbing the human personality in the divine, but rather at a union with God in which the human personality is actually intensified. Repetition and digression sometimes mar an otherwise fine work. B-D

See: AER 138 (1958) 431; CR 44 (1959) 120; CW 186 (1958) v; C 68 (1958) 522; DuR 232 (1958) 175-78; J 5 (1958) 52; S 37 (1958) 64; Ta 211 (1958) 409; T 33 (1958) 458.

————. *The Mind and Heart of Love, Lion and Unicorn: A Study in Eros and Agape.* 2d ed. revised. New York: Meridian, 1956 (1947). 381 pp. Bibliography, index. (M 26)

An analysis of the tension between the self-centered and the self-transcending aspects of love. After critically investigating the divergent theories on love of De Rougemont, Nygren, and others, the author concludes that only in the divine agape can the balance between the two loves be maintained. A penchant for rhetoric vitiates precise philosophical analysis; more formal organization would enhance the book's value. C

See: A 76 (1947) 691; Bl 27 (1946) 432-35; Bl 35 (1954) 348; C 46 (1947) 233-35; IER 68 (1946) 355-56; RP 9 (1947) 504-506; RUO 17 (1947) 363; S 26 (1947) 56; St 35 (1946) 430-31; St 46 (1957) 257; Ta 188 (1946) 9-10.

DAY, Sebastian J. *Intuitive Cognition.* See XVI.

DE COURSEY, Sr. Mary Edwin. *The Theory of Evil in the Metaphysics of St. Thomas and Its Contemporary Significance* (The Catholic University of America. *Philosophical Studies,* No. 102). Washington, D.C.: The Catholic University of America Press, 1948. xiii, 178 pp. Bibliography. (Paper)

A survey of the character of evil according to St. Thomas. The nature of evil is seen against its metaphysical background, and its kinds and causes are studied. Collateral reading. B-C

DESAN, Wilfrid. *The Planetary Man.* See XVII.

DIGGS, Bernard J. *Love and Being: An Investigation Into the Metaphysics of Love in St. Thomas Aquinas.* New York: Vanni, 1947. xi, 180 pp. Bibliography, index.

A penetrating study of the metaphysical components of love in the philosophy of St. Thomas Aquinas. The first section, on the analogy of love, is the most successful. The other sections contain many fine insights concerning the ordered interrelation of the transcendentals and the implications of this structure of being for the various types of love. C

See: RUO 17 (1947) 191*-92*; T 23 (1948) 351-52.

DONDEYNE, Albert. *Contemporary European Thought and Christian Faith.* See VIII.

DRENNEN, Donald A. (ed.) *A Modern Introduction to Metaphysics: Readings from Classical and Contemporary Sources.* Glencoe, Ill.: Free Press, 1962. xxv, 738 pp. Index.

An excellent selection of stimulating readings in the area of metaphysics. Sections on the spirit, method, and schools of metaphysical inquiry pave the way for the main issues. The editor provides not only useful introductions to each section and to the particular readings, but bibliographical material and study aids. The selections, though drawn from a broad spectrum of philosophical thought, are positive and complementary. A challenging instrument for above average students. B-C

DULLES, Avery, DEMSKE, James, and O'CONNELL, Robert. *Introductory Metaphysics.* See II.

FACKENHEIM, Emil. *Metaphysics and Historicity* (The Aquinas Lecture, 1961) . Milwaukee: Marquette University Press, 1961. 100 pp.

A description in clear, vigorous language of the nature of historicity and its metaphysical implications. The work concentrates on the challenge of historicity to the traditional metaphysical notion of the immutability of natures and of truth. The development of the dialectical and subjectivist positions on these topics is traced and evaluated in a clear and well-documented manner. The reader is enabled to perceive the authentic flow of metaphysical enquiry to gauge the precise position of the question at the present time. C-D

See: MS 39 (1962) 298; PS 11 (1961) 309; RUO 31 (1961) 136; St 50 (1961) 459; T 37 (1962) 318.

FARAON, Michael J. *The Metaphysical and Psychological Principles of Love* (The Aquinas Library. Doctrinal Studies, No. 3). Dubuque: Brown, 1952. xx, 93 pp. Bibliography. (Paper)

A well-written study of the nature of love. A review of the metaphysical character of the finite being, its finality and its appetites, provides the context for a psychological review of love as union in terms of affectivity, similarity, and end or goal. B

See: ABR 4 (1953) 269; CER 51 (1953) 354; CR 38 (1953) 568; D 38 (1953) 252; HPR 53 (1953) 862-63; Tm 16 (1953) 593.

FROM AN ABUNDANT SPRING. See II.

GERRITY, Benignus. *Nature, Knowledge, and God.* See II.

GILBY, Thomas. *Phoenix and Turtle.* See IV.

GILSON, Etienne. *Being and Some Philosophers.* 2d ed. revised. Toronto: Pontifical Institute of Mediaeval Studies, 1961 (1949). xi, 235 pp. Bibliography, index.

An exposition and critical analysis of various historical developments, according to which being has been approached as unity, substance, essence, and *esse*. The result is a veritable history of metaphysics up to the time of St. Thomas, the later medieval and modern periods being covered in the author's *Unity of Philosophical Experience.* In the course of the presentation, a sense of the continuous development of metaphysics and the complementary character of various positions is imparted, along with profound insights into many metaphysical notions. The final sections constitute a classical statement of the author's position concerning being in terms of existence and of judgment. An appendix contains an excerpt from a critical review by L. Régis, and an important reply. C-D

See: J. McAllister, ER 121 (1949) 508-11; L. Régis, MS 28 (1951) 111-25; R. Henle, T 24 (1949) 592-97; B. Lonergan, TS 11 (1950) 122-25.

————. *Elements of Christian Philosophy.* See XV.

————. *Wisdom and Love in St. Thomas Aquinas* (The Aquinas Lecture, 1951). Milwaukee: Marquette University Press, 1951. 55 pp.

A statement of the importance of rational desire in achieving true philosophic wisdom. Designating a true Thomist as one who knows because he loves, the author brings out the moral side of Thomistic thought and the role of the will in the study of philosophy. There is food here for meditation as well as speculation. B-C

See: D 37 (1952) 224; NS 27 (1953) 468.

GLENN, Paul J. *Ontology: A Class Manual in Fundamental Metaphysics.* St. Louis: Herder, 1937. x, 340 pp. Index.

This text in metaphysics for the undergraduate is perhaps over-simple. The key elements of ontology are treated, with special emphasis on the transcendental properties. A-B

See: CW 149 (1939) 254.

GRAJEWSKI, Maurice J. *The Formal Distinction of Duns Scotus.* See XVI.

GRENIER, Henri. *Thomistic Philosophy.* See II.

GUARDINI, Romano. *Freedom, Grace and Destiny.* Trans. by J. Murray. New York: Pantheon, 1961. 251 pp.

A discussion of many facets of the relation of freedom to finality in terms of recent philosophical orientations and in relation to the theological problem of grace. Freedom is studied as the form and content of the human act, while the personal religious factors of finality and providence are emphasized in the meeting of freedom and grace. B-C

GUITTON, Jean. *An Essay on Human Love.* See VI.

HARDING, Michael J. *The Science of Metaphysics.* Boston: Boston College (Worcester, Mass.: Rosseel Lithoprint), 1943. 126 pp.

An undergraduate text in metaphysics, written on a basic thesis format, but leaving room for development of definitions and discussion of opinions of Scholastic and non-Scholastic authors. B

HARPER, Thomas. *The Metaphysics of the School.* 3 vols. New York: Smith, 1940 (1879-81).

A reprint of the most extensive work in English on general metaphysics. It is a compendium of Scholastic metaphysical writing up to its original date of publication and provides a clear, orderly, and complete exposition of the key notions. There is a particularly good treatment of the trancendental properties of being. This work is also recommended as a background for more specialized investigations or more recent discussions. C-D

See: NS 16 (1942) 88-90.

HART, Charles. *Thomistic Metaphysics: An Inquiry into the Act of Existence.* Englewood Cliffs, N.J.: Prentice-Hall, 1959. xiii, 413 pp.

A difficult but rewarding undergraduate textbook. After introducing recent clarifications on the relation of metaphysics to the other sciences, the interacting hierarchy of being is unfolded according to the threefold application of potency as limiting act. This is done within the perspective of participation, indicating the principle implications for natural philosophy, ethics, and natural theology. A lengthy treatment of the transcendentals is reserved for the end of the text as an integrating summary manifesting the full results of wisdom. One of the few metaphysics texts which can be counted on to reflect later research on the key issues, it does not, unfortunately, solve the student's terminological problems. There are helpful review questions, and part of the historical material is arranged so that it can be left for collateral reading. B-C

See: M. Wheeler, NS 33 (1959) 244.

HAWKINS, Denis J. *Being and Becoming: An Essay Toward a Critical Metaphysics.* New York: Sheed and Ward, 1954. 176 pp.

A stimulating challenge to a critical rethinking of Thomistic metaphysics for those already familiar with that body of thought, It insists that metaphysical reflection must be rooted in experience. There is valuable material on the principle of sufficient reason and on causality, complementing the author's earlier work, *Causality and Implication.* Original while adhering to the main lines of Aristotelian and Thomistic thought, it will be of service to those of some philosophic sophistication who are interested in a metaphysics viable in the critical climate of English philosophic thought. B-C

See: C. Hart, AER 133 (1955) 61; W. Barden, Bl 36 (1955) 35; D 40 (1955) 310; DR 73 (1955) 192; Mo 14 (1955) 60; W. Clarke, NS 30 (1956) 110; M. Connolly, St 44 (1955) 117; M. Pontifex, T 205 (1955) 62; A. Dulles, TS 16 (1955) 314.

―――. *Causality and Implication.* London: Sheed and Ward, 1937. 122 pp.

A study of causality with special attention to the difficulties of British empiricism. Special attention, which the author has since considered to be excessive, is given to the more purely logical notion of implication as a relation between facts. The principles of implication and causation are studied along with their function in induction and hypothesis. This work sheds considerable light on the problems of causality raised in the Anglo-American philosophical milieu, and will be especially valuable when complemented by the author's later *Being and Becoming.* C

See: A 58 (1938) 479; Bl 19 (1938) 543; DuR 202 (1938) 185; ER 99 (1938) 88; HPR 39 (1939) 888; St 31 (1942) 407; Ta 170 (1937) 558; T 14 (1939) 336-37.

HENLE, Robert J. *Method in Metaphysics* (The Aquinas Lecture, 1950) . Milwaukee: Marquette University Press, 1951. vii, 73 pp.

An exposition of the problem of proceeding from sense knowledge to metaphysical knowledge. The greater part of the book is concerned with an excellent analysis, through reflective consciousness, of intellectual knowledge in general. The remainder is devoted specifically to metaphysical knowledge and its formal concentration on the intelligibility of the concrete existent. C

See: MS 30 (1953) 151; NS 26 (1952) 376.

HOENEN, Peter. *Reality and Judgment According to St. Thomas.* See IV.

HORRIGAN, Alfred F. *Metaphysics as a Principle of Order in the University Curriculum* (The Catholic University of America. *Philosophical Studies,* No. 86) . Washington, D.C.: The Catholic University of America Press, 1944. 241 pp. (Paper)

A study of the function of metaphysics in the university curriculum. The problem is traced historically to the anti-metaphysical elements in the transition from the medieval to the modern university. The pertinence of the ontology course to general college work is shown, with special attention to this problem on the American scene. C

HUGHES, Mary C. *The Intelligibility of the Universe* (The Catholic University of America. *Philosophical Studies,* No. 92) . Washington, D.C.: The Catholic University of America Press, 1946. viii, 172 pp. Bibliography, index.

This study prepares the way toward the understanding of the universe by means of an ontological and cosmological review of its structure, which is then considered in terms of metaphysical truth or intelligibility. The result is a view of the universe as a place of rational action on the part of man and as a manifestation of God as Truth Itself. C

JOHANN, Robert O. *The Meaning of Love: An Essay Towards*

a Metaphysics of Intersubjectivity. Westminster, Md.: Newman, 1955. ix, 133 pp.

An investigation of the ultimate metaphysical intelligibility of
altruistic love and of the good as perfective. A phenomenological
description of friendship is followed by an analysis of interpersonal love, explained within the framework of the Thomistic
metaphysics of participation. This work, which demonstrates the
capacity of Thomism to assimilate the best fruits of modern
existentialism, personalism, and realistic phenomenology, justifies the serious effort required from the reader. C-D

See: A 93 (1955) 53; DR 73 (1955) 392; IER 87 (1952) 312-16; MS 33
(1956) 284; PS (1955) 140; P 30 (1955) 630; Tm 19 (1956) 533.

JOLIVET, Régis. *Man and Metaphysics (Twentieth Century
Encyclopedia of Catholicism,* Vol. 35). Trans. by B. Reardon from *L'homme métaphysique.* New York: Hawthorn,
1961. 144 pp. Bibliography.

A treatment of the contemporary position of the problem of the
nature and possibility of metaphysics, and of the relation between
metaphysics and the sciences, epistemology, psychology, and ethics. There is a helpful glossary of terms. B-C

See: Bl 42 (1961) 528; CR 47 (1962) 526; DR 80 (1962) 294; IER 97
(1962) 207.

JOURNET, Charles. *The Meaning of Evil.* Trans. by M. Barry
from *Le mal.* New York: Kenedy, 1963. xii, 299 pp. Index.

An erudite study of evil within a primarily theological context.
The work emphasizes that the understanding of evil is possible
only through recognition of God as sufficiently powerful and good
to draw good out of evil. There is extensive use of the thought of
philosophers of different ages, and many contemporary issues are
considered. C

See: AM 98 (1963) 29; IER 100 (1963) 68; Lg 51 (1963) 62.

JUNKERSFELD, Mary J. *The Aristotelian-Thomistic Concept
of Chance.* See V.

KANE, William H. *Approach to Philosophy.* See II.

KLUBERTANZ, George P., and HOLLOWAY, Maurice R. *Being and God: An Introduction to the Philosophy of Being and to Natural Theology.* New York: Appleton-Century-Crofts, 1963. v, 382 pp.

A combination of two of the more successful texts on metaphysics and natural theology. Only the less important sections of each text are omitted. The two relate very well in point of view and manner of approach. This combined text will be specially useful for the more brief undergraduate course on these areas, and corresponds well to the renewed appreciation of natural theology as part of metaphysics. B

See: MS 41 (1964) 298.

————. *Introduction to the Philosophy of Being.* 2d ed. revised. New York: Appleton-Century-Crofts, 1963 (1955). v, 336 pp. Bibliography.

An excellent introduction to metaphysics for the college student. It uses a clear, readable, essay approach and contains useful summaries, definitions, bibliography, and excerpts from St. Thomas at the end of the various chapters. It reflects the more existential and subject-centered orientation of contemporary Thomism and contains original contributions by the author on analogy and constructural knowledge. B

See: MS 34 (1957) 139; MS 41 (1964) 302-303; E. Salmon, NS 31 (1957) 126; R. Porreco, NS 38 (1964) 244-46; SJR 48 (1955) 161.

————. *St. Thomas on Analogy: A Textual Analysis and Systematic Synthesis* (Jesuit Studies). Chicago: Loyola, 1960. 319 pp. Bibliography, index, appendices.

A profound, scholarly, and controversial study of the texts of St. Thomas on analogy, intended as a complement to H. Lyttkens, *The Analogy between God and the World.* Particularly valuable are the appendices which contain the Thomistic texts dealing directly with analogy, an analytic index of the texts, and a full bibliography of modern studies on Thomistic analogy. Though important studies do consider it a problem in logic, the possibility of a successful textual study has been questioned when, as here, the metaphysical questions are relegated to a subsequent section on material analogy. C-D

See: W. Ong, A 104 (1961) 574; DR 79 (1961) 369; IPQ 2 (1962) 335; L. Sweeney, MS 39 (1962) 253-62; R. McInerny, NS 36 (1962) 128-34; NRT 83 (1961) 975; PS 11 (1961) 276; T 36 (1961) 464.

KOREN, Henry J. *An Introduction to the Science of Metaphysics.* St. Louis: Herder, 1955. xix, 291 pp. Indices.

A capable explanation of metaphysical problems and solutions in the Thomistic tradition. The introduction gives more than usual attention to an approach to metaphysics from the viewpoint of the three degrees of abstraction. The book is then divided between the philosophy of being in general and the philosophy of finite being. There are helpful chapter summaries and suggested readings which include pertinent periodical articles. B-C

See: ABR 7 (1956) 89; AER 134 (1956) 284; A 94 (1956) 408; AM 82 (1955) 29; CER 54 (1956) 205; R. Blackwell, MS 34 (1957) 139; NS 30 (1956) 246; SJR 48 (1956) 436.

KREYCHE, Robert J. *First Philosophy: An Introductory Text in Metaphysics.* New York: Holt, 1962 (1959). xviii, 328 pp. Bibliography.

A clearly written and simple college text. The presentation of Thomistic metaphysics is integrated with some material pertaining to contemporary developments. The careful attention given to the somewhat schematic method of exposition is an important aid in learning the technical terms, though this is but one step in the profound comprehension towards which metaphysics is aimed. There is a list of leading questions and conclusions and a summary at the end of each chapter. The bibliography offers an excellent selection of modern books and articles. B

See: G. McCool, MS 37 (1960) 328; L. Schumacher, NS 34 (1960) 248; J. St. Denis, RUO 29 (1959) 169.*

KWANT, Remy C. *Encounter* (Duquesne Studies, "Philosophical Series," No. 13). Translated by R. Adolfs from *Wijsbegeerte van de Ontmoeting.* Pittsburgh: Duquesne University Press, 1960 (1959). viii, 86 pp. (Paper)

This study of the import of intersubjective contact for human life can provide valuable contemporary orientations. The contact or "encounter" with other men and through the "word" is studied as a primary element in man's knowledge. Its implications for metaphysics, ethics, and theology are reviewed. C-D

See: G 42 (1961) 587-89; MS 39 (1961) 76; PS 11 (1961) 249; T 36 (1961) 463.

LAVELLE, Louis. *Evil and Suffering*. See XVII.

LeTROQUER, Rene. *What is Man?* See VI.

LUIJPEN, William A. *Existential Phenomenology*. (Duquesne Studies, "Philosophical Series," No. 12) . Trans. by J. Koren from *Existentiële fenomenologie*. Pittsburgh: Duquesne University Press, 1960. 362 pp. (Paper)

An original, personal attempt at a synthesis of existential-phenomenological thought. The attempt to consolidate the results of the inquiries of the second generation of existentialists is of great importance. However, it should not be taken as completely representative of the movement as, due to the difficulty of the task, an element of eclecticism remains. C-D

See: G 42 (1961) 586; IPQ 1 (1961) 533; MS 39 (1962) 398; R. Allers, NS 35 (1961) 541; PS 11 (1961) 247.

LYTTKENS, Hampus. *The Analogy between God and the World: An Investigation of Its Background and Interpretation of Its Use by Thomas of Aquino*. Uppsala: Almqvist and Wiksells, 1952. 493 pp. Bibliography.

A carefully researched study of the notion of analogy in the works of St. Thomas. It also traces the history of analogy, especially in Aristotle and his interpreters. It has led to important re-evaluations of traditional interpretations of analogy, particularly concerning the role played by likeness to cause in the analogy of proper proportionality in man's knowledge of God. Perhaps only the historical survey will be of use to undergraduates doing research papers, but the whole work is an indispensable point of departure for any subsequent scholarly study of the subject. C-D

See: MS 31 (1954) 238.

McCALL, Robert E. *The Reality of Substance* (The Catholic University of America, *Philosophical Studies,* No. 168). Washington, D.C.: The Catholic University of America Press, 1956. 202 pp. Bibliography, index. (Paper)

A study of substance: its existence, nature and intelligibility. The main investigation is preceded by a criticism of modern philosophical positions on the subject. Collateral reading. B-C

See: NS 32 (1958) 139.

McCORMICK, John F. *Being, Its Division and Causes.* Part I of *Scholastic Metaphysics.* Chicago: Loyola University Press, 1940 (1928). 252 pp. Bibliography, index.

A clear and well-organized undergraduate text covering the traditional matter of metaphysics courses, together with a study of the material and formal causes and their realization in man. A general index and bibliography are provided along with particular suggestions for further reading. Instead of presenting formal theses, the text invites the student at the end of each section to establish and explain, on his own, a number of propositions. B

McINERNY, Ralph. *The Logic of Analogy.* See III.

McMORROW, George J. *A Metaphysical Study on the Individual and the Person.* Notre Dame, Ind.: Notre Dame University. (Ann Arbor: Edwards Lithoprint), 1940. iii, 122 pp. Bibliography. (Paper)

A survey of the problems concerning man's metaphysical nature as a person. These include substantial individuation, subsistence, and the rational and free nature of the person. While the work can be of general interest, it raises too many questions to allow for a fully satisfying treatment of any of them. B

MARCEL, Gabriel. *Being and Having.* See XVII.

———. *Creative Fidelity.* See XVII.

———. *The Decline of Wisdom.* See XVII.

————. *The Existential Background of Human Dignity.* See XVII.

————. *Homo viator: Introduction to a Metaphysics of Hope.* See XVII.

————. *Metaphysical Journal.* See XVII.

————. *The Mystery of Being.* See XVII.

————. *The Philosophy of Existence.* See XVII.

MARITAIN, Jacques. *Creative Intuition in Art and Poetry.* See XI.

————. *The Degrees of Knowledge.* See IV.

————. *Existence and the Existent.* Trans. by L. Galantière and G. Phelan from *Court traité de l'existence et de l'existant.* New York: Pantheon, 1949 (1947). vi, 148 pp. (Image: D 45)

An excellent series of studies on the authentically existential character of Thomism. It considers some of the insights of contemporary philosophy and shows how they can be brought to full fruition in the Thomistic synthesis. Of prime interest is the chapter on the intuition of being, with its illuminatng footnotes, and the chapter on subject and person. As collateral reading it will do much toward bringing the undergraduate to a realization of the import of the problems treated in a more technical fashion in class. B-C

See: K. Reinhart, C 49 (1949) 545; M. Hess, CW 169 (1949) 75; D 34 (1949) 53; F. Salmon, T 24 (1949) 725-27.

————. *Freedom in the Modern World.* Trans. by R. O'Sullivan from *Du régime temporel et de la liberté.* New York: Scribner's, 1936 (1933).

A re-examination of some of the foundations upon which social organs and institutions are based. Three essays study the philosophy of freedom, relations between religion and culture, and the means necessary for radical reform of the temporal order. C

See: Bl 16 (1935) 627; CR 11 (1936) 297-304; MS 14 (1937) 45; S 16 (1936) 249; Ta 166 (1935) 202.

————. *A Preface to Metaphysics: Seven Lectures on Being.* Translated from *Sept leçons sur l'être et les premiers principes de la raison spéculative.* New York: Sheed and Ward, 1939 (1934) . 152 pp. (Mentor Omega: MP 403)

A very useful text as preparation for the study of metaphysics. It establishes the differences between metaphysics and other scientific approaches to reality; discusses the role of the imagination in the service of philosophy; and expounds the distinction between problem and mystery. The main tasks of metaphysics are introduced. B

See: CW 151 (1940) 371-72; CR 18 (1940) 63; ER 102 (1940) 541; HPR 40 (1940) 1380-81; S 19 (1940) 697; Ta 175 (1940) 38; Tm 3 (1941) 172.

————. *St. Thomas and the Problem of Evil.* (The Aquinas Lecture, 1942) . 2d ed. Trans. by Mrs. G. Andison. Milwaukee: Marquette University Press, 1958 (1942) . 46 pp.

A brief, illuminating essay on the key issues involved in the problem of evil. It contains original and stimulating comments on the meaning of the existence of evil in the world, and on free will in connection with the cause of moral evil. It concludes that moral evil transpires only when the creature takes the initiative of nothingness, evading the influx of the first cause. Some modes of expression have been considered questionable. B-C

See: Bl 24 (1943) 319; C 37 (1942) 236; D 27 (1942) 288; DuR 212 (1943) 175-78; MS 20 (1943) 109-11; NS 17 (1943) 193-94; RUO 13 (1943) 61-62*; S 22 (1943) 696-97; St 32 (1943) 292.

————. *Science and Wisdom.* See II.

————. *Sin of the Angel: An Essay on a Re-interpretation of Some Thomistic Positions.* Trans. by W. Rossner from *Le péché de l'ange.* Westminster, Md.: Newman, 1959. 106 pp.

A competent rethinking of the old controversy on whether, in a purely natural order, angels could sin. The problem is solved in the affirmative. Along the way much is done to clarify the nature of free will and of evil, though some expressions have been questioned. C

See: D 45 (1960) 175; P. Donnelly, TS 21 (1960) 662.

MARLING, Joseph. *The Order of Nature in the Philosophy of St. Thomas Aquinas* (The Catholic University of America, *Philosophical Studies*, No. 28). Washington, D.C.: The Catholic University of America Press, 1934. xii, 187 pp. Bibliography.

A study of the order of nature and its laws according to the mind of St. Thomas. After surveying the notion of nature and the metaphysics of order, the author presents a study of the order of nature, its necessity, and its laws according to Aristotle, the Stoics, St. Augustine, and St. Thomas. Contemporary objections are also reviewed. Collateral reading, useful in appreciating the metaphysical foundations of natural law. B-C

MARTIN, William O. *Metaphysics and Ideology* (The Aquinas Lecture, 1959). Milwaukee: Marquette University Press, 1959. vii, 104 pp.

A study of the true meaning of metaphysics. The history of the loss of metaphysical thinking is traced. Four criteria are proposed for distinguishing metaphysics with its objective validity from ideology. B

See: PS 9 (1959) 272; P. McShane, St 48 (1959) 241; M. Kelley, Tm 23 (1960) 483-88.

MASCALL, Eric L. *Existence and Analogy, a Sequel to* He Who Is. New York: Longmans, Green, 1949. xix, 188 pp. Index.

A study of theism and analogy. The essentialist approach to theism is contrasted with the existential approach of St. Thomas. The nature of analogy is studied at some length with special attention to the function of the analogy of attribution in relation to that of the analogy of proper proportionality in man's knowledge of God. C

See: DR 68 (1949) 90-93; T. Gilby, DuR 224 (n. 447, 1950) 133-34; O. Trethowan, DR 72 (1954) 16-30; J. O'Mara, S 39 (1950) 236-38.

MEEHAN, Francis X. *Efficient Causality in Aristotle and Saint Thomas* (The Catholic University of America, *Philosophical Studies,* No. 56) . Washington, D.C.: The Catholic University of America Press, 1940. xx, 424 pp. Bibl., index. (Paper)

A treatment of the Aristotelian notion of efficiency and its implications, as amended, modified, and restated by St. Thomas. While some positions—such as that of Aristotle on divine efficiency— have not been substantiated in subsequent research, the work is done with thoroughness and authority. C

MIHALICH, Joseph C. *Existentialism and Thomism.* See XVII.

MILTNER, Charles C. and O'GRADY, Daniel C. *Introduction to Metaphysics.* New York: Macmillan, 1930. 270 pp. Index.

A general survey of metaphysics. To the ordinary contents of a metaphysics course are added some notions on quantity, space, and time. There is a useful author and subject index. B

See: A 45 (1931) 287.

MORRIS, Hilaire. *Philosophy for Beginners.* See II.

MORRISON, Bakewell, and RUEVE, Stephen. *Think and Live.* See II.

MOUNIER, Emmanuel. *Be Not Afraid.* See XVII.

———. *Existentialist Philosophies.* See XVII.

———. *A Personalist Manifesto.* See XVII.

———. *The Spoil of the Violent.* See XVII.

MULLEN, Mary D. *Essence and Operation in the Teaching of St. Thomas and Some Modern Philosophies* (The Catholic University of America, *Philosophical Studies,* No. 58) . Washington, D.C.: The Catholic University of America Press, 1941. xi, 119 pp. Bibliography, index. (Paper)

A study of the relation of substance to activity. Different levels of substantial beings are considered with special attention to their activity and its value. Collateral reading. B-C

NOONAN, John P. *General Metaphysics*. Chicago: Loyola University Press, 1957. 273 pp. Bibliography.

An effective undergraduate text in metaphysics. The usual material is covered in a succinct manner. There is a helpful summation, and glossary. B

> *See:* J. Tiblier, NS 34 (1960) 390.

O'BRIEN, Mary C. *The Antecedents of Being: An Analysis of the Concept "de nihilo" in the Philosophy of St. Thomas Aquinas. A Study in Thomistic Philosophy*. (The Catholic University of America, *Philosophical Studies*, No. 46). Washington, D.C.: The Catholic University of America Press, 1939. 202 pp. (Paper)

An analysis of the concept *nihil* in the philosophy of Saint Thomas. In relation to this there is a presentation and criticism of other philosophical interpretations of reality. The discussions on this topic have developed considerably since this work was written. Collateral reading. B-C

O'BRIEN, Thomas C. *Metaphysics and the Existence of God*. See VIII.

O'NEIL, Charles J. *An Etienne Gilson Tribute*. See II.

OSGNIACH, Augustine J. *Analysis of Objects; or the Four Principle Categories: An Historico-Critical Analysis in the Light of Scholastic Philosophy*. New York: Wagner, 1938. xvii, 302 pp. Bibliography, index.

An analysis of reality which treats the categories of substance, quality, quantity, and relation in a clear and readable manner. C

> *See:* AM 48 (1938) 251; Bl 21 (1940) 115; CSJ 38 (1938) 12a; ER 99 (1938) 297-98; IER 53 (1939) 103; Th 2 (1940) 166-71.

OWENS, Joseph. *The Doctrine of Being in the Aristotelian Meta-*

physics: A Study in the Greek Background of Medieval Thought. 2d ed. revised. Toronto: Pontifical Institute of Mediaeval Studies, 1963 (1951). xi, 535 pp. Bibliography, indices.

A landmark among studies of the Aristotelian metaphysical roots of subsequent Christian philosophy. Each book of the *Metaphysics* is studied in detail, both according to the text and to classical and modern commentators. Being is found to mean, first of all, form and separate entity; it is then extended to all else by a *pros en* analogy. The thesis of the book is still strongly disputed; but no scholar can proceed into this field without coming to grips with the issues it raises. D

See: DS 6 (1953) 234; J. Veatch, MS 30 (1953) 146-51; J. Anderson, NS 26 (1952) 229-39; J. Heuston, PS 2 (1952) 97-109; Th 16 (1953) 300-01; TS 13 (1952) 165; HJ 5 (1964) 233-34.

————. *An Elementary Christian Metaphysics.* Milwaukee: Bruce, 1963 v, 384 pp.

An exceptionally competent text on metaphysics. Considerable attention is paid to the acquisition of the notion of being, which is given a strongly existential interpretation. The rest of metaphysics is developed in this light, with special consideration to the place of man in the hierarchy of being and the relation of all to God. B-C

See: W. Max, CSJ 64 (1964) 70; Lazan, MS 41 (1964) 292-99; T. O'Brien, NS 38 (1964) 270-73.

————. *St. Thomas and the Future of Metaphysics* (The Aquinas Lecture 1957). Milwaukee: Marquette University Press, 1957. vi, 97 pp.

A study of the nature of the contemporary metaphysical task. After surveying the situation of metaphysics in modern thought, the author attempts to clarify its properly philosophic character and to describe the steps required for the elaboration of such a science. Many will not agree with this interpretation of St. Thomas. C

See: NS 32 (1958) 264; PS 7 (1957) 199; St 46 (1957) 361; Tm 21 (1958) 215-20.

PEGIS, Anton. (ed.) *Essays in Modern Scholasticism*. See II.

PETERS, John A. *Metaphysics: A Systematic Survey*. (Duquesne Studies, *Philosophical Series*, No. 16). Pittsburgh: Duquesne University Press, 1963. vi, 529 pp. Index. (Paper)

A metaphysics text of strong phenomenological orientation. An extensive description of types of human knowledge, experience, and insight, lays the foundation for a discussion of the feasibility and necessity of metaphysics. Perception, as temporal and corporeal activity, is shown to direct the mind toward the notion of essence and its principles. The affective life and knowledge of other men and of God are given important attention. This text would seem to be indicated if the phenomenological elements were made the core of the course. B-C

PHELAN, Gerald B. *St. Thomas and Analogy* (The Aquinas Lecture, 1941). Milwaukee: Marquette University Press, 1941. viii, 58 pp. Bibliography.

The clearest introductory outline of the doctrine of analogy. It is too early a work and too general in intent to consider more recent problems on this subject. Nevertheless, it does make an exceptionally effective presentation of the analogy of inequality. B

See: Bl 23 (1942) 159-60; D 27 (1942) 57-58; MS 19 (1942) 36; Th 4 (1942) 544; T 17 (1942) 550-52.

PHILLIPS, Richard P. *Modern Thomistic Philosophy*. See II.

PHILOSOPHY AND FINALITY. See I.

PHILOSOPHY AND UNITY. See I.

PHILOSOPHY OF BEING. See I.

PIEPER, Josef. *The Silence of St. Thomas*. See XV.

PONTIFEX, Mark, and TRETHOWAN, Illtyd. *The Meaning of Existence: A Metaphysical Inquiry*. London: Longmans, Green, 1953. 179 pp.

A series of reflections on the notion of existence. It posits a double notion of existence, and rejects any real distinction between essence and existence or act and potency, reducing the distinction to the conceptual order. It also champions the Anselmian argument for the existence of God. The authors' statement that their approach is "in the spirit of St. Thomas," could be misleading to the reader. They are more correct when they characterize it as Augustinian. C

See: A. MacIntyre, DR 71 (1953) 452; E. Watkin, DuR 228 (1954) 84; IER 81 (1954) 391; P. Stubbs, Ta 201 (1953) 374.

THE PROBLEM OF LIBERTY. See I.

RAEYMAEKER, Louis de. *The Philosophy of Being: A Synthesis of Metaphysics.* Trans. by E. Zieglemeyer from the 2d revised ed. of *Philosophie de l'être (De Metaphysiek van het Zijn).* St. Louis: Herder, 1954 (1944). xii, 360 pp. Bibliography, index.

A contemporary text on metaphysics. It finds the origin of its study in the epistemological area through the apprehension of the ego and the non-ego. Recent insights, such as the import of esse, give a dynamism and unity to the work, which takes up the various sectors of metaphysics and even extends to the study of the creative cause. Excellent summaries of historical disputes are included. C

See: A 91 (1944) 322; ABR 5 (1954) 169; AER 131 (1954) 216; AM 80 (1954) 26; CER 53 (1955) 137; CR 39 (1952) 698; CC 5 (1955) 184; D 39 (1954) 201; IER 85 (1956) 228; Tm 18 (1955) 117; T 29 (1954) 468; R. Blackwell, MS 34 (1957) 139.

—— *et al. Truth and Freedom* (Duquesne Studies, "Philosophical Series," No. 5). Trans. by H. Koren from *Liberté et vérité.* Pittsburgh: Duquesne University Press, 1955 (1954). vii, 133 pp. (Paper)

A collection of essays on freedom by several professors at the University of Louvain. Freedom is studied in relation to truth. The psychological, moral, and social facets of freedom are reviewed, especially in relation to faith, the physical sciences, and literary criticism. C

See: D 40 (1955) 313; HPR 56 (1955) 264; T 19 (1956) 263.

RAMSEY, Ian. (ed.) *Prospect for Metaphysics: Essays of Metaphysical Exploration.* London: Allen and Unwin, 1961. 240 pp.

A series of conferences given at Downside Abbey on the possibility and nature of metaphysics. The compilation is an excellent cooperative venture by Catholic and non-Catholic British philosophers. In it they probe the recent openings for metaphysics and discuss the logical and epistemological problems confronting this science in the context of contemporary analytic thought. Indispensable reading for the professional philosopher. C-D

> *See:* Bl 42 (1961) 530; CR 47 (1962) 526; DR 79 (1961) 364; MS 40 (1963) 194; PS 12 (1963) 283; TS 23 (1962) 358.

REITH, Herman R. *The Metaphysics of St. Thomas Aquinas.* Milwaukee: Bruce, 1958. xvii, 403 pp. Index.

An explanation of metaphysics with special attention to the thought of St. Thomas. It follows the order of the *Commentary on the Metaphysics* with frequent references to that book. The value of studying the philosophy of nature before metaphysics is emphasized. About half the work is a collection of Thomistic and Aristotelian texts, arranged in an order parallel to that of the topics of the various chapters. Some chapters are confusing. As a text, the work would be for the more capable undergraduates; however, as a collection of passages, it will be useful to all undergraduates, whatever their text might be. B-C

> *See:* W. Kane, NS 33 (1959) 252; PS 8 (1959) 233; G. McCool, TS 20 (1959) 663.

RENARD, Henri. *Philosophy of Being.* 2d ed. revised and enlarged. Milwaukee: Bruce, 1946 (1943). x, 262 pp. Bibliography, indices.

A clear and uniform introduction to Thomistic metaphysics. It is especially clear on the need for potency as a limiting principle, the derivation of the categories, distinction, and subsistence. This clarity sometimes leads to an oversimplification of relations to other philosophies and of disputed questions. It is a successful text for brief introductory courses in metaphysics, but should be complemented by recent writings on contemporary problems in this field. Of special note is the 32-page *Student Manual for the Philosophy of Being,* listing pertinent questions, and the companion 38-page *Answer Guide,* both compiled by William L. Rossner and published in Milwaukee by Bruce in 1954. B

See: MS 21 (1944) 120; NS 18 (1944) 391-92; T 19 (1944) 736.

RICKABY, John. *General Metaphysics.* ("Stonyhurst Philosophical Series"). 3rd ed. London: Longmans, Green, 1921 (1890) . 398 pp.

An approach to metaphysics in a rambling, witty style. It treats the notion of being, essence and existence, the transcendentals, and finite and infinite being. This is a refreshing change from the usual textbook fare. B

ROSENBERG, Jean. *Readings in Metaphysics* ("College Reading Series," No. 9) . Westminster, Md.: Newman, 1964. ix, 368 pp. (Paper)

A collection of readings, mostly from recent authors in the neo-Scholastic tradition, on selected topics in the field of metaphysics. The readings are grouped under being, transcendentals, first principles, intrinsic principles, and causes. B-C

ROTHER, Aloysius. *Beauty.* See XI.

————. *Being: A Study in Metaphysics.* St. Louis: Herder, 1911. viii, 127 pp.

A Suarezian textbook in metaphysics. The approach is through being and its modes, with the intrinsic analogy of being given a prominent place. It is not adequate as a text but, especially because of its unaccustomed approach, it can provide useful material for students investigating various ways of working on specific problems. B

See: A 6 (1912) 354.

RUSSELL, John. *Science and Metaphysics* ("The Philosophy of

Science Series"). New York: Sheed and Ward, 1958. 80 pp. (Paper)

A simple, methodical, and elementary comparison of experimental science with metaphysics. Their respective starting points, methods, objects, and conclusions are compared. Special attention is given to the analogical character of metaphysical thought. It can be of service as supplementary reading at the beginning of a metaphysics course. A-B

RYAN, James F. *An Introduction to Philosophy*. See II.

RYAN, John K. *Basic Principles and Problems of Philosophy*. See II.

SALMON, Elizabeth G. *The Good in Existential Metaphysics* (The Aquinas Lecture, 1952). Milwaukee: Marquette University Press, 1953. vi, 93 pp.

A scholarly, well-ordered, and economically written consideration of the good as it actually exists. It treats good as a transcendental and progressively illumines its role, showing that the ontological and moral goods find their relationship only in the supreme good. C

   See: D 38 (1953) 367; Tm 17 (1954) 276.

SCHEU, Sr. Marina. *The Categories of Being in Aristotle and St. Thomas* (The Catholic University of America, *Philosophical Studies,* No. 88). Washington, D.C.: The Catholic University of America Press, 1944. 109 pp. Bibliography, index. (Paper)

A general survey of the problem, with special attention to its logical and metaphysical aspects in the writings of Aristotle. After a survey of the history of the notion up to the time of St. Thomas, the particular notions of substance and accident are studied. Collateral reading. B-C

SHARPE, Alfred. *Evil: Its Nature and Cause*. See VIII.

SHIRCEL, Cyril L. *The Univocity of the Concept of Being in the Philosophy of Duns Scotus.* See XVI.

SIWEK, Paul. *The Philosophy of Evil.* New York: Ronald, 1951. 226 pp.

A study of evil as a human problem: its nature, origins, and effects. The treatment of the problem in the teachings of Aristotle and other ancient and modern philosophers is presented and criticized. Special attention is given to modern pessimism and optimism. A statement of the nature of evil, simply in relation to good rather than in relation to man, would have provided a more adequate context for consideration of these problems. C

See: L. Fley, CER 50 (1952) 498; J. Croteau, RUO 22 (1952) 71*; TL 15 (1952) 522; W. Clarke, TS 13 (1952) 153-55.

SMITH, Sr. Enid. *The Goodness of Being in Thomistic Philosophy and Its Contemporary Significance* (The Catholic University of America, *Philosophical Studies,* No. 98). Washington, D.C.: The Catholic University of America Press, 1947. xi, 143 pp. Bibliography, index. (Paper)

A study of the nature of the good as understood in a Thomistic metaphysical perspective. The good is situated within the context of being and the transcendentals. It is studied in its various aspects, axioms, and kinds, as well as in its relation to evil. B-C

See: Tm 11 (1948) 133-34.

SMITH, Gerard, and KENDZIERSKI, Lottie H. *The Philosophy of Being.* Vol. I of *Metaphysics* ("Christian Wisdom Series"). New York: Macmillan, 1961. xvii, 408 pp. Bibliography.

A textbook on ontology, based largely on Aristotle and St. Thomas, with the text mostly by G. Smith and the notes mostly by L. Kendzierski. In this rather difficult and very personal statement, the work proceeds from a study of passive potency in becoming, to its presence in multiple being and its implication of causality. Hence, the step to the notion of being is made only in the middle of the text and is followed by a study of analogy and an extensive treatment of the transcendentals. C

See: D 46 (1961) 272; G 33 (1962) 611; IER 97 (1962) 207; MS 40 (1962) 70; NS 36 (1962) 400; PS 11 (1961) 278.

————. *The Truth that Frees.* (The Aquinas Lecture, 1956). Milwaukee: Marquette University Press, 1956. x, 89 pp.

A lecture on the elements and usage of truth which allow it to contribute to human freedom. This takes the author into the division of truth, universals, and the real distinction between essence and existence. B-C

See: NS 31 (1957) 578; St 46 (1957) 115.

STEENBERGHEN, Fernand Van. *Ontology* (The Philosophical Series of the Higher Institute of Philosophy. University of Louvain). Trans. by M. Flynn from *Ontologie*. New York: Wagner, 1952 (1946). 279 pp. Bibliography.

A stimulating, personal, criteriological approach to metaphysics, representative of the Louvain school. A sequel to the author's work on epistemology, its style and method depart from that of a manual. It omits many topics normally treated in metaphysics and accepts the Wolfian schema of philosophy. Its interpretation of the five ways has been highly debated. C

See: C. Bruehl, HPR 53 (1953) 668-74; S. Donoghue, IER 83 (1955) 71; T 29 (1954) 475.

STRAELEN, H. Van. *Man the Lonely.* See XVII.

SULLIVAN, James B. *An Examination of the First Principles in Thought and Being in the Light of Aristotle and Aquinas* (The Catholic University of America, *Philosophical Studies*, No. 51). Washington, D.C.: The Catholic University of America Press, 1939. vii, 150 pp. Bibliography, index. (Paper)

A study of the first principles and their origin. After the various elements in the logical order have been considered, the first principles are reviewed individually, finally the basis for each is studied. B-C

THOMAS AQUINAS, Saint. *Commentary on the Metaphysics of Aristotle.* See XV.

————. *On Being and Essence.* See XV.

————. *On Searching into God.* See XV.

————. *On Spiritual Creatures.* See XV.

————. *On the Truth of the Catholic Faith.* See XV.

————. *Summa theologica.* See XV.

————. *Treatise on Separate Substances.* See XV.

————. *Truth.* See XV.

TOURNIER, Paul. *The Meaning of Persons.* Trans. E. Hudson from *Le personnage et la personne.* New York: Harper and Row, 1957. 238 pp.

Simple and direct discussion of the person from the viewpoint of the doctor engaged in continual personal contact. Self-identity, commitment, and the opening of the person ultimately to God, are treated in a way which stresses the relationship between life, liberty, and person. A

VARVELLO, Francesco. *Metaphysics.* Trans. A. Fearon from *Institutiones philosophiae.* San Francisco, Calif.: University of San Francisco Press, 1933. 341 pp.

A general text on ontology, cosmology, philosophical anthropology, and theodicy. The thesis method is used, but the brief statement of the problem, which precedes each thesis, helps to provide a greater continuity to the text. B

VASKE, Martin O. *An Introduction to Metaphysics.* 2d ed. New York: McGraw-Hill, 1963. v, 272 pp. Index.

An up-to-date text in metaphysics, developed in a heavily subdivided manner. Participation and essence are treated in the context of a Thomistic existentialism, with the development of analogy and the transcendentals placed after the consideration of God. B

See: HJ 5 (1964) 198-99; MS 41 (1964) 302.

VIO, Tommaso G. de (Cajetan.) *The Analogy of Names; and The Concept of Being* (Duquesne Studies. "Philosophical Series," No. 4). 2d ed. Trans. by E. Bushinski and H. Koren from *De nominum analogia.* Pittsburgh: Duquesne University Press, 1959 (1506). x, 93 pp. Bibliography, indices. (Paper)

A classical text on analogy accompanied by a clarifying letter on being, written to Sylvester of Ferrara. The work contains that division of analogy which, until recently, provided the context for most discussions on the subject. This is followed by a review of abstraction, definition, predication, and resolution of the analogon. The place of analogy in reasoning is also studied. C-D

See: D 39 (1954) 71.

WALSHE, Thomas A. *The Quest of Reality.* See II.

WARD, Leo R. *Philosophy of Value: An Essay in Constructive Criticism.* New York: Macmillan, 1930. x, 263 pp. Bibliography.

A study of the notion of value, illustrating the deficiencies of the subjective approach and supplying the needed elements from the Thomistic perspective. The lively treatment of such thinkers as Dewey, Whitehead, Russell, and Hobhouse succeeds in being critical without being polemic. At times it remains vague and it contans a possible misreading of Perry and Santayana. B-C

See: A 44 (1930) 193; C 11 (1930) 716; CW 131 (1930) 758; T 5 (1930) 340.

————. *Values and Reality.* New York: Sheed and Ward, 1935. 331 pp.

An explicit and general treatment of value within the scholastic framework. In three steps the author describes the notion of value, seeks its standard, and then investigates some applications of the standard. It is an important pioneering effort, but needs to be complemented to keep apace of the many recent developments in this field. B-C

See: A 53 (1935) 282; DuR 202 (1938) 168.

WATKIN, Edward I. *A Philosophy of Form.* 3d ed. revised and
    enlarged. New York: Sheed and Ward, 1950 (1935). xxviii,
    424 pp. Index.

An eclectic and highly literate study of contemplation. Traditional philosophy, leaning a bit toward the Platonic, is used as a
context for an isolation of contemplation and a study of its relation to intuition, union, and freedom. Contemplation is surveyed
in its axiological, speculative, aesthetic, and religious species. C

> *See:* A 53 (1935) 135; CW 142 (1935) 242; Ta 170 (1937) 386; C. Miltner,
> AM 74 (1951) 90; D 36 (1951) 124.

WILHELMSEN, Frederick O. *The Metaphysics of Love.* New
    York: Sheed and Ward, 1962. 159 pp.

A study of love against the background of the dynamics of existence. This is accomplished by a study of the tragic and ecstatic
dimensions of human existence and a review of the modern and
contemporary philosophers, whose insights concerning being have
been the catalysts for the author's own existential Thomism. It is
written in a free, essay style. B-C

> *See:* A 107 (1962) 502; D 47 (1962) 212; J 10 (1962) 45; MS 40 (1963)
> 195; RR 21 (1962) 383; T 37 (1962) 632.

WOLTER, Allan B. *The Transcendentals and Their Function
    in the Metaphysics of Duns Scotus.* See XVI.

CHAPTER VIII

Theodicy—Natural Theology

This chapter is devoted to works in the field of what is variously termed theodicy, natural theology, or special metaphysics. The contents of the textbooks in this area generally follow a threefold division: man's knowledge of the existence of God, the nature and attributes of God, and God's knowledge, will, causality, and providence.

Many of the works included here study one or another of these questions in relation to the material of other philosophical sciences. Hence, there are special studies of pertinent epistemological problems, of the providence of God in relation to human freedom or moral evil, and of related material in the physical science, cultural, and theological areas. There are also books in the field of the philosophy of religion.

Finally, works on recent history of philosophy are included here when the areas they treat are of special concern to the problem of God. Thus, in a negative sense, some studies of atheism have been introduced when they evaluate this phenomenon in the light of Christian philosophy.

The reader is referred to Chapters III-VI of *A Bibliography of Christian Philosophy and Contemporary Issues* by the same editor.

THE ABSOLUTE AND THE RELATIVE. See I.

ANDERSON, James F. *The Cause of Being: The Philosophy of Creation in St. Thomas.* St. Louis: Herder, 1952. vii, 172 pp. Index.

A study of the nature of creative causality. Special attention is given to the problem of the cause of being as being, which study leads to a gradual clarification of God's most intimate creative indwelling in all things. This opens onto questions concerning the eternity of the world and finality. C

See: Bl 35 (1954) 35; D 38 (1953) 244; HPR 53 (1953) 1036; SJR 46 (1953) 173; St 43 (1954) 105; Tm 16 (1953) 595; T 28 (1953) 632.

————. *Natural Theology: The Metaphysics of God* ("Christian Culture and Philosophy Series") . Milwaukee: Bruce, 1962. xii, 192 pp. Bibliography.

A clear and succinct undergraduate presentation of the central arguments and truths concerning God, as they are known by the light of reason. It follows the usual order in the main presentation of its material, but prefaces the five proofs with some considerations on pre-philosophical knowledge of God. One of the best brief textbooks in the area, it also contains reading lists and a note on the relation of philosophy to theology. B-C

See: MS 40 (1963) 320; R. Baker, NS 38 (1964) 265-67.

ARMSTRONG, A. Hilary, and MARKUS, Robert A. *Christian Faith and Greek Philosophy.* New York: Sheed and Ward, 1964 (1960) . vii, 162 pp. Index.

An investigation of the roots of Christian thought in the world of Greek philosophy. A. Armstrong investigates such questions as creation and transcendence; while R. Markus discusses the relation of love and reason in Greek thought. This brief work is particularly rich in insight. C-D

See: CR 46 (1961) 499; DR 79 (1961) 63; IER 96 (1961) 329; Ta 215 (1961) 14.

AVELING, Francis. *The God of Philosophy.* St. Louis: Herder, 1906. xi, 191 pp.

A philosophical study of the problem of God. This work concentrates on proving His existence. Little attention is given to the divine nature and attributes. B

See: CW 89 (1907) 560.

BAISNEE, Jules A. (ed.) *Readings in Natural Theology.* ("College Reading Series, No. 7"). Westminster, Md.: Newman, 1962. xiii, 321 pp. (Paper)

A selection of readings to accompany an undergraduate course in natural theology. After some readings on the sources of belief and on God in the history of philosophy, the remainder are laid out according to the usual course sequence. The material is drawn from St. Thomas and others, who are for the most part, classically oriented authors. B

BALTHASAR, Hans U. Von. *Science, Religion and Christianity.* Trans. by H. Graff from *Die Gottesfrage des heutigen Menschen.* Westminster, Md.: Newman, 1958 (1956). 155 pp.

A study of the relation of science to Christianity. Though seemingly unconnected, they are related by an intermediate sphere—considered variously as world-view, religion, or philosophy—which must be studied as the ground from which human actions and decisions spring. Special attention is given to anthropology in its broader sense as the study of man. Collateral reading. C

See: CR 44 (1959) 315; CC 9 (1959) 306; CW 190 (1959) 65; DR 77 (1959) 190; J 7 (1959) 44; B. Murchland, Ps 4 (1959) 45; St 48 (1959) 492; W 34 (1959) 9-19.

BASCHAB, Charles R. *A Manual of Neo-Scholastic Philosophy.* See II.

BENEDETTO, Arnold J. *Fundamentals in the Philosophy of God.* New York: Macmillan, 1963. vii, 330 pp. Index.

A simplified text for a brief undergraduate course in philosophy. The unusual sequence in this text begins with the notions of creation and conservation in order to arrive at a personal creator who is unique and supremely perfect. Only then does it take up the question of man's knowledge of God, after which it concludes with a discussion of the divine attributes. A

See: M. Vogel, A 109 (1963) 591; HPR 63 (1963) 822; R. Desharnais, NS 37 (1963) 393.

BITTLE, Celestine N. *God and His Creatures: Theodicy*. Milwaukee: Bruce, 1953. 420 pp.

A textbook on theodicy which covers the usual facets of the course in a rather flowing fashion. Though perhaps too simple, its summaries are of value. A-B

See: L. Delmag, HPR 53 (1953) 1118-20; TS 14 (1953) 657.

BIVORT DE LA SAUDÉE, Jacques. *God, Man and the Universe*. See XIII.

BOEDDER, Bernard. *Natural Theology*. 2d ed. ("Stonyhurst Philosophical Series"). London: Longmans, Green, 1921 (1891). xi, 480 pp.

An old and formal textbook on the philosophical questions concerning God. Its aim is to expose and defend the natural truths which form the basis of Christianity. The chapter about the manner of divine foreknowledge and concurrence in human actions is particularly well done—though not all will agree with the author's viewpoint on this disputed subject. B-C

See: CW 54 (1921) 304.

BORNE, Etienne. *Atheism (Twentieth Century Encyclopedia of Catholicism*, Vol. 91). Trans. by S. Tester from *Dieu n'est pas mort*. New York: Hawthorn, 1961 (1959). 154 pp. Bibliography.

A study of the nature and causes of contemporary atheism. After a statement of the generating principle of atheism in its ancient and modern forms, the author studies atheism as a mass modern cultural phenomenon which evokes a crisis of wisdom. B

See: Bl 43 (1962) 241; CW 194 (1962) 376; DR 80 (1962) 97; HPR 62 (1962) 382; IER 97 (1962) 347; RR 21 (1962) 295.

BRENNAN, Robert E. *Essays in Thomism*. See II.

BROSNAN, William J. *God Infinite, the World and Reason: Some Theses from Natural Theology.* New York: Fordham University Press, 1943. 246 pp.

An adequate textbook on theodicy for the undergraduate in which the usual matters are treated. The thesis manner of presentation is used, with explanations introduced into the earlier part of each thesis and a list of objections and answers at the end. In this presentation the work contains more on modern philosophy than it did in some of its earlier forms which had slightly different titles. B

BRYAR, William. *St. Thomas and the Existence of God: Three Interpretations.* Chicago: Regnery, 1951. xxv, 247 pp. Bibliography, index.

A systematic, interpretive study of St. Thomas' proof from motion for the existence of God. This work restricts itself to distinguishing three lines of meaning contained in one text. In this way it intends to clarify the number and meaning of the terms and to situate the proof within St. Thomas' order of the sciences. It is not concerned with confronting the universe for the sake of defending or opposing the argument of St. Thomas. C-D

See: D 37 (1952) 225; DR 70 (1952) 329; MS 30 (1953) 245; T 16 (1953) 269-79; TS 14 (1953) 418.

BURNABY, John. *Amor Dei.* See XIV.

CANFIELD, Francis X. (ed.) *Philosophy and the Modern Mind.* See II.

CHAUVIN, Remy. *God of the Scientists, God of the Experiment.* Trans. by S. Attanasio from *Dieu de l'expérience.* Baltimore: Helicon, 1960 (1958). 152 pp. Bibliography.

A study of the proof of God's existence in terms of the contemporary scientist. Different types of religious and mystical experience are reviewed. There is a helpful glossary. B-C

See: A 105 (1961) 91; AM 93 (1961) 27; J. Burns, CW 193 (1961) 51; C 76 (1962) 355; D 46 (1961) 188; RPL 60 (1962) 463; RR 20 (1961) 464; Tm 25 (1962) 456.

COLLINS, James D. *God in Modern Philosophy*. Chicago: Regnery, 1959. xii, 476 pp. Bibliography, index.

An excellent historical exposition of the place of the idea and problem of God in the shaping of modern philosophic thought. Extending from the time of Cusa, the writings of the modern period are seen in relation to Kant, and the light they shed on the contemporary situation is noted. The presentation is not only expository, but critical in the light of a realistic theism dependent on causal inference and analogical predication. B-C

See: F. Kerr, Bl 41 (1960) 392; D. Callahan, C 70 (1959) 428; D 45 (1960) 76; W. Martin, MS 37 (1960) 316; NS 34 (1960) 244; TS 20 (1959) 651.

COLLINS, William B. *Metaphysics and Man*. See II.

———. *Speculative Philosophy*. See II.

CONLEY, Kiernan. *A Theology of Wisdom*. Dubuque: Priory, 1963. xiii, 171 pp. Bibliography.

A survey of the dimensions of wisdom. This notion is first reviewed in its ancient Greek and Jewish realizations; then it is studied in its forms in metaphysics, theology, and the spiritual life. B-C

DANIELOU, Jean. *God and the Ways of Knowing* (Greenwich Editions). Trans. by W. Roberts from *Dieu et nous*. New York: Meridian, 1957 (1956). 249 pp. Bibliography. (Meridian: M 96)

An excellent presentation of the various ways in which man can have knowledge of God. It is quite contemporary in its perspectives, and more than merely philosophical in its approach. The chapter on the God of the philosopher is particularly well done, indicating the perfection and limitations of man's approach to God. The translation is not always adequate. B-C

See: A 98 (1957) 350; C 67 (1958) 412; CW 187 (1958) 76; PS 8 (1958) 193-95; T 33 (1958) 464; Tm 21 (1958) 402-405; TS 19 (1958) 248-49.

———. *The Lord of History*. See XIII.

D'ARCY, Martin C. *Mirage and Truth.* New York: Macmillan, 1935. 204 pp.

A contrast of the theistic and Christian ideal with various modern ideals. This work studies the grandeur of theism, its rational justification, the unique character of the Christian ideal, and the necessity of suffering. Its approach is intellectual and apologetic, while its style has unusual force, sobriety, power, and beauty. Though not easy reading, it is recommended for those of wavering faith or as collateral material for the undergraduate. B-C

See: A 53 (1935) 331; Cw 142 (1935) 248; C 22 (1935) 535.

——. *No Absent God: The Relations Between God and Self* ("Religious Perspectives Series," Vol. 6) . New York: Harper and Row, 1962. 157 pp.

A literate discussion of the pertinence of God to our life, based on the 1959 Danforth Lectures at Cornell University. It is an answer to the empiricist challenge to show that the existence of God makes a difference to man. A-C

See: AM 96 (1962) 28; C 17 (1962) 100; HJ 4 (1963) 430; R. Santoni, IPQ 3 (1963) 475; J 10 (1962) 51; J. Disselhorst, RR 22 (1963) 722.

——. *The Pain of this World and the Providence of God.* New York: Longmans, Green, 1952 (1935) . 150 pp.

A clever essay on the place of suffering in an ordered world. An agnostic and others are used in a dialogue which effectively analyzes the place of pain within the providence of God. A-C

See: C 23 (1936) 475; CW 143 (1936) 125.

DONCEEL, Joseph F. *Natural Theology.* New York: Sheed and Ward, 1962. xiii, 178 pp. Bibliography.

A brief natural theology text, attentive to the more Platonic elements in St. Thomas after the nature of the Marechal school. Over half the book is devoted to the first proof for the existence of God, which is developed in relation to an extended treatment of the principle of causality. The rest of the work provides a compressed consideration of the remaining proofs, the nature of God, creation, and providence. B

See: M. Holloway, MS 41 (1963) 101-102; Sr M. Jane Francis, NS 37 (1963) 525-28.

DONDEYNE, Albert. *Contemporary European Thought and Christian Faith* (Duquesne Studies. "Philosophical Series, No. 8"). Trans. by E. McMullin and J. Burnheim from *Foi chrétienne et pensée contemporaine*. Pittsburgh: Duquesne University Press, 1958 (1951). xi, 211 pp. Index. (Paper)

A study of existential phenomenology in itself and its relation to Thomism, especially in the problem area of faith and reason. Existentialism is viewed as a promising attempt to correct the split between naturalism and idealism. The valuable insights into man's historicity and his non-rational aspects are seen to require the correlative recognition of the stable and rational factors in existence. The work is essentially a plea for dialogue between differing viewpoints and is enhanced by the notes contributed by the translators. B-D

See: A 100 (1959) 526; PS 8 (1958) 206-207; RUO 29 (1959) 114*-15*.

————. *Faith and the World* (Duquesne Studies. Theological Series, No. 1). Pittsburgh: Duquesne University Press, 1963. 324 pp.

A profound study of the tensions in the confrontation of faith and the contemporary culture. Reflections on Christianity and civilization and on the problems of truth and freedom in the contemporary world are finally combined in a review of the relations of faith and politics and the problem of tolerance. B-D

See: E. Egan, CC 13 (1963) 491; D 81 (1963) 278; R. Vander Gucht, RN 37 (1963) 542-47.

DONOVAN, Mary A. *The Henological Argument for the Existence of God in the Works of St. Thomas Aquinas.* Notre Dame, Ind.: Notre Dame University (Ann Arbor: Lithoprinted by Edwards), 1946. vii, 146 pp. Bibliography, index. (Paper)

An analysis of the construction of the fourth proof for the existence of God in the context of the notion of participation. After tracing the history of this notion, the author states in its terms

the absolute perfection of God and the limited perfection of creatures. Both are then connected in the form of the fourth way. Collateral reading. B-C

DRISCOLL, John T. *God: Being a Contribution to a Philosophy
of Theism* ("Christian Philosophy"). New York: Benziger,
1904. xxxvi, 382 pp.

A treatment of the material usually covered in a theodicy course.
The existence of God is arrived at through considerations of
man's mental and moral life. The unity and providence of God
are also treated. A-B

See: CW 79 (1904) 547; CW 72 (1900) 279.

DULLES, Avery; DEMSKE, James; and O'CONNELL, Robert.
Introductory Metaphysics. See II.

THE EXISTENCE AND NATURE OF GOD. See I.

GARRIGOU-LAGRANGE, Reginald. *God, His Existence and
His Nature: A Thomistic Solution of Certain Agnostic An-
tinomies.* 2 vols. Trans. by B. Rose from the 5th French ed.
of *Dieu, son existence et sa nature.* St. Louis: Herder, 1955
(1914).

One of the most extensive works on the general field of natural
theology. The whole first volume is devoted to the proofs for the
existence of God, with special attention to the problems raised by
other philosophies. The exposition of the first principles in this
context is one of the best available. The second volume concerns
the nature of God and his attributes. Special attention is given to
the problem of human freedom in relation to divine causality
and to pantheism. Though many new questions have arisen since
this work was written, it remains the best Thomistic explanation
of most questions in theodicy. C-D

See: A 52 (1935) 480; AM 43 (1936) 474; CW 143 (1936) 756.

————. *The One God: A Commentary on the First Part of the
Thomas' Theological* SUMMA. Translated by B. Rose from
De Deo uno. St. Louis: Herder, 1943. viii, 736 pp. Index.

An excellent commentary on questions 1-26 of the first part of the *Summa theologica*. The existence, nature, attributes, and providence of God are studied. C-D

See: AM 58 (1943) 410-11; AER 109 (1943) 313; CW 157 (1943) 665-66; D 29 (1944) 53-54; HPR 44 (1943) 75-76; MS 21 (1944) 237-38; RR 2 (1943) 337-38; SJR 37 (1944) 62; R 19 (1944) 548-50.

————. *Providence*. Trans. by B. Rose from *La providence et la confidence en Dieu*. St. Louis: Herder, 1944 (1932). 389 pp.

A study of divine providence and the response it evokes on the part of man. Providence is studied in relation to the existence and the perfections of God, which it presupposes and includes— especially His justice and mercy. Self-abandonment to God is examined as man's proper response. B-D

————. *The Trinity and God the Creator: A Commentary on St. Thomas' Theological* SUMMA, *I^a, q. 27-119*. Trans. by F. Eckhoff from *De deo trino et creatore*. St. Louis: Herder, 1952 (1943). 675 pp.

A classical commentary on part of the *Summa theologica*. Of special philosophical interest are sections on God as first cause, His governance and conservation of nature, and those on man, his nature, origin, and intellectual functions. This work is of the greatest value to anyone seeking an understanding of the thought of St. Thomas. C-D

See: ABR 3 (1952) 267-68; AM 77 (1953) 314-15; CER 51 (1953) 428; D 37 (1952) 319; HPR 53 (1952) 286; SJR 45 (1953) 296; TS 14 (1953) 101-103; T 16 (1953) 293-94.

GERRITY, Benignus. *Nature, Knowledge, and God*. See II.

GILSON, Etienne. *Christianity and Philosophy*. See II.

————. *Elements of Christian Philosophy*. See XV.

————. *God and Philosophy* (Powell Lectures on Philosophy, Indiana University). New Haven: Yale University Press, 1959 (1941). xviii, 147 pp. (Y 8)

A series of four lectures dealing with the tensions between philosophy and theology on the metaphysical problem of God. This problem, with its causes and implications, is followed through Greek, Christian, modern, and contemporary thought. The work is rich in historical insights. B-C

See: A 65 (1941) 724; Bl 23 (1942) 249-50; CW 8 (1941) 4; D 26 (1941) 182-83; HPR 41 (1941) 1159; MS 19 (1941) 15-16; RP 4 (1942) 223; Ta 79 (1942) 48; T 17 (1942) 326-29.

————. *Reason and Revelation in the Middle Ages* (The Richards Lectures, 1937). New York: Scribner's, 1961 (1938). 114 pp. (SL 37)

A study of the interplay of fideistic and rationalistic tendencies in the Middle Ages, and of the harmonious union of faith and knowledge in Thomas Aquinas. In function of his theory that the recurring philosophical views are intrinsically determined by the ideas themselves, the author works out his thesis by the isolation of families of thinkers. C

See: CR 17 (1939) 62; CW 150 (1940) 621-27; C 29 (1939) 332; J 9 (1961) 44; MS 16 (1939) 67-68; S 18 (1939) 378-79; T 14 (1939) 341-42; T 15 (1940) 129-33.

GLEASON, Robert W. *The Search for God.* New York: Sheed and Ward, 1964. 311 pp.

A survey of the different modes of human thought concerning the divine. The study extends from the Hebrew modes of thought to that of contemporary schools, and from theism to atheism. B-C

GLENN, Paul J. *Theodicy: A Class Manual in the Philosophy of Deity.* St. Louis: Herder, 1938. 300 pp. Index.

The usual matters are covered in a simple and clear manner. The proofs for the existence of God are divided into categories according to the type of causality involved—efficient, formal, or final—with an additional treatment of supplementary proofs. A-B

See: CW 149 (1939) 254; S 17 (1938) 508.

GORNALL, Thomas. *A Philosophy of God: The Elements of Thomist Natural Theology.* New York: Sheed and Ward, 1962. 250 pp.

Following an unusual order, from the introduction on the nature of the subject and its relation to theology, the author proceeds directly to the attributes of God, His knowledge and will. Only then are the proofs for the existence of God undertaken and distinguished from invalid approaches. B

See: M. Vogel, A 109 (1963) 591; Bl 43 (1962) 498; E. Sillem, CR 48 (1963) 596; M. Pontifex, D 81 (1963) 69; IER 99 (1963) 66; L. O'Donovan, TS 24 (1963) 736.

GRABOWSKI, Stanislaus. *The All-present God*. See XIV.

GRENIER, Henri. *Thomistic Philosophy*. See II.

GUARDINI, Romano. *Freedom, Grace and Destiny*. See VII.

GUITTON, Jean. *Unity through Love: Essays in Ecumenism*. New York: Herder and Herder, 1964. 152 pp.

A study of the contemporary religious thought and its philosophical roots. This thought is that expressed in the Second Vatican Council and is traced to the work of Newman and Leibniz. The book will be useful to all capable general readers interested in the sources of contemporary intellectual tensions and their religious expression and implications. B-C

HART, Charles A. (ed.) *Aspects of the New Scholastic Philosophy*. See II.

HAWKINS, Denis J. *Essentials of Theism*. New York: Sheed and Ward, 1949. iv, 151 pp.

An excellent introduction to Scholastic thought concerning the existence and nature of God. The problems of a natural theology are presented in a concise but clear manner, with special attention to the philosophic difficulties commonly found in the positivistically oriented countries. B-C

See: CR 33 (1950) 125-26; C. Milter, AM 72 (1950) 215; D 35 (1950) 285; S. Delehait, ABR 1 (1950) 283; D. Hardwicke, DR 68 (1949) 46-54; F. Ripley HPR 50 (1949) 298; IER 73 (1950) 187-88; E. Quinn, Ta 194 (1949) 298.

HEALY, Emma T. *St. Bonaventure's* DE REDUCTIONE ARTIUM AD THEOLOGIAM. See XVI.

HETTINGER, Franz. *Natural Religion.* Trans. and ed. by H. Bowden from *Apologie des Christentums.* 3d ed. London: Burns and Oates, 1906 (1890). 302 pp. Index.

A general introduction to the field of theodicy. Besides the matters usually treated in such courses, special attention is given to the problems of certainty, the human soul, the end of man, materialism, and pantheism. B

See: CW 51 (1890) 842.

HILL, Owen A. *Psychology and Natural Theology.* See VI.

HOLLOWAY, Maurice R. *An Introduction to Natural Theology.* New York: Appleton-Century-Crofts, 1959. xxv, 492 pp. Index.

One of the most effective textbooks now available for college theodicy courses. Special attention is given to the increasingly interesting questions concerning the nature of natural theology and its relation to metaphysics, sacred theology, religion, and science. The discussions of the proofs for the existence of God make effective use of the author's earlier work on the distinction between first and second causes. The presentation is well organized, each chapter ending with a summary, definitions, and proofs, followed by a selected bibliography. Interesting material on such pertinent topics as atheism, existentialism, and the natural desire for the beatific vision, is included in the appendix. B

See: A. Benedetto, MS 37 (1960) 327; R. Dates, TS 20 (1959) 663.

JAEGER, Werner W. *Humanism and Theology* (The Aquinas Lecture, 1943). Milwaukee: Marquette University Press, 1943. 91 pp.

A lecture on humanism in the medieval context. The contribution of the special characteristics of that age to classical culture is studied, with particular attention to the humanistic aspect of St. Thomas' theocentric view of the world. This is an important work for the general arts student. B-C

See: C 39 (1943) 30; Du R 215 (1944) 175; FS 26 (1945) 84-85; MS 21 (1944) 120; St 32 (1943) 583-84; Th 7 (1944) 133.

JOLIVET, Régis. *The God of Reason (Twentieth Century Encyclopedia of Catholicism,* Vol. 15). Trans. by Mark Pontifex. New York: Hawthorn, 1958 (1956). 127 pp. Bibliography.

A study of the modes which are open to man for approaching God. The moral way is investigated first, then the metaphysical or demonstrative way. The nature of God, His attributes, and providence are also surveyed. The problem of atheism is treated in the conclusion. B-C

See: C 17 (1959) 23; D 44 (1959) 69; IER 92 (1959) 136; St 48 (1959) 483.

JOYCE, George H. *Principles of Natural Theology* ("Stonyhurst Philosophical Series"). 3d ed. revised. London: Longmans, Green, 1951 (1923). viii, 612 pp. Index.

An old and formal textbook on theodicy. It covers the usual topics: the existence of God, His nature and attributes, and His creation of the world. B

See: A 30 (1924) 457; CW 119 (1924) 419.

KANE, Robert. *God or Chaos.* New York: Kenedy, 1912. 243 pp. A general survey of the matter of a theodicy course. After treating the foundations of such knowledge and the existence and nature of God, the author introduces further notions on free will, evil, and faith. A-B

KLUBERTANZ, George P., and HOLLOWAY, Maurice R. *Being and God.* See VII.

LATTEY, Cuthbert. (ed.) *God* (Papers from the Cambridge, England, Summer School of Catholic Studies, 1930). London: Sheed and Ward, 1931. vii, 253 pp.

A collction of lectures on the main problems of theodicy by such speakers as F. J. Sheen and F. J. Sheed. The existence of God, His transcendence, providence, and personal nature are studied in the light of modern philosophic thought. B-C

See: A 46 (1932) 342.

LUBAC, Henri De. *The Discovery of God*. Trans. by A. Dru
from *De la connaissance de Dieu (Sur les chemins de Dieu)*.
New York: Kenedy, 1960 (1946). 212 pp.

A contemporary statement on the manner of coming to a realization of the divine. It treats the origin of the idea of God—a new
and particularly well-done chapter—the search for Him, the
proof of His existence, and man's knowledge concerning Him.
This can be of use to the more advanced student or general
reader and, as collateral reading, to capable undergraduates by
bringing them into contact with present day problems and
insights. B-C

See: DR 79 (1961) 164-67; IER 95 (1961) 64; NS 36 (1962) 119.

————. *The Drama of Atheist Humanism*. Trans. by E. Riley
from *Le drame de l'humanisme athée*. New York: Sheed
and Ward, 1950 (1945). 253 pp. Bibliography, index.
(Meridian Books: M 165)

A study of man's attempt to build a humanism on the denial of
God. After the author states the atheistic positions of Marx,
Nietzsche, and Comte as fairly, forcefully, and sympathetically as
possible, he proceeds to expose their innate deficiencies. The
exposition of the theistic position leads through doubts and
problems, as had by Dostoievski's characters, to an affirmation of
the existence of God. B-C

See: L. Mercier, A 83 (1950) 92; P. Olsen, Bl 31 (1950) 96-97; DR 68
(1950) 228-30; J. Bate, ECQ 8 (1950) 352-54; St 38 (1949) 488; C. Hollis,
Ta 194 (1949) 212-13.

LYTTKENS, Hampus. *The Analogy Between God and the
World*. See VII.

McCORMICK, John F. *Natural Theology*. Part II of *Scholastic
Metaphysics*. Chicago: Loyola University Press, 1943 (1931).
291 pp.

The usual material and order of texts in this field is followed.
An effort is made to present disputed points and various positions with fairness, but without entering into detailed controversy. Each chapter contains readings, points for further study,
and propositions to be explained or demonstrated. B

MARITAIN, Jacques. *Approaches to God* (World Perspectives, Vol. 1). Trans. by P. O'Reilly. New York: Harper, 1954. 128 pp. (Collier)

A general survey of the ways of knowing God exists. After an analysis of man's quasi-spontaneous knowledge of God, the traditional five ways are presented with special attention to modern problems. The concluding chapters are thought provoking and will suggest the possibility of other approaches to the knowledge of God. B-C

> *See:* R. Harvanek, A 92 (1955) 566; L. Ward, C 61 (1955) 589; D 40 (1955) 66; Et 281 (1954) 114; MS 33 (1955) 57-60; G. Phelan, NS 29 (1955) 336; L. Ward, RP 17 (1955) 548; J. Evans, T 30 (1955) 121.

————. *An Essay on Christian Philosophy.* See II.

————. *Man's Approach to God* (Wimmer Lecture, No. 5). Latrobe, Penn.: Archabbey Press, 1960. 53 pp.

A review of the various approaches to God in philosophy and theology. This lecture compares the different types of knowledge all of which are seen as contributing to finding God everywhere and as ordered to contemplation. This is a summary, almost popular, expression of many key themes of the author's *Degrees of Knowledge.* A

> *See:* IER 96 (1961) 261; RR 21 (1962) 485.

MARTINDALE, Cyril C. *Does God Matter for Me?* London: Rich and Cowan, 1937. xi, 238 pp.

An answer to the crisis of meaning at its very core. The role of God in rescuing, enriching, and directing the individual and society is reviewed. This leads to a consideration of the appropriate religious response. A-B

> *See:* A 59 (1938) 93; CW 147 (1938) 510; ER 98 (1938) 581.

MASCALL, Eric L. *Existence and Analogy.* See VII.

————. *He Who Is: A Study in Traditional Theism.* New York: Longmans, Green, 1948 (1943). viii, 210 pp. Bibliography.

An effective natural theology, quite Thomistic in approach. Both the demonstrative and intuitive roads to knowledge of God are studied. The work on God and analogy has been carried further in the author's more recent work under that title. After a consideration of God's attributes the work concludes with treatments of Tennant's cosmic theology and Whitehead's cosmology. C

See: CR 24 (1944) 178-80; Ta 182 (1943) 262.

MAZZEI, Alfred M. *Does God Exist?* Trans. by D. Fornacca from *Esiste Dio?* New York: Society of St. Paul, 1956. 293 pp. Appendices.

A very loosely written discourse on man's appreciation of the existence of God. The section considering the part of reason and the rational proof for the existence of God is placed between those describing various religions and the divinity of Christ. A

MENGES, Matthew C. *The Concept of Univocity Regarding Predication of God and Creatures.* See XVI.

MORRISS, Frank. *The Forgotten Revelation: Essays on God and Nature.* Paterson, N.J.: Franciscan Herald Press, 1964.

A simple presentation of the manifestations of God in nature. The presence of God through nature is seen as the basis for a positive evaluation of the world. A

NEDONCELLE, Maurice. *Is There a Christian Philosophy?* See II.

NEILL, Thomas P. *Religion and Culture: The Christian Idea of Man in Contemporary Society* (The Gabriel Richard Lecture, No. 2). Milwaukee: Bruce, 1952. ix, 102 pp. (Paper)

A statement of the nature of man and the foundation of his hopes. Both the philosophy of progress and the philosophy of despair are rejected and, in the process, the authentic religious dimension of man appears and provides a basis for a balanced view of man's cultural capacities. B

See: A 89 (1953) 138-39; ACSR 14 (1953) 36; CHR 39 (1953) 67-68; MS 31 (1954) 145; SO 3 (1953) 143-44.

O'BRIEN, Thomas C. *Metaphysics and the Existence of God* (The Thomist Press. Texts and Studies, Vol. 1). Washington, D. C.: Thomist Press, 1960. viii, 269 pp. (Paper)

A scholarly inquiry concerning the place of God in the study of metaphysics. The positive knowledge of God is rejected as the point of origin for metaphysics. The author shows the human mind arriving, by the pinciples of limitation and extension, to God as the proper cause of the subject of metaphysics. This work is most important on the nature of both metaphysics and our knowledge of God. C-D

See: AER 146 (1962) 430; D 46 (1961) 68-77; IER 96 (1961) 59.

O'CONNOR, William R. *The Eternal Quest.* See IX.

———. *The Natural Desire for God.* See IX.

O'MAHONY, James E. *Christian Philosophy.* See II.

———. *The Desire of God in the Philosophy of St. Thomas Aquinas.* London: Longmans, Green, 1929. xxvi, 263 pp.

A review of the notion of God as the unifying term of all human effort. The search for unity is seen as reflecting the order of being which ascends to God. Because of its intellectual nature the human mind is seen to be directed toward God for its beautitude. B-C

See: A 43 (1930) 238; C 13 (1931) 277; CW 131 (1930) 498-99.

PATTERSON, Robert L. *The Conception of God in the Philosophy of Aquinas.* London: Allen and Unwin, 1933. 508 pp. Bibliography.

A critical investigation of the thought of St. Thomas on most of the matters covered by the ordinary theodicy course. While generally sympathetic, a number of reservations expressed by the author show that he himself has not solved the dilemma with regard to making God finite and making creatures divine. C-D

See: CR 7 (1934) 441-43; St 23 (1934) 539.

PEGIS, Anton C. *Christian Philosophy and Intellectual Freedom*. See II.

PHELAN, Gerald B. *The Wisdom of Saint Anselm* (Wimmer Lectures, No. 3) . Latrobe, Pa.: Archabbey, 1960. viii, 52 pp.

A lecture on Saint Anselm and his contribution to the intellectual life of the Church. After some considerations of Anselm's life and spirit, this lecture concentrates on his philosophy of God. A-B

See: NS 37 (1963) 401.

PHILLIPS, Richard P. *Modern Thomistic Philosophy*. See II.

THE PHILOSOPHY OF RELIGION. See I.

PIEPER, Josef. *Belief and Faith: A Philosophical Tract*. Trans. by R. Winston and C. Winston from *Über den Glauben*. New York: Pantheon, 1963 (1962) . xii, 106 pp. Index.

A contemporary discussion of faith, emphasizing the insights of the phenomenological and existential schools. The personal term of belief is discussed, as is the relation of faith to freedom. B-D

See: C. Chereso, CCr 15 (1963) 480; MS 41 (1964) 298; P. Knauer, NRT 85 (1963) 989; RM (1964) 481.

———. *The Silence of St. Thomas*. See XV.

PONTIFEX, Mark. *The Existence of God: A Thomistic Essay*. London: Longmans, Green, 1947. xv, 181 pp.

A personal study of the problem of the existence of God. The author's preoccupation with limitations from the positivistic view are particularly evident and limit the degree to which the essay could meaningfully be called Thomistic. It is a useful attempt to face the problems of the day. C

See: J. Ryan, AER 119 (1948) 320; D 32 (1947) 307; DuR 220 (1947) 177-80; St 37 (1948) 119-20; R. Bates, T 23 (1948) 550-51; Ta 190 (1947) 153-54.

————. *Freedom and Providence.* (*Twentieth Century Encyclopedia of Catholicism,* Vol. 22.) New York: Hawthorn, 1960. 135 pp. Bibliography.

A theodicy in the original sense of the word. After a review of man's power of free choice and of God's providence, the problem of evil is raised and a solution proposed. Objections have been raised to the author's statement of the difficult problem of man's freedom in relation to divine power. B

See: CE 32 (1962) 888; CW 192 (1961) 376; DR 79 (1961) 161-62; HJ 2 (1961) 173; RR 21 (1962) 166.

RENARD, Henri. *The Philosophy of God* (Science and Culture Texts). Milwaukee: Bruce, 1951. 241 pp.

A brief, clear textbook for a course in Thomistic natural theology. Consideration of human freedom leads to a series of disputable positions concerning divine knowledge and providence. The chapters are developed according to a common pattern, with most articles followed by incisive summaries. B

See: C. Hart, NS 26 (1952) 98-101.

REYS, Arthur L. *God and His Attributes* ("The Treasury of Faith Series," No. 3). New York: Macmillan, 1929. viii, 86 pp.

A simple presentation of the divine perfections which, however, contains authentically philosophical insights. The attributes of God are reviewed with special attention to divine freedom. A

RICKABY, Joseph. *Studies on God and His Creatures.* London: Longmans, Green, 1924. 205 pp.

A general survey of God and man's relation to Him. There are considerations of the proofs for the existence of God, the unchangeable creator, contingency, and the immortality of the soul. A-B

See: A 31 (1924) 238; CW 119 (1924) 854.

ROBERTS, David E. *Existentialism and Religious Belief.* See XVII.

RYAN, John K. *Philosophical Studies in Honor of I. Smith.* See II.

SCHUMACHER, Magnus A. *The Knowableness of God: Its Relation to the Theory of Knowledge in St. Thomas.* (The Catholic University of America, *Philosophical Studies,* No. 3). Notre Dame, Ind.: University Press, 1905. 200 pp. (Paper)

A survey of the matter of natural theology from the point of view of the types of knowledge employed. The first part surveys the nature and validity of knowledge and, in particular, of the knowledge of causality. The final part traces the uses of knowledge in attaining the fact of the existence of God and in learning something concerning His nature. This work should be supplemented by more contemporary material. B

See: AM 43 (1936) 58.

SHARPE, Alfred B. *Evil: Its Nature and Cause* (Westminster Lectures). London: Sands, 1906. 70 pp.

A brief study of the philosophic principles concerning evil. The nature of evil and its divisions are presented after the positions of optimism and pessimism have been rejected. The work gradually becomes one of theodicy as the ways of God are justified in the face of the fact of evil. A-B

See: CW 84 (1906) 263.

SHEEN, Fulton J. *God and Intelligence in Modern Philosophy: A Critical Study in the Light of the Philosophy of St. Thomas.* London: Longmans, Green, 1935. xii, 295 pp. Index. (Image: D 74)

An investigation of the place of reason or an intellectual element in philosophies of God. There is extensive consideration of its absence in many modern approaches to the question. These are evaluated and complemented by elements from the philosophy of St. Thomas. C

See: C 3 (1926) 264-65; C 12 (1930) 590; A 35 (1926) 238; CW 123 (1926) 281; T 1 (1926) 557.

————. *Philosophy of Religion: The Impact of Modern Knowledge on Religion.* New York: Appleton-Century-Crofts, 1948. xvii, 409 pp. Index.

A study of the relationship to religion of new orientations in the uses of the human reason. This is placed in context by a comparison of the history of the abandonment of reason—the periods when many descended into irrationalism—with the use of reason concerning the existence and nature of God. The impact of the physical and historical sciences on religion is studied, and special attention is given to the approach to God through man instead of through nature. While this work is a study in the area of the philosophy of religion, it does not in itself constitute such a work. C

See: D 33 (1948) 324; J. Maguire, CW 168 (1949) 412; J. Shannon, ER 120 (1949) 357-59; A. Kolnal, T 24 (1949) 732-34.

————. *Religion Without God.* Garden City, N. Y.: Garden City, 1954 (1928) . xiv, 368 pp. Index.

A critical study of modern conceptions of religion. The history of the philosophy of religion is reviewed with special attention to sorting out orientations, such as nominalism and the notion of a uniform method, which have been damaging to a valid theistic perspective. These are evaluated from a Thomistic viewpoint in order to provide a more solid philosophical basis for religious values. C

See: HPR 54 (1954) 1022.

SILLEM, Edward. *Ways of Thinking About God: Thomas Aquinas and Some Recent Problems.* New York: Sheed and Ward, 1962. viii, 190 pp. Bibliography.

A study of the problem of man's knowledge of God. This is seen to be approached by St. Thomas in the general context of a study of the divine nature and transcendence. The author attempts to overcome an excessive delimitation of the value of the five ways by an appeal to their context for a new and more valid statement of the question. This is done in relation to the later statement of the problem. B-C

See: Bl 43 (1962) 43; CR 46 (1961) 494; DR 79 (1961) 359; HJ 2 (1961)

359; J. Reagan, MS 41 (1964) 177-80; RPL 59 (1961) 597-608; J. Dissel-horst, RR 22 (1963) 722; Ta 215 (1961) 490.

SMITH, Gerard. *Natural Theology.* Vol. II of *Metaphysics* (Christian Wisdom Series). New York: Macmillan, 1951. xvi, 297 pp. Bibliography, index.

A personal analysis of the major points in the area of natural theology. It explains and proves all the propositions of meta-physics required for an understanding of natural theology. These are developed in a way that can encourage the exceptionally capable student to think for himself. C

See: H. Reith, AM 75 (1952) 218; D 37 (1952) 66; CER 50 (1952) 423; R. O'Connor, MS 30 (1952) 63-68. F. Van Steenberghen, NS 27 (1953) 114-17; C. O'Neil, NS 27 (1953) 205-09; J. Mullaney, Tm 16 (1953) 122-27.

STUFLER, Johann. *Why God Created the World; or the Pur-pose of the Creator and of Creatures: A Study of the Teaching of St. Thomas Aquinas.* Trans. from the German by E. Sutcliffe. Stanbrook, Worcester: Stanbrook Abbey Press, 1937. 71 pp.

A profound study of the Thomistic position on the finality of creation. This problem is studied from the point of view of both creator and creatures. Attention is given to the order of creatures and to the place of evil and of divine providence. C

See: AER 97 (1937) 216; Bl 19 (1938) 156; IER 50 (1937) 204.

THOMAS Aquinas, Saint. *Compendium of Theology.* See XV.

————. *Nature and Grace.* See XV.

————. *On Searching into God.* See XV.

————. *On the Power of God.* See XV.

————. *On the Truth of the Catholic Faith.* See XV.

————. *On the Ways of God.* See XV.

————. *Providence and Predestination.* See XV.

————. *Summa theologica*. See XV.

————. *Treatise on God*. See XV.

TRESMONTANT, Claude. *The Origins of Christian Philosophy* (*Twentieth Century Encyclopedia of Catholicism*, Vol. 11). Trans. by M. Pontifex from *Les origines de la philosophie chrétienne*. New York: Hawthorn, 1963 (1962). 126 pp. Bibliography.

A discussion of the influences contributing to the development of Christian philosophy. In metaphysics these are traced to the notion of creation as a free act; in anthropology, to the need for clarifying notions in the face of early heresies. This work is a brief presentation of the extensive work done by this author on the subject. B-C

See: HJ 8 (1963) 297; Ta 217 (1963) 765.

————. *Toward the Knowledge of God*. Trans. by R. Olsen from *Essai sur la connaissance de Dieu*. Baltimore: Helicon, 1961 (1959). vii, 120 pp.

A general survey of the actual knowledge man has attained of God. The knowledge attained through the world is studied with special attention to the Kantian and more recent orientations. The religious attainment of the people of the Old and New Testaments is reviewed from a phenomenological point of view. B-C

See: AM 95 (1962) 25; C 75 (1962) 393; IER 100 (1963) 192; R. Murphy, RR 22 (1963) 722; WO 36 (1962) 618.

TRETHOWAN, Illtyd. *The Basis of Belief* (*Twentieth Century Encyclopedia of Catholicism*, Vol. 131). New York: Hawthorn, 1961 (1960). 142 pp. Bibliography. (Paulist)

A study in the philosophy of religion. After recounting, and perhaps in too large part accepting, the difficulties which the empiricists encounter in rational approaches to God, this work attempts to develop a more direct approach to the knowledge of God. The direction is that of Jolivet's "intuition," Daniélou's "encounter," and Marcel's "recollection." The author attempts to justify this position in the face of criticisms noting inadequacies in his previous writings in this field. B

See: E. Sillen, CR 47 (1962) 191; DR 79 (1961) 267; RR 21 (1962) 293.

————. *Certainty, Philosophical and Theological.* Westminster: Dacre, 1949. 170 pp. Index.

A study of the nature of certitude in the realms of both nature and supernature. The nature of certitude is reviewed with special attention to the philosophies of Reid, Ritchie, and Ewing. In this context diverse types of human knowledge of God are evaluated. The problem of faith is broached, particularly as to its freedom and its evidence. On this point the approaches of various modern Dominican and Jesuit authors are compared. The solution to the initial problem of the nature of certitude does not appear adequate, which weakens the whole work. Nonetheless, to the philosophically and theologically capable reader it will provide a valuable confrontation with the train of thought dominant on the Anglo-Saxon scene. C-D

See: D. Nicholl, Bl 30 (1949) 134.

————. *An Essay in Christian Philosophy.* See II.

TROISFONTAINES, Roger. *Existentialism and Christian Thought.* See XVII.

WARD, Leo. *God and World Order: A Study of Nature.* St. Louis: Herder, 1961. 222 pp. Bibliography.

A study of the place of God as a principle of order for the world. The notion of final cause in the thought of Plato, Aristotle, Hume, Kant, Darwin, and Dewey is reviewed. C

See: D 47 (1962) 84; HJ 3 (1962) 309; HPR 62 (1961) 290; MS 40 (1962) 77; NS 37 (1963) 110-12; P. Dent, RR 22 (1963) 588; SJR 54 (1961) 247.

WEIGEL, Gustave. *The Modern God* (Eleanore B. Jeffery Lecture, Goucher College; and the Shaffer Lecture, Northwestern University). New York: Macmillan, 1963 (1959). 168 pp.

A combination of the Jeffery Lecture, "Faith in a Shaken

World," and the Shaffer Lecture, "God, Dead or Alive." These lectures discuss the situation of faith and religion in modern culture and in relation to the public conscience. B-C

See: G. Pepper, CC 13 (1963) 508; CCr 15 (1963) 372; CW 197 (1963) 269; R. Dubuque, Ps 9 (1964) 28; J. Hochban, T 38 (1963) 615.

————, and MADDEN, Arthur G. *Religion and the Knowledge of God.* Englewood Cliffs, N. J.: Prentice-Hall, 1961. viii, 181 pp. Bibliography. (Spectrum: S 21)

An essay on the philosophy of religion. Beginning with Otto's phenomenological description of God as the numinous, the authors examine a variety of ways of approaching God: suggestion, emotion, instinct, and mystical experience. The second part of the work investigates what philosophy can do in the field of religion. The conclusion, concerning the validity of the five ways and their epistemological suppositions, is that metaphysics justifies religion but cannot produce an adequate religion by its own power. This work provides excellent collateral reading on questions not generally treated in natural theology texts. B-C

See: C 75 (1962) 599; RE 57 (1962) 203.

WEISS, Paul. *Religion and Art.* See XI.

WHITE, Victor. *God and the Unconscious.* Chicago: Regnery, 1953. 287 pp. (Meridian: M 120)

A study of the import of the knowledge of God for the workings of the human psyche. The place of God in the work of Freud and Jung is compared to an Aristotelian notion of man. The implications for the ethical character of psychotherapy and for the relation between the analyst and the confessor are reviewed. This can be of use to those concerned with the religious dimensions of human personality. C

See: F. Braceland, A 89 (1953) 251; T. Maher, ACSR 14 (1953) 268; Bl 34 (1953) 104-105; CW 178 (1953) 77; D 38 (1953) 261; O. Sumner, DR 70 (1953) 95-7; C. Burns, DuR 227 (1953) 79-83; R. McCall, NS 28 (1954) 240; D. Hawkins, Ta 201 (1953) 8-9; G. Stevens, TS 14 (1953) 499.

WHITTAKER, Edmund T. *Space and Spirit: Theories of the Universe and the Arguments for the Existence of God*

(Donnellan Lectures, 1946). Hinsdale, Ill.: Regnery, 1948 (1947). vii, 143 pp. Bibliography, index.

A study of the Thomistic proofs in the light of modern science. The work of science is found to provide a number of aids towards strengthening and presenting the traditional five ways. The author is out of sympathy with some Aristotelian logic and principles, for which he would substitute a more Ockhamist orientation. C

See: A. J. McNicholl, Tm 12 (1949) 425-73.

ZUNDEL, Maurice. *In Search of the Unknown God.* New York: Herder and Herder, 1959. 194 pp.

A simple presentation, in question and answer form, of the content of a natural theology course. Considerations of the elements of subjectivity are added, as are observations on the theology of Christ and the Church. The notion of love is stressed. A

See: AM 90 (1959) 28; CR 45 (1960) 316; G. Sloyan, W 34 (1960) 236.

CHAPTER IX

General Ethics

This chapter is composed of works in the field variously termed general ethics, moral philosophy, or axiology. Textbooks in ethics are usually composed of two sections, of which the first is general ethics. In this category are studies of the goal of man, followed by questions concerning the nature and norm of law, morality, conscience, and the virtues. This chapter includes works on these general issues, along with more specialized investigations in the field of psychology and in the metaphysics of good and evil. Many such works contain theological material, but have been listed here when the ethical considerations were dominant or notable.[1]

The reader is referred to Chapters III and VII of *A Bibliography of Christian Philosophy and Contemporary Issues* by the same editor.

---

[1] A related specialized bibliography is: *A Selected Bibliography on Values, Ethics and Esthetics in Behavioral Sciences and Philosophy, 1920-58*, edited by E. M. Albert, C. Kluckhohn, *et al.* (Glencoe, Ill.: Free Press, 1959).

ADLER, Mortimer J. *Art and Prudence.* See XI.

————. *A Dialectic of Morals: Towards the Foundation of Political Philosophy.* New York: Frederick Ungar, 1958 (1941). ix, 117 pp.

An attempt to cast Scholastic ethics in a form pertinent to political philosophy. The presentation uses both a type of Socratic dialogue with the student and an expository method. While more Aristotelian in character, this omits elements found earlier in the order of the *Summa,* which are needed to solidify the foundations of the argument. C-D

See: T 34 (1959) 626.

ARDLEY, Gavin. *Aquinas and Kant.* See XV.

BASTABLE, Patrick K. *Desire for God. Does Man Aspire Naturally to the Beatific Vision? An Analysis of the Question and Its History.* London: Burns, Oates, and Washbourne, 1947. 177 pp.

A somewhat specialized study of the problem of man's desire for God and its relation to beatitude. A history of the problem is presented and the main Scholastic and modern positions are reviewed. C-D

See: CR 29 (1948) 114-15; IER 70 (1948) 88-89; IM 76 (1948) 142-43; St 36 (1947) 510-11.

BITTLE, Celestine N. *Man and Morals: Ethics.* Milwaukee: Bruce, 1950. x, 719 pp. Bibliography, index.

A textbook in ethics for the undergraduate. The usual matters concerning the nature and norm of morality and of particular duties are investigated. The chapters are loosely written, but the summaries are effective. While not generally considered fully satisfactory as a text, parts might still provide useful reading in an ethics course or for a discussion club. B

See: ER 125 (1951) 160; CR 35 (1951) 135-36; HPR 51 (1951) 761-63 F. Tyrell; IER 74 (1950) 560-61.

BOURKE, Vernon J. *Ethics: A Textbook In Moral Philosophy*

("Christian Wisdom Series"). New York: Macmillan, 1951. xii, 497 pp. Bibliography, index.

A college text useful for a six semester-hour course. It closely reflects the ethics of St. Thomas' *Summa* while attempting to answer concrete contemporary questions arising in many areas of life. The book is cast in a very readable essay style. It contains many apt translations from the works of Aquinas and concludes each chapter with a bibliography. B-C

See: CER 50 (1952) 421-23; D 37 (1952) 64; IER 78 (1952) 159-60; NS 27 (1953) 354; TS 13 (1952) 281-84; H. Reith, AM 75 (1952) 282.

————. *St. Thomas and the Greek Moralists* (The Aquinas Lecture, 1947). Milwaukee: Marquette University Press, 1947. vi, 67 pp. Bibliography, index.

A lecture on the influence of Aristotelian and Stoic thought on the moral philosophy of St. Thomas. Special consideration is given to the structure of the moral act, right reason as the rule of morality, and the relation of moral problems to the virtues. This lecture illustrates to what extent the work of reason can be useful in seeking guidelines for human action. B-C

See: D 33 (1948) 242; J. Mullaney, T 23 (1948) 737.

BRENNAN, Sr. Rose Emmanuella. *The Intellectual Virtues*. See VI.

BROSNAHAN, Timothy. *Ethics: Digests of Lectures*. Baltimore: Murphy, 1913. 140 pp.

A simple ethics course. The material is so divided as to become almost an outline of an ethics course emphasizing definitions. Brief and clear, its main usefulness would be as a memory refresher. This work forms Part II of the author's later *Prolegomena to Ethics*. B

See: A 9 (1913) 430.

————. *Prolegomena to Ethics*. Ed. by F. LeBuffe. New York: Fordham University Press, 1941. viii, 367 pp. Indices.

A mature, thoughtful work on the basic concepts of ethics. It contains a just presentation and a scholarly critique of the untenable theories of the major adversaries. This work is intended more as a source book than as a text; an idea of how a text done on this basis would look may be had from Part II which is the author's *Ethics: Digests of Lectures.* B

See: CW 154 (1942) 510-11; HPR 42 (1941) 311-12; MS 19 (1942) 58; NS 16 (1942) 94-97; T 16 (1941) 742.

BROWN, Brendan F. (ed.) *The Natural Law Reader* ("Docket Series," Vol. 13) . New York: Oceana, 1960. 229 pp. (Paper)

A collection of rather brief selections concerning natural law. This contains useful source material coordinating the several facets of natural law jurisprudence. Of special interest is its presentation of the causes of the rise, decline, and contemporary revival of natural law doctrine. A-C

See: CER 59 (1961) 140; M. McGuire, CHR 46 (1961) 511; NS 35 (1961) 132.

BRUEHL, Charles. *This Way Happiness: Ethics, the Science of the Good Life* ("Science and Culture Series") . Milwaukee: Bruce, 1941. xiv, 241 pp. Bibliography, index.

An undergraduate text in ethics. The author follows the traditional division of general and special ethics. The style is clear and readable. It is unfortunate that only 23 pages are devoted to social morality. B

See: A 65 (1941) 358; AM 54 (1941) 257; ER 105 (1941) 233; HPR 41 (1941) 960-62; MS 19 (1941) 18; NS 16 (1942) 94-97; S 21 (1941) 62.

BUCKLEY, Joseph. *Man's Last End.* St. Louis: Herder, 1949. xii, 249 pp.

An investigation of the problem of man's last end in the natural order. It concludes that man has no concrete and determinate end in the natural phychological order. C

See: J. Anderson, RP 12 (1950) 143; H. Beck, C 50 (1949) 397; D 34 (1949) 637; F. Houlahan, CER 49 (1951) 142; J. Jolin, SJR 42 (1949) 207; Joubert, T 8 (1949) 59; B. Lonergan, TS 10 (1949) 578-80; C. Miltner, AM 70 (1949) 442; C. O'Neil, NS 24 (1950) 278; W. O'Connor, T 24 (1949) 740-42; A. Wolter, FS 10 (1950) 198-202.

COLEBURT, Russell. *The Search for Values.* See VII.

CONNELL, Francis. *Morals in Politics and Professions.* See X.

COPPENS, Charles. *A Brief Text-Book of Moral Philosophy.* Revised and enlarged by J. Spalding. New York: Sadler, 1941 (1924). 280 pp.

A clear undergraduate text in ethics in thesis form. After defining ethics, the author divides the material in the ordinary fashion between general and special ethics. There is an additional section devoted to social ethics. B

See: A 23 (1920) 476.

COVENTRY, John. *Morals and Independence: An Introduction to Ethics.* London: Burns, Oates, and Washbourne, 1949. 109 pp.

A general introduction to the need and basis for morality. Duty and freedom are treated in relation to happiness and moral judgment. The relation of the moral law to God is also studied. This work will be of interest as a statement of the major problems of morality and as an indication of the direction for their solutions. B

See: J. Bonsan, Bl 30 (1949) 392; M. Connolly, IM 77 (1949) 539; G. Klubertanz, T 25 (1950) 156; M. Pontifex, DR 67 (1949) 348; M. Pontifex, IER 72 (1949) 565; E. Quinn, Ta 193 (1949) 322.

COX, Ignatius W. *Liberty, Its Use and Abuse: Being the Principles of Ethics, Basic and Applied.* 3d ed. revised. New York: Fordham University Press, 1946 (1936). xii, 442 pp. Bibliography, index.

An adequate undergraduate text covering the matters ordinarily treated in an ethics course. The thesis method is employed, with the addition of lists of readings and of questions for discussion. Appendices review the basic points and indicate important social principles. B

CRONIN, Michael. *The Science of Ethics.* 2 vols. 4th ed. revised. Dublin: Gill, 1939 (1909).

A very extensive presentation of the field of ethics. While its main purpose is to present a full and connected account of the

Aristotelian-Thomistic ethical system, much study is devoted to other systems. The areas where agreement is possible are emphasized. Though it does not reflect current problems, this work provides useful reading on the classical themes. B-C

> *See:* A 1 (1909) 667; ACSR 1 (1940) 225-26; CR 20 (1940) 62-63; CW 90 (1909) 667.

D'ARCY, Eric. *Conscience and Its Right to Freedom.* New York: Sheed and Ward, 1960. 277 pp.

An extensive, and perhaps overstated, defence of freedom of conscience. The positions of classical authors from pagan to modern times are reviewed. The arguments for and against in St. Thomas are stated and then reconstructed in such a way as to stress full freedom. C

> *See:* A 107 (1962) 208; Hamilton, Bl 43 (1962) 13; J. Sheerin, CW 195 (1962) 177; D. Hawkins, CR 47 (1962) 60; M. Novak, C 76 (1962) 92; M. Pontifex, DR 80 (1962) 84; J 10 (1962) 35; J. Mackey, PS 11 (1961) 186-90; RR 21 (1962) 585; SO 12 (1962) 440; St 51 (1962) 333.

D'ARCY, Martin C. *Christian Morals.* London: Longmans, Green, 1937. xi, 195 pp.

A dozen brief essays on the foundations and ideals of Christian morality. The discussions are followed by applications to some modern topics. B

> *See:* CW 147 (1938) 506; S 17 (1938) 571.

DAVITT, Thomas E. *The Nature of Law.* St. Louis: Herder, 1951. v, 274 pp. Bibliography, index.

A scholarly contribution to the controversy concerning the nature of law. The voluntarist and the intellectualist orientations are compared. Conclusions about the obligation of law and the question of purely penal laws will be disputed. The scholarship is solid, however, and makes the work of great value to jurists and professional philosophers. C-D

> *See:* CR 38 (1953) 125-26; CER 50 (1952) 702-705; R. Drinan, A 86 (1952) 594; D 37 (1952) 74-76; FS 13 (1953) 67; R. Jones, AM 75 (1952) 538; MS 30 (1953) 67; NS 26 (1952) 371; SJR 44 (1952) 370; ER 126 (1952) 75.

DeFERRARI, Sr. Teresa Mary. *The Problem of Charity for Self: A Study of Thomistic and Modern Theological Discussions.* Washington, D.C.: The Catholic University of America Press, 1962. vii, 205 pp. Bibliography.

A quite competent study of the speculative basis for the notion of charity for self. After a review of the position—stressing the distinct objects of love and of the kerygmatic philosophy of forgetfulness of self—there is a study of the solutions proposed by recent commentators, based on the premises of the love of God and of the true good. The texts of St. Thomas are found to manifest an emphasis on the self as an active subject, loving; and on the lovable object as an imitation of the Divine goodness. C-D

See: CBQ 25 (1963) 156; HJ 8 (1963) 318; HPR 63 (1963) 455; M. Holloway, MS 41 (1963) 106.

DEPLOIGE, Simon. *The Conflict Between Ethics and Sociology.* Trans. by C. Miltner from *Le conflit de la morale et de la sociologie.* St. Louis: Herder, 1938 (1927). 386 pp.

A comparison of the nature and approaches of ethics and sociology. Both the origin of sociology and the validity of moral philosophy are treated. A difference is noted between the understanding of natural law in the Scholastics and in such philosophers as Rousseau and Hobbes. A resolution of differences through further specification of ethics is suggested. Though social theory has advanced since this was written, it can still be useful to the student seeking to clarify the nature and sources of his knowledge. B-C

See: A 60 (1938) 70; CW 150 (1939) 252; IER 53 (1939) 319; RP 2 (1940) 131-32; SJR 34 (1942) 389.

DOHERTY, Richard T. *The Relation of the Individual to Society in the Light of Christian Principles as Expounded by the Angelic Doctor.* Romae: Officium Libri Catholici, 1957. 84 pp. (Paper)

A study of the one and the many in the social order. Beginning with the analogy of the universe and the framework of the social cosmos, the author presents Aristotle's principles concerning the relation of the individual to the society. The evaluation is made from a Thomistic viewpoint. Theological perspectives are added in the concluding chapter. Though in manuscript form since 1938, the basic principles are sound and will be of use as collateral reading. B-C

DONAHUE, Lester. *Outline of Ethics*. Brooklyn: St. Johns University, 1927. 94 pp.

An extremely simple presentation of ethics. The basic principles are presented in general essay form. A

DOOLAN, Aegidius. *Order and Law*. Westminster, Md.: Newman, 1954. 199 pp.

A general survey of the nature of law. Situated within the order of the universe, law is studied as to its effects and limits. Such basic rights as those to life and property are stated and the international dimension of law is also noted. A

See: AM 80 (1954) 26; CCr 6 (1954) 295; D 39 (1954) 295; IER 82 (1954) 140.

DOUGHERTY, George V. *The Moral Basis of Social Order According to St. Thomas* (The Catholic University of America. *Philosophical Studies*, No. 63). Washington, D.C.: The Catholic University Press, 1941. 81 pp. (Paper)

A study of the philosophical foundations of society. After a survey of its metaphysical principles, the causes of the social order are reviewed and the particular function of justice is highlighted. B

DOUGHERTY, Kenneth. *General Ethics: An Introduction to the Basic Principles of the Moral Life According to St. Thomas Aquinas*. Peekskill, N.Y.: Graymoor Press, 1960 (1959). 183 pp.

A serviceable textbook for the undergraduate course in ethics. The usual matter is treated simply and clearly and modern ethical problems are introduced. Each chapter is preceded by an outline and ends with suggested readings and review questions. B

See: AER 143 (1960) 65; NS 36 (1962) 273; Tm 25 (1962) 189.

DRUMMOND, William F. *Social Justice.* Milwaukee: Bruce, 1955. x, 132 pp. Bibliography, index.

A clearly written study of the meaning of social justice in Catholic philosophy. Social justice is seen to be neither an aggregate concept nor a species of justice separate from legal justice. Special attention is given to the distinction between necessary and superfluous goods. The reasoning is based on natural law, but the main papal encyclicals are often cited. B

> *See:* J. Cantwell, MS 34 (1957) 218; M. Connolly, St 45 (1956) 356; W. Ferree, ACSR 17 (1956) 150; F. McGinnis, HPR 56 (1956) 790; P. Montavon, RP 19 (1957) 136-39; AM 83 (1956) 24; Bl 38 (1957) 397; TS 17 (1956) 438.

ETHICS AND OTHER KNOWLEDGE. See I.

FAGOTHEY, Austin. *Right and Reason: Ethics in Theory and Practice.* 3d ed. St. Louis: Mosby, 1963 (1953). 511 pp. Bibliography, index.

A clear, non-technical ethics textbook for the undergraduate. The problem method of exposition is used. The author's personal assimilation of the traditional doctrine has resulted in a stimulating presentation. References at the end of the chapters and to historical positions are complemented by a fine bibliography. B

> *See:* ACSR 20 (1959) 162; C. Bittle, CSJ 53 (1953) 200; W. Drummond, SO 9 (1959) 291-93; P 38 (1953) 371; Tm 17 (1954) 275.

FARRELL, Walter. *The Natural Law According to St. Thomas and Suarez.* Ditchling: St. Dominic's Press, 1930. 162 pp.

A scholarly study of the character of natural law in Suarez, with a Thomistic critique. The natural law is set in its context by a review of the nature of law and of the eternal law. C-D

FERREE, William. *The Act of Social Justice: An Analysis of the Thomistic Concept of Legal Justice, with Special Reference to the Doctrine of Social Justice Proposed by His Holiness Pope Pius XI in His Encyclicals* QUADRAGESIMO ANNO *and* DIVINAE REDEMPTORIS *to Determine the Precise Nature of the Act of This Virtue.* (The Catholic University of America. *Philosophical Studies*, No. 72) . Washington, D.C.: The Catholic University of America Press, 1945. 221 pp. Bibliography, index. (Paper)

An analysis of social justice in a Thomistic context. Social justice is seen to be an area of legal justice. The mode of completing the thought of St. Thomas on this point is considered, and social justice is analyzed according to its four causes. B-C

See: TS 5 (1944) 222-27.

FERROLI, Domenico. *Moral Science*. 3 vols. Ranchi, India: Catholic Press, 1947. (Paper)

A textbook survey of the field of ethics. The three volumes reflect the division between general principles, personal duties, and social ethics. There are excellent synopses in outline form and lists of readings for each chapter. B

FROM AN ABUNDANT SPRING. See II.

GARRIGOU-LAGRANGE, Reginald. *Beatitude, a Commentary on St. Thomas' Theological* SUMMA, *I^a-II^{ae}, qq. 1-54.* Trans. by P. Cummins from *De beatitudine*. St. Louis: Herder, 1956 (1951) . vi, 397 pp. Index.

An excellent commentary on the section of the *Summa* on general ethics. The introduction concerns the nature of moral science and various ethical systems. A treatment of the ultimate goal is followed by a discussion of the voluntary and moral character of human acts. The relevance of passions and habits is investigated. C

See: AM 85 (1957) 24; NS 31 (1957) 556-59; Tm 20 (1957) 114.

GERHARD, William A. *Infra-Rational Knowledge and the Intellectual Virtue of Prudence*. Notre Dame, Ind.: Notre Dame University Press, 1948. vi, 87 pp. (Paper)

A study of the pertinence of prudence to knowledge which is not fully rational. Empirical knowledge and the non-rational estimation of practical values are reviewed, and, in relation to this, the author analyzes the nature of prudence. This work can be of use as collateral reading for undergraduates by mining a facet of the thought of St. Thomas pertinent to some contemporary approaches to knowledge. C

GILSON, Etienne. *Moral Values and the Moral Life*. Trans. by L. Ward from *Saint Thomas d'Aquin*. 2d ed. Hamden, Conn.: Shoe String Press, 1961 (1931). 337 pp. Bibliography.

An excellent study in the ethics of Thomism. The volume begins with an essay on St. Thomas and the significance of his moral system. This is followed by a presentation, substantially in the words of Aquinas, of the general principles involved in his ethics. The work suffers in translation but has benefited by the inclusion of a topical index. B-C

See: A 45 (1931) 509; CW (1931) 247.

GLENN, Paul J. *Ethics: General and Special*. 3d ed. St. Louis: Herder, 1933 (1930). xiv, 302 pp.

A text on Thomistic ethics in which the usual matter is treated. The presentation is too simplified for the college level, but might be effective for discussion clubs or the general reader. A

GRENIER, Henri. *Thomistic Philosophy*. See II.

GUARDINI, Romano. *Conscience*. Trans. by A. Lane from *Das Gute, das Gewissen, und die Sammlung*. New York: Benziger, 1932 (1931). ix, 103 pp.

A simple exposition of the nature and import of conscience. Conscience is viewed in relation to the good, to God, and to recollection. The last part of the work is theological in character. A-B

See: A 48 (1932) 167.

———. *Freedom, Grace and Destiny*. See VII.

———. *Power and Responsibility*. Trans. by E. Briefs from *Die Macht: Versuch einer Wegweisung*. Chicago: Regnery, 1961 (1951). xiv, 104 pp.

An investigation of the possibility of using power without destroying oneself. The nature of power is discussed along with more recent orientations in the appreciation of man. Against this background the possibilities of action are considered. This work is notably theological in orientation. B-C

See: A 105 (1961) 109; AM 93 (1961) 27-28; CER 60 (1962) 350; HPR 61 (1961) 1099; J 9 (1964) 43; P 17 (1961) 695; RR 21 (1962) 473.

GUITTON, Jean. *An Essay on Human Love.* See VI.

HART, Charles A. (ed.) *Aspects of the New Scholastic Philosophy.* See II.

HAWKINS, Denis J. *Christian Ethics. (Twentieth Century Encyclopedia of Catholicism,* Vol. LVIII). New York: Hawthorn, 1963. 122 pp.

A brief, interesting survey of contemporary ethics. The present situation is studied, and the intentions and values in man's understanding of himself, of evil, and of wisdom are reviewed. A series of particular areas of special ethical problems is studied, with particular insights contributed by the Christian context. B

———. *Man and Morals.* New York: Sheed and Ward, 1961 (1960). vii, 104 pp.

A clear and simple introduction to Scholastic ethical thinking. It is written without theistic or religious presuppositions and uses both ancient and modern philosophers. Because a large field is covered in few pages, some of the language and distinctions employed seem incompatible with the details of Thomism. The treatment of the nature of man might also be supplemented. B

See: HJ 1 (1960) 343; ITQ 27 (1960) 343; NS 36 (1962) 261; MS 39 (1962) 409; E. O'Doherty, Bl 41 (1960) 391; PS 11 (1961) 333; St 50 (1961) 105; Ta 214 (1960) 604; TS 22 (1961) 520; Tm 25 (1962) 190.

HIGGINS, Thomas J. *Man as Man: The Science and Art of Ethics.* Revised ed. Milwaukee: Bruce, 1958 (1949). xiii, 585 pp. Bibliography, index.

A college textbook for the field of moral philosophy. It follows the usual threefold division: general principles of morality, individual ethics, and social ethics. Some effort is made to compare

Scholastic and non-Scholastic thought. The thesis format is used with numerous corollaries; a bibliography follows each chapter, and there is a helpful index. B

See: BR 9 (1958) 131; E. Naughton, NS 33 (1959) 385.

HILDEBRAND, Dietrich Von. *Christian Ethics.* New York: McKay, 1953. 470 pp.

A phenomenological defense of the objectivity and supremacy of moral values as an alternative to eudaemonism. For a deductive ethics based on the importance of the means-end relation, there is substituted an intuited and self-intelligible "due relation" between moral values and the proper response of the person to them. This book contains matter of significance on the philosophy of value, freedom of the will, and the importance and spirituality of many non-volitional affective responses. The distinctive character of Christian ethics is underlined. B-C

See: IM 8 (1954) 42; H. Davis, DR 228 (1954) 98; B. Gilligan, T 28 (1953) 113; J. Lawler, W 27 (1953) 477; A. Nevins, HPR 54 (1954) 661-62; R. Russell, DR 72 (1954) 190; B. Schwartz, A 89 (1953) 442; R. Springer, TS 14 (1953) 638.

——. *Fundamental Moral Attitudes.* Trans. by A. Jourdain from *Sittliche Grundhaltungen.* New York: Longmans, Green, 1950 (1946). 72 pp.

A review of the place of man in creation and the moral characteristics appropriate to rational nature. Motivation is emphasized in an analysis of the moral values of reverence, faithfulness, responsibility, veracity, and goodness. B

See: J. Clune, CW 171 (1950) 78; R. Gleason, A 82, (1950) 702; J. Johnston, C 51 (1950) 635.

——, and JOURDAIN, Alice. *Graven Images: Substitutes for True Morality.* New York: McKay, 1957 (1950). vii, 204 pp.

An evaluation of some modern systems of morality in comparison with Christian morality. It methodically examines some substitutes for true morality which, in contemporary culture, are replacing sounder values. Relativism, in its lack of an absolute order, is seen as insufficient—even for an understanding of the relative. The painstaking analysis makes challenging but technical reading, suited to the more capable or advanced student. C

―――. *True Morality and Its Counterfeits.* New York: McKay, 1955. ix, 179 pp.

A critique, from a phenomenological perspective, of the situation ethics and sin mysticism of the existential systems. There are apt illustrations from the field of literature. A Papal allocution on the new morality is included in the appendix. B-C

See: N. Logal, CW 182 (1955) 72-74; L. Ward, C 63 (1955) 150; J 3 (1955) 54; RR 15 (1956) 106; J. Hardon, TS 17 (1956) 118.

HILL, Owen A. *Ethics, General and Special.* New York: Macmillan, 1920. 414 pp.

An undergraduate text in moral philosophy. The usual material is covered, but with some originality. The thesis method is followed and its parts are well reasoned. Some of the special questions treated are now outmoded but the greater part of the work retains its value. B

See: A 24 (1920) 18; CW 112 (1921) 690.

JAFFA, Harry V. *Thomism and Aristotelianism, a Study of the Commentary by Thomas Aquinas on the* NICOMACHEAN ETHICS. Chicago: The University of Chicago Press, 1952. viii, 230 pp. Bibliography, index.

A study of the progress in ethical theory in St. Thomas as compared to Aristotle. The notions of courage and the virtues, and of magnanimity and the limits of morality, lead to a comparison between natural right and natural law. Through this, the Christian ethic in St. Thomas emerges as distinct from that of Aristotle. This work is for the specialist. D

See: D 37 (1952) 335; DR 70 (1953) 89-90; PS 3 (1953) 122; SO 3 (1953) 333.

JOURNET, Charles. *The Meaning of Evil.* See VII.

JUSTICE. See I.

KAVANAUGH, James. *Manual of Social Ethics.* Dublin: Gill, 1956 (1954). 182 pp. Bibliography, index.

A simple summary of ethical principles in the social sphere. The general notions of natural law and human dignity are presented as the context within which the family, education, and property are studied. The material is well divided. A-B

See: IER 83 (1955) 309; St 43 (1954) 470.

KEANE, Henry. *A Primer of Moral Philosophy* (Philosopher's Library). New York: Kenedy, 1927. 212 pp.

A simple undergraduate text in ethics. The usual order is followed, proceeding from the notion of ethics, to the notions of moral obligation and natural law, and thence to personal and social duties. Questions are listed in order to stimulate reflection on the part of the student. Parts I and II were republished by the Catholic Social Guild of Oxford in 1942 and contain all but the social philosophy. A-B

See: A 36 (1927) 364; T 2 (1927) 342.

LATTEY, Cuthbert. (ed.) *St. Thomas Aquinas.* See XV.

LAVELLE, Louis. *Evil and Suffering.* See XVII.

LAWLOR, Monica. *Personal Responsibility.* (*Twentieth Century Encyclopedia of Catholicism,* Vol. 33). New York: Hawthorn, 1963. 142 pp.

A study of the person in predominantly psychological and sociological terms. The nature of man is studied for the roots of his activity and the social demands placed upon it. His development in conciliating these is then reviewed. A-B

LECLERCQ, Jacques. *Christ and the Modern Conscience.* Trans. by R. Mathews from *Saisir la vie à pleines mains.* New York: Sheed and Ward, 1962 (1961). 289 pp. Index.

A discussion of morality in the modern world, with a strong theological orientation. After stating the problem of morality, this work compares wisdom and code moralities and draws the implications for a new appreciation of morality and moral values in the present world. B-C

See: E. Egan, CC 13 (1963) 498; R. Doherty, CCr 16 (1964) 122; Pr 19 (1963) 602; E. Spittler, RR 23 (1964) 105; M. Sweetman, St 52 (1963) 334; Ta 217 (1963) 111.

LEIBELL, Jane F. (ed.) *Readings in Ethics.* Chicago: Loyola University Press, 1926. xv, 1098 pp. Index.

A comprehensive arrangement, under eight headings, of nearly two hundred papers by recognized writers. It is fully indexed and covers the entire field of general and special ethics with wide readings on each topic. There is a clear Scholastic explanation of basic ethical problems. B

See: A 36 (1927) 435; CW 125 (1927) 429.

LINEHAN, James C. *The Rational Nature of a Man.* See VI.

McALLISTER, Joseph B. *Ethics, With Special Application to the Medical and Nursing Professions.* 2d ed. Philadelphia: Saunders, 1955 (1947). xiii, 423 pp. Bibliography, index, appendices.

A clearly and effectively written basic text on ethics. The major portion of the book is divided between the usual mater of general ethics (goal, guide, criterium, conscience, and the virtues), and special ethics (the self, the other, and society). Appendices provide most of the particular orientation concerning the nursing profession and include the pertinent codes. A helpful summary and bibliography is provided for each chapter. B

See: AM 65 (1947) 794; CER 46 (1948) 405; D 32 (1947) 298; T. Davitt, MS 26 (1948) 75-76; HPR 49 (1949) 336; S 27 (1947) 55.

McGILLIVRAY, George J. (ed.) *Moral Principles and Practice* (Papers from the Cambridge, England, Summer School of Catholic Studies, 1932). New York: Sheed and Ward, 1933. viii, 326 pp. Bibliography.

Although moral theology is not entirely omitted, this book is of particular use to the philosopher. It provides a clear, reasoned, and scientific presentation of the norms of ethical conduct, with

applications to the family, state, and international communities.
C

McGLYNN, James V., and TONER, Jules J. *Modern Ethical Theories*. Milwaukee: Bruce, 1962 (1961). vii, 167 pp. (Impact)

This work distinguishes ethical facts from ethical systems. The moral sense as well as the Kantian, utilitarian, naturalistic, analytic, and existentialistic approaches are examined; the relation of psychoanalysis to ethical theory is considered; and all is placed in the broad context of man's moral life. B-C

See: CSJ 62 (1962) 19; RPL 60 (1962) 477; J. Hoffman, RR 23 (1964) 105.

McLEAN, George F. (ed.) *Philosophy in a Technological Culture*. Washington, D.C.: The Catholic University of America Press, 1964. 438 pp. Bibliography, index. (Paper)

A study of the effects of contemporary technological culture on philosophy, and of the contributions which philosophy must make toward a proper orientation of this culture. After investigating the relation of philosophy to science and of science to technology in order to establish the ontological and epistemological foundations, the influence of technology on the appreciation of the person is studied. These two lines of approach combine in reflections upon the domestic and international ethical problems of a technological culture. B-C

MARITAIN, Jacques. *Moral Philosophy: An Historical and Critical Survey of the Great Systems*. New York: Scribner's, 1964. xiii, 468 pp.

An important survey of the development of moral theory through the history of Western philosophy. The approach by reason is traced from both Greek and Judeo-Christian roots, through the Fathers of the Church and Kant, to its contrasting realizations in both Positivism and idealism. The contemporary crisis is discussed in relation to the existential emphasis on person and freedom, and to the thought of Dewey and Bergson. C-D.

————. *The Person and the Common Good.* Trans. by J. Fitzgerald from *La personne et le bien commun.* New York: Scribner's, 1947 (1946). 98 pp.

Two lectures concerning the relation of man to society. The positions of St. Thomas on the orientation of man to God as his ultimate end and on the distinction between individuality and personality are treated. Special attention is given to man in communistic, totalitarian, and individualistic societies. C

See: CWK 14 (1948) 4; C 47 (1948) 330; D 33 (1948) 34-35; S 27 (1948) 75; TS 9 (1948) 334-35.

————. *The Rights of Man and Natural Law.* Trans. by D. Anson from *Les droits de l'homme et la loi naturelle.* New York: Scribner's, 1947 (1942). vi, 119 pp. Index.

An effective introduction to Maritain's political philosophy: an outline of principles and inferences rather than a detailed discussion. The nature of the human person, society, and natural law, are discussed, as are the rights of the individual as a person, citizen, and worker. B

See: A 69 (1943) 526; Bl 26 (1945) 66-69; C 38 (1943) 396-97; CW 157 (1943) 660; D 28 (1943) 206-207; ER 110 (1944) 198-99; HPR 44 (1944) 711-12; IER 64 (1943) 140; RP 7 (1945) 247; St 34 (1945) 286-87; Ts 4 (1943) 645-47.

————. *Saint Thomas and the Problem of Evil.* See VII.

————. *True Humanism.* Trans. by M. Adamson from *Humanisme intégral.* London: Bles, 1941 (1938). xvii, 304 pp. Appendix.

A discussion of the possibilities of moral reconstruction in a democratic society. It first describes the crisis of humanism during the depression and as the Second World War approached. This is followed by a discussion of the place of the Christian in the world and of the possibilities of reconstructing a new Christian social order. B-C

See: CW 149 (1939) 246-47; DR 204 (1939) 404-406; MS 16 (1939) 42; Th 1 (1939) 286-91.

MENASCE, Giovanni De. *The Dynamics of Morality.* New York: Sheed and Ward, 1961. 353 pp. Bibliography.

A study of the moral dimension of the positive and dynamic elements in the human adventure. Moral life is considered in relation to experience, order, and creative intelligence. The latter is found in emotional life, and both intelligence and love are considered in their relation to man's ultimate goal. This work is somewhat loosely organized. B-C

See: D 47 (1962) 72; HPR 62 (1962) 462; MS 40 (1962) 80; Ps 7 (1962) 24; TS 23 (1962) 354.

MESSNER, Johannes. *Ethics and Facts: The Puzzling Pattern of Human Experience.* St. Louis: Herder, 1952. 327 pp. Bibliography, index.

An erudite and penetrating analysis of five basic impulses of human nature: sex, happiness, liberty, society, and knowledge. Sociological data are used, together with Christian and Thomistic principles. In these terms there is a critical appraisal of Freudianism, anthropologism, Kantianism, existentialism, dialectical materialism, and logical positivism. C

See: A 89 (1953) 51; C. Miltner, AM 77 (1953) 184-5; R. Bode, CER 51 (1953) 64-66; CR 39 (1954) 183; D 39 (1954) 69; MS 31 (1954) 224; L. Ward, NS 28 (1954) 115; SJR 45 (1952) 224; SO 3 (1953) 25.

————. *Social Ethics: Natural Law in the Modern World.* Trans. from the German by J. Doherty. St. Louis: Herder, 1949. xiii, 1018 pp. Bibliography, index.

A truly outstanding work on social ethics. In its profound analysis of the nature of man as a social being, it delineates the basis of natural law. In this context a thorough investigation is made of the ethics of society in general, of the political community, and of the social economy. Attention is paid to social and economic theory and to the Papal encyclicals. While too extensive in scope for use as a class text it is an indispensable source book. C-D

See: D 34 (1949) 318; C. Bruehl, SJR 42 (1949) 171; W. Gough, CW 171 (1950) 397; T. Higgins, T 24 (1949) 511-13; G. Kelly, C 51 (1950) 542; W. McDonald, CER 49 (1951) 354; H. Reith, AM 70 (1949) 603; I. Smith, ER 121 (1949) 511-13.

MILTNER, Charles C. *The Elements of Ethics*. 2d ed., revised. New York: Macmillan, 1946 (1925). 378 pp. Bibliography.

A text on moral philosophy in which the usual material from general and special ethics is included. There are helpful study questions. B

See: A 34 (1925) 166; A 56 (1937) 503; C 4 (1926) 220; CW 146 (1937) 125.

MIRON, Cyril H. *The Problem of Altruism in the Philosophy of St. Thomas: A Study in Social Philosophy* (The Catholic University of America, *Philosophical Studies,* No. 41). Washington, D.C.: The Catholic University of America Press, 1939. ix, 130 pp. Bibliography, index. (Paper)

A study of altruism, whose foundation is discovered to be in love and whose objects are placed in a hierarchical order. Other systems, such as individualism and collectivism, are reviewed in relation to these subjects. B-C

MOORE, Thomas V. *A Historical Introduction to Ethics*. New York: American, 1915. 164 pp.

A preliminary survey of the field of ethics, rather than a history or a textbook. The fundamental preambles of ethics, such as man's nature and destiny, are considered. Although, various ancient and modern philosophical positions on these notions are explained and criticized deftly and with impartiality, because of its age, this book has no specific reference to contemporary problems concerning the meaning of life. B

See: A 13 (1915) 159.

———. *Principles of Ethics*. 5th ed., revised by G. Stevens. Philadelphia: Lippincott, 1959 (1935). xiii, 282 pp. Bibliography, index.

A general textbook of practical ethics, originally written as a manual for nurses. Not a formal treatise on moral philosophy or theology, it treats everyday moral problems and broadly discusses the fundamental principles involved. There is a list of practical topics for discussion at the end of each chapter, and a section on medical ethics. B

See: C 22 (1935) 222; CW 141 (1935) 382; D 44 (1959) 194.

MURRAY, Michael V. *Problems in Conduct.* New York: Holt, Rinehart and Winston, 1963. vii, 335 pp. Bibliography.

A study in special ethics which is a continuation of the author's earlier work, *Problems of Ethics.* It is divided according to the virtues of prudence, fortitude, justice, and religion. These categories lead to the particular problems concerning life, truth, property, and the various societies. B

————. *Problems in Ethics.* New York: Holt, Rinehart and Winston, 1960. 404 pp. Bibliography, index.

A study of the principles of ethics. Stress is given to their speculative foundation, and they are placed in subalternation to moral theology. Questions concerning the nature of the morality of human actions, law, conscience, and virtue are discussed. The work follows the *Summa* of St. Thomas rather than his *Ethics,* and considers man as an existential unity oriented by right thinking. B

See: ACSR 21 (1960) 89; P. Campbell, CE 30 (1960) 773; M. O'Donnell, PS 10 (1960) 303; L. Schumacher, NS 35 (1961) 275.

NAUS, John E. *The Nature of the Practical Intellect According to Saint Thomas Aquinas* (Pontificia Universitas Gregoriana, *Analecta Gregoriana,* No. 108). Romae: Pontificia Universitas Gregoriana, 1959. 220 pp. Bibliography. (Paper)

A study of the practical intellect and its virtues. After distinguishing between the speculative and the practical intellect, the knowledge and virtues that derive from the latter are studied in some detail. Particular attention is given to art, faith, prudence, and connatural knowledge. C

See: R. Johann, TS 21 (1960) 688.

NEWMAN, Jeremiah. *Foundations of Justice: An Historico-Critical Study in Thomism.* Cork: Cork University Press, 1954. xvii, 130 pp. Bibliography, index.

A study of legal justice in the thought of St. Thomas. By studying such notions as justice, the common good, justice, and order, the author prepares the basis for a final review of the Thomistic synthesis. D

See: Bl 36 (1955) 305; IER 82 (1954) 290-94; RP 16 (1954) 508; TS 14 (1954) 661; St 43 (1954) 469; NS 30 (1956) 386.

NICHOLL, Donald. *Recent Thought in Focus.* See II.

NOONAN, John P. *General and Special Ethics.* Chicago: Loyola University Press, 1947. x, 310 pp. Bibliography.

An introductory text covering the entire field of general and special ethics. The treatment is brief but clear. Appropriate examples elucidate the morality of double effect, and there is an interesting discussion of the state's authority and of relations between capital and labor. Its handling of false theories of morality is, however, rather inadequate. B

See: CE 46 (1948) 256-58; CSJ 47 (1947) 36a.

O'BRIEN, Mary C. *Christian Social Principles.* New York: Kenedy, 1941. xvi, 621 pp. Index.

A basic text for college students on the social thought of St. Thomas. Theories are distinguished from the established principles which are diligently sought out. Each chapter is supplemented by quotations from the writings of St. Thomas and the encyclicals, a chapter summary, questions for study and discussion, and suggested collateral reading. A-B

See: ACSR 2 (1941) 260; CER 40 (1942) 123-24; CW 154 (1941) 117; D 27 (1942) 46-47; AER 107 (1942) 16; MS 19 (1941) 17; TS 3 (1942) 150-53.

O'BRIEN, Patrick. *Emotions and Morals: Their Place and Purpose in Harmonious Living.* New York: Grune and Stratton, 1950. xiii, 241 pp. Bibliography, index.

A study of the relation of emotions to moral responsibility. The nature of emotions is investigated, with special attention being given to their influence on free acts. In this context anger, desire, and fear are studied in detail. A-B

See: F. Houlihan, CER 48 (1950) 285; R. Lange, AM 71 (1950) 666.

O'CONNOR, Daniel A. (ed.) *Catholic Social Doctrine.* Westminster, Md.: Newman, 1956. xii, 204 pp. Index.

An introduction to the moral facets of social thought. A large portion of Part I consists of a translation of P. Van Gestel's *Introduction a l'enseignement social de l'église.* The remainder of the book deals with the magisterial authority of the Church and a summary, mainly by quotation, of the teachings of Pope Pius XII on peace, the individual, marriage, and the family. It is not a comprehensive survey of Catholic social doctrine. A-B

See: CR 41 (1956) 628; HPR 56 (1956) 964; SJR 50 (1957) 68.

O'CONNOR, William R. *The Eternal Quest: The Teaching of St. Thomas Aquinas on the Natural Desire for God.* New York: Longmans, Green, 1947. ix, 290 pp. Bibliography, index.

An exegesis of seemingly contradictory texts in St. Thomas concerning man's natural desire to see God. It contains a methodical exposition of opinions of the outstanding commentators. The solution follows a metaphysical and psychological study of the natural desire for knowledge and happiness. There are four brief appendices on closely related subjects, as well as copious notes. C-D

See: A 78 (1948) 416; C 47 (1948) 452; D 33 (1948) 49-50; RR 7 (1948) 109; TS 9 (1948) 125-27.

———. *The Natural Desire for God.* (The Aquinas Lecture, 1948). Milwaukee: Marquette University Press, 1948. vii, 90 pp. Bibliography.

A survey of the history of philosophic thought concerning the natural desire for God. The notion is traced from Plato and Aristotle, through Plotinus, Augustine, St. Thomas, and Scotus, to modern contemporary positions. B

See: D 34 (1949) 157; Donnelly, T 24 (1949) 545.

OESTERLE, John A. *Ethics: The Introduction to Moral Science.*

Englewood Cliffs, N.J.: Prentice-Hall, 1957. xvii, 269 pp. Bibliography, index.

An outstanding general ethics textbook for college students. The work is based upon Aristotle's *Nicomachean Ethics* and St. Thomas' corresponding *Commentary*. It carefully distinguishes ethics from metaphysics and from moral theology. Attention is given to principles, rather than to cases, and the role of the virtues in moral life is stressed. The style is readable and invites personal reflection. Each chapter contains an outline, review questions, practical points for discussion, and a short bibliography. Since there is no explicit treatment of special ethics, the material could be covered in one semester. B

See: AM 86 (1957) 23; D 43 (1958) 178; NS 32 (1958) 287; Tm 22 (1959) 128.

O'NEIL, Charles. *Imprudence in St. Thomas Aquinas* (The Aquinas Lecture, 1955). Milwaukee: Marquette University Press, 1955. 165 pp.

A lecture on the work of prudence. After a review of this virtue in Aristotle, its structure and acts are examined according to the mind of St. Thomas in their relationship to love and to divine help. B

See: NS 30 (1956) 512; St 46 (1957) 115; Tm 19 (1956) 402.

PASSERIN d'ENTREVES, Allessandro. (ed.) *Natural Law: An Introduction to Legal Philosophy* (Hutchinson's University Library: *Philosophy*). London: Hutchinson, 1951. 126 pp.

A study of the import of natural law for legal philosophy. The book's central theme is the existence of natural law and its relation to positive law in providing the ultimate norm of human actions. B

See: Tm 15 (1952) 534; SO 4 (1954) 235.

PHILOSOPHY OF ORDER. See I.

PIEPER, Josef. *Fortitude and Temperance.* Trans. by D. Coogan from *Vom Sinn der Tapferkeit,* and *Zucht und Mass.* New York: Pantheon, 1954 (1934). 128 pp.

An excellent series of essays on the Christian conception of fortitude and temperance. Based upon Thomistic principles and applied to current problems, the essays realistically show the true worth and far-reaching significance of these two cardinal virtues. Modern errors are skillfully refuted and common misconceptions dispelled. A-C

See: Bl 36 (1955) 246; D 39 (1954) 200; HPR 55 (1955) 801; Ta 205 (1955) 374; Tm 19 (1956) 145; W 28 (1954) 391.

―――. *Happiness and Contemplation.* Trans. by R. and C. Winston from *Glück und Kontemplation.* New York: Pantheon, 1958 (1957) . 125 pp.

A series of reflections on the nature of happiness and on contemplation as a foretaste in this life of the perfect happiness of heaven. St. Thomas' position, that ultimate human happiness is found in contemplation, is developed and evaluated in the light of ancient and modern thinkers. A-C

See: D 43 (1958) 324; DR 78 (1960) 307; P. Donovan, APJ (1958) 46; F. Harkins, A 99 (1958) 593; O'Sullivan, APR 8 (1957) 377; J 6 (1958) 46; SR 29 (1958) 335; NS 33 (1959) 254; Ta 213 (1959) 488; W 33 (1959) 127.

―――. *Justice.* Trans. by L. Lynch from *Über die Gerechtigkeit.* New York: Pantheon, 1955 (1953) . 121 pp.

A survey of the cardinal virtue of justice. The basic elements, in both their simple and profound senses, are seen in the Greeks, the Bible, Kant, and especially in St. Thomas. Apt applications are made to later social and political conditions, though there is no mention of social justice as such. A-C

See: AM 83 (1956) 23; CW 182 (1956) 397; C 63 (1955) 335; Bl 38 (1957) 337; DR 75 (57) 281; NS 30 (1956) 511; Ta 209 (1957) 471.

―――. *Prudence: The First of the Cardinal Virtues.* Trans by R. and C. Winston from *Traktat über die Klugheit.* New York: Pantheon, 1959 (1939) . 96 pp.

A stimulating introduction to Thomistic teaching on the virtue of prudence. The traditional doctrine on prudence is expressed in a personal, clear, and modern manner and related to the other virtues. The well-chosen notes at the end serve as an excellent

review for anyone who has made a thorough study of this virtue.
A-C

> See: H. Nolan, A 102 (1959) 161; AM 91 (1960) 26; D 45 (1960) 81; DR
> 78 (1960) 307; HPR 60 (1960) 490; J 7 (1959) 49; W. Buchler, NS 34
> (1960) 533; G. McMurrow, W 34 (1959) 56.

POLAND, William J. *Fundamental Ethics: An Ethical Analysis,
Conducted by Way of Question and Answer for Use in
Classes of Moral Philosophy*. Chicago: Loyola University
Press, 1921. 138 pp.

A survey of general ethics, in which the questions are grouped
according to articles. The question-and-answer approach limits
its interest to those seeking simple definitions. A

RENARD, Henri. *The Philosophy of Morality* ("Science and
Culture Series"). Milwaukee: Bruce, 1953. 252 pp.

An undergraduate text on ethics. It concentrates especially on the
matter of the *Summa Theologica*, I-II, but distinguishes the philosophical from the theological. There is a special treatment of
the ultimate destiny of man. The work is well-arranged, with excellent pedagogical devices such as summaries and discussion suggestions after each chapter. B

> See: CR 39 (1954) 507; NS 28 (1954) 353; S 33 (1953) 67; T 29 (1954)
> 474.

RICKABY, Joseph. *Four Square; or, the Cardinal Virtues: Addresses to Young Men*. New York: Wagner, 1908. 93 pp.

A simple review of the meaning and order of the virtues in daily
life. The nature and division of the virtues are stated, and the
cardinal virtues are treated singly. A

————. *Moral Philosophy: Or Ethics, Deontology, and Natural
Law* ("Stonyhurst Philosophical Series"). 4th ed. London:
Longmans, Green, 1918 (1888). xv, 379 pp.

An early neo-Scholastic discussion of the perennial moral problems. After a study of the nature of human acts, the sources of
obligation and law are reviewed, along with their implications in

relation to God, self, and the various societies. The positions of Mill, Spencer, and Huxley, though contrasted with Aristotle and St. Thomas, are fairly stated, and whatever is true or valuable in them is accepted. B

See: CW 49 (1889) 137.

ROMMEN, Heinrich A. *The Natural Law: A Study in Legal and Social History and Philosophy.* Trans. by T. Hanley from *Die ewige Wiederkehr des Naturrechts.* St. Louis: Herder, 1947 (1936). xii, 290 pp. Bibliography, index.

A comprehensive study of natural law, the history of which is traced from the Greeks to the problems of the eighteenth century and the challenges of positivism in the nineteenth. The nature and content of natural law are examined and compared with those of positive law. The notes, index, and references help to make this an extremely useful reference work. C-D

See: AM 66 (1947) 666; CR 29 (1948) 202-205; E. Littlejohn, C 46 (1947) 360-61; D 32 (1947) 216-17; MS 25 (1948) 282-85; TS 8 (1947) 709-11; T 22 (1947) 757-59.

ROSS, John E. *Christian Ethics: A Textbook of Right Living (Ethics from the Standpoint of Scholastic Philosophy).* New York: Devin-Adair, 1948 (1919). 367 pp.

The section on general ethics contains the usual considerations of man's final destiny, the norm of morality, and law. The section on special ethics contains subsections on both the individual and society. It is well-divided and contains lists of suggested readings. B

RYAN, James F. *An Introduction to Philosophy.* See II.

RYAN, John K. *Philosophical Studies in Honor of Ignatius Smith.* See II.

SCHUYLER, Henry C. *Life's Final Goal: Charting a Course by the Light of Reason.* Philadelphia: Reilly, 1939. x, 365 pp.

A popular introduction to the field of morality. A study of the

unity and goodness of man and the world lays the groundwork
for a review of motivation in human actions. A-B

See: A 62 (1940) 528; AER 101 (1939) 576.

SCHWARZ, Balduin V. *The Human Person and the World of*
Values: A Tribute to Dietrich von Hildebrand by His
Friends in Philosophy ("The Orestes Brownson Series on
Contemporary Thought and Affairs," No. 3). New York:
Fordham University Press, 1960. xiii, 210 pp.

An excellent collection of essays by such distinguished American
and European Christian philosophers as Marcel, Maritain,
Sciacca, and others. Centering on the dignity of human values in
the contemporary situation, it manifests that breadth of vision of
which the work of D. von Hildebrand has ever been a model. B-D

See: M. Novak, C 73 (1961) 616; MS 39 (1961) 65; SO 10 (1960) 421;
J. Diemert, T 35 (1960) 605-607.

SHEED, Francis J. *Society and Sanity*. New York: Sheed and
Ward, 1953. 274 pp.

A general discussion of man and his social duties. The nature of
man is reviewed as a basis for an analysis of his place in the family and civil societies. A-B

See: D. Campion, A 88 (1953) 654; G. Schnepp, ACSR 14 (1953) 179;
Bl 34 (1953) 242-44; CSJ 53 (1953) 33; CR 38 (1953) 314-15; J. Kittleson, C 57 (1953) 635; DR 72 (1954) 115; A. Nevins, HPR 54 (1954) 362;
IER 80 (1953) 209; J. Madden, S 32 (1953) 65-66; K. Quinn, St 42
(1953) 470; Ta 201 (53) 399; TS 14 (1953) 522; Th 17 (54) 124.

SHEEN, Fulton J. *The Moral Universe: A Preface to Christian*
Living. Milwaukee: Bruce, 1936. vii, 170 pp. (Paper)

A series of discourses on the principles of moral living. The appreciation of man's authentic destiny and the moral problem of
living according to this end are presented as the problems to be
faced. The rhetorical manner of exposition does not always favor
philosophical precision. A-B

See: A 55 (1936) 235.

SIMON, Yves. *A General Theory of Authority.* Notre Dame, Ind.: University of Notre Dame Press, 1962. ix, 167 pp.

A discussion of authority within the context of related modern problems. Forces militating against an appreciation of authority are outlined, while the grounds for authority are laid in the notions of common good and common action. The special problem of the freedom of the intellect and authority is studied. C-D

See: A 108 (1963) 574; AM 97 (1963) 28; C 78 (1963) 229; HPR 63 (1963) 638; J 11 (1963) 46; RF 169 (1964) 208.

————. *Nature and Functions of Authority* (The Aquinas Lecture, 1940). Milwaukee: Marquette University Press, 1940. 78 pp.

A lecture on the meaning of freedom, in which are studied the nature of authority, its essential functions in relation to subordinates and their liberty, and its contrast with anarchy and tyranny. There are effective notes. B-C

See: Bl 21 (1940) 716-17; CW 153 (1941) 125; CSA 5 (1940) 358-60; C 33 (1940) 85; RP 3 (1941) 250-54; RUO 11 (1941) 133.

SMITH, Elwood F., and RYAN, Louis A. *Preface to Happiness.* Vol. II of *Guidebook to the* SUMMA. New York: Benziger, 1950. xx, 281 pp. Index.

A guide, rather than a substitute for, the *Summa theologica,* I-II. It contains aids for studying the *Summa* itself, such as historical summaries of each problem from St. Thomas' predecessors to the present, a glossary, and textual citations. A-B

See: D 35 (1950) 263.

SULLIVAN, Joseph F. *General Ethics: A Digest of Lectures.* 7th ed. Worcester, Mass.: Holy Cross College Press, 1949 (1926). vii, 239 pp. Bibliography, index.

The notions of good and end provide the context for the study of such concepts as law and conscience. The material is presented in a schematic thesis form. B

See: A 43 (1930) 46; CW 132 (1930) 253.

————. *Special Ethics: A Digest of Lectures.* 8th ed. Worcester, Mass.: Holy Cross College Press, 1949 (1929). 288 pp.

The perennial values of the individual and of society are studied in relation to the problems arising on the modern industrial, civil, and international levels. The work is presented in thesis form. B

SULLIVAN, Robert P. *Man's Thirst for Good* (Thomistic Studies, No. 4). Westminster, Md.: Newman, 1952. 120 pp. Bibliography.

A study of man's reasoned and responsible direction toward the good, assembling relevant texts in response to a notion proposed by W. O'Connor on the nature of the natural appetite and the extent of necessitation in the human will. The position of the classical commentators is indicated and shown to be found seminally in Aquinas. C

SWITALSKI, Bruno. *Plotinus and the Ethics of St. Augustine.* See XIV.

THOMAS AQUINAS, Saint. *Aquinas Ethicus.* See XV.

————. *The Commandments of God: Conferences on the Two Precepts of Charity and the Ten Commandments.* See XV.

————. *On Aristotle's Love and Friendship,* ETHICS, *Books VIII-IX.* See XV.

————. *On Charity.* See XV.

————. *On Free Choice.* See XV.

————. *On the Truth of the Catholic Faith.* See XV.

————. *On the Virtues in General.* See XV.

————. *Summa theologica.* See XV.

————. *Treatise on Happiness.* See XV.

————. *Treatise on Law.* See XV.

TODD, John M. (ed.) *The Springs of Morality: A Catholic Symposium.* New York: Macmillan, 1956. vii, 327 pp.

A collection of essays on the sources of moral philosophy. Historical influences on Western ethical attitudes, especially the existential and communist positions on morality, are studied. Though the whole lacks inner unity, the individual essays, especially those concerning insights into morality made by the secondary sciences, are of high quality. B-C

> *See:* Bl 37 (1956) 534; CR 42 (1957) 116; DR 75 (1957) 85; ITQ 24 (1957) 189; SJR 50 (1957) 100; T. Gregory, Ta 208 (1956) 428; G. Sloyan, W 31 (1957) 188-99.

TRETHOWAN, Illtyd. *An Essay in Christian Philosophy.* See II.

VANN, Gerald. *The Heart of Man.* New York: Longmans, Green, 1945. vii, 182 pp. (Image: D 103)

An essay on creative human subjectivity. The perspective is set by a review of human love in relation to the vision of good and evil. Man is then viewed as a maker in the fields of art, family life, the world, and the Church. B-C

> *See:* AM 63 (1946) 506; Bl 25 (1944) 126-27; C 43 (1945) 210-11; HPR 46 (1946) 399; JRI 16 (1946) 680-83; LA 14 (1946) 68; MS 23 (1946) 109-10; RP 8 (1946) 537; RR 5 (1946) 68; S 25 (1945) 49; Ta 184 (1944) 45; TS 7 (1946) 182-83.

————. *Morals and Man.* Revised ed. New York: Sheed and Ward, 1960 (1937). 223 pp.

A revised edition of *Morals Makyth Man.* The moral principles of St. Thomas are presented and applied to contemporary problems in the fields of politics, economics, and ethics. It does not go back to Thomism, but carries that thought forward. The Thomistic synthesis is compared with other philosophies of morality. B-C

> *See:* NS 36 (1962) 106; TS 22 (1961) 339.

VERSFELD, Martin. *The Perennial Order.* See II.

WALLACE, William A. *The Role of Demonstration in Moral Theology: A Study of Methodology in St. Thomas Aquinas* (The Thomist Press, *Texts and Studies,* Vol. 2). Washington, D.C.: Thomist Press, 1962. ix, 254 pp. Bibliography. (Paper)

A work on method in moral philosophy and moral theology. It contains a thorough discussion of moral philosophy as a demonstrative science, of Christian moral philosophy, and of the latter's relation to theology and the traditional science of ethics. C-D

See: D 47 (1962) 308.

WARD, Leo R. *Christian Ethics: An Introduction for College Students.* St. Louis: Herder, 1952. vi, 298 pp. Bibliography, index.

An informal treatment of general ethical principles. There are numerous inductive examples from great philosophers and from American life. In the central chapter, consideration is given to Maritain's Christian personalism. A-B

See: A 89 (1953) 51-52; L. Schumacher, AER 129 (1953) 287; P. Glenn, AM 76 (1952) 538; CR 39 (1954) 183; D 38 (1953) 369; C. Bruehl, HPR 54 (1954) 367-68; T. Higgins, NS 27 (1953) 485; W. Buehler, SJR 46 (1953) 135; E. Hynes, W 27 (1953) 331-32.

————. *God and World Order.* See I.

————. *Philosophy of Values.* See I.

————. *Values and Reality.* See I.

WELTY, Eberhard. *A Handbook of Christian Social Ethics.* 2 vols. Trans. by G. Kirstein from *Herders Sozialkatechismus,* 2d German ed., and revised by J. Fitzsimons. Freiburg: Herder, 1960-63. 395 pp. Bibliography.

An introductory work on social ethics. After a determination of the nature of social ethics, the core of each problem is stated, and concise solutions are presented. The question-answer format is advantageous for quick reference. The work includes relevant Papal teachings, and a selective, annotated, and up-to-date bibliography. A-B

See: CE 32 (1962) 806; CC 11 (1961) 384; F 12 (1961) 330; RSE 19 (1961) 77; SJR 53 (1961) 353.

WILMS, Jerome. *The Divine Friendship According to St. Thomas*. Trans. by Sr. M. Fulgence from *Die Gottesschaft nach dem hl. Thomas*. Dubuque: Priory, 1964 (1958). 162 pp.

A study of charity with emphasis on its theological elements. The fact, nature, and effects of charity are studied, along with man's entrance and re-entrance into this state. A-B

WOOD, Robert. *Principles and Problems of Ethics*. St. Louis: Herder, 1962. 184 pp.

A textbook on ethics. After reviewing such notions as the existence of God, man's destiny, and the nature of morality, the author proceeds to a series of related questions and answers. This work is more catechetical than scientific. A-B

See: MS 90 (1962) 95.

WOODS, Henry. *A First Book in Ethics*. New York: Wagner, 1923. 295 pp.

An undergraduate text of general and special ethics. Among the usual matters treated in such a course, special attention is given to man in his social relations. The thesis form is used. B

See: CW 118 (1924) 859.

WU, John C. *Fountain of Justice: A Study in the Natural Law*. New York: Sheed and Ward, 1955. ix, 287 pp. Index.

A study of the roots and nature of natural law. American jurisprudence is seen to be veering away from positivism and mechanism. A relationship is developed between natural law and common law as it has developed in England and the United States. The teachings of St. Thomas and Confucius are found to meet in the Christian position. The work is copiously annotated. C

See: A 94 (1955) 786; ACSR 16 (1956) 69; AM 83 (1956) 24; CW 182 (1956) 318; FL 24 (1955) 729-39; GLR 44 (1956) 539; HPR 56 (1956) 608.

ZIMMERMANN, Otto. *The Problem of Evil and Human Destiny.* Trans. by J. Zybura from *Warum Schuld und Schmerz.* St. Louis: Herder, 1924 (1918) . xvi, 135 pp.

A series of reflections on evil. These are made within the framework of such positive considerations as goodness, freedom, self-fulfillment, and the infinity of God. A-B

See: A 32 (1925) 284; C 1 (1925) 443.

CHAPTER X

Special Ethics

This chapter is composed of works in the field of special ethics which constitute the second half of most ethics textbooks. As these texts, along with comprehensive surveys of special ethics,[1] have been listed in the previous chapter, they will not be repeated here. Special ethics studies the broad area of the duties of man to God, to self, and to society. This area has been divided, according to the plan of an extensive bibliography of special ethics by Austin Fagothy,[2] into ten sections:

The reader is referred to Chapters III and VII of *A Bibliography of Christian Philosophy and Contemporary Issues* by the same editor.

- A. Legal Ethics: rights, law, justice
- B. Medical Ethics: life, health
- C. Sociological Ethics: society, community
- D. Domestic Ethics: marriage, family
- E. Political Ethics. state, government
- F. Economic Ethics: property, business
- G. Industrial Ethics: management, labor
- H. Marxian Ethics: communism, socialism
- I. International Ethics: world community, war, peace

As a practical science, special ethics has a particularly important relation to the concrete situation in which its problems

---

[1] Michael V. Murray, *Problems in Conduct* (New York: Holt, Rinehart and Winston, 1963); Joseph F. Sullivan, *Special Ethics* (Worcester: Holy Cross College Press, 1949).

[2] *Right and Reason: Ethics in Theory and Practice* (3d ed.; St. Louis: Mosby, 1963), 481-92.

are realized. For this reason, a number of titles from the above-mentioned bibliography, which would not otherwise be included, have been listed below, though without annotation.

In considering problems of special ethics, many works draw extensively on material from the social encyclicals. Where this material turns to natural law for its content, the works have been included as expressions of authentic and extensive ethical reflection on the part of the Christian community. On the other hand, ethical works rendered irrelevant by changes in the social situations to which they were addressed have been omitted.

A. LEGAL ETHICS: RIGHTS, LAW, JUSTICE [3]

BROWN, Brendan, F. (ed.) *The Natural Law Reader.* See IX.

DAVITT, Thomas E. *The Nature of Law.* See IX.

DOOLAN, Aegidius. *Order and Law.* See IX.

FARRELL, Walter. *The Natural Law.* See IX.

GERHART, Eugene C. *American Liberty and "Natural Law."* Boston: Beacon Press, 1953.

HAINES, Charles G. *Revival of Natural Law Concepts.* New York: Russell and Russell, 1965 (1930).

HARDING, Arthur L. (ed.) *Natural Law and Natural Rights.* Dallas: Southern Methodist Press, 1955.

HUMAN RIGHTS (A symposium ed. by UNESCO). London: Wingate, n.d.

KELSEN, Hans. (ed.) *What Is Justice?* Berkeley: University of California Press, 1957.

KREILKAMP, Karl. *The Metaphysical Foundations of Thomistic Jurisprudence* (The Catholic University of America, *Philosophical Studies,* No. 53). Washington, D.C.: The Catholic University of America Press, 1939. 183 pp. Bibliography. (Paper)
A study of the nature of law according to the mind of St. Thomas Aquinas. On the basis of the metaphysics of nature and order, it reviews natural law, its social and obligatory nature, and its variations. B

---

[3] Works on the general nature of law and on natural law have been included in the previous chapter on general ethics.

LeBUFFE, Francis P., and HAYES, James V. *The American Philosophy of Law with Cases to Illustrate Principles.* New York: Jesuit Educational Association, 1953. xxvii, 418 pp. Indices, appendix.

Formerly entitled *Jurisprudence,* this is a study of the nature of law and its understanding in America. The work begins with a basic statement concerning the nature of law and of natural law. A description of the philosophy of law prevalent in the United States follows. This lays the groundwork for a more extensive treatment of justice, rights, and their conflicts.

See: A 60 (1939). 263; CW 148 (1939) 764.

McKINNON, Harold. *The Higher Law.* Berkeley, Calif.: Gillick, 1946.

MARITAIN, Jacques. *The Rights of Man and Natural Law.* See IX.

MESSNER, Johannes. *Social Ethics.* See IX.

THE NATURAL LAW AND INTERNATIONAL RELATIONS. See I.

NEWMAN, Jeremiah. *Foundations of Justice.* See IX.

PASSERIN d'ENTREVES, Allesandro. (ed.) *Natural Law.* See IX.

RITCHIE, David G. *Natural Rights.* London: Allen and Unwin, 1952 (1894).

ROMMEN, Heinrich A. *The Natural Law.* See IX.

ST. JOHN-STEVAS, Norman. *Life, Death, and the Law.* See X.

STRAUSS, Leo. *Natural Rights and History.* Chicago, Ill.: University of Chicago Press, 1953.

WU, John C. *Fountain of Justice,* See IX.

B. MEDICAL ETHICS: LIFE, HEALTH

BIRMINGHAM, William, and CUNNEEN, Joseph E. (eds.)
Cross Currents of Psychiatry and Catholic Morality. New
York: Pantheon, 1964 (1963). 396 pp. (Paper)

A collection of articles on psychiatry and morality from *Cross
Currents.* Along with particular studies of psychiatry and the
Church, there are some important investigations on the contributions of psychiatry to an appreciation of freedom and its implications for morality and for religious belief. Also treated are the
implications of recent scientific research on man's understanding
of ethical behavior. B-C

BONNAR, Alphonsus. *The Catholic Doctor.* New York: Kenedy,
1950 (1939). xvi, 184 pp. Appendix.

A study of moral problems and principles relevant to a doctor's
practice. The principles of natural law are discussed, and in their
light the author considers various types of cases, such as problems
of scandal, scruples, and psychotherapy. B

See: CR 37 (1952) 57; IM 79 (1951) 456; T 14 (1939) 515.

BOUSCAREN, T. L. *The Ethics of Ectopic Operations.* Milwaukee: Bruce, 1944.

BRACELAND, Francis. (ed.) *Faith, Reason, and Modern Psychiatry.* Garden City, N.Y.: Doubleday, 1963 (1955). xv,
346 pp.

A symposium of doctors and scholars on the philosophical and
theological context of psychiatry. The papers treat problems of
belief, the existential crisis, man, and spiritual direction in relation to psychiatry. This is an exceptionally able treatment of
these questions. C-D

See: F. Flach, A 94 (1955) 106; ACSR 16 (1956) 55; AER 133 (1955)
428-32; AM 82 (1955) 24; V. White, BL 37 (1956) 82; CER 26 (1956)
534; D 41 (1956) 67; S. Lando, HPR 56 (1956) 436-38; J 3 (1956) 46; E.
O'Doherty, St 45 (1956) 110.

COPPENS, Charles. *Moral Principles and Medical Practice*. New York: Benziger, 1921 (1897) . 320 pp. Bibliography, index, appendix.

A classical work on the basic moral and legal principles relevant to medical practice. The foundations of jurisprudence and the relation of insanity and the law are discussed, as well as particular medical problem areas. Interest in this standard work is still maintained. B

See: A 25 (1921) 406; CW 66 (1921) 410-11; D 114 (1921) 251.

CUNNINGHAM, Bert. *Morality of Organic Transplantation*. Washington, D.C.: Catholic University Press, 1944.

DUFFEY, Felix D. *Psychiatry and Asceticism*. St. Louis: Herder, 1950.

FICARRA, Bernard J. *Newer Ethical Problems in Medicine and Surgery*. Westminster, Md.: Newman, 1951. xx, 168 pp. Index.

A study of particular areas of medico-moral problems. Two chapters are devoted to the moral aspects of professional conduct and of finances. B

See: M. Coyne, AM 76 (1952) 155; CR 38 (1953) 126; D 37 (1952) 90; J. McLaughlin, TS 13 (1952) 284.

FINNEY, Patrick, and O'BRIEN, Patrick. *Moral Problems in Hospital Practice: A Practical Handbook*. St. Louis: Herder, 1956 (1922) . xiii, 208 pp.

A study of problems concerning the life of patients, especially in relation to difficulties arising in childbirth. These questions are treated in detail, but the conclusions need to be verified in the light of subsequent information. B

See: A 27 (1922) 596; CW 115 (1922) 831.

FLOOD, Peter. (ed.) *The Ethics of Brain Surgery*. Chicago: Regnery, 1955.

———. *New Problems in Medical Ethics* ("Divine Word").

4 vols. Trans. by M. Carroll from *Cahiers Laënnec*. Westminster, Md.: Newman, 1953-60. (Paper)

A collection of articles on a broad series of medico-moral problems. Areas treated range from the usual problems of the physical order to the juridical, psychological, and spiritual condition of the patient. This series is particularly well done. B-C

See: Vol 1: AM 78 (1953) 25; CR 38 (1953) 632; D 38 (1953) 250; DR 71 (1953) 456; A. Welsh, HPR 54 (1953) 276; R. Havard, Ta 202 (1953) 38; J. McLaughlin, TS 15 (1954) 159. Vol 2: G. Stevens, AER 131 (1954) 430; CR 40 (1955) 115; IER 83 (1955) 73 G. Kelley, SO 5 (1955) 190. Vol 3: A 97 (1957) 129; CR 42 (1957) 560; DR 75 (1957) 394; IER 88 (1957) 292; J. Coogan, P 17 (1961) 528; T. O'Donnell, TS 22 (1961) 141.

————. *Medical Experimentation on Man*. Chicago: Regnery, 1955.

GODIN, Edgar, and O'HANLEY, J. P. E. *Hospital Ethics*. Bathurst, N.B., Canada: Hotel Dieu Hospital, 1957.

GOOD, Frederick, and KELLY, Otis. *Marriage, Morals and Medical Ethics*. New York: Kenedy, 1951.

HAGMAIER, George, and GLEASON, Robert W. *Counseling the Catholic: Modern Techniques and Emotional Conflicts*. New York: Sheed and Ward, 1960.

HAYES, Edward, HAYES, Paul, and KELLY, Ellen. *Moral Handbook of Nursing*. New York: Macmillan, 1957. xvi, 180 pp.

A general handbook for all aspects of the life of the nurse. There is an extensive section on the relevant moral and ethical principles concerning the origin and destruction of life. B

HEALY, Edwin F. *Medical Ethics*. Chicago: Loyola University Press, 1956. xxii, 440 pp. Appendix.

An exceptionally fine work on the moral problems which confront doctors. The general ethical principles are explained, along with the obligations of doctors. Special problems are treated in detail, including those areas in which the work of the doctor opens onto the spiritual needs of the patient. A code of ethics is appended. B-C

See: CR 42 (1957) 114; D 42 (1957) 53; IER 87 (1957) 474.

JOHNSON, Brian D. *The Catholic Nurse.* London: Burns, Oates and Washbourne, 1950. 160 pp.

A manual for all phases of the life of a nurse. There is a section on ethical problems which provides a summary statement of the fundamental principles, along with indications concerning a few particular areas. A-B

See: CR 36 (1951) 203; A. D'Abreu, Ta 197 (1951) 152.

JUSTICE. See I.

KELLY, Gerald. *Medico-Moral Problems.* Parts I-V. St. Louis: Catholic Hospital Association, 1949-52.

A collection of booklets dealing with a broad variety of moral problems that arise in the field of medicine. The treatment is particularly well done. B-C

KENNY, John P. *Principles of Medical Ethics.* Westminster, Md.: Newman, 1961 (1952). xvi, 274 pp. Bibliography, index, appendix.

An effective work on moral problems in the practice of medicine. After a consideration of the general principles, and of justice and charity as they effect this area, particular problem areas are viewed, among which are some recent problems in mutilation. The appendix contains a set of ethical and religious directives for Catholic hospitals. B-C

See: A. Rosso, CER 51 (1953) 497; CR 39 (1954) 249; D 38 (1953) 134; F 5 (1954) 58; A. Welsh, HPR (1953) 853-56; G. Klubertanz, LQ 20 (1953) 50; T 28 (1953) 632; J. McCarthy, Th 17 (1954) 100-104; TS 14 (1953) 520.

LAROCHELLE, Stanislas A., and FINK, C. T. *Handbook of Medical Ethics.* Trans. by M. Poupore from *Précis de morale médicale pour infirmières.* Westminster, Md.: Newman, 1943 (1940). 369 pp.

The mode of the formation of conscience is introduced, along with the general principles concerning voluntary acts. The treatment of particular areas is expanded to include the exercise of charity and secrecy in the professional life of the doctor. B-C

See: D. 28 (1943) 131-33; S 22 (1943) 636.

LEHANE, Joseph. *Morality of American Civil Legislation Concerning Eugenical Sterilization.* Washington, D.C.: Catholic University Press, 1944.

MARSHALL, John. *Medicine and Morals (Twentieth Century Encyclopedia of Catholicism,* Vol. CXXIX). New York: Hawthorn, 1960. 140 pp. Bibliography.

A study of the basic elements of medical ethics. The nature of man, the origin of the moral law, and the doctor's religious dimensions are reviewed as the context for a discussion of the key problem areas for the moral decisions involved in the field of medicine. A-B

See: J. Royce, A 104 (1961) 573; AM 93 (1961) 25; F. Filas, CR 19 (1961) 62; T. Wassmer, CW 192 (1961) 376; LQ 29 (1962); TA 215 (1961) 386.

McALLISTER, Joseph B. *Ethics, with Special Application to the Medical and Nursing Professions.* See IX.

McFADDEN, Charles. *Medical Ethics.* Philadelphia: Davis, 1962 (1946). xxi, 441 pp. Index, appendix.

A standard text on the moral problems in the practice of medicine. It follows the usual sequence, from a discussion of the principles to problems related to marriage and birth, the right of life, and various types of operations. Professional secrecy and the sacraments are also treated. This is a text of proven value. B-C

See: AER 147 (1962) 70; Bl 43 (1962) 440; FS 6 (1946) 503; HJ 3 (1962) 401; IER 98 (1962) 268; IER 88 (1957) 139; RR 21 (1962) 586; SJR 40 (1948) 319; Ta 216 (1962) 1050; TS 22 (1961) 722.

MAVES, Paul B. *The Church and Mental Health.* New York: Scribner's, 1953.

O'DONNELL, Thomas. *Morals in Medicine.* 2d ed., revised. Westminster, Md.: Newman, 1960 (1956). xxx, 398 pp. Index.

A text on ethical problems in the medical profession. An explanation of the fundamental principles and of the inviolability of human life leads to the discussion of problems involved in pregnancy and mutilation. The care of the dying is given special attention. There is also a set of ethical directives for Catholic hospitals. This is an effective work on the subject. B

See: DR 79 (1961) 271; S. McDonald, NRT 85 (1963) 883.

O'MALLEY, Austin. *The Ethics of Medical Homicide and Mutilation.* New York: Devin Adair, 1919.

REGAN, Robert. *Professional Secrecy in the Light of Moral Principles, with an Application to Several Important Professions.* Washington, D.C.: Augustinian Press, 1943.

RYAN, John A. *Moral Aspects of Sterilization.* Washington, D.C.: National Catholic Welfare Conference, 1930.

ST. JOHN-STEVAS, Norman. *Life, Death, and the Law: Law and Christian Morals in England and the United States.* Bloomington, Ind.: Indiana University Press, 1961. 375 pp. Bibliography, appendices.

A study of the relation of law to morals in modern society. After a general introductory consideration of the relationship, its history is traced in particular problem areas such as contraception, suicide, and euthanasia. C

See: A 105 (1961) 666; CL 7 (1961) 320; W. Ball CW 193 (1961) 260; D 47 (1962) 218; DR 79 (1961) 372-76; I 75 (1961) 59; J 9 (1961) 41; C. Palms, NLF 7 (1962) 190; C. Sheedy, NDL 36 (1961) 610; R. Drinan, RE 56 (1961) 452; J. Dunsford, SO 11 (1961) 470; L. Fairfield, Ta 215 (1961) 280; TS 23 (1962) 316; J. Hassett, T 37 (1962) 137; F. Cohen, UDL 39 (1961) 257-65; WJ 4 (1962) 250.

SCHMIEDELER, Edgar. *Sterilization in the United States.* Washington, D.C.: National Catholic Welfare Conference, 1943.

SULLIVAN, Joseph V. *The Morality of Mercy Killing.* Westminster, Md.: Newman Press, 1950.

TOURNIER, Paul. *The Meaning of the Person.* See VII.

VAN der VELDT, James H., and ODENWALD, Robert. *Psychiatry and Catholicism.* New York: McGraw-Hill, 1957 (1952).

C. SOCIOLOGICAL ETHICS: SOCIETY, COMMUNITY

CAHILL, Edward. *Framework of a Christian State.* Dublin: Gill, 1932.

CALVEZ, Jean-Yves. *The Social Thought of John XXIII.* Chicago: Regnery, 1964.
A sequel to *The Church and Social Justice* presenting subsequent developments in this field. The work centers around *Mater et Magistra* and studies the opening of the thought of Pope John onto other social positions. C-D

CASSERLEY, J. V. Langmead. *The Bent World.* New York: Oxford University Press, 1955.

CHRISTIAN PHILOSOPHY AND THE SOCIAL SCIENCES. See I.

DEPLOIGE, Simon. *The Conflict Between Ethics and Sociology.* See IX.

DOHERTY, Richard T. *The Relation of the Individual to Society.* See IX.

DOUGHERTY, George F. *The Moral Basis of Social Order.* See IX.

DRUMMOND, William F. *Social Justice.* See IX.

DURKHEIM, Emile. *Suicide.* Glencoe, Ill.: Free Press, 1951.

GILBY, Thomas. *Between the Community and Society.* New York: Longmans, Green, 1953. 344 pp. Index.
A study of the nature and purpose of human society. After a survey of the historical background for an understanding of Thomistic thought on this question, there is a detailed analysis of the ideas of community, society, and state. To this is added a commentary on the treatise "On Law" in St. Thomas' *Summa Theologica,* I-II. B-C

HAAS, Francis. *Man and Society.* New York: Appleton-Century-Crofts, 1952.

JÜNGER, Friedrich. *The Failure of Technology.* Chicago, Ill.: Regnery, 1956.

KAVANAGH, James. *Manual of Social Ethics.* See IX.

LIPPMANN, Walter. *The Good Society.* New York: Universal Library, 1956 (1937).

McKENNY, Charles. *Moral Problems in Social Work.* Milwaukee: Bruce, 1951.

MARCEL, Gabriel. *The Decline of Wisdom.* See XVII.

————. *Man Against Mass Society.* See XVII.

MASSE, Benjamin. *Justice for All: An Introduction to the Social Teaching of the Catholic Church.* Milwaukee: Bruce, 1964. ix, 196 pp.
A relatively brief survey of the social thought of the Church. Special attention is given to the meaning of social justice for the problems of the American scene. A-B

MESSNER, Johannes. *Social Ethics.* See XVII.

MICHEL, Virgil. *Christian Social Reconstruction: Some Fundamentals of the* QUADRAGESIMO ANNO. Milwaukee: Bruce, 1938. viii, 137 pp. Index.

A simplified analysis of the fundamental principles of *Quadragesimo anno*. There is an excellent application of these principles to the social problems of everyday life, such as social justice, private ownership, wages, and labor. The inclusion of the encyclical itself would have been helpful. A-B

See: CW 147 (1938) 125; LA 6 (1937) 105-107.

O'BRIEN, Mary C. *Christian Social Principles*. See IX.

OSGNIACH, Augustine. *Must It Be Communism?* New York: Wagner, 1950.

PHILOSOPHY AND SOCIETY. See I.

PHILOSOPHY AND UNITY. See I.

SOROKIN, Pitirim. *The Crisis of Our Age*. New York: Dutton, 1941.

WELTY, Eberhard. *A Handbook of Christian Social Ethics*. See IX.

D. DOMESTIC ETHICS: MARRIAGE, FAMILY

BAUM, Gregory *et al. Contraception and Holiness*. St. Louis: Herder and Herder, 1964.

A collection of essays on the moral and social problems of family planning and contraception. The work is a strong appeal for change from the previous positions of classical ethics. B

BIRMINGHAM, William. *What Modern Catholics Think about Birth Control*. New York: New American Library, 1964. 256 pp. (Signet: T2577)

A symposium on family planning. The moral principles involved are first discussed in the fields of ethics, history, and authority. There follows a survey of the particular problems involved in such areas as psychiatry, sociology, and demography, with a concluding section reflecting the experience of married couples. B-C

CLEMENS, Alphonse. *Marriage and the Family.* Englewood Cliffs, N.J.: Prentice-Hall, 1957.

DE GUCHTENEERE, Raoul. *Judgment on Birth Control.* New York: Macmillan, 1931.

DUPRE, Louis K. *Contraception and Catholics: A New Appraisal.* Baltimore, Md.: Helicon, 1964. 94 pp.
A study of the problem of family planning in the light of recent emphases in moral philosophy and theology. In the philosophical section are discussed natural law and natural purpose or end, and there is a review of the solutions of the moral problem in the light of the development of the question of the end of marriage. This work is a key to understanding the later discussions in this field. B-C

FOERSTER, Friedrich W. *Marriage and the Sex Problem.* New York: Stokes, 1912.

GERRARD, Thomas. *Marriage and Parenthood.* New York: Wagner, 1937.

GILBY, Thomas. *Morals and Marriage.* London: Longmans, Green, 1952 (1936 under pseud. T. G. Wayne).

HANDREN, Walter. *No Longer Two: Commentary on* CASTI CONNUBII. Westminster, Md.: Newman, 1955.

HEALY, Edwin. *Marriage Guidance.* Chicago, Ill.: Loyola University Press, 1958 (1949).

HILDEBRAND, Dietrich von. *In Defense of Purity.* New York: Sheed and Ward, 1938.

————. *Marriage*. New York: Longmans, Green, 1942.

HOPE, Wingfield. *Life Together*. New York: Sheed and Ward, 1944.

JOYCE, George. *Christian Marriage*. London: Sheed and Ward, 1948.

LECLERCQ, Jacques. *Marriage and the Family*. New York: Pustet, 1942.

MAGNER, James. *The Art of Happy Marriage*. Milwaukee: Bruce, 1947.

MIHANOVICH, Clement, SCHNEPP, Bro. Gerald, and THOMAS, John. *Marriage and the Family*. Milwaukee: Bruce, 1952.

MOORE, Edward. *The Case Against Birth Control*. New York: Century, 1931.

MORRISON, Robert. *God Is Its Founder*. Milwaukee: Bruce, 1946.

O'BRIEN, John A. *Sex-Love-Marriage*. St. Louis: Herder and Herder, 1964.
A collection of papers on marital ethics and the related disciplines. A broad spectrum of specialists and views is represented. A-B

O'CONNOR, Daniel A. (ed.) *Catholic Social Doctrine*. See IX.

SCHMIEDELER, Edgar. *Marriage and the Family*. New York: McGraw-Hill, 1946.

THIBON, Gustave. *What God Has Joined Together*. Chicago, Ill.: Regnery, 1952.

THOMAS, John L. *Marriage and Rhythm*. Westminster, Md.: Newman Press, 1957.

WELTY, Eberhard. *A Handbook of Christian Social Ethics*. See IX.

E. POLITICAL ETHICS: STATE, GOVERNMENT

BIGONGIARI, Dino. (ed.) *The Political Ideas of St. Thomas Aquinas: Representative Selections* (*The Hafner Library of Classics*, No. 15). New York: Hafner, 1953. 217 pp.

A useful collection of excerpts on political topics from the writings of St. Thomas. The passages are drawn from the *Summa theologica*, I-II, qq. 90-97 and II-II, *passim*. There is also an extensive portion of St. Thomas' *On Kingship*. B-D

CAHILL, Edward. *Framework of a Christian State: An Introduction to Social Science*. Dublin: Gill, 1932. xxvii, 701 pp. Appendices.

An historical and speculative study of political philosophy. The historical section extends from ancient to modern times, and might be considered rather overly polemic in the style of its time. In the speculative section is considered the whole series of social units and virtues; thus political philosophy is placed in an extensive context of social thought. B

See: A 47 (1932) 479; AER 101 (1939) 243.

CATLIN, George. *The Story of Political Philosophers*. New York: McGraw-Hill, 1939.

COGLEY, John. (ed.) *Natural Law and Modern Society*. Cleveland: World, 1963. 285 pp. Index.

A collection of articles on natural law in relation to various facets of modern life. Of special philosophical interest are the studies on its implications for law, religion, and teleology, the last of which is considered with special attention to the Greeks and Kant. Qustions of public consensus, sociology, and culture are also investigated. B-C

See: C 77 (1963) 405.

CONNELL, Francis J. *Morals in Politics and Professions:* A *Guide for Catholics in Public Life*. Westminster, Md.: Newman, 1946. vi, 187 pp. Index.

This work is broader in scope than its title indicates. There is a chapter on moral problems of each of the professions and a general concluding chapter on social justice and charity. Quite theological in orientation, it still contains most of the relevant ethical considerations. B

See: AM 65 (1947) 26; CER 45 (1947) 124-25; CW 165 (1947) 477-78; D 32 (1947) 38-39; AER 116 (1947) 236; HPR 47 (1947) 1024; S 26 (1947) 55; T 22 (1947) 567.

DEANE, Herbert A. *The Political and Social Ideas of St. Augustine*. See XIV.

DOUGLAS, Paul H. *Ethics in Government*. Cambridge, Mass.: Harvard University Press, 1952.

FIGGIS, John. *The Divine Right of Kings*. Cambridge: Cambridge University Press, 1914. (Harper: TB 1191)

————. *The Political Aspects of St. Augustine's City of God*. See XIV.

GARDINER, Harold. *Catholic Viewpoint on Censorship*. Garden City, N. Y.: Hanover House, 1961. (Image: D 125)

GILBY, Thomas. *The Political Thought of Thomas Aquinas*. Chicago, Ill.: University of Chicago Press, 1958. 357 pp.

A thorough study of the state in the system of St. Thomas. The author first surveys the pertinent events, institutions, and ideas in the fields of theology, law, social history, and philosophy. The systematization of this material by St. Thomas is then traced and recapitulated in the concluding summary. C

See: D 44 (1959) 62; Ms 4 (1960) 174.

GRAHAM, George A. *Morality in American Politics.* New York: Random House, 1952.

McCOY, Charles N. *The Structure of Political Thought.* New York: McGraw-Hill, 1963. v, 323 pp.

An historically oriented study of political thought concerning its philosophical foundations. The unfolding of this thought is traced from the ancients to the Marxists. There is a special consideration of the problem of natural law in the modern world. This is perhaps the most adequate book of its kind, and will be of interest to the graduate student in philosophy, history and the political and social sciences. C

McGOVERN, William. *From Luther to Hitler.* Boston: Houghton Mifflin, 1941.

MARITAIN, Jacques. *Man and the State* (Charles R. Walgreen Foundation Lecture). Ed. R. O'Sullivan. London: Hollis and Carter, 1954. 197 pp. (Phoenix: P 5)

An important book in political philosophy developed from lectures given in 1949. Perennial Thomistic thought is applied to the new political situations in order to make abiding human values the norm of true progress. After nation, body politic, state, and people have been distinguished, there are discussions regarding sovereignty, popular control of the state, the rights of man, democracy, Church and state, and world government. Stimulating and profoundly original, the work demands careful reading. B-C

See: J. Fitzsimmons, Bl 36 (1955) 29; J. Collins, JER 83 (1955) 469; G. Beck, Ta 204 (1954) 600.

————. *Scholasticism and Politics.* Trans. and ed. by M. Adler. 2d ed. London: Centenary Press, 1945 (1940). 197 pp. (Image: D 98)

A series of lectures that summarize Maritain's political philosophy in terms of his integral humanism. The work centers on the human person, his dignity and capacities in the moral, cultural, and political domains. There are important considerations of Catholic and political action, science and philosophy, Freudianism and psychoanalysis, and democracy and authority. B-C

See: AM 54 (1941) 58; Bl 21 (1940) 717-18; CW 153 (1941) 372-74; C 33 (1940) 211; D 25 (1940) 263; MS 18 (1941) 38; NS 15 (1941) 189; RP 4 (1942) 517-18; SJR 33 (1941) 357.

————. *Social and Political Writings of Jacques Maritain: Selected Readings.* Eds. Joseph W. Evans and Leo R. Ward. New York: Scribner's, 1955. 375 pp.

A collection of writings representative of various areas of political and social philosophy. The individual is studied as regards his freedom, rights, property, and place in political society. The religious and cultural aspects of this society are considered, as are the possibilities of constituting a new social order. B-C

See: M. Scott, Bl 38 (1957) 84; Bt 14 (1955) 18; CR 42 (1957) 185; N. Logal, CW 181 (1955) 397; D 40 (1955) 407; J. Haddox, NS 32 (1958) 391-93.

MESSNER, Johannes. *Social Ethics.* See IX.

MURPHY, Edward F. *St. Thomas' Political Doctrine and Democracy* (The Catholic University of America, *Philosophical Studies,* No. 10). Washington, D. C.: The Catholic University of America Press, 1921. xiv, 297 pp. Index (Paper)

A study of the relative positions of person and state. The nature of government—its purpose and power—is reviewed, with special attention given to the situation of the individual, his rights, and liberties. This study is based principally on the point of view of St. Thomas, but comparison is made with modern philosophic thought pertinent to the questions discussed. B

MURRAY, John C. *We Hold These Truths.* New York: Sheed and Ward, 1960.

A study of the issues in American political philosophy of special relevance to the place of the Catholic Church in American life.

The nature of unity and of social pluralism is investigated as the context for a more detailed review of some highly discussed public issues. B-C

See: G. Shuster, A 104 (1960) 183; ACSR 21 (1960) 371; AM 92 (1960) 18; F. Wilson, CHR 47 (1961) 41; T. Neill, CR 19 (1960) 23; CW 192 (1961) 217-21; J. Lerch, CM 25 (1961) 278; T. Corbishley, CR 47 (1962) 427; CC 11 (1961) 79-83; G. Dyer, D 46 (1961) 54-61; DR 80 (1962) 175; J. Costelloe, HPR 61 (1961) 808-14; I 74 (1960) 58; IER 97 (1962) 205; IR 34 (1961) 142; J. Hoffman, RR 21 (1962) 74; A. Hennessy, S 40 (1960) 68; SJR 53 (1961) 375-77; E. McCarthy, SO 11 (1961) 178; T 36 (1961) 149; TM 24 (1961) 111.

NEWMAN, Jeremiah. *Studies in Political Morality.* Dublin: Scepter, 1962.

PASSERIN d'ENTREVES, Allessandro. (ed.) *Aquinas: Selected Political Writings.* Trans. by J. Dawson. New York: Macmillan, 1959 (1954). 199 pp. Bibliography.

A selection of texts reflecting the political thought of St. Thomas. The context is provided in the introduction by a discussion of St. Thomas' approach and his notion of political obligation. The excerpts are from the chief political works, the *Summae,* and the *Commentaries* on the *Ethics* and the *Sentences.* B-D

PHILOSOPHY AND RECONSTRUCTION. See I.

PHILOSOPHY OF DEMOCRACY. See I.

PHILOSOPHY OF THE STATE. See I.

POLITICAL PHILOSOPHY. See I.

POWERS, Francis J. (ed.) *Papal Pronouncements on the Political Order.* Westminster, Md.: Newman, 1952. xii, 256 pp. Bibliography, index.

A thorough survey of the Catholic viewpoint on the social order. Excerpts from the writings of the Popes from Leo XIII to Pius XII concern the Church and citizens in the social order, the origin and nature of the state and civil authority, the purpose and function of the state, Church and state, law and liberty, and the international order. There are skillful chapter introductions and subtitles, along with an index and a bibliography of Papal documents in English. A-D

See: ABR 3 (1952) 374-75; ACSR 13 (1952) 139; AER 126 (1952) 480; AM 76 (1952) 58; CHR 39 (1953) 104-105; CR 37 (1952) 376; D 37 (1952) 314-15; HPR 52 (1952) 1123-26; SJR 46 (1954) 354; T 27 (1952) 600-601; Tm 16 (1953) 149-50; TS 13 (1952) 291; W 26 (1952) 383.

ROMMEN, Heinrich A. *The State in Catholic Thought: A Treatise in Political Philosophy.* St. Louis: Herder, 1945 (1935) . 745 pp. Index.

A comprehensive treatment of political philosophy conditioned by theology and revelation. A fine index makes it a valuable reference work as well as a source of collateral reading material for both teachers and students. The context is set by a review of the individual and social nature of man, and of the foundations of natural law and order. A study is made of the philosophy of the state in itself and its relations to the Church and to the community of nations. C-D

See: ACSR 7 (1946) 68-69; AM 63 (1946) 635; CHR 32 (1946) 224-25; C 44 (1946) 218-20; D 31 (1946) 52; HB 24 (1946) 94; HPR 47 (1946) 76; MS 24 (1947) 252-54; R 7 (1947) 317-18; RR 5 (1946) 139; Rp 9 (1947) 381-83; SJR 39 (1946) 171; T 22 (1947) 558-60.

RYAN, John A., and BOLAND, Francis J. *Catholic Principles of Politics (The State and the Church).* New York: Macmillan, 1940 (1922) . viii, 366 pp. Index.

The science of politics is discussed in the light of Catholic moral philosophy and theology concerning man as an independent social being, living under a natural moral law, and in possession of a supernatural destiny. The state is seen to exist for man, and political problems are solved in this context. C

See: A 27 (1922) 253; CW 117 (1923) 701-703.

SIMON, Yves R. *The Philosophy of Democratic Government* (Charles R. Walgreen Foundation Lecture, No. 2). Chicago, Ill.: University of Chicago Press, 1951. 324 pp. (Phoenix, P 67)

A scholarly presentation of democratic theory grounded on rational principles. The general theory of government is studied, with special attention to such elements as sovereignty, freedom, and equality. Catholic principles are seen to be compatible with those of democracy. B-C

> *See:* J. Meaney, C 55 (1951) 232-34; K. von Schuschnigg, MS 30 (1953) 242-4; L. Strauss, NS 26 (1952) 379-83; A. Hermens, RP 14 (1952) 556-58; K. von Schuschnigg, SO 2 (1952) 29-36; R. Allers, BT 10 (1951) 76.

THOMAS AQUINAS, Saint. *On Kingship to the King of Cyprus.* See XV.

———. *The Political Ideas of St. Thomas Aquinas.* See XV.

WARD, Leo. (ed.) *Ethics and the Social Sciences.* Notre Dame, Ind.: Notre Dame University Press, 1959. xiii, 127 pp. Bibliography.

A collection of papers that emphasize the philosophical foundations of relations between various cultures and societies. Man's knowledge of values and their relation to the social sciences are studied. This opens onto an excellent essay on culture and ethics by Christopher Dawson, which is followed by reflections on the philosophical presuppositions of dialogue between various cultures, societies, and faiths. B

> *See:* ACSR 20 (1959) 350; W. Drummond, SO 10 (1960) 329; RP 23 (1961) 110.

F. ECONOMIC ETHICS: PROPERTY, BUSINESS

BELLOC, Hilaire. *The Restoration of Property.* New York: Sheed and Ward, 1936.

———. *The Servile State.* London: Foulis, 1912.

BUNTING, James W. *Ethics for Modern Business Practice.* New York: Prentice-Hall, 1953.

CASSELMAN, Paul. *The Cooperative Movement.* New York: Philosophical Library, 1952.

CHESTERTON, G. K. *What's Wrong With the World.* New York: Dodd, Mead, 1910.

FLUBACHER, Joseph. *The Concept of Ethics in the History of Economics.* New York: Vintage Press, 1950.

GARRETT, Thomas. *Ethics in Business.* New York: Sheed and Ward, 1963. 181 pp. Bibliography, appendices.
A survey of the general principles and particular problems involved in business ethics. The work begins with a study of the notion of responsibility, the relation of the businessman to society, and the virtue of honesty. Special problems surveyed include the ethics of expense accounts, decision making, and personality testing. A-B
See: R. Baumhart, A 109 (1963) 360; W. Neidhart, AM 98 (1963) 25; A. Giunta, BS 23 (1963) 204; D. O'Shea, CR 22 (1963-1964) 81; D. O'Shea, CW 198 (1963) 188; T. McMahon, HPR 64 (1963) 268; T. Tobin, LG 52 (1964) 61; H. Johnston, S 43 (1963) 71.

————. *An Introduction into Some Ethical Problems of Modern American Advertising (Studia Socialia,* 6). Romae: Pontificia Universitas Gregoriana, 1961. 209 pp. Bibliography.
A fairly advanced study of the ethics of advertising. The general character and value of advertising are surveyed, followed by a study of the responsibilities implied in the power it exerts. C
See: SO 12 (1962) 91.

GEORGE, Henry. *Progress and Poverty.* New York: Schalkenbach Foundation, 1955 (1879).

GILL, Eric. *Money and Morals.* London: Faber and Faber, 1937.

HARTMAN, R. S. (ed.) *Profit Sharing Manual.* Columbus, Ohio: Council of Profit Sharing Industries, 1948.

HEWES, Thomas. *Decentralize for Liberty.* New York: Dutton, 1947.

JOHNSTON, Herbert. *Business Ethics.* 2d ed., revised. New York: Putnam, 1961 (1956). 305 pp.

A general survey of the principles and special areas of business ethics. The nature of ethics, rights, and justice is first investigated. This is followed by special studies of cooperation in injustice, problems of capital and labor, and other special areas. B-C

> *See:* CBE 8 (1956) 61; C. Quick, CW 184 (1956) 234; D 41 (1956) 386; J. Cronin, NS 31 (1957) 265; P. Harris, SO 7 (1957) 140.

KELSO, Louis, and ADLER, Mortimer. *The Capitalist Manifesto.* New York: Random House, 1958.

McDONALD, William J. *The Social Value of Property According to St. Thomas Aquinas: A Study in Social Philosophy* (The Catholic University of America, *Philosophical Studies,* No. 48). Washington, D. C.: The Catholic University of America Press, 1939. viii, 200 pp. Bibliography, index. (Paper)

A study of property in the philosophy of St. Thomas. The nature of property and of private ownership are studied both philosophically and historically. In this context their social dimension is underlined and related to modern social theories. B-C

> *See:* ER 101 (1939) 462.

McLEAN, George F. (ed.) *Philosophy in a Technological Culture.* See IX.

MERRILL, Harwood, *Responsibilities of Business Leadership.* Cambridge, Mass.: Harvard University Press, 1948.

MULCAHY, Richard. *Economics of Heinrich Pesch.* New York: Holt, Rinehart and Winston, 1952.

QUINN, Francis X. (ed.) *Ethics, Advertising and Responsibility.* Westminster: Canterbury, 1963.

ROSS, John E. *Cooperative Plenty.* St. Louis: Herder, 1941.

THOMPSON, Kenneth M. *Profit Sharing.* New York: Harper, 1949.

WARBASSE, James P. *Cooperative Democracy.* New York: Harper, 1942.

WIRTENBERGER, Henri J. *Morality and Business.* Chicago, Ill.: Loyola University Press, 1962.

WOELFEL, Br. LaSalle. *Business and Christian Virtues.* Austin, Texas: St. Edwards University Press, 1961. vii, 106 pp. Index.

A simple discussion of moral perspectives relevant to the businessman. The Christian conscience and the purpose of things are reflected upon. This provides the context for a review of the various virtues and their demands in the conduct of business. A-B

See: CBER 14 (1936) 28-32.

G. INDUSTRIAL ETHICS: MANAGEMENT, LABOR

ARES, Richard. *What Is Corporative Organization?* St. Louis: Central Bureau Press, 1939.

BORNE, Etienne, and HENRY, François. *The Philosophy of Work.* Trans. by F. Jackson from *Le travail et l'homme.* New York: Sheed and Ward, 1938 (1937). 221 pp.

A study of the history and nature of work. The history is traced from ancient times to the modern problems of workers in an industrialized society. In this section the book reflects the European conditions of the study's place and time of authorship. The social, moral, and religious dimensions of work are emphasized. A-B

BRUEHL, Charles. *The Pope's Plan for Social Reconstruction.* New York: Devin-Adair, 1939.

See: A 60 (1939) 577; D 24 (1939) 71-72; MS 16 (1939) 42; S 18 (1939) 376-77.

CALLAHAN, John D. *The Catholic Attitude toward a Familial Minimum Wage.* Washington, D. C.: Catholic University Press, 1936.

CRONIN, John F. *Catholic Social Action.* Milwaukee: Bruce, 1948.

————. *Catholic Social Principles: The Social Teachings of the Catholic Church Applied to American Economic Life.* Milwaukee: Bruce, 1955 (1950). xxviii, 803 pp. Index, appendices.

An application of social philosophies to the American economic scene. The principles of a Christian social order are studied in their philosophical foundations and compared to the positions of other philosophies. Particular attention is then given to problems of capital and labor, private property, and the state. Particular movements and problems in the United States are also studied. This work makes effective use of philosophy as well as economics. B-C

See: J. Schuyler, A 83 (1950) 627; J. Walsh, ACSR 11 (1950) 191-93; F. Drinkwater, AER 123 (1950) 437-42; Br. Justin, CE 21 (1950) 175; S. Theisen, CER 49 (1951) 211-12; J. Fitzsimmons, CR 35 (1951) 35-36; D 36 (1951) 49; F. Tyrrell, HPR 51 (1950) 88; G. Kelly, RR 10 (1951) 93-95; D. Boyle, S 30 (1950) 72; J. Redding, T 26 (1951) 615.

————. *Social Principles and Economic Life.* Milwaukee: Bruce, 1959. xxiii, 436 pp. Bibliography, index.

An exposition of the social order that addresses itself to both philosophical and Christian principles. Excerpts from Papal encyclicals are included, along with an extensive, up-to-date reading list and bibliography. A-B

See: B. Masse, A 101 (1959) 595; AM 90 (1959) 422; D 44 (1959) 27; IER 94 (1960) 256; IR 33 (1960) 24; S 38 (1959) 59; L. Brown, SO 9 (1959) 343; K. Quinn, St 49 (1960) 334.

DRUMMOND, William. *Social Justice*. Milwaukee: Bruce, 1955.

ENGLISH, Michael, and WADE, William. *Rebuilding the Social Order*. Chicago, Ill.: Loyola University Press, 1939.

FERREE, William. *The Act of Social Justice*. See X.

HUGHES, Philip. *The Pope's New Order*. New York: Macmillan, 1944.

HUSSLEIN, Joseph. *Christian Social Manifesto*. Milwaukee: Bruce, 1931. xxiv, 329 pp.
A presentation of the social thought of the encyclicals *Rerum novarum* of Leo XIII and *Quadragesimo anno* of Pius XI. The modern problem is stated and a study is made of the demands of justice and charity concerning property, state versus private ownership, and occupational groups. The importance of the social apostolate is indicated. B
   See: A 46 (1932) 582; CW 136 (1932) 251.

KILLEEN, Sylvester M. *The Philosophy of Labor According to St. Thomas Aquinas* (The Catholic University of America, *Philosophical Studies,* No. 49). Washington, D. C.: The Catholic University of America Press, 1939. xx, 148 pp. Bibliography, index. (Paper)
A study of the nature of labor within the framework of the philosophy of St. Thomas Aquinas. Its meaning, division, and dignity are reviewed, and the contemporary problem of the relation to rest and leisure is considered. B

KWANT, Remy C. *Philosophy of Labor* (Duquesne Studies, "Philosophical Series," No. 10). Trans. from *Arbeid en Leven*. Pittsburgh: Duquesne University Press, 1960. xi, 163 pp. Indices.
A profound, contemporary study of the paradox of human labor. The evolution of human thought on this subject is traced, and the Marxist position is given special attention. After the author has presented his own position, he proceeds to a discussion of

various contemporary practical questions, such as the world organization and humanization of labor, as well as the problem of the spiritual attitude of the worker. B-C

See: W. Willigan, ACSR 21 (1960) 182; D. Hodges, MS 38 (1961) 345; R. Allers, NS 35 (1961) 248; Sa 17 (1962) 138; SJR 53 (1960) 182.

McLEAN, Donald. *Morality of the Strike.* New York: Kenedy, 1921.

McLEAN, George F. (ed.) *Philosophy in a Technological Culture.* See X.

MELSEN, Andrew G. Van. *Science and Technology.* See V.

MICHEL, Virgil. *Christian Social Reconstruction.* See X.

MILLER, Raymond. *Forty Years After: Pius XI on the Social Order.* St. Paul: Radio Replies Press, 1948.

MUNIER, Joseph D. *Some Approximations to Pius X's "Industries and Professions."* Washington, D. C.: Catholic University Press, 1943.

NAUGHTON, James. *Pius XII on World Problems.* New York: America Press, 1943.

RE-ORGANIZATION OF SOCIAL ECONOMY: The Social Encyclical Developed and Explained, by Nell-Breuning, O. Trans. by B. Dempsey from *Die Soziale Enzyklika.* Milwaukee: Bruce, 1936. xi, 451 pp. Bibliography, index.

A thorough, authoritative analysis of the encyclical *Quadragesimo anno.* Suggestions in this encyclical are correlated with corresponding suggestions in *Rerum novarum,* the entire text of both encyclicals being appended. The discussion for the most part is restricted to the principles of a vocational order of society and economics. Abstract points are illustrated by practical examples. B-D

See: Bl 18 (1937) 870; CW 145 (1937) 382; S 16 (1937) 700.

RYAN, John A. *A Better Economic Order*. New York: Harper, 1935.

————. *Distributive Justice: The Right and Wrong of Our Present Distribution of Wealth*. 3d ed., revised. New York: Macmillan, 1942 (1916). xi, 357 pp. Bibliography, index. A classical study of distributive justice. The revision brings the statistics, economic developments, and social legislation up to the date of publication. Moral aspects of monopolies and wages are presented clearly, and the problem of unemployment is treated. A-C

See: CER 40 (1942) 378-80; CW 157 (1943) 336.

SMITH, William J. *Spotlight on Labor Unions*. New York: Duell, Sloan and Pearce, 1946.

————. *Spotlight on Social Order*. Rochester, N. Y.: Christopher Press, 1953.

TANNENBAUM, Frank. *A Philosophy of Labor*. New York: Knopf, 1951.

TONER, Jerome. *The Closed Shop*. Washington, D. C.: American Council on Public Affairs, 1944.

TREHEY, Harold F. *Foundations of a Modern Guild System*. Washington, D. C.: Catholic University Press, 1940.

WELTY, Eberhard. *A Handbook of Christian Social Ethics*. See X.

H. MARXIAN ETHICS: COMMUNISM, SOCIALISM

BERDYAEV, Nicholas. *The Origin of Russian Communism*. London: Bles, 1937.

BOBER, Mandell M. *Karl Marx's Interpretation of History.* Cambridge, Mass.: Harvard University Press, 1948.

BOCHENSKI, Innocentius M. *The Dogmatic Principles of Soviet Philosophy as of 1958.* Trans. by T. Blakeley from *Die dog-matischen Grundlagen der sowjetischen Philosophie.* Dord-recht, Holland: Reidel, 1964. xii, 78 pp. Index.
A synopsis of the principles in the official *Osnovy Marksistskoj filosofii.* The key official positions on the structure of dialectical materialism and its historical realization are stated in single sentences without commentary. D

BÖHM von BAWERK, Eugen. *Karl Marx and the Close of His System.* New York: Kelley, 1949.

CAMERON, James M. *Scrutiny of Marxism.* New York: Macmillan, 1948.

COLE, George D. *Meaning of Marxism.* London: Gollancz, 1948.

CONZE, Edward. *Introduction to Dialectical Materialism.* London: Chapman and Hall, 1935.

CORNFORTH, Maurice. *Dialectical Materialism: Introductory Course.* London: Lawrence and Wishart, 1952.

CROCE, Benedetto. *Historical Materialism and the Economics of Marx.* New York: Macmillan, 1914.

CROSSMAN, R. H. S. (ed.) *The God That Failed.* New York: Harper, 1949.

D'ARCY, Martin. *Communism and Christianity.* New York: Devin-Adair, 1957.

EASTMAN, Max. *Marxism: Is It a Science?* New York: Norton, 1940.

FEDERN, Karl. *Materialist Conception of History*. London: Macmillan, 1939.

GUEST, David. *Textbook of Dialectical Materialism*. New York: International Publishers, 1939.

GURIAN, Waldemar. *Bolshevism: Theory and Practice*. New York: Sheed and Ward, 1932.

———. (ed.) *The Soviet Union: Background, Ideology, and Reality*. Notre Dame: University of Notre Dame Press, 1951.

HOOK, Sidney. *From Hegel to Marx*. New York: Humanities Press, 1950.

———. *Toward the Understanding of Karl Marx*. New York: John Day, 1933.

HUNT, R. N. Carew. *Marxism, Past and Present*. New York: Macmillan, 1955.

———. *Theory and Practice of Communism*. New York: Macmillan, 1951.

HYDE, Douglas. *The Answer to Communism*. London: Paternoster Publications, 1949.

———. *I Believed*. New York: Putnam, 1950.

JOSEPH, Horace. *The Labor Theory of Value in Karl Marx*. London: Oxford University Press, 1923.

KAUTSKY, Karl. *Ethics and the Materialist Conception of History*. Chicago, Ill.: Kerr, 1907.

LINDSAY, Alexander. *Karl Marx's Capital*. London: Oxford University Press, 1925.

LUNN, Arnold. *The Science of World Revolution*. New York: Sheed and Ward, 1938.

McFADDEN, Charles J. *The Philosophy of Communism*. New York: Benziger, 1939. xx, 345 pp. Bibliography, index.
An eminently clear exposition and evaluation of communist philosophy. The first part consists of an orderly objective presentation of Marxist doctrine on nature, mind, history, the state, morality, revolution, and society. In the second part, in a parallel series of chapters, the philosophy of communism on these points is criticized. B-C
> See: AM 51 (1940) 250; C 31 (1939) 100; CHR 26 (1940) 143; CW 150 (1940) 503; D 24 (1939) 290-91; HPR 40 (1940) 814; MS 17 (1940) 38-39; S 19 (1940) 381; T 15 (1940) 177-78; Tm 2 (1940) 307-308.

MacMURRAY, John. *Philosophy of Communism*. London: Faber and Faber, 1933.

MARCUSE, Herbert. *Reason and Revolution: Hegel and the Rise of Social Theory*. New York: Humanities Press, 1954.

MAURIAC, François, *et al*. *Communism and Christians*. Westminster, Md.: Newman Press, 1949.

MAYO, Henry B. *Democracy and Marxism*. New York: Oxford University Press, 1955.

NEILL, Thomas, and COLLINS, James. *Communism: Why It Is and How It Works*. New York: Sheed and Ward, 1964. viii, 216 pp.
A study of the history and philosophy of Communism. The development of this thought is reviewed and its concrete realization is considered. B

PLAMENATZ, John. *What Is Communism?* London: National News Letter, 1947.

POSSONY, Stefan. *A Century of Conflict: Communist Techniques of World Revolution*. Chicago, Ill.: Regnery, 1953.

SCHUMPETER, Joseph. *Capitalism, Socialism, and Democracy.*
New York: Harper, 1950.

SELSAM, Howard. *Socialism and Ethics.* London: Lawrence,
1949.

SHAW, George Bernard, *et al. Essays in Fabian Socialism.* London: Constable, 1932.

SHEED, Frank. *Communism and Man.* London: Sheed and
Ward, 1938. xii, 247 pp.
A study of the questions raised by communism and their solution
in a Christian perspective. After an extensive study of communism, a Christian philosophy of man as a rational, social creature
is developed. The investigation of the insufficiencies of man leads
the author to a more detailed statement of man's relation to God.
A-B

> *See:* A 59 (1938) 525; AM 48 (1938) 346; C 28 (1938) 412; CHR 25 (1939)
> 251; DR 56 (1938) 500; S 18 (1938) 62; Ta 171 (1938) 770-71.

SHEEN, Fulton J. *Communism and the Conscience of the West.*
Indianapolis: Bobbs-Merrill, 1948.

SOMERVILLE, John. *Soviet Philosophy.* New York: Philosophical Library, 1946.

STRACHEY, John. *The Theory and Practice of Socialism.* New
York: Random House, 1936.

SWEEZY, Paul. *Socialism.* New York: McGraw-Hill, 1949.

VON MISES, Ludwig. *Socialism.* New Haven: Yale University
Press, 1951.

WETTER, Gustav A. *Dialectical Materialism: A Historical and
Systematic Survey of Philosophy in the Soviet Union.* Trans.
and revised by P. Heath from the 4th German ed. of *Der
dialektische Materialismus (Il materialismo dialettico sovie-*

tico). New York: Praeger, 1963 (1950). 609 pp. Bibliography. (Paper: U 536)

A profound study, written by an outstanding authority on communism, of the philosophy of communism in the historical perspective, not only of the Hegelian-Marxist dialectic, but of its official Soviet interpretation. The present volume is restricted to logic and the philosophy of nature, including the theory of knowledge. In a later volume, the notions of state, society, economy, religion, and historical materialism each will be studied. It is the author's thesis that this thought is not a philosophy, but a godless theology. The criticism is effective and original. C-D

See: Q. Lauer, A 100 (1959) 696; M. Harrington, C 70 (1959) 60; C. Mertens, NRT 85 (1963) 653; C. McFadden, NS 34 (1960) 384; A. Caponigi, PS 9 (1959) 152; R. Delaney, S 38 (1959) 63; J. Calvez, SO 9 (1959) 383; J. Reid, Tm 22 (1959) 580; C. Kassel, T 35 (1960) 299.

I. INTERNATIONAL ETHICS: WORLD COMMUNITY, WAR, PEACE[1]

ADLER, Mortimer. *How To Think About War and Peace.* New York: Simon and Schuster, 1944.

BATCHELDER, Robert. *The Irreversible Decision.* Boston: Houghton-Mifflin, 1962.

BENNETT, John. *Christians and the State.* New York: Scribner's, 1958.

DAWSON, Christopher. *Judgment of the Nations.* London: Sheed and Ward, 1943. v, 154 pp.

Principles for the reconstruction of the disintegrating pattern of Western culture at the time of the Second World War. The philosophical and religious roots of the disintegration are traced and

---

[1] See Noel Brown, "The Moral Problem of Modern Warfare: A Bibliography," in *Morality and Modern Warfare: The State of the Question,* ed. William J. Nagle (Baltimore: Helicon, 1960), pp. 151-68.

a statement is made of the need for the renewal of man's appreciation of Christian social principles of unity and order. This is a particularly literate statement concerning the modern dilemma and the need of religious insight for an understanding of the heritage of the West. B-C

See: ACSR 5 (1944) 70-71; AM 58 (1943) 122-23; Th 8 (1945) 136-46.

EPPSTEIN, John. *Catholic Tradition and the Law of Nations.* London: Burns, Oates, and Washbourne, 1935. xix, 525 pp. Index, appendix.

An erudite study of the relation of the development of the law of nations to the pattern of Catholic thought. This is studied first of all in the philosophy and theology of war and peace and the ethics of war. From this is seen to derive a more developed notion of the society of nations and its law. C-D

See: A 54 (1936) 479; AER 95 (1936) 319; Bl 17 (1936) 148; CER 34 (1936) 186; CHR 22 (1936) 64; CR 11 (1936) 253-55; CW 143 (1936) 326; DR 58 (1936) 281; IER 47 (1936) 549; JRI 6 (1936) 943; S 15 (1936) 445-46.

GIGON, Henri. *The Ethics of Peace and War.* London: Burns, Oates and Washbourne, 1935.

GONELLA, Guido. *A World To Reconstruct.* Trans. by T. Bouscaren from *Presupposti di un Ordine Internazionale.* Milwaukee: Bruce, 1944 (1942). xxx, 335 pp. Appendix.

Originally a series of articles written during the Second World War, concerning the foundations upon which a new international order could be built. These are seen to be, not force, but good faith, justice, and the rights of man. The implications of these principles for the distribution of wealth and other problems of the international sphere are developed. B-C

See: ACSR 5 (1944) 262-63; AM 60 (1944) 189; C 40 (1944) 573; CER 43 (1945) 120-21; AER 111 (1944) 473-74; D 29 (1944) 271-72; HB 23 (1945) 72; HPR 45 (1944) 79-80; IER 6 (1945) 70-71; RP 6 (1944) 529-30; RR 3 (1944) 422-23; S 24 (1944) 105; SJR 37 (1944) 247; T 20 (1945) 126-29; TS 5 (1944) 560-61.

HODGSON, Peter. *Nuclear Physics in Peace and War.* New York: Hawthorn, 1961.

HUTCHINS, Robert M. *St. Thomas and the World State* (The Aquinas Lecture, 1949) . Milwaukee: Marquette University Press, 1949. x, 58 pp.

A lecture on the universal dimensions of the political theory of St. Thomas Aquinas. These are shown to imply a notion of world law and of world government which can be a significant contribution to contemporary efforts. B-C

See: J. McKenna, A 83 (1950) 22; Bl 31 (1950) 345; F. Grogen, T 25 (1950) 348.

THE INTERNATIONAL UNION OF SOCIAL STUDIES. *Code of International Ethics*. Trans. and commentary by John Eppstein. Westminster, Md.: Newman, 1953. xiv, 256 pp. Index, appendices.

A translation of and commentary on the *Malines Code*, drawn up after the First World War by a group directed by Cardinal Mercier. The code concerns the rights and duties of states in war and peace. It takes into account the unequal development of various states and looks for the meaning of natural law in international society. The individual conscience is related to international morality. There is an extensive commentary preceding the text of the *Code*. B-D

JARRETT, Bede. *Social Theories of the Middle Ages*. New York: Frederick Ungar, 1966 (1926).

KAHN, Herman. *On Thermonuclear War*. Princeton: Princeton University Press, 1961.

KNOX, Ronald A. *God and the Atom*. New York: Sheed and Ward, 1945. viii, 166 pp.

An extended essay on moral adjustment to the atomic age. In the concrete context of the bombing of Japan, attitudes toward doubt and despair are examined and modes of hope are founded. A-B

See: C 43 (1946) 602-604; CW 163 (1946) 201; D 31 (1946) 68; HPR 46 (1946) 982; IM 74 (1946) 89-90; RP 8 (1946) 537; S 25 (1946) 544.

MacLEAN, Donald. *Dynamic World Order*. Milwaukee: Bruce, 1945.

MURRAY, Thomas E. *Nuclear Policy for War and Peace*. Cleveland: World, 1960.

NAGLE, William J. *Morality and Modern Warfare: The State of the Question*. Baltimore: Helicon, 1960.

THE NATURAL LAW AND INTERNATIONAL RELATIONS. See I.

PLATER, Charles. *A Primer of Peace and War*. New York: Kenedy, 1915.

PRINCIPLES FOR PEACE. Washington, D.C.: National Catholic Welfare Conference, 1943.

RAMSEY, Paul. *War and the Christian Conscience*. Durham, N.C.: Duke University Press, 1961.

RYAN, John K. *Modern War and Basic Ethics*. Milwaukee: Bruce, 1940 (1933). ix, 142 pp. Bibliography, index.
A survey of Thomistic principles pertinent to a moral evaluation of modern warfare. Within a basic understanding of the nature of peace and war, the character of a just modern war and its execution is discussed. B

> *See:* A 64 (1941) 444; CHR 27 (1942) 528; CW 152 (1941) 759; ER 104 (1941) 91; ER 116 (1947) 421; MS 18 (1941) 39.

SCOTT, James B. *The Catholic Conception of International Law*. Washington, D.C.: Georgetown University Press, 1934.

STEIN, Walter. *Nuclear Weapons: A Catholic Response*. New York: Sheed and Ward, 1961.

STRATMANN, Franziskus. *The Church and War*. New York: Kenedy, 1929.

———. *War and Christianity Today*. London: Blackfriars, 1956.

STURZO, Luigi. *Nationalism and Internationalism.* New York: Roy, 1946.

THOMPSON, Charles S. (ed.) *Morals and Missiles.* London: Clarke, 1959.

VANN, Gerald. *Morality and War.* London: Burns, Oates and Washbourne, 1939.

WRIGHT, John J. *National Patriotism in Papal Teaching.* Westminster, Md.: Newman, 1943.

CHAPTER XI

Esthetics: Philosophy of Art

This chapter contains works on beauty, esthetics, the philosophy of art, and artistic intuition. The works reflect investigations carried out: in rational psychology, toward an analysis of the faculties operative in the perception of beauty; in metaphysics, toward an understanding of beauty itself as a transcendental; in the arts, as objects of reflection as to their processes; and in ethics, for the social implications of the arts and for their contribution to a unified appreciation of all the elements in a given act. This last element has led to works of considerable epistemological value, which compare the artistic with the mystical experience and study the contribution to knowledge made by the affective powers of the subject. Such works, when primarily epistemological in character, have been included in Chapter IV; those concentrating on the elements of artistic experience have been included in this section.

The reader is referred to Chapter III of *A Bibliography of Christian Philosophy and Contemporary Issues* by the same editor.

ADLER, Mortimer J. *Art and Prudence: A Study in Practical Philosophy.* New York: Longmans, Green, 1937. xiv, 686 pp.

A study of the problem of moral and political criticism of the fine arts. Seeing the problem as occasioned by conflicts in the operation of prudence and art, the author discusses the relation of these virtues, and places this discussion in the context of politics and of the various modern art forms. There are extensive notes. C

See: Bl 18 (1937) 853-56; A 59 (1938) 190; C 28 (1938) 221-22; CW 145 (1937) 505; LA 6 (1938) 151-53; NS 11 (1937) 272-75.

CALLAHAN, John L. *A Theory of Esthetics, According To the Principles of St. Thomas Aquinas* (The Catholic University of America, *Philosophical Studies,* No. 16). Washington, D.C.: The Catholic University of America Press, 1947 (1927). 132 pp. Bibliography. (Paper)

An outline of the theory of esthetics as found in St. Thomas Aquinas. The subject is studied first in its passive aspects by a review of the nature and conditions of beauty and its relation to the true and the good. Then the active aspects of art, its morality, and its relation to the ideal and the real are studied. The discussion of metaphysical beauty is rather confusedly related to the problems of art. B-C

CHAPMAN, Emmanuel. *St. Augustine's Philosophy of Beauty.* See XIV.

CORY, Herbert E. *The Significance of Beauty in Nature and Art.* Milwaukee: Bruce, 1947. xv, 248 pp. Bibliography, index.

A study of the nature and meaning of art. There is a sympathetic presentation of subjective and objective views of art from prehistoric to modern times, with special emphasis on St. Thomas Aquinas and Aristotle. The analysis of post-Renaissance and contemporary non-Scholastic esthetics is critical, with the synthesis of modern and Thomistic speculations not fully successful. The relation of esthetics to the other major branches of philosophy is reviewed. The style is more lyrical than scientific. A-B

See: CW 167 (1948) 85-86; TS 9 (1948) 333-34.

DUFFY, John A. *A Philosophy of Poetry Based on Thomistic Principles* (The Catholic University of America, *Philosophical Studies*, No. 83) . Washington, D.C.: The Catholic University of America Press, 1945. xi, 258 pp. Bibliography, index. (Paper)

A study of the philosophical principles pertinent to a comprehension of the nature of poetry. A discussion of the nature and experience of beauty provides the context for a review of the psychology and metaphysics of art. This, in turn, is the basis on which the author studies the genesis of poetry, including the function of word and will. C

See: BL 28 (1947) 77; MS 24 (1947) 186-87; Tm 9 (1946) 588-97.

GILBY, Thomas. *Poetic Experience: An Introduction to Thomist Aesthetic* ("Essays in Order," No. 137) . London: Sheed and Ward, 1934. 114 pp.

A helpful general statement of Thomistic esthetics, leaning rather toward romanticism. Rational knowledge is contrasted with the poetic experience. This is situated not in emotion or sense, but in an intuition understood as a moving experience in which the mind possesses a substance. This position would be disputed by many scholars. B-C

See: A 53 (1935) 136; C 21 (1935) 686; CW 140 (1935) 634.

GILSON, Etienne. *Choir of Muses.* Trans. by M. Ward from *L'école des Muses.* New York: Sheed and Ward, 1953 (1951) . 196 pp.

A statement of general principles on the nature of art drawn from the stories of six artists, in which poetic vision is continually related to mystical experience. In the final two chapters art is related to Eros, and the artist to the saint. B

See: M. Gable, ABR 5 (1954) 358; R. Sharrock, Bl 34 (1953) 565; J. Simons, C 59 (1953) 96; E. Peters, CW 78 (1953) 156; B. Moss, DR 72 (1954) 122; E. Sewell, DR 228 (1954) 477; M. Grace, Rn 7 (1954) 91; S 33 (1953) 76.

———. *Painting and Reality* ("Bollingen Series," No. 35; The A. W. Mellon Lectures in the Fine Arts, No. 4) . New York: Pantheon, 1957. 367 pp. Bibliography. (Meridian: M 79)

A review of traditional esthetic issues, with special emphasis on modern art. Attention is given to the material realizations of form in relation to imitation, creation, and beauty. There is a philosophical analysis in which the intellectual significance of painting is contrasted with the merely representative value of pictures. B-C

See: G. Carey, CAQ 21 (1957) 28-31; Sa 15 (1960) 150; M. McNamee, T 33 (1958) 123; Ta 211 (1958) 360-61.

HAMM, Victor M. *Language, Truth and Poetry* (The Aquinas Lecture, 1960). Milwaukee: Marquette University Press, 1960. 74 pp.

A lecture on whether poetry can be said to express truth. The positions of the logical positivists and the mythologists are examined. The author then proceeds to show how poetry expresses truth by the use of symbols and figures. B-C

See: PS 11 (1961) 310; St 50 (1961) 459.

LaDRIERE, James C. *Directions in Contemporary Criticism and Literary Censorship* (The Gabriel Richard Lecture, 1953). Milwaukee: Bruce, 1953. 114 pp.

A study of the situation of literary criticism in America today. Various trends are noted and evaluated. There is an indication of the philosophical foundations of these orientations. B-C

LECHNER, Robert. *The Aesthetic Experience.* Chicago, Ill.: Regnery, 1953. 144 pp. Bibliography.

A compressed account and evaluation of some modern understanding of the esthetic experience, in which Maurice de Wulf and Jacques Maritain are given particular attention. The author's personal views on the subject, it has been suggested, would benefit by greater attention to the importance of analogy to the subject. B-C

See: C. Lehner, NS 28 (1954) 482; J. Collins, T 29 (1954) 292.

LEEUW, Gerardus Van der. *Sacred and Profane Beauty.* Trans. by D. Green from *Vom Heiligen in der Kunst.* New York:

Holt, Rinehart and Winston, 1963 (1932). 357 pp. Bibliography, index.

A phenomenological approach to the relation of art to religion. By using the dance as the dominating image, art is related to religion in terms of the movement of God toward man and man toward God. The problem of sacred images is treated, and apparent divergences between art and religion are likened to those between the flesh and the spirit. B-C

See: A 109 (1963) 180; C 78 (63) 513; F. Burkel, IPQ 4 (1964) 162; HPR 63 (1963) 997.

LITTLE, Arthur. *The Nature of Art: The Shield of Pallas.* London: Longmans, Green, 1947. x, 264 pp.

A study of the nature and dimensions of art, in which art is related to human reason rather than to mystical experience. While realized by human craftmanship, its end, it is noted, is not simply the beauty of the work itself. Instead, art is seen as pleasing by the invocation of beauty which is beyond art itself, and which invites contemplation. B-C

See: CR 28 (1947) 209-11; IR 75 (1947) 454-57; Ta 190 (1947) 170.

MARITAIN, Jacques. *Art and Poetry.* Trans. by E. Mathews from *Frontières de la poésie et autres essais.* London: P. L., Editions Poetry London, 1945 (1935). 75 pp.

A threefold analysis of esthetics, clear in thought and expression, in which painting, the novel, and music are discussed in relation to outstanding figures in these fields. Esthetics is seen to be directed to a theological end and an analogy is drawn between poetic knowledge and the creative knowledge of God. Though philosophical, the work is at times overly impressionistic. B

See: C 39 (1943) 42-43; CER 42 (1944) 61-62; CW 158 (1943) 212-13; FS 25 (1944) 197-98; LA 12 (1944) 92; S 23 (1944) 380.

————. *Art and Scholasticism* and *The Frontiers of Poetry.* Trans. by J. Evans from the 3d ed., revised, of *Art et scholastique.* New York: Scribner's, 1964 (1930). vi, 234 pp. Bibliography, appendices. (Paper)

A classical statement of Scholastic philosophy on the fine arts.

Art is presented as a habit of the practical intellect. Much is made of the necessity of judging art by intrinsic esthetic norms. The approach is vigorous, penetrating, and at times difficult. Extensive notes, four appendices on St. Thomas Aquinas and religious art, and "The Frontiers of Poetry" complete the volume. B

See: A 43 (1930) 214; C 12 (1930) 530; C 76 (1962) 383; CW 132 (1930) 249; DR 187 (1930) 201-15; DR 188 (1931) 134-36 (reply); A. Little, St 19 (1930) 467-80; T 5 (1930) 261-71.

————. *Creative Intuition in Art and Poetry* ("Bollingen Series," No. 35; The A. W. Mellon Lectures in the Fine Arts, No. 1). New York: Pantheon, 1955. 339 pp. (Meridian: M 8)

A series of lectures on creative intuition as the basis of artistic genius. There is a penetrating survey of ancient and modern philosophy, and of Eastern and Western art. The intellectual character of the poetic process is presented, along with a well-balanced understanding of the subjective elements. This leads to a search for a place in the Scholastic synthesis on man for a union of the intellectual and subjective elements. The import of this in the actual works of art themselves is studied and examples are quoted. B-D

See: V. Hamm, A 89 (1953) 302; D. Moody, Bl 35 (1954) 491; J. Ryan, CAQ 19 (1955) 29; CC 4 (1953) 79; C. Hart, CER 51 (1953) 706; J. Sheerin, CW 177 (1953) 476; P. Kelley, DR 73 (1955) 199-203; L. Bondy, LA 21 (1953) 131; C. Hart, NS 28 (1954) 231; P. Connolly, PS 7 (1957) 193; F. Connolly, S 20 (1953) 89-94; W. Lynch, T 28 (1953) 459; A. Bertram, Ta 203 (1954) 271; T. Heath, Th 17 (1954) 583.

————. *The Responsibility of the Artist.* New York: Scribner's, 1960. 120 pp.

A study of the relation of art to morality. The stress on inner norms of evaluation in *Art and Scholasticism* is balanced here by a review of the artist's relation to the community. This provides the context for such considerations as "art for art's sake" or for the people, censorship, and the artist's love of truth. B-C

See: H. Kenny, C 18 (1960) 26; J 7 (1960) 48; J. Charlot, LA 28 (1960) 111; T. Gilby, NLF 6 (1961) 161; T. Heath, Th 23 (1960) 613.

————, and MARITAIN, Raïssa. *The Situation of Poetry: Four*

Essays on the Relations between Poetry, Mysticism, Magic, and Knowledge. Trans. by M. Suther from *Situation de la poésie.* New York: Philosophical Library, 1955 (1938). 85 pp.

A technical and penetrating philosophical discussion of the nature of poetry. Raïssa Maritain compares magic, poetry, and mysticism for their various contents and approaches. Jacques Maritain presents a profound analysis of poetic knowledge and the creative character of poetic experience. The remarkable amount of wisdom and insight in this work demands some knowledge of ontology. B-C

See: AER 132 (1955) 283-84; AM 82 (1955) 23; CW 181 (1955) 238; D 40 (1955) 297; SJR 49 (1956) 63.

ROTHER, Aloysius J. *Beauty: A Study in Philosophy.* Philadelphia: Reilly, 1924 (1917). 137 pp.

A survey of questions concerning beauty—its nature, its relation to God, and its objective character and standards. A-B

See: A 16 (1917) 500; CW 105 (1917) 123.

SPARGO, Emma J. *The Category of the Aesthetic in the Philosophy of St. Bonaventure.* See XVI.

VERSFELD, Martin. *The Perennial Order.* See II.

WATKIN, Edward I. *Poets and Mystics.* New York: Sheed and Ward, 1953. 318 pp.

A collection of essays on the individual spiritual writers referred to in the title as poets and mystics. These particular essays are complemented by two comparative studies on poetry and mysticism and on drama and religion. Esthetic consciousness as expressive is distinguished from mystic consciousness as experiencing, while their relation to the same ultimate goal is recognized. While the work manifests clarity and erudition, at times it involves caricature. B-C

See: C. Boehm, AM 79 (1954) 25; R. Sharrock, Bl 34 (1953) 565-66; E. Geissman, C 60 (1954) 121; P. Duhamel, A 91 (1954) 384; CCr 6 (1954)

240; IER 82 (1954) 455; J. Morral, St 44 (1955) 124; J. Sabastian, T 30 (1955) 136; D. Schlezal, Ta 202 (1953) 473.

WULF, Maurice De. *Art and Beauty*. Trans. by M. Udell from *Art et beauté*. St. Louis: Herder, 1950 (1920). ix, 213 pp. Index.

A readable and illuminating series of lectures reestablishing objectivism in art. Esthetics is considered in relation to metaphysics, ethics, and psychology. The inductive examination of works of art themselves is considered. A-B

See: C. Miltner, AM 73 (1951) 730; D 36 (1951) 127; B. Byrne, ABR 2 (1951) 120.

WEISS, Paul. *Religion and Art* (The Aquinas Lecture, 1963). Milwaukee: Marquette University Press, 1963. 112 pp.

A discussion of various aspects of art in relation to the fulfillment of human life and to religion. Beginning from the premise that man cannot do all that he ought in order to have a full life, the spheres of art and religion are investigated and the special character of religious art as having value for both is noted. B-C

See: A 109 (1963) 180; C. McNaspy, LA 31 (1963) 118; R. Blackwell, MS 41 (1963) 85; V. Duminuco, TS 24 (1963) 738.

CHAPTER XII

Philosophy of Education

This chapter is composed principally of general works on the philosophy of education. Few of the works are exclusively philosophical, since most add material from experimental psychology, educational methods, administration, and history. The philosophical content is drawn principally from rational psychology and ethics, though some works turn effectively to logic, epistemology and metaphysics. The extent of the philosophical content is usually indicated in the annotations below.

Along with general works on the philosophy of education, there are also some books of a more concentrated character on particular problems. These concern the particular function of philosophy in integrating college education, the role of the state, the interrelation of freedom and formation, and the particular contribution demanded of education in the present cultural situation.

The reader is referred to Chapter VIII of *A Bibliography of Christian Philosophy and Contemporary Issues* by the same editor.

AVALOS, Beatrice. *New Men for New Times: A Christian Philosophy of Education.* New York: Sheed and Ward, 1962. 182 pp.

A plan for the education of the modern Christian. The origin of the problematic of contemporary man is described along with the naturalistic solutions of Marx and Dewey. The principles of Christian thought which have special relevance to contemporary man are stated, and a plan for education is drawn in their light. A-B

See: J. Sanders, RR 22 (1963) 595.

BROWN, Anthony. *Discipline Concepts in Education.* Boston: St. Paul, 1964.

A study of the understanding of the relation of discipline to the field of education. The various philosophies of education are reviewed on this topic. C

CARRON, Malcolm, and CAVANAUGH, Alfred D. (eds.) *Readings in the Philosophy of Education.* 3d ed. Detroit: University of Detroit Press, 1963 (1959). 423 pp.

A collection of papers by some of the most outstanding and forward-looking philosophers of recent times. They treat the nature of the human intelligence and its learning processes, as well as the type of Christian intellectualism needed and the way of developing it through teaching. B-C

CONWAY, Pierre H. *Principles of Education: A Thomistic Approach.* Washington, D.C.: Thomist Press, 1960. xiii, 204 pp. Bibliography, index, exercises.

A study of the meaning of the educational process, strongly emphasizing the role of the three societies: family, church, and state. Within this framework, the four causes of education are detailed. This outline is technical in nature. B-C

See: CE 32 (1961) 198; CER 59 (1961) 275; P. Philibert, D 46 (1961) 61-65; IER 96 (1961) 261; MS 39 (1962) 303.

COSTANZO, Joseph F. *This Nation Under God: Church, State and Schools in America.* New York: Herder and Herder, 1964. 448 pp. Appendix, index.

A study of the place of religion in education in America. The first half of the work reviews the history of religious liberty and the place of religion in the public school system. The remainder of the work is concerned with the problem of federal aid and the religious school. A-B

CUNNINGHAM, William. *The Pivotal Problems of Education: An Introduction to the Christian Philosophy of Education.* New York: Macmillan, 1949. xix, 588 pp. Bibliography, index, appendix.

A strongly developed text on the philosophy relevant to the education of the Christian. Four basically different modern approaches to the philosophy of education are indicated, as is the philosophical context for an appreciation of the ends of the education of man as a social being and as a Christian. The required means are then detailed. The philosophy of the curriculum, and values in American democracy are considered, though the distinction between philosophy and theology is not well observed. B-C

DAWSON, Christopher. *Crisis of Western Education.* New York: Sheed and Ward, 1961. vi, 246 pp.

A study of education within the broad framework of the history of Western culture. Liberal education is related to the humanist, nationalist, and technological influences. In contrast, Christian education is related to its cultural context and to its theological foundations. Specific programs by John J. Malloy for the study of Christian culture are included. B-C

> *See:* A 105 (1961) 85; AER 146 (1962) 283; AM 94 (1961) 20; M. Wileman, Bl 43 (1962) 148; P. Hallinan, CHR 47 (1961) 398; G. Beck, CR 47 (1962) 379; C 74 (1961) 356; CSJ 61 (1961) 6; D 46 (1961) 250-54; DR 80 (1962) 185; HPR 61 (1961) 915; F. Wade, MS 39 (1962) 263-67; B. Schlesinger, RE 56 (1961) 458; L. Ward, RP 25 (1961) 531-34; RR 21 (1962) 290; T. Neill, SJ 54 (1961) 124; A. Beales, Ta 215 (1961) 1048; J. Lawler, TS 22 (1961) 504.

DEFERRARI, Roy J. *A Complete System of Catholic Education Is Necessary.* Boston: St. Paul, 1964. 72 pp.

A reply to the work of M. Ryan, *Are Parochial Schools the Answer?* The author sets his consideration of this question within the context of an explanation of the philosophy of education which stresses its integration. A

DUBAY, Thomas E. *The Philosophy of the State as Educator.* Milwaukee: Bruce, 1959. xii, 237 pp.

A study of the place of the state in the educational field. The foundation of the study is laid in a comparison of the natural law understanding of man and society with other philosophical positions on the relation of the individual and the state. The question of the state as the primary educator is discussed. A-C

See: G. Timone, CL 6 (1960) 331-37; CE 31 (1960) 242; J. Whalen, CER 58 (1960) 63.

DUPUIS, Adrian, and NORDBERG, Robert. *Philosophy and Education: A Total View.* Milwaukee: Bruce, 1964. 334 pp.

A history of the philosophy of education from early Christian times to today. The context is set by a statement of the conflict in modern education, and special attention is given to the many contemporary American philosophies and to the understanding of education which they imply. C

FITZPATRICK, Edward. *Philosophy of Education.* Milwaukee: Bruce, 1953. xiv, 477 pp. Index, glossary.

A broadly ranging reflective study of many matters relevant to education. Strictly philosophical issues are treated very briefly. Along with a consideration of the nature of man, there are chapters on psychology, sociology, and religion. B

See: J. Tracy, CSJ 53 (1943) 28; J. Wise, TS 14 (1953) 645.

GALLAGHER, Donald and Idella. (eds.) *The Education of Man: The Educational Philosophy of Jacques Maritain.* Garden City, N.Y.: Doubleday, 1962. 191 pp. Bibliography, index, appendices.

A collection of the writings of Maritain which, together with his *Education at the Crossroads,* constitutes a broad survey of his thought in the field of education. The work includes studies on the Christian philosophy of education and its relation to the humanities, morality, and freedom. B-C

See: A 108 (1963) 101; CC 13 (1963) 127.

————. (ed.) *Some Philosophers on Education*. Milwaukee: Marquette University Press, 1956. xiii, 95 pp.

A collection of papers on the educational philosophy of thinkers from Aristotle to Dewey. The topics are capably treated, and the whole work shows the insight which can be provided by philosophy concerning the role of education in a Christian humanism. B-C

See: CSJ 57 (1957) 42; A. Farrell, NS 32 (1958) 415-17; T. Openaker, P 19 (1963) 848; St 46 (1957) 368.

HOVRE, Franz De. *Catholicism and Education*. Trans. by E. Jordan from *Le Catholicisme: ses pédagogues; sa pédagogie*. New York: Benziger, 1934 (1930) . xx, 501 pp.

A study of the principles of Catholic philosophy of education and of its most outstanding proponents. After outlining the principles of a Catholic philosophy of life and of education, the author describes the development of this thought by such men as J. Spalding, J. Newman, D. Mercier, and O. Willman. B-C

See: AER 91 (1934) 324; CHR 21 (1936) 491; MS 12 (1935) 44; T 10 (1935) 142-46.

————. *Philosophy and Education: The Modern Educational Theories of Naturalism, Socialism and Naturalism; a Textbook for Normal Schools and Teacher's Colleges*. Trans. by E. Jordan from *Essai de philosophie pédagogique*. New York: Benziger, 1931 (1927) . 443 pp. Bibliography.

This study of the variety of modern educational philosophies was followed by his *Catholicism and Education,* which presents a more positive statement of his own Christian philosophy of education. B-C

See: G. Shuster, CER 29 (1921) 321-27.

JOHNSTON, Herbert. *A Philosophy of Education*. New York: McGraw-Hill, 1963. xv, 362 pp.

The context for this study is set by a review of the sciences and of the nature of man. The nature, types, and aims of education, as well as modern philosophies of education are then discussed. B

See: E. Kevane, CER 61 (1963) 350.

KANE, William T. *Some Principles of Education.* Chicago, Ill.: Loyola University Press, 1938. ix, 215 pp.

A study of some fundamental questions dealing with education. The work is not very philosophical, except for some sections on the person to be educated and on the objectives of the educational process. These points are accompanied by sections on the agencies and processes of education. A

See: CER 37 (1939) 283; MS 16 (1939) 93.

KELLY, William A. *Educational Psychology* ("Science and Culture Series"). 4th ed. Milwaukee: Bruce, 1956 (1953). xxiv, 597 pp.

A classical treatment of the psychology of the educational process. The nature of the mental powers and their growth and adjustment are treated. The work is philosophically aware, but does not enter deeply into philosophical questions. B

See: CW 138 (1934) 761; HPR 34 (1934) 778; MS 12 (1935) 44.

KEVANE, Eugene. *Augustine the Educator: A Study in the Fundamentals of Christian Formation.* Westminster, Md.: Newman, 1964. xiv, 446 pp. Bibliography, index.

A study of the thought of Augustine on education and its significance for the modern world. The education of Augustine himself is reviewed, along with his thought on Christian philosophy and the pattern of the arts. This material is then related to the modern scene in a number of chapters. C

LEEN, Edward. *What Is Education?* New York: Sheed and Ward, 1944. 288 pp.

A penetrating, but nontechnical discussion of a series of questions on the nature of education and its orientation. These range from the mind, the relative place of the different subjects, and the work of unfolding the personality, to the determination of the authentically true, good, and beautiful. A-B

See: A 71 (1944) 133; ACSR 5 (1944) 138-39; AER 111 (1944) 153-54; AM 60 (1944) 13; Bl 25 (1944) 310; D 29 (1944) 124-25; HPR 44 (1944) 947-48; IER 63 (1944) 67; St 32 (1943) 577-79; T 19 (1944) 504-507; Ta 183 (1944) 249; Th 7 (1944) 421-25.

McGUCKEN, William. *The Catholic Way in Education* ("Religion and Culture Series"). Milwaukee: Bruce, 1937. xvii, 131 pp. Index, appendix.

A study of the more properly spiritual and Catholic concerns in the educational process. The nature of a liberal education is described. The development of character formation, with its implications for the supernatural, is treated against a background of modern educational trends. The philosophical elements infuse the whole, but are not given a developed separate treatment. A-B

See: A 51 (1934) 354; AER 91 (1934) 631; CW 140 (1934) 248; HPR 36 (1936) 1006; MS 12 (1935) 44; S 13 (1934) 700; T 9 (1934) 498.

McLEAN, George F. (ed.) *Philosophy and the Integration of Contemporary Catholic Education.* Washington, D.C.: The Catholic University of America Press, 1962. x, 366 pp. Bibliography, index. (Paper)

A study of the contribution of philosophy to the unification of college education. The capacity of the mind to know and the unity of truth provide the basic principles for this study, which includes an investigation of the relation of philosophy to the various parts of the curriculum. The meaning of this insight into unity and order for the personal development of the student is also studied. B-C

MARIQUE, Pierre. *The Philosophy of Christian Education* ("Prentice-Hall Education Series"). New York: Prentice-Hall, 1939. xv, 347 pp. Index.

A simple text on the nature and aims of the philosophy of education. Various types of philosophy and their educational implications are discussed and the different areas and systems of education are singled out for separate attention. A-B

See: AM 49 (1939) 666; C 29 (1939) 612-13; MS 16 (1939) 92; NS 14 (1940) 84; T 14 (1939) 315.

MARITAIN, Jacques. *Education at the Crossroads*. New Haven: Yale University Press, 1963 (1943). 120 pp. Index. (Yale Paperbounds: Y 15)

A particularly literate discussion of the aims and dynamics of education. The place of the liberal arts is stressed, and the problems of the times are reviewed with pertinent suggestions for their confrontation. This work will long remain a classic to be read by all concerned with the nature of education in our society. B-C

See: A 71 (1944) 499-500; C 38 (1943) 542-43; CER 43 (1945) 53-55; D 29 (1944) 40-41; FS 25 (1944) 110-11; MS 21 (1943) 53-54; Ta 183 (1944) 296; Th 7 (1944) 415-18.

O'BRIEN, Kevin J. *The Proximate Aim of Education*. Washington, D.C.: The Catholic University of America Press, 1958. x, 267 pp.

A doctoral study of the goal toward which the educational process is directed. The general nature of final causality is used as a background for the review of various opinions on the purpose of education, which is then studied more in depth within the context of the cooperation of man and God, with the implications being drawn for the field of education. C-D

See: J. Whalen, CER 56 (1958) 566; CSJ 58 (1958) 8; D 44 (1959) 200; HPR 59 (1959) 393; P. Birch, PS 8 (1958) 236.

PHILOSOPHY OF EDUCATION. See I.

REDDEN, John D. and RYAN, Francis A. *A Catholic Philosophy of Education*. Revised ed. Milwaukee: Bruce, 1956 (1942). ix, 601 pp. Bibliography, index.

An extensive text that combines a study of philosophical trends, with their implications for the various aspects of education. The first part studies those to be educated and the relation of the various disciplines in the overall process of education. The second part is a study of various philosophies of education and a review of the characteristics which should be possessed by education in a democratic society. This work has proven to be one of the most effective for capable students. B-C

See: A 67 (1942) 635; CER 40 (1942) 565; CSJ 42 (1942) 17; CW 153

(1942) 366-67; JRI 13 (1943) 404; MS 20 (1942) 51-52; S 22 (1942) 252-53; T17 (1942) 571.

THE ROLE OF PHILOSOPHY IN THE CATHOLIC LIB-
ERAL COLLEGE. See I.

RYAN, John A., and MILLAR, F. X. *Catholic Principles of
Politics*. See X.

SHIELDS, Thomas E. *Philosophy of Education* ("The Catholic
University of America Pedagogical Series," No. 5) . Washington, D.C.: Catholic Educational Press, 1917. 446 pp.

A collection of reflections, not intended to constitute a text, in
which the nature, aims, and agencies of education are discussed.
A

See: A 17 (1917) 220.

SMITH, Vincent E. *The School Examined: Its Aim and Content*.
Milwaukee: Bruce, 1960. xiii, 300 pp.

An excellent treatment of the problem of integrating the college
curriculum. The accent is on organizing content according to the
order of knowledge, which should be reflected in the order of the
parts of philosophy. This work has been called the best single
work on education. It might also be termed the most meaningful
on the order in which philosophy should be studied. B-C

See: A 104 (1961) 522; BR 16 (1961) 79; CE 32 (1961) 362; CER 59
(1961) 205; D 46 (1961) 156; MS 38 (1961) 350-54; TS 22 (1961) 348; Tm
24 (1961) 667.

WADE, Francis C. *Teaching and Morality*. Chicago, Ill.: Loyola
University Press, 1963. vii, 270 pp.

A very capable discussion of the relation of teaching to moral
training. The problem studied is the relation of education to
both knowledge and value. The solution is developed through reflections on the nature of reasoned assent, the place of subject
matter in this assent, and its relation to moral choice. This work
will be important in assisting the philosophically aware teacher
to exercise his profession with full recognition of the freedom of
the student in his pursuit of truth. C

WARD, Leo. *Philosophy of Education*. Chicago, Ill.: Regnery, 1963. 311 pp.

A freely ranging discussion of some key issues in the field of education. The place of the teacher and the student, together with the ends of education and values are treated. Liberal education is considered in relation to the American scene. A-B

See: P. Lambert, A 109 (1963) 316; AM 98 (1963) 28; C 78 (1963) 567; J. Maguire, CC 8 (1963) 33; E. Kevane, CER 61 (1963) 350.

WOLFE, John M. *Introduction to the Study of Human Conduct and Character. A Discussion of the Elements and Agencies That Factor in Character Education*. New York: Benziger, 1930. 213 pp. xxviii, 213 pp.

A statement of those philosophical principles concerning a man's moral character which are important in the field of social work. In relation to modern ethical systems the nature of free will, imputability, and self-control are studied. Practical orientation is given concerning aids in character education. Of use to most social workers. A-B

YZERMANS, Vincent A. (ed.) *Pope Pius XII and Catholic Education*. St. Meinrad, Ind.: Grail, 1957. xv, 180 pp. (Paper)

Twenty-one addresses of Pius XII, chosen for their value as typical expressions of the thinking of the Church about various areas of education. The teacher, the student, the content of the curriculum, and the relation of its parts are considered and related to the religious training of the student. A-C

CHAPTER XIII

Philosophy of History

This chapter is composed of works on the philosophy of history.[1] These works often have notable theological elements, rooted in the position that history, as more than a mere chronicle, is founded on the appreciation of God as creator and heightened by an appreciation of Christ as Savior. Since the first of these notions is also philosophical, the thought which it specifies retains an authentically philosophical character. These works often contain extensive critical studies of philosophies of history outside the area of Christian philosophy. It might also be noted that Chapter XIII contains relevant studies of the importance of time in the unfolding of human potentialities.

The reader is referred to Chapter II of *A Bibliography of Christian Philosophy and Contemporary Issues* by the same editor.

---

[1] See J. C. Rule, *Bibliography of Works in the Philosophy of History, 1945-1957*, supplement I to *History and Theory*, II (1961).

BIVORT DE LA SAUDÉE, Jacques De. (ed.) *God, Man and the Universe: An Answer to Modern Materialism.* Trans. from *Essai sur Dieu, l'homme et l'univers.* New York: Kenedy, 1954 (1950). xvi, 421 pp. Bibliography.

A collection of papers by the more outstanding contemporary Christian authors on the position of man in his material universe. The human condition in this world, with its economic problems and materialistic philosophies, is reviewed in the light of the nature of man and his relation to God. B-C

> *See:* ABR 6 (1955) 117; L. Bright, Bl 35 (1954) 379; H. Reinhold, C 61 (1954) 173; G. Sloyan, CHR 41 (1955) 191; J. Sheerin, CW 180 (1954) 234; K. Taggart, DR 12 (1954) 316; IER 85 (1956) 221; J. O'Connell, ITQ 23 (1956) 188; C. Barrett, St 44 (1955) 231; E. Watkin, Ta 203 (1954) 474; G. Glanzman, TS 16 (1955) 120; K. Stern, W 29 (1955) 173.

CALLAHAN, John F. *Four Views on Time in Ancient Philosophy.* See XIV.

CAPONIGRI, Alphonsus R. *Time and Idea: The Theory of History in Giambattista Vico.* Chicago, Ill.: Regnery, 1953. viii, 225 pp. Index.

A study of the philosophy of history as developed by a seminal mind for modern Christian thought. As the expression of man, history is considered the place for man to discover himself as subject and spirit. Human history is related to providence, and the significance of the poetic and mythical is suggested. C-D

> *See:* MS 33 (1955) 51; R. Tsanoff, NS 28 (1954) 494-96; W. Shanahan, RP 17 (1955) 136; J. Walsh, TS 15 (1954) 503.

The Catholic Philosophy of History (Papers of the American Catholic Historical Association, Vol. III). Ed. Peter Guilday. New York: Kenedy, 1936. xvi, 270 pp. Index.

A collection of papers on the philosophy of history within the Catholic perspective, especially as reflected by some of its chief architects. The subject is treated in general and in its economic relevance, and traced through Otto of Freising, Aquinas, Dante, Bossuet, and Vico. B-C

See: A (1936) 550; MS 14 (1937) 43; S 16 (1937) 50-58.

DANILOU, Jean. *The Lord of History: Reflections on the Inner Meaning of History.* Trans. by N. Abercrombie from *Essai sur le mystère de l'histoire.* Chicago, Ill.: Regnery, 1958 (1953) . viii, 375 pp.

A study of the meaning of Christianity for the philosophy of history. History, as more than mere chronicle, is considered possible only on the basis of a notion of God as creator. This is contrasted to the Marxian position and related to the nature of continuity proper to history. B-C

See: W. Abbott, A 100 (1958) 348; J. Mahoney, AM 89 (1959) 27; Bl 40 (1959) 92; B. Murchland, C 69 (1959) 440; C. Ceplecha, CHR 45 (1959) 368; J. Burns, CR 44 (1959) 694; C. Stuhlmueller, Cr 17 (1959) 36; A. Woods, CW 189 (1959) 72; D 44 (1959) 214; E. John, DR 77 (1958) 82; B. Marthaler, HPR 59 (1959) 590; IER 92 (1959) 63; P. Corish, ITQ 26 (1959) 197; PR 15 (1959) 676; P. Andrews, ST 48 (1959) 125; R. Barry, T 35 (1960) 309; L. Johnston, Ta 213 (1959) 58; J. DeVault, TS 20 (1959) 443-45; G. Sloyan W 33 (1959) 371.

D'ARCY, Martin C. *The Sense of History, Secular and Sacred (The Meaning and Matter of History: A Christian View).* London: Faber and Faber, 1959. 309 pp. Index.

A preface to a critique of philosophies of history, this work evaluates the deterministic idealist, behaviorist, and Marxist philosophies of history. In a constructive effort it details the importance of the notion of providence for the development of the Christian philosophy of history. B-C

See: W. Clarke, A 102 (1960) 469; R. Mohan, AER 143 (1960) 352; AM 91 (1960) 28; K. Foster, Bl 40 (1959) 330-35; W. Arnold, C 71 (1960) 500-501; J. Reardon, CC 10 (1960) 409; D. Shea, CHR 46 (1960) 209; M. Crowe, PS 9 (1959) 213-18; St 49 (1960) 90; T. Gregory, Ta 213 (1959) 693-94; J. Coffey, Th 23 (1960) 125-30.

DAWSON, Christopher. *The Dynamics of World History.* Ed. John J. Mulloy. New York: Sheed and Ward, 1956. xi, 489 pp. Index.

A study concerning the sociology and philosophy of history. Following an extensive review of the social forces in history, the author turns to a comparative study of the Christian and non-Christian vision of history. The import of Christianity for this vision is detailed, and the philosophy of history of the major classical and modern figures in the field is critically reviewed. B-C

See: ACSR 18 (1957) 251; R. Mohan, AER 137 (1957) 433; AM 85 (1957) 23; G. Mathew, Bl 39 (1958) 189; F. Gallagher, BS 17 (1957) 37; BT 15 (1957) 305; CC 7 (1957) 184; M. McGuire, CHR 44 (1958) 32; CR 43 (1958) 114; CW 23 (1957) 7; D 42 (1957) 279; P. McKevitt, ITQ 25 (1958) 84; S 36 (1957) 65; Ta 210 (1957) 337; J. Coffey, Th 21 (1958) 118.

GUARDINI, Romano. *The End of the Modern World.* Ed. F. Wilhelmsen. Trans. by J. Theman and H. Burke from *Das Ende der Neuzeit.* New York: Sheed and Ward, 1956 (1950). 133 pp.

Three lectures on the roots of the contemporary cultural situation and the orientations needed for the future. This is based on a review of the sense of being and the world picture of the medieval period, in the light of which the modern world, its recent problems, and its future needs, are seen more deeply. B-C

MARITAIN, Jacques. *On the Philosophy of History.* Ed. Joseph W. Evans. New York: Scribner's, 1957. xi, 180 pp. Index.

A series of lectures that have been extensively edited and reorganized. The place of various principles and levels of interpretation is studied in chapters on functional and vectoral laws. The place of man's knowledge of God in this context is also investigated. B-C

See: W. Clarke 98 (1958) 516; K. Foster, Bl 40 (1959) 330-35; R. Mohan, CHR 44 (1958) 330; CR 44 (1959) 696; C. Fecher, NLF 3 (1958) 210-19; R. Barry, NS 33 (1959) 367; F. Keegan, RP 20 (1958) 383-86; T. Berry, S 37 (1958) 68; St 49 (1960) 90; C. Loughran, T 33 (1958) 141-43; R. Coffey, Th 21 (1958) 569-74; J. Somerville, TS 19 (1958) 298.

————. *Some Reflections on Culture and Liberty.* Chicago, Ill.: University of Chicago Press, 1933. 51 pp.

A lecture on freedom in the context of modern culture. Freedom is studied for the purpose of identifying a foundation, extending beyond the simply human, that is adequate for its sustenance and draws man into a valid area of spiritual and social activity. This work is in both French and English. A-C

MARROU, Henri. *The Meaning of History*. Baltimore, Md.: Helicon, 1964.

A study of the philosophical and theological roots of history. The problem of the truth of history and the principles underlying its understanding are studied. C

PHILOSOPHY AND RECONSTRUCTION. See I.

PIEPER, Josef. *The End of Time: A Meditation on the Philosophy of History*. Trans. by M. Bullock from *Über das Ende der Zeit*. London: Faber and Faber, 1954. 157 pp. Index.

A study of the philosophy of history, its nature and its view of the conditions of a future life. The importance of history's relation to theology is investigated, as are the views of modern philosophers on an understanding of the end of time and of the Antichrist. This book presents the student of history with a broad view of the implications of his work. B-C

See: B. Chudoba, A 92 (1955) 364; ABR 6 (1955) 116; AM 80 (1954) 24; G. Vann, Bl 35 (1954) 386; F. Gannon, BS 14 (1954) 79; G. Gargan, BT 13 (1954) 64; CER 53 (1955) 422; CHR 41 (1955) 364; B. Hunt, CW 180 (1954) 155; D 40 (1955) 81; M. Wilson, DR 72 (1954) 319; H. Fallon, In 9 (1954) 40; P. Nash, MS 33 (1956) 127-31; SO 5 (1955) 142; T. Gregory, Ta 204 (1954) 228.

PART II

Schools of Christian Philosophy: 1900-1964

CHAPTER XIV

Augustinian Philosophy

This chapter consists of works on the philosophy of St. Augustine and the Augustinian school. The source material has been restricted to works by St. Augustine himself. Most of the studies are general in character, while those on particular topics which are of distinctive importance to other chapters have been noted by cross references in those chapters. It would be impossible to isolate those works in the other chapters which reflect the perennial and increasing influence of the thought of St. Augustine. However, some of the more notable examples are indicated by cross references in this chapter. Some general research instruments in this area may also be consulted with profit.[1]

The reader is referred to Chapters I and VIII of *A Bibliography of Christian Philosophy and Contemporary Issues* by the same editor.

---

[1] C. Andresen (ed.), *Bibliographia Augustiniana* (Darmstadt: Wissenschaftliche Buchgesellschaft, 1962).
T. Van Bavel and F. Van der Zande, *Répertoire bibliographique de S. Augustin* (The Hague: Nijhoff, 1963).
Concordantiae Augustinianae, 2 vols. (Brussels: Culture et Civilization, 1963).
E. Nebreda, *Bibliografia Augustiniana* (Romae: "Cuore di Maria," 1928; Dubuque, Iowa: Brown, 1963).

SOURCES
AUGUSTINE, SAINT [2]

The Works of Aureuus Augustinus. 16 vols. Ed. by Marcus Dods. Edinburgh: Clark, 1871-1876.

Basic Writings of Saint Augustine. 2 vols. Ed. by Whitney J. Oates. New York: Random, 1948.

The City of God. (Fathers of the Church, ed. by Ludwig Schopp and Roy J. Deferrari, Nos. 8, 14 and 24). 3 vols. Trans. by G. Walsh *et al.* Brooklyn, N.Y.: Fathers of the Church, 1950-1954.

Confessions (Fathers of the Church, No. 21) . Trans. by V. Bourke. Brooklyn, N.Y.: Fathers of the Church, 1953.

Divine Providence and the Problem of Evil. Trans. by R. Russell. New York: Cosmopolitan, 1942.

The Greatness of the Soul: The Teacher (Ancient Christian Writers, No. 9) . Trans. by J. Colleran. Westminster, Md.: Newman, 1950.

Letters (Fathers of the Church, Nos. 12, 18, 20, 30, 32) . 5 vols. Trans. by W. Parson. Brooklyn, N.Y.: Fathers of the Church, 1951-1956.

The Problem of Free Choice (Ancient Christian Writers, No. 22) . Trans. by M. Pontifex. Westminster, Md.: Newman, 1955.

The Trinity (Fathers of the Church, No. 45) . Trans. by S. McKenna. Brooklyn, N.Y.: Fathers of the Church, 1963.

An Augustine Synthesis. Ed. by Erich Przywara. New York: Harper, 1958 (1936) . (TB 35) .

---

[2] A selection of the more philosophically relevant texts are included here. For a list of the major series English translations see Henri Marrou, *St. Augustine and His Influence Through the Ages.* (New York: Harper, 1957), 182-86.

The Essential Augustine. Ed. by Vernon J. Bourke. New York: Mentor, 1964.

Introduction to the Philosophy of Saint Augustine: Selected Readings and Commentaries. University Park, Pa.: Pennsylvania University Press, 1964.

Studies

ADAM, Karl. *Saint Augustine: The Odyssey of His Soul.* Trans. by M. McCann from *Die geistige Entwicklung des heiligen Augustinus.* New York: Macmillan, 1932 (1931).

A commemorative address on the spirit of Saint Augustine. The spiritual development of the Saint is studied in relation to his intellectual growth. B

BARRACHINA, Ignatius M. *The Spiritual Doctrine of Saint Augustine.* Trans. by E. Schuster. ("Cross and Crown Series on Spirituality," No. 25). St. Louis: Herder, 1963. xiv, 264 pp.

A study of the thought of St. Augustine on the roots of the spiritual life. The first part investigates his understanding of man, including the place of man in the world, and his relation to God. The second part treats the mystical phases of this relationship. A-B

See: C. Farrell, To 48 (1964) 28.

BATTENHOUSE, Roy W. (ed.) *A Companion to the Study of St. Augustine.* New York: Oxford University Press, 1955. xiii, 425 pp. Index.

A collection of papers by a group of Protestant professors on the general theme of the continuing vitality of the thought of St. Augustine. In three sections the papers survey his life, his major writings, and a series of special questions concerning his thought. B-C

See: E. Hill, Bl 36 (1955) 397; CHR 41 (1955) 329; DR 74 (1955) 67; T. Clarke, TS 16 (1955) 454.

BONNER, Gerald. *St. Augustine of Hippo: Life and Controversies.* Philadelphia: Westminster, 1964 (1963). 428 pp. Bibliography, appendices.

A study of the background of St. Augustine's work concerned with the intellectual disputes in which he engaged. The life of St. Augustine is surveyed, as are his writings against the Manicheans, the Donatists, and the Pelagians. C

See: D. Brass, Ta 218 (1964) 102.

BOURKE, Vernon J. *Augustine's Quest of Wisdom: Life and Philosophy of the Bishop of Hippo.* Milwaukee: Bruce, 1945. xi, 323 pp. Index, appendices.

A life of Augustine, written with special attention to his intellectual development. This excellent work contains an extensive study of his development as a Christian philosopher and a study of his major works, with discussion of the key philosophical questions concerning his thought. Appendices detail the chronology of his life and writings. B-C

See: A 73 (1945) 499-500; AM 62 (1945) 413; Bl 26 (1945) 476-77; CHR 31 (1946) 477-79; CR 26 (1946) 277-79; AER 114 (1946) 151-53; D 30 (1945) 203-204; FS 6 (1946) 238-40; HPR 46 (1946) 398-99; IER 67 (1946) 139; MS 23 (1947) 228-30; NS 20 (1946) 73-74; RR 4 (1945) 427; RUO 16 (1946) 123; S 25 (1945) 50; St 34 (1945) 419-22; T 9 (1946) 170-72; Th 9 (1946) 126; TS 7 (1946) 623-26.

BROOKES, Edgar H. *The City of God and the Politics of Crisis.* London: Oxford University Press, 1960. x, 111 pp. Index.

An application of the political philosophy of St. Augustine to recent political tensions. Such questions as the place of the state and the rights of the individual, and law and the rights of protest are reviewed in relation to the thought of St. Augustine on these matters, especially as presented in *The City of God*. A-B

See: S. Bond, J 8 (1961) 46; D. Brass, Ta 214 (1960) 372.

BURLEIGH, John H. *The City of God: A Study of St. Augustine's Philosophy* (Croall Lectures, 1944). London: Nisbet, 1949. vii, 266 pp. Index.

A series of lectures setting St. Augustine's philosophy of history within the full context of his thought. The situation of his times is described, along with his search for a Christian philosophy. With the theological and social perspectives, this provides the full context for a statement of St. Augustine's philosophy of history. B-C

BURNABY, John. *Amor Dei: A Study of the Religion of St. Augustine* (The Hulsean Lectures, 1938). Naperville, Ill.: Allenson, 1960 (1938). xi, 338 pp. Indices, appendix.

A study of the Neo-Platonic-Christian philosophy of love in St. Augustine. The centrality of this love is identified as the Platonic element which becomes Christian as it is ultimately identified with God's own being and His gift to men. The meaning and order of love, the love of God, grace, and sin are studied, and the history of the notion of pure love since Augustine's time is traced. C-D

See: Ta 174 (1939) 361-62.

CALLAHAN, John F. *Four Views on Time in Ancient Philosophy*. Cambridge: Harvard University Press, 1948. ix, 209 pp. Bibliography.

A survey of the appreciation of time among early philosophers, which draws on and reveals the development of philosophical insight during this period. Plato, Aristotle, Plotinus, and St. Augustine are each studied. C

CHAPMAN, Emmanuel. *Saint Augustine's Philosophy of Beauty* (St. Michael's Mediaeval Studies, "Monograph Series"). New York: Sheed and Ward, 1939. xiii, 113 pp.

A study of beauty and art in the work of St. Augustine. The experience of the beautiful is discussed as an introduction to the study of the nature and judgment of beauty. This leads to a discussion of the meaning of art and a review of modern painting in the light of the Augustinian esthetic. B

See: A 61 (1939) 525; C 30 (1939) 166-67; LA 7 (1939) 17; MS 17 (1939) 17; NS 13 (1939) 381-85; T 15 (1940) 139; Tm 1 (1939) 450-58.

CLARK, Mary T. *Augustine, Philosopher of Freedom: A Study in Comparative Philosophy*. New York: Desclée, 1958. 273 pp. Bibliography, index.

A study of the nature of freedom in the Christian philosophy of St. Augustine. Though the work centers on St. Augustine, an extensive comparison is made of St. Augustine's views vis-à-vis those of the pagan philosophers, as well as those of later Christian and present-day philosophers. St. Augustine's notion of freedom is followed through his major writings, and analyzed for its theological and philosophical implications and its Plotinian references. C

See: B. Kennedy, DR 78 (1960) 235-36; F. de la Vega, NS 33 (1959) 538-40; RPL 59 (1961) 543; R. Russell, Tm 22 (1959) 585-87; T. Clarke, TS 20 (1959) 463-64

D'ARCY, Martin C., *et al. Saint Augustine (A Monument to Augustine).* New York: Meridian Books, 1957 (1930) . 367 pp. Index. (M 51)

A collection of articles on St. Augustine's thought by a group of the most capable writers on the subject. The background of his thought is reviewed and his philosophy is elucidated in relation to St. Thomas and to the modern world. C

DEANE, Herbert A. *The Political and Social Ideas of St. Augustine.* New York: Columbia University Press, 1963. xix, 356 pp. Bibliography, index.

A study of the Augustinian understanding of the relation of man and the state, cast against the background of his theology and psychology of fallen man. The general notions of justice and state, as well as particular questions such as those of war and church-state relations are considered. C-D

See: R. O'Connell, IPQ 3 (1963) 631; J. Burns, M 30 (1963) 304; E. Hill, Ta 217 (1963) 1091.

FIGGIS, John N. *The Political Aspects of St. Augustine's* CITY OF GOD. Gloucester: Smith, 1963 (1921) . 132 pp. Bibliography, index.

A series of lectures delivered on the general theme of St. Augustine's philosophy of society. Both state and Church are considered in a study that extends through St. Augustine's philosophy of history and its implications for the Middle Ages and modern times. C-D

See: CW 113 (1921) 696.

GARVEY, Mary P. *St. Augustine: Christian or Neo-Platonist?* Milwaukee: Bruce, 1939. 267 pp. Bibliography, index.

In this study of the writings of St. Augustine a search is made for typically Neoplatonic and Christian elements. These elements are stated and compared, and in their light St. Augustine's works are reviewed for the purpose of drawing a conclusion concerning the relation between the two traditions. C

See: CHR 26 (1940) 401-402; NS 14 (1940) 80-84; T 15 (1940) 355-56.

GEIGER, James A. *The Origin of the Soul: An Augustinian Dilemma.* Romae: Pontificia Universitas Gregoriana, 1957. 91 pp.

A study of various trends in the understanding of the origin of the soul. The background of these trends is sought in Plato and in the psychology of the early Fathers. St. Augustine is found to remain undecided between creationism and traducianism. D

GILSON, Etienne. *The Christian Philosophy of Saint Augustine.* Trans. by L. Lynch from *Introduction à l'étude de saint Augustin.* London: Gollancz, 1961 (1929). xii, 398 pp. Bibliography, index.

A study of the philosophy of St. Augustine, from the viewpoint of his understanding of the progress of man toward God as love. Knowledge and faith are examined, as well as the notions of will, love, and freedom. This examination leads to a study of nature as a place for the contemplation of God. C-D

See: A 104 (1961) 522; Bl 42 (1961) 480; C 74 (1961) 84; G. McCool, MS 38 (1961) 334; NS 37 (1963) 99-101; PS 11 (1961) 279; A. Armstrong, Ta 215 (1961) 634; T. Clarke, TS 22 (1961) 298.

GRABOWSKI, Stanislaus J. *The All-Present God: A Study in St. Augustine.* St. Louis: Herder, 1954. xi, 327 pp.

A study of the presence of God, in both its static and dynamic aspects, conducted against the background of a presentation of

St. Augustine's position on the relation of philosophy to theology, and on the philosophies of his day as they tended toward pantheism and dualism. The particular presence of God in human life is stressed. C

See: F. Rosaly, CB 31 (1954) 47; V. Bourke, MS 33 (1955) 288; J. de la Vega, NS 29 (1955) 356; J. Mara, TS 16 (1955) 255-58.

————. *The Church*. St. Louis: Herder, 1957. xviii, 673 pp.

A predominantly theological synthesis of the thought of St. Augustine. Important insights into his philosophy are also included. C

GREENWOOD, David. *St. Augustine*. New York: Vantage, 1957. 155 pp. Appendix, index.

A general survey of the life and work of St. Augustine. Following a survey of his life and its main religious events, the Donatist and Pelagian controversies are reviewed, along with *The City of God*. A-B

HENRY, Paul. *Saint Augustine on Personality* (The Saint Augustine Lecture, 1959). New York: Macmillan, 1960. viii, 44 pp.

A lecture on the contribution of St. Augustine to the development of an understanding of the individual. It is evident that St. Augustine's fundamental analogy is the substitution of man for the world, an analogy that deepens the appreciation of the moral responsibility and freedom of the individual. This insight is related to the needs of modern times. C-D

See: J. Haddox, AM 92 (1960) 25; Bl 41 (1960) 437; D 45 (1960) 374; NS 36 (1962) 246; A. Jansen, T 36 (1961) 146; Th 24 (1961) 126; TS 21 (1960) 628.

LEFF, Gordon. *Medieval Thought from St. Augustine to Ockham: A Survey of the Dominant Ideas and Thinkers of the Middle Ages, and of Their Sources and Influences*. Harmondsworth: Penguin, 1958. ix, 316 pp. (Pelican: A 424)

A study of the history of philosophy during the Middle Ages. Special attention is given to the problems of the relation between man and God and between reason and faith. B-C

See: V. Bourke, MS 36 (1959) 303; T. Gilby, Ta 212 (1958) 16.

McDOUGALL, Eleanor. *St. Augustine: A Study in His Personal Religion.* London: Student Christian Movement Press, 1930 (1928). 125 pp.

A study of the personal religious development of St. Augustine. With particular reference to the *Confessions,* the author investigates the inner life of St. Augustine in order to trace his acceptance of the will of God. A

McKEOUGH, Michael J. *The Meaning of the "Rationes Seminales" in St. Augustine* (The Catholic University of America, Philosophical Studies, No. 15). Washington, D.C.: The Catholic University of America Press, 1926. xiii, 115 pp. Bibliography. (Paper)

A study of the notion of *rationes seminales* in the complex of St. Augustine's thought. Their origin, nature, and development are investigated. This study is set against the background of the philosophy of preceding times, and implications are drawn for modern evolution. C

See: A 36 (1927) 604.

MARROU, Henri. *St. Augustine and His Influence through the Ages* ("Men of Wisdom"). Trans. by P. Hepburne-Scott from *Saint Augustin et l'augustinisme.* New York: Harper, 1957 (1955). 191 pp. Bibliography. (Paper)

A simple but literate presentation of St. Augustine and his influence. His life and works are presented with a view to their broad cultural and religious significance. Included is an extensive collection of brief texts from his own writings. A-B

See: R. Markus, Bl 39 (1958) 93; CR 43 (1958) 505; E. John, DR 76 (1958) 185; IER 89 (1958) 231.

MEER, Frederik Van Der. *Augustine, the Bishop: The Life and*

Work of a Father of the Church. Trans. by B. Battershaw and G. Lamb from *Augustine de Zielzorger*. New York: Sheed and Ward, 1961. xxiii, 679 pp. Index.

An extensive work on St. Augustine, concentrating more on the pattern of his life in the Church than on his philosophy. The initial survey of the situation of the Church of Hippo is followed by a survey of the work of St. Augustine in liturgy, preaching, and teaching. B-C

MONTGOMERY, W. *St. Augustine: Aspects of His Life and Thought*. New York: Hodder and Stoughton, 1914. xi, 225 pp.

A general background study of St. Augustine, with emphasis on the psychological aspects of St. Augustine as an individual. The work surveys his conversion and his philosophical and theological contributions. B

O'CONNOR, William. *The Concept of the Human Soul According to St. Augustine* (The Catholic University of America, *Philosophical Studies*, No. 11). Washington, D.C.: The Catholic University of America Press, 1921. 85 pp. (Paper)

A brief survey of questions concerning the soul in the works of St. Augustine. The nature, spirituality, and immortality of the soul, and the origin of its concept are discussed. B

O'MEARA, John. *Charter of Christendom: The Significance of* THE CITY OF GOD (The Saint Augustine Lecture, 1961). New York: Macmillan, 1961. xvii, 120 pp.

A study of *The City of God* for the purpose of illuminating its central theme of pointing the way to salvation as the worship of the one true God. This theme is traced through earlier writings of St. Augustine, and is then presented as Augustine debated it in *The City of God* in relation to the Bible, Greek philosophy, and Rome. This work is also a helpful clarification of Augustine's political thought. B-C

See: Bl 43 (1962) 435; DR 80 (1962) 178; HJ 4 (1963) 82; HPR 62 (1962) 472; IER 98 (1962) 198; PS 12 (1963) 292; RR 21 (1962) 478; TS 23 (1962) 347.

————. *The Young Augustine: The Growth of St. Augustine's Mind Up to His Conversion*. New York: Longmans, Green, 1954. xv, 215 pp. Bibliography, index.

A study of the development of St. Augustine during his earlier life. Extensive consideration is given to the various philosophical currents which he encountered and their contribution to the shaping of his thought. D

See: E. Eller, A 93 (1955) 568; E. Hill, B 136 (1955) 93; DR 74 (1955) 67; St 44 (1955) 171-80; J. Kelley, Ta 204 (1954) 542; T. Clarke, TS 16 (1955) 288.

PAPINI, Giovanni. *Saint Augustine*. Trans. by M. Agnetti from *Sant' Agostino*. London: Hodder and Stoughton, 1930 (1929) . 336 pp.

A general biography of St. Augustine. The main events of his life are reviewed, and his writings are studied in order to identify the spirit of the saint. The work is not particularly attentive to the philosophical issues. A-B

POPE, Hugh. *Saint Augustine of Hippo: Essays Dealing with His Life and Times and Some Features of His Work*. Westminster, Md.: Newman, 1949 (1937) . xix, 408 pp. Index. (Image: D 119)

A series of addresses on the life and thought of St. Augustine. Each deals with a different phase of his life, one of which is St. Augustine and the world of nature. A chronological table of his works is included. A-B

See: Bl 18 (1938) 873; DR 56 (1938) 108; IER 51 (1938) 211; St 27 (1934) 148; Ta 170 (1937) 486.

PORTALIE, Eugene. *A Guide to the Thought of Saint Augustine* (Library of Living Catholic Thought). Trans. by R. Bastian from "Augustin, Saint," *Dictionnaire de Théologie Catholique, I*. Chicago, Ill.: Regnery, 1960. xxxvii, 428 pp. Bibliography, index, appendix.

A very competent study of the philosophy and theology of St. Augustine, cast against the background of his life and writings, and an investigation of the Neoplatonic influences. The subjects studied include: religious knowledge, the divine nature, and creatures. The special place of charity in his moral theology is noted, and the subsequent influence of Augustine is traced. C-D

See: A 104; (1961) 24; R. Callahan, AER 144 (1961) 522; AM 93 (1961) 24; C 74 (1961) 84; E. Kevan, CER 58 (1960) 625; CR 47 (1962) 255; D. Faul, F 12 (1961) 137; HPR 61 (1960) 304; NS 35 (1961) 389; RR 20 (1961) 307; Th 24 (1961) 680; T. Clarke, TS 22 (1961) 298.

PRZYWARA, Erich. (ed.) *An Augustine Synthesis.* New York: Harper, 1958 (1936) . xvi, 496 pp.

A selection of brief passages from the writings of St. Augustine. These are arranged in order to provide an overall view of the wisdom of St. Augustine. The texts generally proceed from the question of knowledge to the notion of God. Thence, the perspective turns to man and his return to God. A-B

See: A 55 (1936) 91-92; Bl 17 (1936) 313; CW 143 (1936) 427; CR 11 (1936) 427; AER 94 (1936) 540; HPR 36 (1937) 332; IER 49 (1937) 332; S 15 (1936) 639; T 12 (1937) 347.

RICKABY, Joseph. *St. Augustine's* CITY OF GOD: *A View of the Contents.* London: Burns, Oates and Washbourne, 1925. 119 pp.

A summary of the contents of *The City of God,* book by book. The author draws out the salient points and interprets them well. A-B

SULLIVAN, John E. *The Image of God.* See VI.

SWITALSKI, Bruno. *Plotinus and the Ethics of St. Augustine (Neoplatonism and the Ethics of St. Augustine,* Vol. I) . New York: Polish Institute of Arts and Sciences in America, 1946. xxxii, 114 pp. Bibliography, index.

A study of the influence of Plotinus on the ethics of St. Augustine. The main features of the ethics of the two men are detailed, and the presence of the influence of Plotinus is sought both in the conversion of St. Augustine and in his ethical theory. The evidence for this, which is introduced, consists in nominal references, literal citations, and similarity of ideas. D

See: D 32 (1947) 41-42; RUO 17 (1947) 131*-32*; T 22 (1947) 171-73; Th 10 (1947) 128-29.

TOLLEY, William P. *The Idea of God in the Philosophy of St. Augustine.* New York: Smith, 1930. 214 pp. Bibliography.

A general study of St. Augustine's thought on the knowledge and nature of God. The general lines of his philosophy are traced, and proofs of God's existence are shown to manifest Him as the source of being, knowledge, and goodness. C

See: A 45 (1931) 503; C 14 (1931) 369; IJE 4 (1931) 49.

VEGA, Angel C. *Saint Augustine: His Philosophy.* Trans. by D. Kavanagh from *Introducción a la filosofía de san Agustín.* Philadelphia: Reilly, 1931. xi, 264 pp. Bibliography, index.

A discussion of the value of St. Augustine as a philosopher, rather than a presentation of his philosophy. The author describes the typical ways in which St. Augustine philosophized. His value for modern thought is also noted, as are various interpretations of Augustine's accomplishments. B-C

See: C 14 (1931) 330; T 7 (1932) 309-13.

VERSFELD, Marthinus. *A Guide to* THE CITY OF GOD. New York: Sheed and Ward, 1958. xii, 141 pp. Index.

A statement of the main lines of *The City of God,* intended to introduce the student to reading the work itself. Selected books are singled out, and their special import and structure analyzed. This work can serve as a general introduction to the thought of St. Augustine as well as to *The City of God* itself. B

CHAPTER XV

Saint Thomas Aquinas

This chapter consists of sources and studies. The former comprises a list of the works of St. Thomas which are of philosophical interest and which have appeared in English translation. It is prefaced by two catalogues of the complete works of St. Thomas and by a list of volumes composed of selections of varying lengths from many of his works. The subdivision in this listing has been simplified to four categories: *Summae, Disputed Questions, Commentaries* on the works of Aristotle, with all other pertinent works listed as *Opuscula*. For a division more reflective of the literary genre of each work, the catalogue by I. Eschmann, listed in this chapter, may be consulted.

The section of studies is composed of books on St. Thomas Aquinas and his philosophy. It includes works on his life and on the philosophical situation of his times. It also includes works on his philosophy as a personal synthesis and on the part played in this synthesis by classical Greek authors. It has been difficult to separate from many of these works the general surveys of Thomistic philosophy in Chapter II. This has been accomplished by reserving for this final section those studies directed toward the philosophy of St. Thomas as an individual, while those reflecting the school of philosophy which he founded have been placed in Chapter II.

The reader is referred to Chapters I and VIII of *A Bibliography of Christian Philosophy and Contemporary Issues* by the same editor.

SOURCES
THOMAS AQUINAS, SAINT [1]

A. General Catalogues [2]

BOURKE, Vernon J. *Introduction to the Works of St. Thomas Aquinas.* (Reprint from S. Thomae Aquinatis, *Opera omnia,* Vol. I). New York: Musurgia, 1948.

---

[1] Only works of philosophical interest are included here. Other English translations of the works of St. Thomas include:

Apology for Religious Orders, ed. John Procter (St. Louis: Herder, 1902).

Blessed Sacrament and the Mass, trans. F. O'Neill (London: Blackfriars, 1955).

The Catechetical Instructions of St. Thomas Aquinas, trans. J. Collins (New York: Wagner, 1939).

The Commandments of God: Conferences on the Two Precepts of Charity and the Ten Commandments, trans. L. Shapcote (London: Burns, Oates and Washbourne, 1937).

Meditations for Every Day, trans. E. McEniry (Somerset: Rosary Press, 1939).

The Religious State: The Episcopate and the Priestly Office, ed. J. Proctor (Westminster, Md.: Newman, 1950).

Teaching of St. Thomas on Prayer and the Contemplative Life, trans. H. Pope (New York: Benziger, 1935).

The Three Greatest Prayers: Commentaries on the Our Father, the Hail Mary, and the Apostles Creed, trans. L. Shapcote (Westminster, Md.: Newman, 1956).

[2] See the annotated presentation of these catalogues in the second section of this chapter. Along with the works of Bernard Wuellner listed there, the following may be of service:

Peter di Bergamo, *Tabula aurea: In omnia opera s. Thomae Aquinatis* (Parma: Fiaccadori, 1873).

E. Gilson, *Index scolastico-cartésien* (Paris: Alcan, 1912).

Indices auctoritatum omniumque rerum notabilium occurrentium in SUMMA THEOLOGIAE *et in* SUMMA CONTRA GENTILES *S. Thomae de Aquino Doctoris Angelici.* (Romae: ed Leonina, 1948), vol. XVI.

L. Schütz, *Thomas-Lexikon* (New York: Musurgia, 1949).

N. Signoriello, *Lexicon peripateticum philosophico-theologicum in quo Scholasticorum distinctiones et effata praecipua explicantur* (Romae: Officium Bibl. Cat. Scrip., 1931).

C. Suermondt, *Tabulae schematicae cum introductione de principiis et compositione comparatis* SUMMA THEOLOGIAE *et* SUMMA CONTRA GENTILES *s. Thomae Aquinatis* (Rome: Marietti, 1942).

DEFERRARI, Roy J., and BARRY, (Sr.) Mary I. *A Complete Index of the* SUMMA THEOLOGICA *of St. Thomas Aquinas.* See I.

―――. *A Latin-English Dictionary of St. Thomas Aquinas, Based on the* SUMMA THEOLOGICA *and Selected Passages of His Other Works.* See I.

―――, and BARRY, (Sr.) Mary I. *A Lexicon of St. Thomas Aquinas Based on the* SUMMA THEOLOGICA *and Selected Passages of His Other Works.* See I.

ESCHMANN, I. T. "A Catalogue of St. Thomas' Works: Bibliographical Notes," in Etienne Gilson, *The Christian Philosophy of St. Thomas Aquinas.* New York: Random House, 1956. Pp. 381-439.

B. Compilations and Selections [3]

Basic Writings of Saint Thomas Aquinas. 2 vols. Ed. by Anton C. Pegis. New York: Random House, 1944.

Introduction to Saint Thomas Aquinas. Ed. by Anton C. Pegis. New York: Modern Library, 1948.

New Things and Old in Saint Thomas Aquinas: A Translation of Various Writings and Treatises of the Angelic Doctor. Ed. and trans. by H. C. O'Neill. London: Dent, 1909.

The Pocket Aquinas: Selections from the Writings of St. Thomas. Ed. with some passages newly trans. by Vernon J. Bourke. New York: Washington Square Press, 1960. (W 575)

――――――――――

[3] This section, "Compilations and Selections," lists only those which are general in character. Those of a more specialized nature are listed under "Thomas Aquinas, St." in their appropriate chapters. Such works include: James F. Anderson, *Introduction to Metaphysics;* Dino Bigongiari, *Political Ideas;* A. M. Fairweather, *Nature and Grace;* and A. Passerin d'Entreves, *Aquinas: Selected Political Writings.* There are also innumerable general collections of a number of authors either from this period or on a special theme which include a more or less extensive passage from the writings of St. Thomas.

St. Thomas Aquinas: Philosophical Texts. Trans. by Thomas Gilby. New York: Oxford University Press, 1960. (Gallaxy)

St. Thomas Aquinas: Theological Texts. Trans. by Thomas Gilby. New York: Oxford University Press, 1951.

Thomas Aquinas: Selected Writings. Ed. by Martin D'Arcy. New York: E. P. Dutton, 1940.

C. Summae

SUMMA CONTRA GENTILES

On the Truth of the Catholic Faith. 5 vols. Trans. by A. C. Pegis, J. F. Anderson, V. J. Bourke, and C. J. O'Neil. Garden City, N.Y.: Doubleday, 1955-57. (Image)

The Summa contra Gentiles. 5 vols. Trans. by the English Dominican Fathers. New York: Benziger, 1924-29.

Of God and His Creatures. Trans. and ed. by Joseph Rickaby. London: Burns and Oates, 1905.

SUMMA THEOLOGIAE

Summa theologica. 22 vols. Trans. by the Fathers of the English Dominican Province. 2d ed. London: Burns and Oates, 1912-36.

Summa theologica. 3 vols. Trans. by the Fathers of the English Dominican Province. New York: Benziger, 1947-48.

Summa theologiae (Great Books of the Western World, Vols. 19-20). Ed. by Daniel J. Sullivan. Trans. by the Fathers of the English Dominican Province, with notes from the Ottawa ed. of the Dominican Fathers and the Institute of Medieval Studies, Albert the Great, University of Montreal. Chicago, Ill.: Encyclopaedia Britannica, 1952-55.

Summa theologiae. Ed. by Thomas Gilby. New York: McGraw-Hill, 1964—.

Aquinas ethicus, or The Moral Teaching of St. Thomas: A Translation of the Principal Portions of the Second Part of the SUMMA THEOLOGICA. 2 vols. Trans. by Joseph Rickaby. London: Burns and Oates, 1892.

God and His Works: Selections from Part I of the SUMMA THEOLOGICA ("Texts for Studies Series") . Trans. by A. G. Herbert. New York: Macmillan, 1936.

Nature and Grace: Selections from the SUMMA THEOLOGICA (Library of Christian Classics, No. 11) . London: Westminster, 1954.

On Man. (I, qq. 75-79). Trans. by L. Shapcote, and rev. by A. Pegis. Chicago, Ill.: Regnery, 1951. (Paper)

Treatise on God. (I, qq. 1-26). Trans. by J. Anderson. Englewood Cliffs, N.J.: Prentice-Hall, 1963.

Treatise on Happiness. (I-II, qq. 1-21). Trans. by J. Oesterle. Englewood Cliffs, N.J.: Prentice-Hall, 1964.

Treatise on Law. (I-II, qq. 90-97). Introduction by Stanley Parry. Chicago, Ill.: Regnery, 1949. (Gateway: 6032)

Treatise on Man. (I, qq. 75-88). Trans. by J. Anderson, Englewood Cliffs, N.J.: Prentice-Hall, 1962. (Paper)

Truth and Falsity: On Human Knowledge. (I, qq. 16-17; 84-88) Chicago, Ill.: Regnery. 1949.

D. Disputed Questions

DE ANIMA

The Soul. Trans. by J. Rowan. St. Louis: Herder, 1949.

DE CARITATE

On Charity. Trans. by L. Kendzierski. Milwaukee: Marquette University Press, 1960.

DE POTENTIA

On the Power of God. Trans. by the English Dominican Fathers. Westminster, Md.: Newman, 1952.

DE SPIRITUALIBUS CREATURIS

On Spiritual Creatures. Trans. by M. Fitzpatrick and J. Wellmuth. Milwaukee: Marquette University Press, 1949. (Paper)

DE VERITATE

Truth. 3 vols. Trans. by R. W. Mulligan, J. V. McGlynn, and R. W. Schmidt. Chicago, Ill.: Regnery, 1952-54.

The Teacher-The Mind. (Qq. 10 & 11). Trans. J. McGlynn. Chicago, Ill.: Regnery, 1961. (Gateway: 6046)

Providence and Predestination. (Qq. 5 & 6). Trans. R. W. Mulligan. Chicago, Ill.: Regnery, 1961. (Gateway)

DE VIRTUTIBUS

On the Virtues in General. Trans. J. Reid. Providence: Providence College Press, 1951.

E. Expositions of Aristotelian Works

Thomistic Texts: First Lectures of All Expositions of Aristotle with Allied Translations from St. Thomas. Trans. P. Conway. Columbus, Ohio: College of St. Mary of the Springs. (Paper)

IN LIBROS DE ANIMA

Aristotle's DE ANIMA *with Commentary of St. Thomas Aquinas.* Trans. K. Foster and S. Humphries. New Haven: Yale University Press, 1951.

IN LIBROS DE COELO ET MUNDO

Exposition of ON THE HEAVENS. Trans. P. Conway. Columbus, Ohio: College of St. Mary of the Springs. (Paper)

IN DECEM LIBROS ETHICORUM

Commentary on the NICOMACHEAN ETHICS. 2 vols. Trans. C. I. Litzinger. Chicago, Ill.: Regnery, 1964.

St. Thomas Aquinas on Aristotle's LOVE AND FRIENDSHIP, Ethics, VIII-IX. Trans. Pierre Conway. Providence: Providence College Press, 1951.

IN LIBROS DE GENERATIONE ET CORRUPTIONE

Exposition of ON GENERATION. Trans. P. Conway. Columbus, Ohio: College of St. Mary of the Springs. (Paper)

IN DUODECIM LIBROS METAPHYSICORUM

Commentary on the METAPHYSICS *of Aristotle.* 2 vols. Trans. J. Rowan. Chicago, Ill.: Regnery, 1961.

Exposition of the METAPHYSICS *of Aristotle:* A Summary. Trans. P. Conway. Columbus, Ohio: College of St. Mary of the Springs. (Paper)

In libros Meterologicorum

Exposition of the Meteorology. Trans. by P. Conway. Columbus, Ohio: College of St. Mary of the Springs. (Paper)

Latin Treatises on Comets between 1238 and 1368. Ed. by Lynn Thorndike. Chicago, Ill.: University of Chicago Press, 1950. Includes I, lect. 8-10 on pp. 77-86.

In libros Peri Hermeneias

Aristotle, On Interpretation, *Commentary by St. Thomas and Cajetan* (Mediaeval Philosophical Texts in Translation, No. 11). Trans. by J. Oesterle. Milwaukee: Marquette University Press, 1962. (Paper)

In octo libros Physicorum

Commentary on Aristotle's Physics. Trans. by R. Blackwell, R. Spath, and W. Thirlkel. London: Routledge and Kegan Paul, 1963.

Exposition of the Physics *of Aristotle* (Complete except for Books I and II). Trans. by R. Larcher and P. Conway. Columbus, Ohio: College of St. Mary of the Springs. (Paper)

An Introduction to the Philosophy of Nature. Compiled by Roman A. Kocourek. St. Paul: North Central, 1948. Includes I and II on pp. 25-161.

McWILLIAMS, James A. *Physics and Philosophy: A Study of Saint Thomas'* Commentary on the Eight Books of Aristotle's Physics. Washington, D. C.: The American Catholic Philosophical Association, 1945. Includes III, lect. 1-5 on pp. 28-49.

IN LIBROS POSTERIORUM ANALYTICORUM

Exposition of the POSTERIOR ANALYTICS. Trans. by P. Conway and W. H. Kane. Quebec: M. Doyon, 1961.

F. *Opuscula*

COMPENDIUM THEOLOGIAE

Compendium of Theology. Trans. by C. Vollert. St. Louis: Herder, 1948.

DE DEMONSTRATIONE

"Demonstration: A Disputed Work." Trans. by V. Larkin in *Readings in Logic.* Ed. Roland Houde. Dubuque: Brown, 1958. Pp. 148-52.

DE EMPTIONE ET VENDITIONE AD TEMPUS

O'RAHILLY, A. "Notes on St. Thomas on Credit," *Irish Ecclesiastical Record,* xxxi (1928), 164-65.

DE ENTE ET ESSENTIA

On Being and Essence (St. Michael's Philosophy Texts). Revised ed. Trans. by C. Riedl. Toronto: St. Michael's College, 1937.

Concerning Being and Essence. Trans. by G. Leckie. New York: Appleton-Century, 1937.

On Being and Essence. Trans. by A. Maurer. Toronto: The Pontifical Institute of Mediaeval Studies, 1949.

DE MIXTIONE ELEMENTORUM

"On Combining of the Elements." Trans. by V. Larkin in *Isis,*
LI (1960), 67-70.

DE MODO STUDENDI

WHITE, Victor, O.P. "The Letter of St. Thomas to Brother
John: 'De modo studendi'—Translation and Exposition,"
Blackfriars, XXV (1944), Supplement: *The Life of the
Spirit,* No. 10 (December), pp. 103-104.

DE MOTU CORDIS

"On the Movement of the Heart." Trans. by V. Larkin in *Journal of the History of Medicine and Allied Science,* XV
(1960), 22-30.

DE OCCULTIS OPERATIONIBUS NATURAE

*The Letter of Saint Thomas Aquinas, "De occultis operationibus
naturae ad quemdam militem ultramontanum."* Trans. by
J. McAllister. Washington, D. C.: The Catholic University
of America Press, 1939.

DE PRINCIPIIS NATURAE

The Principles of Nature. Trans. by R. Kocourek. St. Paul:
North Central, 1948.

Principles of Nature. Trans. by P. Conway. Columbus, Ohio:
College of St. Mary of the Springs. (Paper)

DE REGIMINE JUDAEORUM

Aquinas' Selected Political Writings. Trans. by J. Dawson; ed. by Allessandro Passerin d'Entreves. Oxford: Blackwell, 1954. Pp. 85-95.

DE REGIMINE PRINCIPUM (DE REGNO)

St. Thomas Aquinas ON KINGSHIP TO THE KING OF CYPRUS. Trans. G. Phelan, revised by I. T. Eschmann. Toronto: The Pontifical Institute of Mediaeval Studies, 1949.

DE SUBSTANTIIS SEPARATIS, SEU DE ANGELORUM NATURA

Treatise on Separate Substances. Trans. by F. Lescoe. West Hartford: St. Joseph College, 1959 (Latin-English edition, 1963). (Paper)

SUPER LIBRUM BOETHII DE TRINITATE

The Trinity and The Unicity of the Intellect. Trans. by Sr. Rose Emmanuella Brennan. St. Louis: Herder, 1946.

The Division and Methods of the Sciences (Qq. V and VI). Trans. by A. Maurer. Toronto: The Pontifical Institute of Mediaeval Studies, 1953.

On Searching into God (Q. 2). Trans. by V. White. New York: Oxford University Press, 1947.

DE UNITATE INTELLECTUS, CONTRA AVERROISTAS

The Trinity and The Unicity of the Intellect. Trans. by Sr. Rose Emmanuella Brennan. St. Louis, Herder, 1946.

Studies

ADLER, Mortimer J. *St. Thomas and the Gentiles* (The Aquinas Lecture, 1938). Milwaukee: Marquette University Press, 1938. vi, 111 pp.

A lecture on the perennial validity of the thought of St. Thomas. In order to make a case for this philosophy, the author develops the notion of abiding philosophical truth, and concludes to the necessity of returning to the method and spirit of St. Thomas. This scholarly work contains extensive notes. B-C

See: Bl 19 (1938) 509-16; ER 99 (1938) 391; MS 16 (1939) 43.

ANSCOMBE, G. E. M., and GEACH, P. T. *Three Philosophers.* Ithaca, N. Y.: Cornell University Press, 1961. xx, 162 pp.

An investigation of Aristotle, Aquinas, and Frege, carried out according to the methods of the analytic school. In this manner the terms in St. Thomas—"form," "matter," "esse," "operations," and "tendencies"—are analyzed. D

See: D. Hawkins, DR 80 (1962) 274; Ta 216 (1962) 329.

ARDLEY, Gavin. *Aquinas and Kant: The Foundations of Modern Sciences.* London: Longmans, Green, 1950. ix, 256 pp.

A study of the pertinence of Thomistic thought to the problems of post-Kantian science. The influence of Kant is traced through the various branches of modern science such as mathematics, psychology, and the social sciences. In this perspective the area of possible scholastic contribution is outlined. C

See: CR 34 (1950) 353-55; C. Howard, DR 68 (1950) 490-93; J. Collins, T 26 (1951) 150; E. Quinn, T 196 (1950) 575.

BONJOANNES, Bernardus. *Compendium of the* SUMMA THEO-LOGICA *of St. Thomas Aquinas:* PARS PRIMA. Trans. by A. J. M. Revised by W. Lescher. New York: Benziger, 1906 (1560). 310 pp. Introduction, appendix, glossary.

A summary of the key points of the first part of the *Summa theologica.* Each question of this part is presented in a three- or four-page chapter, without special attention to the division of the question into articles. A-B

BOURKE, Vernon. *St. Thomas and the Greek Moralists.* See IX.

BRODE, W. R. *From Plotinus to St. Thomas Aquinas: Being Studies in the Later Phases of Greek Philosophy.* London: Faith, 1926. vi, 104 pp.

A survey of the great philosophers from Plotinus to St. Thomas. A chapter is devoted to each figure, and within this pattern an attempt is made to indicate the sequence of thought. A-B

CHESTERTON, G. K. *St. Thomas Aquinas.* New York: Sheed and Ward, 1933. xii, 248 pp. (Image: D 36)

A study of the life and influence of St. Thomas. Written in Chesterton's inimitable style, it is an appealing introduction to the greatness and power of the scholastic synthesis and its significance for mankind. A-B

See: A 50 (1931) 622; AER 90 (1938) 436; CHR 20 (1934) 186; CW 138 (1934) 502; MS 11 (1934) 71; RUO 6 (1936) 114*; S 13 (1934) 506; T 10 (1935) 340.

COFFEY, Reginald M. *The Man from Rocca Sicca.* Milwaukee: Bruce, 1944. xi, 140 pp.

A brief study of St. Thomas as a person. The information is quite exact, but centers on Brother Thomas himself rather than on his intellectual attainment. A-B

See: AM 59 (1944) 410-11; CW 160 (1944) 93; D 29 (1944) 31; ER 111 (1944) 76-77; HPR 44 (1944) 796; RR 3 (1944) 204; S 23 (1944) 611.

CONWAY, John P. *Saint Thomas Aquinas of the Order of Preachers (1225-1274): A Biographical Study of the Angelic Doctor.* London: Longmans, Green, 1912. 119 pp.

A brief study of the life of St. Thomas. The work is divided according to the morning, noon, evening, and night of the saint's life. A

See: CW 93 (1911) 547.

COPLESTON, Frederick C. *Aquinas*. Baltimore: Penguin, 1957
(1955). ix, 263 pp. Bibliography, index. (Pelican: A 349)
A brief account of the major aspects of Aquinas' philosophical
thought. Perhaps the most successful of such attempts, it contains a valuable chapter surveying contemporary Thomism. B-C
See: Bl 37 (1956) 37; Ph 19 (1956) 283; Ta 206 (1955) 398.

————. *Medieval Philosophy*. New York: Philosophical Library,
1952. 194 pp. Bibliography, index. (Harper Torchbook;
Cloister Library: TB 76)
A highly recommended introductory sketch of medieval philosophy. It begins with the origins of medieval thought in pa-
tristic speculation and extends through Nicholas of Cusa. There
is a remarkably lucid chapter on William of Ockham. B
See: Bl 33 (1952) 329; DR 70 (1952) 449-50; T 28 (1953) 287; Ta 200
(1952) 191; Tm 16 (1953) 150.

CURTIS, Stanley J. *A Short History of Western Philosophy in
the Middle Ages*. London: MacDonald, 1950. 286 pp.
A brief survey of Christian philosophy from St. Augustine to
Nicholas of Cusa. There is a chronological chart of the principal
Western thinkers and a scheme illustrating the chain of being in
the philosophy of Aquinas. B
See: G. McCool, A 84 (1950) 112; CR 34 (1950) 283; L. Lynch, NS 25
(1951) 488-92; H. Carpenter, Ta 196 (1950) 51.

D'ARCY, Martin C. *St. Thomas Aquinas*. Westminster, Md.:
Newman, 1954. 292 pp.
A general introduction to the philosophy of St. Thomas. The
realism of Thomism is illustrated by comparison with some other
philosophies. The chapter on modern Thomism is felt to be in
need of revision. B
See: R. Hunt, AM 79 (1954) 26; G. Vann, Bl 35 (1954) 348; IER 81
(1954) 236.

FOSTER, Kenelm. (ed) *The Life of St. Thomas Aquinas:
Biographical Documents*. Trans. by K. Foster. Baltimore,
Md.: Helicon, 1959. 172 pp. Bibliography.

A fluent translation of biographical documents from St. Thomas' contemporaries, including the bulk of Gui's life of Aquinas. This unusual book contains an informative introduction, scholarly notes, and a chronology. C-D

See: V. Shooner, Bl 40 (1959) 276-78; D 44 (1959) 187; IER 92 (1959) 205; P. McKevitt, ITQ 26 (1959) 382; M. Crowe, St 48 (1959) 368-70; T. Gregory, Ta 213 (1959) 277; TS 20 (1959) 659.

FREMANTLE, Anne. (ed.) *The Age of Belief: The Medieval Philosophers* (The Great Ages of Western Philosophy, Vol. 1). Boston: Houghton, Mifflin, 1955. 218 pp. Bibliography, index. (Mentor: MS 126)

A presentation of the thought of major medieval philosophers. The descriptive matter is interspersed with numerous selections from the philosophers themselves. The interpretive commentary, however, is not always adequate. A-B

See: A 93 (1955) 23; AM 81 (1955) 24; CB 34 (1957) 10; CW 181 (1955) 77; D 40 (1955) 211; SJR 47 (1955) 389; Tm 19 (1956) 147.

GILSON, Etienne. *The Christian Philosophy of St. Thomas Aquinas.* Trans. by L. Shook from the 5th French ed. of *Le Thomisme.* New York: Random House, 1956 (1920). x, 502 pp. Bibliography, index.

A survey of the philosophy of St. Thomas by one of its most profound contemporary students. The material is divided under the headings: God, Nature, and Morality. Remarkable for its originality, many would question the extent to which the philosophy of St. Thomas is made to depend on his theology. The work includes notes, analytical and nominal indices, and a most valuable catalogue of St. Thomas' works by I. T. Eschmann. B-D

See: W. Grace, AM 84 (1956) 24; C. O'Neil, NS 32 (1958) 387-91; J. Kleinz, P 12 (1956) 1050-51; D. Hawkins, Ta 210 (1957) 81.

――――. *Elements of Christian Philosophy.* New York: New American, 1963 (1960). viii, 380 pp. Bibliography, indices. (Mentor Omega: MT 489)

A valuable and comprehensive recapulation of Gilson's work centering on St. Thomas, but including the related positions of

other philosophers of that time. Half the text is devoted to revelation and to God. This is followed by sections on being and
man. There are copious notes. C

See: W. May, CSJ 64 (1964) 84; CW 192 (1961) 251; MS 38 (1961) 257;
G. McCool, MS 38 (1961) 334; G. McCool, TS 22 (1961) 142.

————. *History of Christian Philosophy in the Middle Ages*
(The Random House Lifetime Library). New York: Random House, 1955. 829 pp.

A clear, scholarly presentation of philosophy from the Greek
apologists to Nicholas of Cusa, deriving from Gilson's own class
lectures. There are extensive notes, giving biographical details,
primary sources, and critical editions. C-D

See: A 92 (1955) 568; K. Foster, Bl 37 (1956) 276; CHR 41 (1956) 475;
C 62 (1955) 260; CR 43 (1958) 59; D 40 (1955) 409; J. Mourant, FS 18
(1958) 96; IER 86 (1956) 366; ITQ 23 (1956) 165-71; D. Sullivan, LA 26
(1958) 63; MS 33 (1956) 122; NRT 77 (1955) 882; NS 30 (1956) 107; J.
Bastable, PS 6 (56) 142-46; Ta 207 (1956) 228; Th 30 (1955) 460.

————, and PEGIS, Anton. *St. Thomas Aquinas and Philosophy*.
West Hartford, Conn.: Saint Joseph's College Press, 1960.
30 pp. (Paper)

Two McAuley lectures of outstanding interest. In the light of
modern research, Etienne Gilson treats the problem of proving
the existence of God, while Anton Pegis studies the problem of
Thomism as a philosophy. B-C

————. *The Spirit of Medieval Philosophy* (Gifford Lectures,
1931-1932). Trans. by A. Downs. New York: Scribner's,
1936. ix, 490 pp.

A survey of Christian thought on the main philosophic problems. It develops the thesis that the spirit of medieval philosophy
is that of Christianity penetrating the Greek tradition and drawing from it a specifically Christian view of the world. B-C

See: A 56 (1936) 28; C 25 (1937) 366; CF 2 (1937) 112; CW 146 (1938)
759; DuR 193 (1933) 213; T 12 (1937) 160.

GLENN, Paul J. *A Tour of the* SUMMA. St. Louis: Herder, 1960.
466 pp.

A readable and practical introduction to the *Summa* of St. Thomas. It contains what the author considers to be the nucleus of each article and is intended to lead to consultation of the original. A

See: D 46 (1961) 259; HPR 61 (1961) 722; IER 95 (1961) 354; RR 20 (1961) 463; SJ 53 (1961) 389.

GRABMANN, Martin. *Interior Life of St. Thomas Aquinas, Presented from His Works and the Acts of His Canonization Process.* Trans. by N. Ashenbrener from *Das Seelenleben des heiligen Thomas von Aquin.* Milwaukee: Bruce, 1951 (1923) . 92 pp.

A series of lectures on the personal foundations of St. Thomas' intellectual accomplishments. The interior life of St. Thomas is investigated, especially in regard to the Saint's resources of wisdom and charity, the mainspring of his work in philosophy and theology. B-D

See: Bl 33 (1952) 142-44; J. Kittleson, C 55 (1951) 206; CR 37 (1952) 188; D 36 (1951) 327-28; RP 11 (1952) 53.

————. *Introduction to the Theological* SUMMA *of St. Thomas.* Trans. by J. Zybura from the 2d ed., revised, of *Einführung in die* SUMMA THEOLOGIAE *des heiligen Thomas von Aquin.* St. Louis: Herder, 1930 (1928) . x, 220 pp.

A general introduction to the use of the *Summa.* Through a series of considerations on the history, spirit, exposition, and structure of the work, the author provides orientation on its aim, method, and plan. B-C

See: A 44 (1930) 243; CW 132 (1931) 629; T 7 (1932) 310-15.

————. *Thomas Aquinas: His Personality and Thought.* Trans. by V. Michel from *Thomas von Aquin.* New York: Russell and Russell, 1963 (1913) . 191 pp. Bibliography.

An excellent historical introduction to St. Thomas and his work by one of the foremost research scholars on the subject. The first third of the work is a living portrait of the sources, personality, and work of St. Thomas. This is followed by a concise, well-balanced presentation of the philosophical and theological synthesis of St. Thomas as found in the *Summa theologica*. B-C

> *See:* A 40 (1929) 414; CW 129 (1929) 761; T 3 (1929) 699-701.

GILSON, Etienne. *The Spirit of Thomism*. New York: Kenedy, 1964. 127 pp.

Four lectures on Thomism delivered at Georgetown University as the Fenwick 175th Anniversary Lectures. The different types of knowledge, the order of creation, and man's knowledge of God are reviewed. B-C

HAWKINS, Denis J. *A Sketch of Medieval Philosophy*. New York: Sheed and Ward, 1947. vii, 174 pp. Index.

A brief description of Christian philosophy from Scotus Erigena to the Renaissance. The sketch, while accurate and readable, is too synoptic to convey the reality of philosophical experience. A-B

> *See:* A 78 (1947) 164; AM 66 (1947) 346; Bl 28 (1947) 346; C 46 (1947) 312-13; CR 26 (1946) 543; D 32 (1947) 221; HPR 48 (1947) 77-78; IER 69 (1947) 69; IM 74 (1946) 406-409; T 23 (1948) 171-72; Ta 187 (1946) 294.

HENLE, Robert J. *Saint Thomas and Platonism: A Study of the Plato and Platonici Texts in the Writings of Saint Thomas*. The Hague: Nijhoff, 1956. xxii, 487 pp.

An excellent study of the nature of the Platonic content in the writings of St. Thomas. An extensive history of the pertinent texts from the works of St. Thomas is provided, and the author establishes a distinction between a *via* and a *positio*. St. Thomas, it is made evident, retains a basic Aristotelianism, even while accepting many particular Platonic positions. D

> *See:* T 32 (1957) 437-43.

KENNEDY, Daniel. *St. Thomas Aquinas and Medieval Philosophy*. New York: Encyclopedia, 1919. 128 pp.

A survey of the position of St. Thomas in the context of his times. After a study of the historical background and the general state of Scholasticism at that time, there is a review of the influence of St. Thomas on philosophy and a statement of the manner in which he developed the *Summa theologica*. There is a useful synoptic chart of the *Summa*. A-B

LITTLE, Arthur. *The Platonic Heritage of Thomism*. Dublin: Golden Eagle, 1953. 290 pp.

An investigation of the Platonic content in the thought of St. Thomas. The work centers on the notion of participation, the fourth way, and the character of passive potency. Considerable reserve has been expressed concerning its precise formulation of these notions. However, the work stands as an important contribution to such studies. C-D

> *See:* I. Trethowan, DR 70 (1952) 322; M. Sweetman, IM 81 (1953) 246; L. Eslick, MS 31 (1954) 225; J. Horgan, PS 2 (1952) 89; C. Hart, Th 17 (1954) 264.

MARITAIN, Jacques. *St. Thomas Aquinas (Angelic Doctor)*. Newly trans. and revised by J. Evans and P. O'Reilly. New York: Meridian, 1958 (1931). 281 pp. Appendices and bibliographies. (M 55)

A simple but eloquent portrayal of St. Thomas. He is studied as the saint, the philosophical architect, the apostle of modern times, and the common Christian doctor. Appendices include in full the four chief modern Papal documents on Thomism and bibliographies of writings by and about St. Thomas. A-B

> *See:* J. Bastable, PS 8 (1958) 235.

MEYER, Hans. *The Philosophy of St. Thomas Aquinas*. Trans. by F. Eckhoff from *Thomas von Aquin: Sein System und seine geistesgeschichtliche Stellung*. St. Louis: Herder, 1944 (1938). viii, 581 pp. Bibliography, index.

An extensive and comprehensive introduction and companion to the work of St. Thomas. His sources are indicated, as are his true genius in developing this material into his own philosophic system. The structure of the individual and of the hierarchy of being, and the origin and order of the universe are described. The influence of the thought of St. Thomas is traced to the present day. The presentation of the distinction of form and matter and of esse and essence is not entirely adequate, and the bibliography and footnotes have unfortunately been abridged in the translation. Nevertheless, this remains a key presentation of the Thomistic synthesis. B-C

See: A 71 (1944) 457-58; AER 113 (1945) 478-79; AM 61 (1945) 125; Bl 26 (1945) 316; C 40 (1944) 379-80; CSJ 44 (1944) 213; CW 160 (1945) 478; D 29 (1944) 268-69; FS 26 (1945) 81-83; MS 22 (1945) 170-72; RR 4 (1945) 70-72; SJR 38 (1945) 61; TS 5 (1944) 551-54.

MULLANE, Donald T. *Aristotelianism in St. Thomas* (The Catholic University of America, *Philosophical Studies*, No. 17). Washington, D.C.: The Catholic University of America Press, 1929. x, 128 pp. (Paper)

An historical study of the connection between Aristotle and St. Thomas. The transmission of Aristotelianism is studied in the ancient and medieval periods in order to provide the context for the direct evaluation of this element in the spirit and content of the thought of St. Thomas. The bibliography, like the text, does not of course reflect the important work done in this area in recent decades. B-C

PEGIS, Anton C. *St. Thomas and Philosophy* (The Aquinas Lecture, 1964). Milwaukee: Marquette University Press, 1964. 89 pp.

A lecture on the effect of the theological context of the thought of St. Thomas on its philosophical content. The notions of history and providence are seen to be specified by the notion of creation. C

————. *St. Thomas and the Greeks* (The Aquinas Lecture, 1939). Milwaukee: Marquette University Press, 1939. vi, 107 pp.

A lecture emphasizing the milieu in which St. Thomas' principles were presented. The differences between St. Thomas' philosophy and that of the Greeks is seen to be centered on the question of creation. The superiority of Thomas over Plotinus in both rhetoric and dialectic is noted. B-C

See: Bl 22 (1939) 821; C 30 (1939) 543; CW 151 (1940) 124; T 15 (1940) 133-35; Ta 174 (1939) 339; Tm 2 (1940) 309.

PEGUES, Thomas. *Catechism of the* SUMMA THEOLOGICA *of Saint Thomas Aquinas for the Use of the Faithful.* Trans. by A. Whitacre from *La* SOMME THEOLOGIQUE *de Saint Thomas d'Aquin, en forme de catéchisme pour tous les fidèles.* Westminister, Md.: Newman, 1950 (1907). xvi, 315 pp.

A survey of the *Summa theologica* in question-and-answer form. The order of the material proceeds from God to man and then to Christ and the Sacraments.

See: J. Ryan, CER 49 (1951) 285.

PETITOT, Henri. *The Life and Spirit of Thomas Aquinas.* Dubuque: Priory, 1964.

A study of the life of St. Thomas as a man and as a saint. The context for the work of St. Thomas is set without any developed study of the work itself. A

PHELAN, Gerald B. *Some Illustrations of St. Thomas' Development of the Wisdom of St. Augustine* (The Mu Nu Sigma Lecture, 1946). Chicago, Ill.: Argus, 1946. 57 pp.

A lecture on some facets of the continuity of Christian philosophy. After a general introduction, the areas of God, human knowledge, and the form of being are investigated, in order to determine more precisely the character of this continuity. C

See: Tm 10 (1947) 129-30.

PIEPER, Josef. *Guide to Thomas Aquinas (Introduction to Thomas Aquinas).* Trans. by R. and C. Winston from *Hinführung zu Thomas von Aquin.* New York: Pantheon, 1962 (1958). ix, 182 pp. Bibliography.

A panoramic, yet scholarly and well-documented introduction to the life and works of St. Thomas, in which St. Thomas is seen as having solved conflicts of thirteenth-century ideologies not unlike the present-day cleavage between science and religion. A-B

See: C 76 (1962) 478; D 47 (1962) 312; W. Quinn, NS 38 (1964) 259-62.

———. (ed.) *The Human Wisdom of St. Thomas: A Breviary of Philosophy from the Works of St. Thomas Aquinas.* Trans.

D. MacLaren. New York: Sheed and Ward, 1948 (1947).
111 pp. Bibliography.

A catalogue of very brief quotations on the main topics of the
synthesis of St. Thomas. The themes: evil, intellect, morals, and
God are especially represented. A-B

See: F. Cassidy, AER 119 (1948) 155; C. Miltner, AM 68 (1948) 474; G.
Ekbery, Bl 30 (1949) 133; CR 31 (1949) 354-55; CW 167 (1948) 477; J.
McHugh, HPR 50 (1949) 201; NS 23 (1949) 124; J. Mullaney, T 24
(1949) 166.

————. *Scholasticism: Personalities and Problems of Medieval
Philosophy.* Trans. by R. and C. Winston from *Scholastik.*
New York: Pantheon, 1960. 192 pp.

A brilliant, concise survey of Scholasticism from Boethius to Ockham. Avoiding oversimplification, it is more informative than
many larger works. It includes a well-documented summation of
recent studies and offers new insight into the Tempier condemna-
tion of 1277. An epilogue evaluates the educational enterprise of
medieval Schoolmen. B

See: W. Reilly, A 104 F (1961) 538; J. Haddox, AM 93 (1961) 25; Bl 43
(1962) 191; D 46 (1961) 161; DR 80 (1962) 191; A. Hayen, NRT
82 (1960) 881; P 17 (1961) 619; M. Crowe, PS 10 (1960) 304; RR 21
(1962) 485; M. Crowe, St. 52 (1963) 438; T 36 (1961) 465.

————. *The Silence of St. Thomas.* Trans. by J. Murray and D.
O'Connor from *Ueber Thomas von Aquin und Philosophia
Negativa.* New York: Pantheon, 1957 (1949), 122 pp.

An excellent correlation of some basic insights of St. Thomas
concerning some themes of contemporary thought. It relates the
mystery of being to the response of the human intellect. A negative element is found in creation insofar as *ex nihilo* involves
each finite being in a certain lack of intelligibility. C-D

See: D 42 (1957) 351; NS 32 (1958) 393; Ta 210 (1957) 510.

ROENSCH, Frederick J. *Early Thomistic School.* Dubuque: Priory, 1964. xxii, 351 pp.

An excellent specialized study concerning the origins of the long
series of followers of St. Thomas. The early English and French

schools are studied in relation to their defense against objections coming from the Augustinian thinkers. D

SCHARLEMANN, Robert P. *Thomas Aquinas and John Gerhard (Yale Publications in Religion,* No. 7). New Haven: Yale University Press, 1964. xi, 271 pp.

A comparative study of the thought of St. Thomas and Gerhard on the freedom of God and man. St. Thomas is seen to have presented a freedom of form, and is compared to John Gerhard who developed a dialectic of obedience. The meaning of this comparison for grace, charity, and freedom is then detailed. C-D

SERTILLANGES, Antonin. *Foundations of Thomistic Philosophy.* (Catholic Library of Religious Knowledge, No. 20). Trans. by G. Anstruther from *Les grandes thèses de la philosophie thomiste.* Springfield: Templegate, 1956 (1928). 254 pp.

A simple, brief and synthetic treatment of Thomism by Thomistic scholars of this century. A-B

See: A 49 (1933) 187; CR 43 (1958) 250; CW 137 (1933) 371; T 10 (1935) 340.

————. *St. Thomas Aquinas and His Work* (Coll. "Grands Coeurs"). Trans. by G. Anstruther from *Saint Thomas d'Aquin.* London: Burns, Oates, and Washbourne, 1957 (1930). ix, 159 pp.

A splendid, popular introduction to the mind of St. Thomas. There is a survey of the biographical facts, together with an analysis of his method and influence upon his own and subsequent ages. There is neither index nor bibliography. B

STEINER, Rudolf. *The Redemption of Thinking: A Study in the Philosophy of Thomas Aquinas.* Trans. by A. Shepherd and M. Nicoll. London: Hodder and Stoughton, 1956. 191 pp. Appendices, index.

A collection of class lectures delivered in 1920 on the philosophy of St. Thomas. There is an introduction and general survey, followed by three lectures—on St. Thomas and St. Augustine, the essence of Thomism, and its place in present-day thought. Anthropologically orientated appendices complete the volume. B

See: PS 7 (1957) 178.

VANN, Gerald. *Saint Thomas Aquinas.* New York: Benziger, 1947 (1940). xxvii, 185 pp.

An evaluation of the thought of St. Thomas that depends extensively on Gilson and Dawson for historical background. The author sees ample room for intuition, contemplation, and mysticism in St. Thomas' philosophy, where characteristics of Eastern culture can be synthesized with Western thought. A-B

See: A 78 (1947) 20; AM 54 (1941) 346-47; AM 67 (1948) 90; Bl 22 (1941) 145-46; C 47 (1947) 19; CR 21 (1941) 352-54; D 26 (1941) 255-56; HPR 48 (1948) 638; T 16 (1941) 418-20; Ta 177 (1941) 133.

WALZ, Angelus M. *Saint Thomas Aquinas: A Biographical Study.* Trans. by S. Bullough from *Delineatio vitae S. Thomas de Aquino.* Westminster, Md.: Newman, 1951 (1926). xi, 254 pp. Bibliography.

An excellent scientific biography by an archivist who employs his resources to sift facts from legend. A scholarly analysis of the historical context of Thomas' thinking judiciously clarifies chronological uncertainties. Included are interesting information on universities and their curricula, a map, and chronological table. A-B

See: A. Gabriel, CHR 38 (1953) 414-15; K. Sullivan, HPR 53 (1953) 480-84; J. Collins, T 28 (1953) 287.

WHEELER, Mother Mary C. *Philosophy and the* SUMMA THEOLOGICA *of St. Thomas Aquinas* (The Catholic University of America, *Philosophical Studies,* No. 169). Washington, D.C.: The Catholic University of America Press, 1956. ix, 109 pp. Bibliography. (Paper)

A study of the place of philosophy and its influence in the *Summa theologica.* The historical, metaphysical, and psychological background of the relation between philosophy and theology in the mind of St. Thomas is reviewed as the context for a direct investigation of the *Summa* itself. There, the contributions of philosophy to the method, order, and content are reviewed along with the relation of philosophy to the materially theological sections. C

WULF, Maurice De. *History of Medieval Philosophy*. Trans. by E. Messenger from *Histoire de la philosophie médiévale*. Vol. I, New York: Dover, 1952; Vol. II, New York: Longmans, Green, 1938 (1900).

A relatively thorough survey of medieval philosophy. The first volume extends through the twelfth century, while the second volume covers the period from Thomas Aquinas through the early sixteenth century. The connection between civilization and philosophy, and the law of continuity underlying the history of philosophy are emphasized. The work is presently in need of revision in the light of recent research. B-C

> *See:* A 34 (1926) 622; A 36 (1927) 483; Bl 19 (1938) 707-709; C 4 (1926) 106-108; C 5 (1927) 334; C 23 (1936) 390; C 29 (1939) 446; CW 123 (1926) 853-54; CW 125 (1937) 709; CW 144 (1936) 253; DuR 204 (1939) 179-82; ER 99 (1938) 94.

————. *An Introduction to Scholastic Philosophy (Scholasticism, Old and New: An Introduction to Scholastic Philosophy, Medieval and Modern)*. Trans. by P. Coffey from *Introduction à la philosophie Néo-scolastique*. New York: Dover, 1956 (1903). 327 pp. (Paper)

A brief but connected view of the teachings and history of Scholasticism in the Middle Ages and modern times. The nature, methods, and disciplines of this philosophy are surveyed. The teachings are compared point by point, and the sources of differences are sought out. Though written by one of the foremost historians of Scholastic philosophy, it should now be complemented by the results of more recent research. B

————. *Philosophy and Civilization in the Middle Ages*. New York: Dover, 1953 (1922). 312 pp. (Paper)

A study of medieval philosophy in the context of its culture. This work supplements the author's presentation of medieval philosophy by linking it with the art, architecture, literature, science, and sociology of the thirteenth century. This provides a good introduction to a period when unity amid diversity was achieved. A-B

See: A 27 (1922) 163; C (1925) 1357.

———. *The System of St. Thomas (Medieval Philosophy Illustrated from the System of Thomas Aquinas).* Trans. by E. Messenger. New York: Dover, 1961 (1922). 152 pp. (Paper)
A study of the entire field of Thomistic philosophy. It deliberately excludes medieval civilization and theological problems, while concentrating on material that is strictly philosophical. Technical terminology is explained in modern equivalents. A-B

CHAPTER XVI

Franciscan Philosophy

This chapter is composed of works on the Franciscan school of philosophy. As the members of this school differ quite noticeably among themselves, the material available consists mainly of historical studies of the main figures. Those chosen as particularly representative are St. Bonaventure, John Duns Scotus, and William of Ockham. To have added more [1] would have been to divert this chapter from the direction of the total work. The material on these figures and on the school in general is divided into two sections: sources and studies. In both areas there are general bibliographical collections.[2]

The reader is referred to Chapter I of *A Bibliography of Christian Philosophy and Contemporary Issues* by the same editor.

---

[1] Of special note are Charles McKeon, *Study of the Summa philosophiae of the Pseudo-Grosseteste* (New York: Columbia University Press, 1948); and a number of studies of Roger Bacon.

[2] *Bibliographia Franciscana*, 11 vols. (Romae: Instituto Storico dei Frati Minori Cappuccini, 1931—).

Boletín Bibliográfico de ciencias del espíritu (Zaragoza: Centro de Estudios Superiores de Padres Capuchinos).

SOURCES

BONAVENTURE, SAINT [3]

The Breviloquium (The Works of Bonaventure, Vol. II). Trans. by J. de Vinck. Paterson, N.J.: St. Anthony Guild Press, 1963. xviii, 326 pp.

Commentary on the SENTENCES, I, d. 3, p. 1 in *Selections from Medieval Philosophers* (Modern Student's Library of Philosophy). Ed. by Richard McKeon. New York: Scribner's, 1959. II, 118-49.

De reductione artium ad theologiam. See Healy below.

Disputed Questions on Christ's Knowledge, Q. 4, "Whether Whatever Is Known by Us with Certitude is Known in the Eternal Reasons Themselves," in *A Scholastic Miscellany: Anselm to Ockham,* ed. by Eugene R. Fairweather *(Library of Christian Classics,* Vol. X). London: C.S.M., 1956. Pp. 379-401.

Itinerarium mentis in Deum (Works of Bonaventure). Trans. by P. Böhner. St. Bonaventure, N.Y.: Franciscan Institute, 1956. 132 pp. Also published as *The Mind's Road to God.* Trans. by George Boas. New York: Liberal Arts, 1953. (Paper)

Mystical Opuscula (The Journey of the Mind to God: The Triple Way, or Love Enkindled; The Tree of Life; The Mystical Vine; On the Perfection of Life; The Works of Bonaventure, Vol. I). Trans. by J. de Vinck. Paterson, N.J.: St. Anthony Guild Press, 1960. xii, 266 pp.

The Triple Way (The Enkindling of Love). Ed. by William I. Joffee. Paterson, N.J.: St. Anthony Guild Press, 1957 (1956). 71 pp.

---

[3] Antonius Maria a Vicentia and J. A. Rubino, *Lexicon Bonaventurianum philosophico-theologicum.* (Venetiis: 1880).

JOHN DUNS SCOTUS [4]

The DE PRINCIPIO *of John Duns Scotus* (Franciscan Institute, "Philosophy Series," No. 5). Ed. and trans. by Evan Roche. St. Bonaventure, N.Y.: The Franciscan Institute, 1949. xvii, 153 pp.

Duns Scotus: Philosophical Writings. See Wolter below.

WILLIAM OF OCKHAM [5]

Ockham: Philosophical Writings. See Böhner below.

BETTONI, Ephrem. *Duns Scotus: The Basic Principles of His Philosophy.* Ed. and trans. by Bernadine Bonansea from *Duns Scoto.* Washington, D.C.: The Catholic University of America Press, 1961 (1946). 220 pp. Bibliography.

An introduction to the philosophy of Scotus by one of the foremost scholars in the field. The various sectors of Scotus' philosophy and its particular problems are discussed, with special attention given to comparisons with alternative Scholastic positions. B

See: PS 11 (1961) 306; RUO 33 (1963) 139; TS 24 (1963) 169.

---

[4] E. Bettoni, Efrem, *Vent'anni di studi scotisti, 1920-1940* (Milano: Rivista di filosofia neoscolastica, 1943).

"Bibliographie Scotiste de langue française, 1900-1934," *La France Franciscaine,* XVIII (1935), 292-361.

M. F. Garcia, *Lexicon scholasticum philosophico-theologicum: Scotus* (Quarrachi: Typ. Collegii S. Bonaventurae, 1910).

Maurice J. Grajewski, "Scotistic Bibliography of the Last Decade (1929-1939), *Franciscan Studies,* I (1941), II (1942).

———. "Duns Scotus in the Light of Modern Research," *Proceedings of the American Catholic Philosophical Association,* XVIII (1942) 168-85.

P. Minges, *Franziskanische Studien,* IV (1917), 49-67 and 177-98.

O. Schäfer, *Bibliographia de vita, operibus, et doctrina I. D. Scoti . . . saec. XIX-XX* (Romae: Herder, 1955).

S. Simonis, *Antonianum,* III (1928), 451-84.

[5] V. Heynck, "Ockham Literatur, 1919-1949," *Franziskanische Studien,* XXXII (1950), 164-83.

————. *St. Bonaventure.* Trans. by A. Gambatese from *S. Bonaventura.* South Bend, Ind.: University of Notre Dame Press, 1964. 127 pp. (PL 4)

A brief presentation of the life and thought of St. Bonaventure by one of the world's leading experts on the subject. The progress of his thought, from his conception of knowledge, wisdom, and God as exemplar, to the structure of the creature, man's activity, and his return to God, is discussed, with emphasis on its dynamic aspect. B

BÖHNER, Philotheus. *Collected Articles on Ockham* (Franciscan Institute, "Philosophy Series," No. 12). Ed. by Eligius M. Buytaert. St. Bonaventure, N.Y.: The Franciscan Institute, 1958. x, 482 pp.

A series of articles drawn from the much more extensive work on this subject by one of the most profound scholars of Ockham's work. The articles range from reports of work done on manuscripts to the metaphysics and politics of Ockham. However, they naturally center on questions of material and formal logic. C-D

————. *The History of the Franciscan School.* 4 vols. (mimeographed). Detroit: Duns Scotus College, 1946-47 (1943). Bibliography.

Four studies of the Franciscan School, centering on A. of Hales, St. Bonaventure, Scotus, and Ockham, prepared for the author's classes on these subjects. The philosophical development of this group of scholars is followed in sure but brief lines. B-C

————. (ed.) *Ockham: Philosophical Writings* (Nelson Philosophical Texts). London: Nelson, 1957. lix, 154 pp. Index.

A collection of texts from widely scattered parts of the writings of William of Ockham, which, when gathered under general headings, represent practically all sectors of philosophical thought. The logical problems occupy half the volume, and the exceptionally long introduction constitutes an important summary of the philosophy of Ockham. C-D

————. *The* TRACTATUS DE PRAEDESTINATIONE ET DE PRAESCIENTIA DEI DE FUTURIS CONTINGENTIBUS *of William of Ockham* (Franciscan Institute, "Philosophy Series," No. 2) . St. Bonaventure, N.Y.: The Franciscan Institute, 1945. xi, 139 pp. Appendices. (Paper)

An untranslated presentation of the *De praedestinatione,* accompanied by extensive interpretation and appendices from the writings of Ockham, Aureolus, and Rimini. The author not only discusses the authenticity of the text, but goes deeply into its various definitions and main thesis. There is also an important study of Ockham's position on three-valued logic. D

BOUGEROL, J. Guy. *Introduction to the Works of St. Bonaventure.* Trans. by J. de Vinck. Paterson, N.J.: St. Anthony Guild Press, 1963. 240 pp. Bibliography, index, appendices.

An advanced introduction to the writings of St. Bonaventure. The sources are reviewed in detail, and St. Bonaventure's technique and his work itself are analyzed. C-D

> *See:* E. Watkin, DR 81 (1963) 72; IER 100 (1963) 263; PS 12 (1963) 266.

CAMPBELL, Bertrand J. *The Problem of One or Plural Substantial Forms in Man as Found in the Works of St. Thomas Aquinas and John Duns Scotus.* See VI.

DADY, Sr. Mary R. *The Theory of Knowledge of Saint Bonaventure* (The Catholic University of America, *Philosophical Studies,* No. 52) . Washington, D.C.: The Catholic University of America Press, 1939. 102 pp. Bibliography, index. (Paper)

A survey of numerous questions concerning knowledge in the philosophy of St. Bonaventure. The study ranges from the soul and its faculties to the knowledge process, the problem of the *rationes aeternae,* and the problem of truth and certitude. C

DAY, Sebastian J. *Intuitive Cognition: A Key to the Significance of the Later Scholastics* (Franciscan Institute, "Philosophy Series," No. 4) . St. Bonaventure, N.Y.: The Franciscan Institute, 1947. xiii, 217 pp. (Paper)

A study of the understanding of intuition in the texts of Scotus and Ockham, carried out in relation to the problem as it arose through the Aristotelian-Scholastic milieu. The subject is treated systematically and some vital distinctions are uncovered. C-D

See: V. Fochtman, FS 9 (1949) 77-79; L. Kendzierski, NS 23 (1949) 110-12.

EFFLER, Roy R. *John Duns Scotus and the Principle: "Omne quod movetur ab alio movetur"* (Franciscan Institute, "Philosophy Series," No. 15). Louvain: Nauwelaerts, 1962. vii, 208 pp.

A study of the problem of motion as understood by Scotus. The historical context is established and the problem of motion and self-motion is surveyed. Particular attention is given to the problems of gravity and to the motion involved in intellection and willing. D

See: IER 101 (1964) 141.

FUCHS, Oswald. *The Psychology of Habit According to William of Ockham* (Franciscan Institute, "Philosophy Series," No. 8). St. Bonaventure, N.Y.: The Franciscan Institute, 1952. xix, 110 pp. Bibliography, index. (Paper)

A study of habit in Ockham's philosophy of knowledge and appetite. The general notion of habit is discussed, as also its realization in the processes of knowledge. There is an extensive review of habit's realization in the conative processes of appetite, passion, and will, and the implications for moral behavior are drawn. C

See: V. Bourke, NS 28 (1954) 220.

GILSON, Etienne. *The Philosophy of St. Bonaventure.* Trans. by I. Trethowan and F. Sheed from *La philosophie de saint Bonaventure.* Paterson, N.J.: St. Anthony's Guild Press, 1965 (1924). xiii, 551 pp. Bibliography, index.

An excellent and detailed study of the philosophy of St. Bonaventure in all its aspects. St. Bonaventure, the man, and his evaluation of earlier philosophers are analyzed; the Saint's thought on God, creation, and various levels of creatures is presented. C-D

See: CHR 25 (1939) 229-30; DR 204 (1939) 179-82; T 14 (1939) 492-93.

GRAJEWSKI, Maurice J. *The Formal Distinction of Duns Scotus* (The Catholic University of America, *Philosophical Studies,* No. 40). Washington, D.C.: The Catholic University of America Press, 1944. xv, 211 pp. Bibliography, Index. (Paper)

A study of the formal distinction and its uses in the philosophy of Scotus. The background to this study is the history of the problem of formal, as opposed to real and virtual, distinctions. Types of distinctions in Scotus' thought are detailed, in order to identify the precise meaning of his formal distinction, which is then traced through his metaphysics, psychology, and theodicy. C

See: Bl 28 (1947) 44; FS 7 (1947) 361; MS 24 (1947) 120-21; St 36 (1947) 125-27.

HARRIS, Charles R. *Duns Scotus.* 2 vols. New York: Humanities, 1959 (1927). Bibliography.

The first volume of this extensive study of the philosophy of Duns Scotus centers on the place of his philosophy within the general context of the age and the immediate context of his faith and theology. In the second volume, each aspect of his philosophy is discussed in detail. D

See: A 38 (1927) 45; C 7 (1928) 1158; CW 128 (1928) 245.

HEALY, Sr. Emma T. *Saint Bonaventure's* DE REDUCTIONE ARTIUM AD THEOLOGIAM *(Works of Bonaventure)*. St. Bonaventure, N.Y.: The Franciscan Institute, 1955 (1939). 158 pp. (Paper)

A translation and commentary on the *De reductione.* The commentary outlines the division of the types of knowledge according to the four "lights" and investigates the relation of philosophy to theology according to this pattern. C-D

See: HPR 42 (1941) 92-93; IER 57 (1941) 479.

LEFF, Gordon. *Medieval Thought from Augustine to Ockham.* See XIV.

MENGES, Mathew C. *The Concept of Univocity Regarding the Predication of God and Creature According to William Ockham* (Franciscan Institute, "Philosophy Series," No. 9). St. Bonaventure, N.Y.: Franciscan Institute, 1952. xi, 196 pp. Bibliography, index. (Paper)

A study of univocity in relation to equivocity and analogy in predication concerning God. This study draws on an analysis of univocity in relation to signification and then in relation to similarity. Following Ockham's thought to the fact of predication about God, which is neither equivocal nor analogical, the author then shows how one univocal concept about God and creature is abstracted, and in this way investigates the concept of being. C-D

See: MS 31 (1954) 143.

MOODY, Ernest A. *The Logic of William Ockham*. London: Sheed and Ward, 1935. xiv, 322 pp. Bibliography, indices.

This survey is introduced by a statement of the relation of Ockham to the Scholastic tradition, and investigates Ockham's logic of terms and such notions as universal, category, signification, demonstration, and consequences. C-D

See: A 55 (1936) 211; AER 95 (1936) 322; Bl 19 (1938) 469; C 23 (1936) 700; CW 143 (1936) 373; DR 54 (1936) 268; HPR 36 (1936) 1220; IER 47 (1936) 443; MS 14 (1937) 93; T 167 (1936) 10.

————. *Truth and Consequence in Medieval Logic*. See III.

O'DONNELL, Clement M. *The Psychology of St. Bonaventure and St. Thomas Aquinas* (The Catholic University of America, *Philosophical Studies*, No. 36). Washington, D.C.: The Catholic University of America Press, 1937. 111 pp. Bibliography, index. (Paper)

In this general survey, man's soul is studied extensively as to its origin, immortality, and individuation. Knowledge and the relative superiority of the will are also considered. C

PRENTICE, Robert P. *Psychology of Love According to St. Bonaventure* (Franciscan Institute, "Philosophy Series," No. 6).

St. Bonaventure, N.Y.: Franciscan Institute, 1957. xiv, 136 pp. (Paper)

A survey of the nature and problems of love in the philosophy of Bonaventure. Love is set in the context of the affective, and its divisions, especially as regards egocentricity and alterocentricity, are discussed in detail. C

SAINT MAURICE, Béraud de. *John Duns Scotus: A Teacher for Our Times.* Trans. by C. Duffy from *Jean Duns Scot, un docteur des temps nouveaux.* St. Bonaventure, N.Y.: Franciscan Institute, 1955 (1944).

The philosophical issues discussed here are: the univocity of being, the formal distinction, the primacy of the will, and the morality of human acts. Theological issues and those characteristics of his thought especially significant for modern thought are also treated. C

See: ER 113 (1945) 240; FS 6 (1946) 236-38; MS 23 (1946) 227-28.

SHAPIRO, Herman. *The Notion of Time and Place According to William of Ockham* (Franciscan Institute, "Philosophy Series," No. 13). St. Bonaventure, N.Y.: Franciscan Institute, 1957. viii, 151 pp. Bibliography.

A study of the reality of motion as seen by Ockham, with his special emphasis on its distinction from both substantial beings and abstract entities. Against the background of science at that time, the author achieves new insights concerning the mechanics of Ockham and his philosophy of external relations. C-D

SHARP, Dorothy E. *Franciscan Philosophy at Oxford in the Thirteenth Century.* New York: Russell and Russell, 1964 (1930). 419 pp. Bibliography, index.

Each philosopher is considered singly in studies subdivided according to the key philosophical issues. There is a concluding summary. C-D

SHIRCEL, Cyril L. *The Univocity of the Concept of Being in the Philosophy of Duns Scotus* (The Catholic University of

America, *Philosophical Studies*, No. 67). Washington, D.C.: The Catholic University of America Press, 1942. 187 pp. (Paper)

The notion of univocity is compared to that of analogy and investigated in relation to being as the object of the intellect and the subject of metaphysics. C-D

See: FS 25 (1944) 295-96; HPR 44 (1944) 634-35.

SPARGO, Emma J. *The Category of the Aesthetic in the Philosophy of St. Bonaventure*. (Franciscan Institute, "Philosophy Series," No. 11). St. Bonaventure, N.Y.: Franciscan Institute, 1953. xi, 162 pp. Bibliography. (Paper)

A study of beauty in the fully transcendental dimensions which it possesses in the philosophy of St. Bonaventure. The nature of beauty is identified, along with its realization in the material world as an imitation of uncreated beauty. C

See: Sr. M. Rachael, FS 15 (1955) 91-92.

TORNAY, Stephen C. *Ockham: Studies and Selections*. LaSalle, Ill.: Open Court, 1938. viii, 207 pp.

This includes a survey of Ockham's positions in logic, natural philosophy, and ethics. The texts are on the same subject areas, with additional selections on natural theology. Often they are only brief fragments, but the compilation constitutes an interesting summary of Ockham's philosophy in his own words. B-C

VIER, Peter C. *Evidence and Its Function According to John Duns Scotus* (Franciscan Institute, "Philosophy Series," No. 7). St. Bonaventure, N.Y.: Franciscan Institute, 1951. xi, 174 pp. Bibliography. (Paper)

A study of the problem of evidence in relation to previous interpretations of the notion of illumination. The background to the problem having been set, the question of the evidence of principles and syllogisms is taken up, along with the problem of evidence for other kinds of knowledge, such as knowledge of internal acts and sensations. C

See: J. Brady, NS 27 (1953) 239-40.

WEBERING, Damascene. *Theory of Demonstration According to William of Ockham* (Franciscan Institute, "Philosophy Series," No. 10). St. Bonaventure, N.Y.: Franciscan Institute, 1953. xii, 186 pp. Bibliography, index. (Paper)

In this study of Ockham's thought on the nature and object of demonstration, demonstrative proof is studied in its terms and propositions. It is also studied on the questions of the demonstrability of existence, definitions, and proper attributes. D

WOLTER, Allan B. (ed.) *Duns Scotus: Philosophical Writings* (Nelson Philosophical Texts). London: Nelson, 1962. xxiii, 360 pp. Bibliography.

A collection of questions from the *Ordinatio* on problems concerning metaphysics, knowledge of God and of his unicity, human knowledge, and the spirituality of the soul. Since well-translated selections generally embrace such problems in their entirety, material for serious work on the intrinsic thought of Scotus is provided. B-D

See: MS 25 (1947) 85-87.

————. *The Transcendentals and Their Function in the Metaphysics of Duns Scotus* (The Catholic University of America, "Philosophical Studies," No. 96). Washington, D.C.: The Catholic University of America Press, 1946. xvi, 204 pp. (Paper)

A study of the broad range of transcendental notions in the philosophy of Scotus. An investigation of the nature of transcendentals in general is followed by a more detailed study of the particularities of being, pure perfections, and the coextensive and disjunctive transcendentals. C-D

CHAPTER XVII

Personalist-Existential-Phenomenological Philosophy

This chapter is composed of works in Christian philosophy on evolutionary, personalist, existential, or phenomenological thought. As these orientations have had a broad influence on contemporary philosophy, they are manifest in a large number of the more recent works in Part I. The present chapter includes not only works specifically concerned with personalism, existentialism, and phenomenology, but those written by and about the seminal philosophers in those groups who have developed their philosophy along the lines of Christian philosophy.[1] Numerous bibliographies and dictionaries of this orientation will be helpful.[2] While an equally extensive confrontation and complementation has not taken place

---

[1] In delving further into the context of this philosophical orientation, the reader may be aided by the following books which do not fall within the area of annotation of this bibliography:

W. Barrett, *Irrational Man: A Study in Existential Philosophy* (Garden City, N.Y.: Doubleday, 1962).

———, *What Is Existentialism?* (New York: Grove, 1964).

D. Bonhoeffer, *Act and Being*. Trans. B. Noble (London: Collins, 1962).

F. Heinemann, *Existentialism and the Modern Predicament* (London: Black, 1953).

W. Kaufmann (ed.), *Existentialism from Dostoevsky to Sartre* (New York: Meridian, 1956).

J. MacQuarrie, *An Existentialist Theology: A Comparison of Heidegger and Bultmann* (London: S.C.M., 1955).

F. Molina, *Existentialism as Philosophy* (Englewood Cliffs, N.J.: Prentice-Hall, 1962).

R. Olson, *An Introduction to Existentialism* (New York: Dover, 1962).

[2] K. Douglas, *A Critical Bibliography of Existentialism: The Paris School* (New Haven: Yale University Press, 1959).

R. B. Winn, *A Concise Dictionary of Existentialism* (New York: Philosophical Library, 1960).

between Christian philosophy and the directions of philosophic thought more characteristic of the English-speaking world, some work has begun.[3]

The reader is referred to Chapters II and IV of *A Bibliography of Christian Philosophy and Contemporary Issues* by the same editor.

H. Spiegelberg, *The Phenomenological Movement* (The Hague: Nijhoff, 1960), II, 708-28.

H. Feick, *Index zu Heideggers Sein und Zeit* (Tübingen: Niemeyer, 1961).

H. Lübbe, "Bibliographie der Heidegger-Literatur, 1917-1955," *Zeitschrift für philosophische Forschung*, XI (1957), 401-52.

G. Schneeberger, *Ergänzungen zu einer Heidegger-Bibliographie* (Bern: A. G. Suhr, 1960).

H. L. Van Breda, "Bibliographie der bis zum 30. Juni 1959 veröffentlichten Schriften Husserls," in *Edmund Husserl, 1859-1959* (The Hague: Nijhoff, 1959), pp. 289-306.

L. Eley, "Husserl-Bibliographie," *Zeitschrift für philosophische Forschung*, XIII (1959), 357-69.

J. Patocka, "Husserl bibliographie," *Revue Internationale de Philosophie*, I (1939), 379-97.

J. Raes, "Supplément à la bibliographie de Husserl," *Revue Internationale de Philosophie*, XIV (1950), 469-75.

J. D. Robert, "Elements de bibliographie Husserlienne," *Tijdschrift voor Philosophie*, XX (1958), 534-44.

A. Robinet, *Merleau-Ponty, sa vie, son oeuvre* (Paris: Presses Universitaires de France, 1963), pp. 67-74.

D. F. Vansina, "Bibliographie de Paul Ricoeur (—June 30, 1962)" in *Revue Philosophique de Louvain*, LX (1962), 394-413.

[3] Along with the investigations listed below, under the series of Ph.D. theses, the following will be of some help in this area:

Analytic Philosophy, see I.

J. Blewett (ed.), *John Dewey: His Thought and Influence* ("The Orestes Brownson Series on Contemporary Thought and Affairs," No. 2; New York: Fordham University Press, 1960).

R. Butler, *The Mind of Santayana* (Chicago, Ill.: Regnery, 1955).

M. Charlesworth, *Philosophy and Linguistic Analysis*, see IV.

Contemporary American Philosophy, see I.

Current British and American Realism, see I.

I. Leclerc, *Whitehead's Metaphysics: An Introductory Exposition* (New York: Macmillan, 1958).

G. Marcel, *Royce's Metaphysics*. Trans. by V. and G. Ringer (Chicago, Ill.: Regnery, 1956).

ALLEN, Edgar L. *Existentialism from Within.* London: Routledge and Kegan Paul, 1953. ix, 185 pp. Index.

A literate but relatively simple introduction to the dialectic within the existentialist group. The background of the movement is sketched; the process of thought is traced from negative aspects of existence, through an attempt to realize freedom, to its transcendent fulfillment. The work of leading existentialists, concluding with Marcel, is surveyed. B

> *See:* Bl 34 (1953) 297; DR 71 (1953) 454; Trethowan, DuR 227 (1953) 203.

ALLER, Catherine. *The Challenge of Pierre Teilhard de Chardin.* New York: Exposition, 1964. 56 pp.

A general survey of the thought of this thinker. The work centers on *The Phenomenon of Man.* A

BLACKHAM, Harold H. *Six Existentialist Thinkers.* London: Routledge and Kegan Paul, 1952. 173 pp. Bibliography, index.

An exposition of the thought of the leading existential thinkers from Kierkegaard to Sartre and Heidegger. Nietzsche, Jaspers, and Marcel also receive separate chapters, and in the final chapter an attempt is made to underline some of the dominant themes and allay some of the misinformed criticism on this subject. B

BOBBIO, Norberto. *The Philosophy of Decadentism: A Study in Existentialism.* Trans. by D. Moore. Oxford: Blackwell, 1948 (1944). viii, 60 pp. Appendix.

An extremely strong critique of existentialism. Its birth in crisis is seen to be reflected in its own difficulties, which are traced through its philosophy of knowledge, man, and morality. The work has special relevance to the Italy of the Second World War years. C

> *See:* D. Nicholl, Bl 29 (1948) 485.

BONHOEFFER, Dietrich. *Act and Being.* Trans. by B. Noble. New York: Harper, 1962. 192 pp.

A study of ultimate perspectives based on being and on act. It was presented as the author's inaugural dissertation. The contingency of act is contrasted to the givenness of being as the basic contrast in modern and contemporary thinkers. A synthesis is outlined on the basis of revelation in a community of persons. C

BUGBEE, Henry G. *The Inward Morning: A Philosophical Exploration in Journal Form.* New York: Collier, 1961 (1958). 232 pp.

A philosophical diary, August 26, 1952—November 5, 1953, strongly related to the thought of Gabriel Marcel. The dominant theme is that of finality: finding the meaning of reality realized in true decision and tracing the freedom of man to its ultimate ground. This is a uniquely personal document of rich existential insight. B-C

See: D 48 (1963) 254; T. Heath, TS 25 (1964) 100.

CHISHOLM, Roderick M. (ed.) *Realism and the Background of Phenomenology.* Glencoe, Ill.: Free Press, 1960. viii, 308 pp. Bibliography, index.

A collection of writings from the sources of phenomenology and of various kinds of English and American realism. The first half of the book, devoted mostly to Brentano and Husserl, provides substantial insight into their contribution to the foundation of phenomenology. C

COLLINS, James. *The Existentialists: A Critical Study.* Chicago, Ill.: Regnery, 1959 (1952). xiv, 268 pp. Bibliography, index. (Gateway)

A study of the origin of existentialism, its principal exponents, and its basic themes. The major portion of the book is devoted to an analysis of Sartre, Jaspers, Marcel, and Heidegger, by means of which the demand for the transcendent and its roots in man's being become increasingly clear. The concluding "Five Existential Themes" summarizes the acquired insights concerning the nature of philosophy and of man in relation to his fellows and to God. This exposition contains a most effective critique of the subject. B-D

See: J. La Farge, A 87 (1952) 403-404; R. Harper, MS 30 (1953) 175-79; K. Reinhardt, NS 27 (1953) 217-18; V. Yanitelli, TS 13 (1952) 628; V. Smith, Th 15 (1952) 658-60.

CROONENBURG, Engelbert J. Van. *Gateway to Reality: An Introduction.* See II.

DESAN, Wilfrid. *The Planetary Man (A Noetic Prelude to a United World,* Vol. I) . Washington, D.C.: Georgetown University Press, 1961. 132 pp.

A study of man's place in the universe, as seen against a background of contemporary existential themes. Considerable effort is made to carry this thought further by showing the realization of the authenticity of the individual to be possible only in relation to the whole and to God. This work of personal reflection is an important contribution to contemporary thought. C-D

See: G 44 (1963) 409; NRT 85 (1963) 546.

————. *The Tragic Finale: An Essay on the Philosophy of Jean-Paul Sartre.* Revised ed. New York: Harper, 1960 (1954) . xxv, 228 pp. Bibliography, indices. (TB 1030)

An exceptionally capable exposition and critique of the philosophy of Sartre. The exposition covers the basic themes of the for-itself, in-itself, and freedom. The critique attends to these points and finds them open to a radical subjectivism, to which the author suggests a positive corrective in his work, *The Planetary Man.* C-D

See: J. Gurr, SO 5 (1955) 414.

DONDEYNE, Albert. *Contemporary European Thought and Christian Faith.* See VIII.

————. *Faith and the World.* See VIII.

DUPRE, Louis. *Kierkegaard as Theologian: The Dialectic of Christian Existence.* Trans. of *Kierkegaard's Theologie.* New York: Sheed and Ward, 1963 (1958) . 229 pp.

In this work on the religious thought of a seminal existential thinker, the initiation of Kierkegaard's religious questions—concerning the dialectic of sin, grace, faith, and the imitation of Christ—are studied. The specific characteristics of a Protestant existentialism are also noted. B-D

See: A 108 (1963) 775; B. Endres, CCr 15 (1963) 380; J. McNassar, E 70 (1964) 89; Q. Lauer, TS 24 (1963) 510.

FRANCOEUR, Robert T. *The World of Teilhard*. Baltimore, Md.: Helicon, 1961. 208 pp. Bibliography, index.

A collection of articles on the thought of Teilhard de Chardin. The papers, by specialists in diverse fields, study this thought as a point of synthesis for various approaches to nature and to man. The articles are sympathetic while retaining an independence for criticism. B-C

GALLAGHER, Kenneth. *The Philosophy of Gabriel Marcel* ("The Orestes Brownson Series on Contemporary Thought and Affairs"). New York: Fordham University Press, 1962. xvi, 179 pp. Bibliography.

A study of the philosophy of Marcel in its entirety, which stresses its metaphysical rather than its phenomenological aspects. His mode of philosophizing is studied, and the material is organized on the basis of a threefold participation on the levels of incarnation, communion, and transcendence. C

See: A 107 (1962) 749; Bl 44 (1963) 186; C 77 (1962) 19; IPQ 3 (1963) 334; V. Miceli, J 38 (1963) 307; R. Fisher, MS 41 (1963) 90; M. Reilly, PS 11 (1963) 446; J. Sikora, RR 22 (1963) 714.

HARPER, Ralph. *Existentialism: A Theory of Man*. Cambridge: Harvard University Press, 1949 (1948). xii, 163 pp. Appendix.

A study of various existential approaches to the understanding of man. The problem is first stated in existential terms and the general contemporary experience is surveyed. Subsequent chapters are concerned in particular with the dialectic of Kierkegaard, the ontological nihilism of Heidegger, and the new humanism of Sartre. Rousselot's interiorized scholasticism is also noted. B-C

See: D. Nicholl, Bl 30 (1949) 235.

————. *The Sleeping Beauty*. New York: Harper, 1955. 144 pp.
A philosophical study, existential in orientation, organized according to the pattern of the sequence of the periods of day and night. The structure of *Sleeping Beauty* is used to indicate the developing awareness of man's existential dimensions and their social implications. C

HERBERG, Will. *Four Existentialist Theologians: A Reader from the Works of Jacques Maritain, Nicolas Berdyaev, Martin Buber, and Paul Tillich*. Garden City, N.J.: Doubleday, 1958. x, 346 pp. (Anchor)
A collection of writings by leading contemporary thinkers who have been influenced by the existential perspective. The selections from Maritain: on the desire to see God, on the existent, on the individual, and on the state and the natural and moral laws, are typical of the breadth of interest of the total volume. B-C

See: D 43 (1958) 324-28.

KINGSTON, Frederick Temple. *French Existentialism: A Christian Critique*. Toronto: University of Toronto Press, 1961. xv, 221 pp. Bibliography, index.
A basically sympathetic study of one sector of existential thought, with special attention to its relevance to the development of theistic and Christian thought. The basic themes of existentialism are reviewed in consideration not only of the situation of philosophical thought and its orientation toward God, but of the epistemological openings of new modes of approach favorable to ecumenical dialogue. B-C

KOPP, Joseph. *Teilhard de Chardin*. New York: Paulist, 1964. (Deus Books)
A general survey of the thought of Teilhard de Chardin. The thought is set in the framework of his life and work. A-B

LANGAN, Thomas. *The Meaning of Heidegger: A Critical Study of an Existentialist Phenomenology*. New York: Columbia University Press, 1959. ix, 247 pp. Bibliography, index.

A critical study in which is constructed the outline of Heidegger's philosophical thought along the lines projected in the introduction to *Sein und Zeit*. In the first part, time is set as the horizon of the question concerning being, while an attempt is made to establish that the nature of authentic existence derives from originative thinking. In the second part, the Heideggerian evaluation of the historical sequence of Western metaphysics is followed. The presentation is fundamentally sound, though it has been questioned on a number of points. The author is in sympathy with the thought of his subject, while remaining sufficiently critical to make some important recommendations. C

See: Q. Lauer, IPQ 1 (1961) 178-82; Q. Lauer, MS 38 (1961) 161; R. Allers, NS 36 (1962) 445-74; Q. Lauer, T 35 (1960) 457.

LAUER, J. Quentin. *The Triumph of Subjectivity: An Introduction to Transcendental Phenomenology* ("The Orestes Brownson Series on Contemporary Thought and Affairs," No. 1). New York: Fordham University Press, 1958. ix, 185 pp. (*Phenomenology: Its Senses and Prospect;* Harper: TB 1169)

A genetic study of phenomenology, centering on the intentionality of consciousness, especially in the later Husserl. It traces the orientation toward the development of a transcendental subjectivity and the explanation of "the other" within this perspective. C-D

See: T. Langan, MS 38 (1960) 64-68; NS 34 (1960) 523; F. Crosson, PS (1958) 207-209; R. Hinners, T 34 (1959) 136.

LAVELLE, Louis. *Evil and Suffering*. Trans. by B. Murchland from *Le mal et la souffrance*. New York: Macmillan, 1963. 159 pp.

A combination of the two essays, "Evil and Suffering" and "Those Who Are Separated and United." It is not restricted to the subjects that comprise its title, but shows also how these provide a

means of reaching a deeper appreciation of the individual and
his communion with others. B-C

See: H. Fenton, CC 16 (1964) 110.

MARCEL, Gabriel. *Being and Having*. Trans. by K. Farrer from
Etre et avoir. Boston: Beacon, 1951 (1935) . 240 pp. (Harper: TB 310)

A series of metaphysical and religious reflections. The first section
is composed of the author's metaphysical diary during the period
1928-1933, together with an outline of a phenomenology of having. The other section consists of a comparison between irreligion
and faith, with a special study of the position of Peter Wust on
the nature of piety. B-D

See: D. Nicholl, Bl 31 (1950) 43; CW 17 (1951) 5; DR 67 (1949) 460-63;
R. Harvanek, MS 29 (1952) 345-49; Ta 194 (1949) 137-38.

————. *Creative Fidelity*. Trans. by R. Rosthal from *Du refus à
l'invocation*. New York: Farrar, Straus, 1964 (1940) . 261
pp. Index.

An excellent summary of Marcel's philosophy. Identifying incar-
nate being as that from which philosophizing begins, Marcel pro-
gresses from the notions of act and person to the subjects of transcendence and God. The implications for tolerance and ecumenism are drawn. B-D

See: D. Drennen, A 110 (1964) 320; M. Anthony, BS 23 (1964) 386.

————. *The Decline of Wisdom*. Trans. by M. Harari from *Le
déclin de la sagesse*. London: Harvill, 1955 (1954). 56 pp.

A plea for the reconstitution of wisdom. This is seen to be particularly required in view of the restrictions of industrial civilization, while man's spiritual heritage manifests that such a recom-
position is within his capabilities. B-C

See: F. Wihelmsen, C 62 (1955) 623; D. DeSousa, CER 54 (1956) 283;
CR 40 (1955) 505; R. Richard, NS 30 (1956) 389; RUO 26 (1956) 249*;
W. Krolikowski, SO 6 (1956) 295.

————. *The Existential Background of Human Dignity* (William
James Lectures, 1961-1962) . Cambridge: Harvard University Press, 1963. 178 pp. Index.

A study of the place of man within a context of being in which his dignity is assured. The ultimate perspective set is one of participation in existence. In this, is found the basis for a resolution of human ambiguity and an appreciation of man's dignity.

―――. *Homo Viator: Introduction to a Metaphysics of Hope.* Trans. by E. Crawford from *Homo viator: prolégomènes à une métaphysique de l'espérance.* Chicago, Ill.: Regnery, 1951 (1944). 270 pp. (Paper)

A strong rejection of the pessimism of other existentialists such as Sartre and Camus, and an attempt to constitute a perspective productive of hope. This is achieved on a phenomenological basis, and leads to the necessity of recognizing a source of being and value as the only alternative to a conception of man as absurd. B-C

See: M. Harrington, CW 18 (1952) 4; C. Cary-Elwes, DuR 227 (1953) 210; J. Collins, SO 3 (1953) 42-43.

―――. *Man Against Mass Society (Man Against Humanity).* Trans. by G. Fraser from *Les hommes contre l'humain.* Chicago, Ill.: Regnery, 1962 (1952). 273 pp. (Gateway: 6077)

A study of the threat to the realization of the authentic person, and of the steps that need to be taken as a corrective. The loss of freedom of the individual in modern society, and the loss of an appreciation of the individual in favor of a philosophical abstraction are seen to be the modern dangers. The dignity of the person in the light of the transcendent is considered to be the only antidote to the predominance of the masses. C

See: G. Sloyan, A 88 (1953) 708; C. Ryan, Bl 33 (1952) 528; E. Littlejohn, C 57 (1953) 386; I. Trethowan, DR 70 (1952) 427; C. Cary-Elwes, DuR 227 (1953) 210; E. Weis, SO 3 (1953) 462; V. Yanitelli, TS 14 (1953) 528.

―――. *Metaphysical Journal.* Trans. by B. Wall from *Journal métaphysique.* Chicago, Ill.: Regnery, 1960 (1914-1923). xii. 344 pp. Index, appendix.

A series of entries of a personally reflective character, written between 1914-1923. They manifest Marcel in the process of a gradual separation from idealistic and systematic presuppositions as he lays the foundations of his future philosophical development. C-D

See: C. Ryan, Bl 33 (1952) 528-29; J. Mullaney, C 56 (1952) 636; J. Collins, T 28 (1953) 306; D. Schlegel, Ta 200 (1952) 210; V. Yanitelli, TS 13 (1952) 630.

―――. The Mystery of Being (Gifford Lectures, 1949). 2 vols. Trans. by G. Fraser and R. Hague from Le mystère de l'être. Chicago, Ill.: Regnery, 1960 (1949). (Gateway: 6054-55)

The closest approximation to a systematic presentation of the position of this existential thinker. The first volume, Reflection and Mystery, is methodological· in character, relating to the phenomenological approach of other existentialists and centering the process of philosophizing on interior reflection by the person in free communion with other subjects. The second volume, Faith and Reality, proceeds to the study of being, identifying the notions of faith, freedom, and hope, which correspond to the participated character of this human existence. B-D

See: Vol. I: C. Ryan, Bl 32 (1951) 110-13; DR 69 (1951) 255; J. Macmillan, DuR 224 (1950) 127-30; R. Harvanek, MS 29 (1952) 345-49; NS 26 (1952) 257-59; F. Copleston, Ta 197 (1951) 30. Vol. II: I. Trethowan, DR 69 (1951) 255; R. Harvanek, MS 29 (1952) 345-49; R. Richard, NS 27 (1953) 234-35; F. Copleston, Ta 198 (1951) 398; V. Yanitelli, TS 13 (1952) 279-81; A. Portz, Wo 26 (1952) 159-60.

―――. The Philosophy of Existentialism (Philosophy of Existence). Trans. by M. Harari. New York: Citadel, 1962 (1933-1947). 128 pp. (Paper)

A collection of four essays, of which one is autobiographical, another a critique of Sartre, and the remaining two outlines of the main features of the author's own philosophy. This work provides a fine introduction to a study of Marcel or of existentialism. B-C

See: E. Kilzer, ACSR 10 (1949) 287; D. Nicholl, Bl 30 (1949) 135-37; D 34 (1949) 236; I. Trethowan, DR 67 (1949) 101-102; R. Allers, NS 24 (1950) 461-63; V. Yanitelli, T 24 (1949) 732; Th 13 (1950) 631-33.

MIHALICH, Joseph C. *Existentialism and Thomism*. New York: Philosophical Library, 1960. 91 pp. (Paper)

A collection of essays on Sartre's concept of freedom, Marcel's ontology of love, Heideggerian and Sartrian cognition, and Husserl. Special attention is given to their pertinence to Thomism. A-B

See: MS 39 (1962) 296; SJR 54 (1961) 102.

MOUNIER, Emmanuel. *Be Not Afraid (Personalism)*. Trans. by C. Rowland from *Qu'est ce que le personalisme* and *La petite peur de XXᵉ Siècle*. New York: Sheed and Ward, 1962 (1946-1948). xxvii, 203 pp.

A translation of two works in personalist philosophy. The first studies the postwar crisis of culture, the technological threat to the person, and the meaning of Christianity in this situation. In the second, individualism is first treated more speculatively by means of a study of the notions of individuality and of engagement; then man's situation is related to the actual crisis of modern times and the ambiguity which it implies for the present. This work is essential for all interested in the roots of modern and contemporary personalism. C

See: F. Harkins, A 92 (1955) 486; ACSR 24 (1963) 95; AM 92 (1962) 26; CCr 15 (1963) 226; D 48 (1963) 78; SO 13 (1963) 44; J. O'Mara, St 41 (1952) 238; W. Tome, TS 14 (1954) 662.

———. *The Character of Man*. Trans. by C. Rowland from *Traité du caractère*. New York: Harper, 1956 (1947). x, 341 pp.

An attempt to identify what it is to be human in the contemporary crisis of meaning. The answer is found in a philosophy of acting and in choosing values that have a vital response to others. B-C

See: A 61 (1939) 261-62; AM 48 (1938) 634; Bl 19 (1938) 936; AER 101 (1939) 374-75; C 28 (1938) 590; CW 148 (1939) 759-60; DuR 204 (1939) 406; HPR 40 (1939) 207-208; IER 53 (1939) 218-21; Ta 172 (1938) 674.

———. *Existentialist Philosophies: An Introduction*. Trans. by E. Blow from *Introduction aux existentialismes*. New York:

Macmillan, 1949 (1947). vii, 142 pp. Bibliography, appendices.

A brief, but excellent and authoritative study of the main existential themes. The negative manifestations of a corrupted existence are detailed, and there follows a description of the road to a reconstitution of personal authenticity through an interior road leading to contact with others and with God. B-C

————. *Personalism*. Trans. by P. Mairet from *Le personnalisme*. London: Routledge and Kegan Paul, 1952 (1950). xx, 132 pp. Index.

A seminal study of the principal insights of personalist philosophy. The key themes of personalism—embodiment, engagement, freedom, and conversion—are surveyed in relation to the transcendent. C

See: J. Egan, In 7 (1953) 41-43; J. O'Mara, St 41 (1952) 238.

————. *A Personalist Manifesto*. Trans. by the monks of St. John's Abbey from a special issue of *Esprit* (1936). New York: Longmans, Green, 1938 (1936). xxii, 298 pp.

A basic statement of the nature and structures of personalism. The forces leading to the destruction of the person are detailed. and the significance of the person—through whom the freedom and community of persons is reaffirmed—is emphasized. The social structures of this community are outlined and the principles of personalist action detailed. B-D

See: F. Harkins, A 97 (1957) 327; CC 7 (1958) 187; DR 231 (1957) 156-61; MS 36 (1958) 38; SO 8 (1958) 38; J. Donceel, T 33 (1958) 137; Th 21 (1958) 98-101; TS 19 (1958) 283-86.

————. *The Spoil of the Violent*. Trans. by K. Watson from *L'affrontement Chrétien*. London: Harvill, 1955. 85 pp.

A statement of the crisis in modern society and its remedy. The collapse of Christianity in recent times is described. The solution of the resulting dilemma is considered to be in the realization of a new freedom rooted in a transcendent perspective. B-C

See: Bl 36 (1955) 400; CR 41 (1956) 44; TS 17 (1956) 288.

O'MEARA, Thomas A., and WEISSER, Celestin D. *Paul Tillich in Catholic Thought*. Dubuque: Priory, 1964. xxiii, 323 pp.

A collection of papers by Catholics on the thought of Paul Tillich, accompanied by their evaluation of their subject, after the pattern of "The Library of Living Philosophers." The papers are mostly theological, but the philosophy of this existential thinker is studied and evaluated. B-C

PETERS, John A. *Metaphysics: A Systematic Survey*. See VII.

RABUT, Olivier. *Teilhard de Chardin: A Critical Study*. Trans. from *Dialogue avec Teilhard de Chardin*. New York: Sheed and Ward, 1961. 247 pp.

A threefold study of the thought of Teihard de Chardin. The cosmological and philosophical issues are first investigated, and special attention is given to the theological questions. The work is positive and constructive in its criticism. C

See: AER 146 (1962) 67; A 106 (1961) 94; AM 95 (1962) 28; CW 194 (1961) 21-27; D 46 (1961) 346; HRP 62 (1962) 826; ITQ 28 (1961) 319; NRT 84 (1962) 205; T 37 (1962) 317; TS 23 (1962) 337.

RAVEN, Charles E. *Teilhard de Chardin: Scientist and Seer*. New York: Harper and Row, 1962. 221 pp. Index.

A study of the thought of Teilhard de Chardin. The work reviews this thought concerning the world, man's place in the world, and the orientation of this understanding toward the religious questions and the problem of evil. C

See: Bl 44 (1963) 141; C 78 (1963) 287; C. Vollert, TS 25 (1963) 514; HPR 42 (1941) 92-93; IER 57 (1941) 479.

REINHARDT, Kurt F. *The Existentialist Revolt: The Main Themes and Phases of Existentialism*. New York: Frederick Ungar, 1960 (1952). ix, 281 pp. Bibliography, index, appendix. (Paper)

A study of the development of existentialism by means of a presentation of its main representatives from Kierkegaard to Marcel. Both Marcel and Heidegger are seen against the despair of Sartre. The evaluation by Marcel and Heidegger of the position of man, according to his nearness to being, is thought to open the way to a renewal of metaphysics. Taken as a whole, this is a capable introduction to existentialism, though the multiplication of figures studied may be a source of confusion to some readers. C

RINTELEN, J. Von. *Beyond Existentialism*. Trans. by H. Graef from *Philosophie der Endlichkeit*. London: Allen and Unwin, 1961 (1951). 264 pp. Index.

An investigation of existentialism and its need for transcendence. The abandonment of the transcendent perspective is studied, along with the existential attempts to construct a philosophy of mere finiteness. Against this background are detailed the efforts of Jaspers, Heidegger, and Marcel to establish, each in his own way, a transcendent view. C-D

See: HJ 8 (1963) 296; MS 40 (1963) 290.

ROBERTS, David E. *Existentialism and Religious Belief*. Ed. by Roger Hazelton. New York: Oxford University Press, 1957. viii, 341 pp. Index.

A discussion of the religious significance of existentialism by means of a survey of the work of those who have contributed to its development, from Pascal and Kierkegaard to Heidegger and Marcel. The treatment is sympathetic, with special attention being given to the insight of this school concerning the dangers to the individual in recent Western culture, and the problems of freedom and of faith and reason. This work will be of use in interpreting the precise religious contribution of such figures as Marcel. C

See: R. Richard, NS 32 (1958) 291; Q. Lauer, T 33 (1958) 301; J. Mullaney, Th 20 (1957) 525.

STRAELEN, Henricus Van. *Man the Lonely: Preface to Existentialism*. Tokyo: Maruzen, 1952. 62 pp. Bibliography.

A paper on the general content of the existentialist movement. Its origins in European thought are traced and the thought is evaluated. A-B

STRASSER, Stephen. *Phenomenology of the Human Sciences*. See VI.

————. *The Soul in Metaphysics and Empirical Psychology.* See VI.

TEILHARD DE CHARDIN, Pierre. *Le Milieu Divin: An Essay on the Interior Life.* Trans. by A. Dru, N. Lindsay, D. Mac-kinnon, and B. Wall. London: Collins, 1961 (1957). 160 pp. Index.

A study of the opening of the world to God. The first section points to the religious implications of the world's interactions and developments as ways of fulfilling the world in Christ and of exercising a religious detachment allied to the cross. The spiritual power of matter is indicated, along with the way in which all nature increasingly participates in Christ. B-D

————. *The Future of Man.* Trans. by N. Denny from *L'avenir de l'homme.* New York: Harper and Row, 1964. 319 pp.

A chronological presentation of papers written between 1920 and 1953 concerning the realization of evolution on the human level. Stressing the distinctive nature of human evolution, the author points to the development of a new man closer to the omega point with whom union is beatitude. The spiritual appreciation of man is expressed in terms relevant to modern evolutionary insights. This work is also significant for its reconciliation of divergent philosophic approaches to the ethical problem. B-D

————. *Letters from a Traveller.* Trans. of *Lettres de voyage 1923-1939* and *Nouvelles lettres de voyage 1939-1955.* New York: Harper, 1962 (1956). 386 pp. Index.

A collection of correspondence by Teilhard de Chardin. In part directed to key modern thinkers, the letters reflect the development of the thought of their author on the subject of man and his place in a developing pattern. B-C

————. *The Phenomenon of Man.* Trans. by B. Wall from *Le phénomène humain.* London: Collins, 1961 (1947). 320 pp. Index. (TB 83)

A study of evolutionary development as manifested in a scientific phenomenology. The process is traced from its most simple manifestations on the material level, through plant and animal life, to the human and social spheres. The pattern of unity and some of its principles are indicated. Some questions about the methodology employed have raised doubts concerning the sufficiency of the explanation of these principles. B-D

TROISFONTAINES, Roger. *Existentialism and Christian Thought.* Trans. by M. Jarrett-Kerr from *Existentialisme et pensée Chrétienne.* London: Adam, Black, 1949 (1946). ix, 76 pp. Glossary.

A comparison between existentialism and Christian thought on such key notions as subjectivity and freedom. This was an early and brief outline of work that has since been done much more thoroughly by the author. A-B

See: L. Gaggero, DR 68 (1950) 508-509; E. Watkin, DuR 225 (1951) 112-14.

WILD, John D. *The Challenge of Existentialism.* Bloomington, Ind.: Indiana Univ. Press, 1964 (1955), vii, 297 pp. Bibliography, index.

A critical but sympathetic study of existentialism. The roots of this thought in Kierkegaard and its conception of man and ethics are detailed. The evaluation is made from the standpoint of a realistic philosophy; the positive contributions of existential thought to this philosophy are underlined. C

INDEX

A B C of Schol. Phil., Cotter, 12
Absolute and the Relative, The, Vol. XXII, *ACPA* *, 4
Achievement of J. and R. Maritain, Gallagher, 6
Act and Being, Bonhoeffer, 321
Adam, Karl, *St. Augustine*, 271
Adler, Mortimer:
  Art and Prudence, 245
  Arts of Learning, 40
  Capitalist Manifesto, 229
  Dialectic, 40
  Dialectic of Morals, 173
  How to Think about War and Peace, 239
  Problems for Thomists, 85
  St. Thomas and Gentiles, 293
  What Man Has Made of Man, 85
Aesthetic Experience, Lechner, 247
Age of Belief, Fremantle, 296
Allen, Edgar, *Existentialism from Within*, 321
Aller, Catherine, *Challenge of Teilhard de Chardin*, 321
All-Present God, Grabowski, 275
American Catholic Philosophical Association Proceedings, 4
American Liberty and "Natural Law," Gerhart, 208
American Phil. of Law, LeBuffe and Hayes, 209
Amor Dei, Burnaby, 273
Anable, Raymond, *Phil. Psych.*, 85
Analogy between God and the World, The, Lyttkens, 127
Analogy of Learning, The, Guzie, 96
Analogy of Names, The, Vio, 143
Analysis of Objects, Osgniach, 133

Analytic Philosophy, Vol. XXXIV, *ACPA*, 4
Anderson, James:
  Bond of Being, 114
  Cause of Being, 146
  Intro. to Metaph. of Thomas Aquinas, 114
  Natural Theology, 146
Anscombe, G. E. M., *Three Philosophers*, 293
Answer to Communism, Hyde, 236
Antecedents of Being, The, O'Brien, 133
Approach to Phil., Hawkins, 19
Approach to Phil., Kane, 19
Approaches to God, Maritain, 160
Aquinas, Copleston, 295
Aquinas and Kant, Ardley, 293
Aquinas Ethicus, Rickaby, 286
Aquinas: Selected Political Writings, Passerin d'Entreves, 225
Ardley, Gavin, *Aquinas and Kant*, 293
Ares, Richard, *What Is Corporative Organization?*, 230
Aristotelianism in Thomas, Mullane, 301
Aristotelian-Thomistic Concept of Chance, Junkersfeld, 72
Aristotle, ON INTERPRETATION, Thomas Aquinas, 289
Aristotle's DE ANIMA, Thomas Aquinas, 288
Aristotle's Sluggish Earth, Ashley, 68
Armchair Phil., Lord, 21
Armstrong, Arthur, *Chris. Faith and Greek Phil.*, 9, 146
Art and Beauty, Wulf, 251

* American Catholic Philosophical Association Proceedings.

Art and Poetry, Maritain, 248
Art and Prudence, Adler, 245
Art and Scholasticism and the Frontiers of Poetry, Maritain, 248
Art of Happy Marriage, Magner, 220
Arts of Learning, Ashley, 40
Ashley, Benedict:
  Aristotle's Sluggish Earth, 68
  Arts of Learning, 40
  Liberal Arts, 12
  Science in Synthesis, 72
Aspects of the New Schol. Phil., Hart, 18
Atheism, Borne, 148
At the Origins of the Thom. Notion of Man, Pegis, 104
Augustine, Meer, 277
Augustine, St., works in English, *see* 270
Augustine Synthesis, Przywara, 270, 280
Augustine the Educator, Kevane, 257
Augustine's Quest of Wisdom, Bourke, 272
Aveling, Francis:
  God of Phil., 146
  Immortality of Soul, 85
Avalos, Beatrice, *New Men,* 253
Awake in Heaven, Vann, 111

Bachhuber, Andrew, *Intro. to Logic,* 40
Baisnée, Jules, *Readings in Nat. Theol.,* 147
Baker, Richard, *Thom. Theory of Passions,* 86
Balthasar, Hans Von, *Science, Religion and Chris.,* 147
Bandas, Rudolph, *Phil. and Thom. Principles,* 9
Barbara Celarent, Gilby, 44
Barrachina, Ignatius, *Spiritual Doctrine of Augustine,* 271
Barrett, James:
  Elements of Psych., 86
  This Creature, Man, 86
Barron, Joseph, *Elements of Epist.,* 54
Barry, Sr. Mary, *A Complete Index of Summa,* 5
Baschab, Charles, *Manual of Neo-Schol. Phil.,* 9
Basic Logic, McCall, 47

Basic Principles and Problems of Phil., Ryan, 33
Basic Writings of Augustine, Oates, 270
Basic Writings of St. Thomas, Pegis, 284
Basis of Belief, Trethowan, 168
Bastable, Patrick, *Desire for God,* 173
Batchelder, Robert, *Irreversible Decision,* 239
Battenhouse, Roy, *A Companion to the Study of Augustine,* 271
Baum, Gregory, *Contraception and Holiness,* 218
Beatitude, Garrigou-Lagrange, 181
Beauty, Rother, 250
Being, McCormick, 128
Being, Rother, 138
Being and Becoming, Hawkins, 122
Being and God, Klubertanz, 125
Being and Having, Marcel, 327
Being and Some Phil., Gilson, 119
Belief and Faith, Pieper, 163
Belloc, Hilaire:
  Restoration of Property, 227
  Servile State, 227
Benedetto, Arnold, *Fundamentals in Phil. of God,* 147
Bennett, John, *Christians and State,* 239
Bennett, Owen, *Nature of Demonstrative Proof,* 40
Be Not Afraid, Mounier, 330
Bent World, Langmead Casserley, 216
Berdyaev, Nicolai, *Origin of Russian Communism,* 234
Better Economic Order, Ryan, 234
Bettoni, Ephrem:
  Duns Scotus, 310
  St. Bonaventure, 311
Between the Community and Society, Gilby, 217
Beyond Existentialism, Rintelen, 333
Bigongiari, Dino, *Political Ideas of St. Thomas,* 221
Biot, René, *What Is Life,* 86
Birmingham, William:
  Cross Currents of Psychiatry, 210
  What Modern Catholics Think about Birth Control, 218
Bittle, Celestine:
  Domain of Being, 114
  From Aether to Cosmos, 68

Bittle, Celestine (cont.):
  God and His Creatures, 148
  Man and Morals, 173
  Reality and the Mind, 54
  Science of Correct Thinking, The,
    41
  Whole Man, The, 87
Bivort de la Saudée, Jacques de, God,
    Man and Universe, 263
Blackham, Harold, Six Existentialist
    Thinkers, 321
Bobbio, Norberto, Phil. of Decadent-
    ism, 321
Bober, Mandell, Karl Marx's Inter-
    pretation of History, 235
Bochenski, Innocentius:
  Dogmatic Principles of Soviet Phi-
    losophy, 235
  Philosophy, 9
Bodkin, Richard:
  How to Reason, 41
  Logic for All, 41
Boedder, Bernard, Natural Theol.,
    148
Boelen, Bernard, Symposium on Evo-
    lution, 87
Böhm von Bawerk, Eugen, Karl Marx
    and the Close of His System,
    235
Böhner, Philotheus:
  Collected Articles: Ockham, 311
  History of Franciscan School, 311
  Ockham, 311
  Tractatus de Praedestinatione et de
    praescientia, 312
Boland, Francis, Cath. Social Princi-
    ples, 226
Bolshevism, Gurian, 236
Bonaventure, St., works in English,
    see 309
Bond of Being, Anderson, 114
Act and Being, Bonhoeffer, 321
Bonjoannes, Bernardus, Compendium
    of Summa Theologica, 293
Bonnar, Alphonsus, Catholic Doctor,
    210
Bonner, Gerald, St. Augustine, 272
Books for Cath. Colleges, Peterson, 6
Borne, Etienne:
  Atheism, 148
  Philosophy of Work, 230
Bougerol, J. Guy, Intro. to the Works
    of St. Bonaventure, 312

Bourke, Vernon:
  Augustine's Quest of Wisdom, 272
  Essential Augustine, 271
  Ethics, 173
  Intro. to Works of Thomas, 283
  Pocket Aquinas: Selections from
    the Writings of St. Thomas,
    284
  St. Thomas and Greek Moralists,
    174
  Thomistic Bibliog., 5
  Will in Western Thought, 87
Bouscaren, T., Ethics of Ectopic Op-
    erations, 210
Braceland, Francis, Faith, Reason,
    and Modern Psychiatry, 210
Brauer, Theodore, Thom. Princi-
    ples, 9
Bremond, André, Phil. in the Mak-
    ing, 10
Brennan, Sr. M. Rose Emmanuella,
    Intellectual Virtues, 89
Brennan, Robert:
  Essays in Thom., 10
  General Psych., 87
  History of Psych., 88
  Image of His Maker, 88
  Thomistic Psych., 88
Breviloquium, 309
Brief Text-Book of Moral Phil.,
    Coppens, 176
Brode, W. R., From Plotinus to St.
    Thomas, 294
Brookes, Edgar, City of God and
    Politics of Crisis, 272
Brosnahan, Timothy:
  Ethics, 174
  Prolegomena to Ethics, 174
Brosnan, William, God Infinite, 149
Brown, Anthony, Discipline Con-
    cepts in Education, 253
Brown, Brendan, Natural Law
    Reader, 175
Bruckmann, Williams, Keystones and
    Theories of Phil., 10
Bruehl, Charles:
  Pope's Plan for Social Reconstruc-
    tion, 231
  This Way Happiness, 175
Bruni, Gerardo, Progressive Schol.,
    10
Brunner, August, Fund. Questions of
    Phil., 11

Bryar, William, *St. Thomas and Existence of God*, 149

Buckley, George, *Nature and Unity of Metaph.*, 114

Buckley, Joseph, *Man's Last End*, 175

Bugbee, Henry, *Inward Morning*, 322

Bunting, James, *Ethics for Modern Business*, 227

Burleigh, John, *City of God*, 272

Burnaby, John, *Amor Dei*, 273

Business and Christian Virtues, Woelfel, 230

Business Ethics, Johnston, 229

Cahill, Edward, *Framework of a Christian State*, 216, 221

Callahan, John:
 Catholic Attitude toward Minimum Wage, 231
 Four Views on Time, 273
 Theory of Esthetics, 245

Calvez, Jean-Yves, *Social Thought of John XXIII*, 216

Cameron, James, *Scrutiny of Marxism*, 235

Campbell, Bertrand, *Problem of One or Plural Substantial Forms*, 89

Canfield, Francis, *Phil. and Modern Mind*, 11

Capitalism, Socialism, and Democracy, Schumpeter, 238

Capitalist Manifesto, Kelso and Adler, 229

Caponigri, Alphonsus, *Time and Idea*, 263

Carron, Malcolm, *Readings in Phil. of Educ.*, 253

Caruso, Igor, *Existential Psych.*, 89

Case Against Birth Control, Moore, 220

Casey, Joseph, *Primacy of Metaph.*, 115

Cass, John, *Quest of Certainty*, 115

Casselman, Paul, *Cooperative Movement*, 227

Catalogue of St. Thomas' Works, Eschmann, 284

Catechism of the SUMMA, Pegues, 302

Categories of Being, Scheu, 139

Category of the Aesthetic in the Phil. of Bonaventure, The, Spargo, 250

Catholicism and Educ., Hovre, 256

Catholic Attitude toward a Familial Minimum Wage, Callahan, 231

Cath. Booklist, 5

Cath. Bookman's Guide, Reynolds, 6

Cath. Church and Phil., McNabb, 23

Cath. Conception of International Law, Scott, 242

Cath. Doctor, Bonnar, 210

Cath. in Psych., Misiak and Studt, 101

Cath. Nurse, Johnson, 213

Cath. Phil. of Educ., Redden and Ryan, 259

Cath. Phil of History, Guilday, 263

Cath. Principles of Politics, Ryan and Boland, 226

Cath. Social Action, Cronin, 231

Cath. Social Doctrine, O'Connor, 194

Cath. Social Principles, Cronin, 231

Cath. Tradition and the Law of Nations, Eppstein, 240

Cath. Viewpoint on Censorship, Gardiner, 222

Cath. Way in Educ., McGucken, 258

Catlin, George, *Story of Political Phil.*, 221

Causality and Implication, Hawkins, 122

Causality in Current Philosophy, Vol. XIV, *ACPA*, 4

Cause of Being, Anderson, 146

Cavanaugh, Alfred, *Readings in Phil. of Educ.*, 253

Century of Conflict, Possony, 237

Certainty, Phil. and Theol., Trethowan, 169

Certitude, Rother, 63

Challenge of Existentialism, Wild, 335

Challenge of Teilhard de Chardin, Aller, 321

Chapman, Emmanuel, *St. Augustine's Phil. of Beauty*, 273

Character of Man, Mounier, 330

Charlesworth, Maxwell, *Phil. and Linguistic Analysis*, 54

Charter of Christendom, O'Meara, 278

Chauvin, Rémy, *God of the Scientists*, 149

Chesterton, G. K.:
 St. Thomas Aquinas, 294
 What's Wrong with the World, 228

Chisholm, Roderick, *Realism and Background of Phenomenology*, 322
Choir of Muses, Gilson, 246
Christ and the Modern Conscience, Leclercq, 186
Christian Ethics, Hawkins, 183
Chris. Ethics, Hildebrand, 184
Chris. Ethics, Ross, 198
Chris. Ethics, Ward, 203
Chris. Faith and Greek Phil., Armstrong and Markus, 9, 146
Chris. Marriage, Joyce, 220
Chris. Morals, D'Arcy, 177
Chris. Phil., Driscoll, 92
Chris. Phil., O'Mahony, 28
Chris. Phil. and Intel. Freedom, Pegis, 28
Chris. Phil. and the Social Sciences, Vol. XII, *ACPA*, 4
Chris. Phil. of Life, Wuellner, 36
Chris. Phil. of St. Augustine, Gilson, 275
Chris. Phil. of St. Thomas, Gilson, 296
Chris. Social Manifesto, Husslein, 232
Chris. Social Principles, O'Brien, 193
Chris. Social Reconstruction, Michel, 218
Chris. Wisdom, McGannon, Cooke, and Klubertanz, 22
Christianity and Phil., Gilson, 16
Christians and the State, Bennett, 239
Church, Grabowski, 276
Church and Mental Health, Maves, 214
Church and War, Stratmann, 242
City of God, Augustine, 270
City of God, Burleigh, 272
City of God and the Politics of Crisis, Brookes, 272
Clark, Joseph, *Conventional Logic and Modern Logic*, 42
Clark, Mary, *Augustine, Phil. of Freedom*, 273
Clarke, Richard, *Logic*, 42
Clemens, Alphonse, *Marriage and Family*, 219
Closed Shop, Toner, 234
Coady, Mary, *Phantasm*, 90
Code of International Ethics, 241

Coffey, Peter:
  Epistemology, 55
  Ontology, 115
  Science of Logic, 42
Coffey, Reginald, *Man from Rocca Sicca*, 294
Cogley, John, *Nat. Law and Modern Society*, 221
Cole, George, *Meaning of Marxism*, 235
Coleburt, Russell, *Search for Values*, 116
Collected Articles: Ockham, Böhner, 311
Colligan, John, *Cosmology*, 68
Collin, Rémy, *Evolution*, 90
Collingwood, Francis:
  Man's Physical and Spiritual Nature, 90
  Phil. of Nature, 68
Collins, James:
  Communism, 237
  Existentialists, 322
  God in Modern Phil., 150
  Lure of Wisdom, 116
Collins, William:
  Metaph. and Man, 11
  Speculative Phil., 12
Commentary on Aristotle's PHYSICS, Thomas Aquinas, 289
Com. on the METAPHYSICS *of Aristotle*, Thomas Aquinas, 288
Com. on the NICOMACHEAN ETHICS, Thomas Aquinas, 288
Com. on the SENTENCES, St. Bonaventure, 309
Communism, Neill and Collins, 237
Communism and Christianity, D'Arcy, 235
Communism and Christians, Mauriac, 237
Communism and Man, Sheed, 238
Communism and the Conscience of the West, Sheen, 238
Companion to the Study of Augustine, Battenhouse, 271
Companion to the SUMMA, Farrell, 14
Compendium of the SUMMA THEOLOGICA, Bonjoannes, 293
Compendium of Theology, Thomas Aquinas, 290
Complete Index of the SUMMA, Deferrari, 5

Complete System of Cath. Educ. Is Necessary, Deferrari, 254
Concept in Thom., Peifer, 105
Concept of Ethics, Flubacher, 228
Concept of Freedom, Grindel, 94
Concept of Matter, McMullin, 75
Concept of the Human Soul, O'Connor, 278
Concept of Univocity: Ockham, Menges, 315
Conception of God, Patterson, 162
Concerning Being and Essence, Thomas Aquinas, 290
Confessions, St. Augustine, 270
Conflict Between Ethics and Sociology, Deploige, 178
Conley, Kiernan, *Theol. of Wisdom*, 150
Connell, Francis, *Morals in Politics*, 222
Connolly, Frederick, *Science Versus Phil.*, 12
Conscience, Guardini, R., 182
Conscience and Its Right to Freedom, D'Arcy, 177
Contemporary American Philosophy, Vol. XXXIII, *ACPA*, 4
Cont. European Thought and Chris. Faith, Dondeyne, 152
Cont. Phil., Copleston, 55
Cont. Phil. and Thom. Principles, Bandas, 9
Contraception and Catholics, Dupré, 219
Contraception and Holiness, Baum, 218
Conventional Logic and Modern Logic, Clark, 42
Conway, John, *St. Thomas*, 294
Conway, Pierre:
 Liberal Arts, 12
 Princ. of Educ., 253
Conze, Edward, *Intro. to Dialectical Materialism*, 235
Cooke, Bernard, *Chris. Wisdom*, 22
Cooperative Democracy, Warbasse, 230
Cooperative Movement, Casselman, 227
Cooperative Plenty, Ross, 230
Copleston, Frederick:
 Aquinas, 295

Copleston, Frederick (*cont.*):
 Cont. Phil., 55
 Medieval Philosophy, 295
Coppens, Charles:
 Brief Text-Book of Moral Phil., 176
 Moral Principles and Medical Practice, 270
Corcoran, John, *Science in Synthesis*, 72
Cornforth, Maurice, *Dialectical Materialism*, 235
Corté, Nicholas, *Origins of Man*, 91
Cory, Herbert, *Significance of Beauty*, 245
Cosmology, Colligan, 68
Cosmology, Dougherty, 69
Cosmology, Foley, 69
Cosmology, Gardeil, 70
Cosmology, Glenn, 71
Cosmology, McWilliams, 75
Cosmology, Nys, 78
Cosmology, O'Grady, 78
Cosmology, O'Neill, 78
Cosmology, Renoirte, 79
Cosmology for All, Rabbitte, 79
Costanzo, Joseph, *This Nation Under God*, 253
Cotter, Anthony:
 A B C of Schol. Phil., 12
 Logic and Epist., 43
 Natural Species, 91
Counseling the Catholic, Hagmaier, 212
Coventry, John, *Morals and Independence*, 176
Cox, Ignatius, *Liberty*, 176
Creative Fidelity, Marcel, 327
Creative Intuition in Art and Poetry, Maritain, 249
Crisis of Our Age, Sorokin, 218
Crisis of Western Educ., Dawson, 254
Cristiani, Leon, *Origins of Man*, 91
Criteriology, Glenn, 57
Critical Value of Concepts, Dalos, 56
Criticism of Experience, Hawkins, 58
Croce, Benedetto, *Historical Materialism*, 235
Cronan, Edward, *Dignity of Human Person*, 91
Cronin, John:
 Catholic Social Action, 231

Cronin, John: (*cont.*):
Catholic Social Principles, 231
Social Principles and Economic
Life, 231
Cronin, Michael, *Science of Ethics*,
176
Croonenburg, Engelbert Van, *Gateway to Reality*, 12
Cross Currents of Psychiatry, Birmingham and Cunneen, 210
Crossen, Frederick, *Modeling of
Mind*, 107
Crossman, R., *God That Failed*, 235
Crucial Prob. of Modern Phil., Hawkins, 19
Crumley, Thomas, *Logic*, 43
Cunneen, Joseph, *Cross Currents of
Psychiatry*, 210
Cunningham, Bert, *Morality of Organic Transplantation*, 210
Cunningham, Walter, *Notes on Epist.*,
56
Cunningham, William, *Pivotal Prob.
of Educ.*, 254
Current British and American Realism, Vol. VIII, *ACPA*, 4
Curtis, Stanley, *Short History of
Western Phil. in Middle Ages*, 295

Dady, Sr. Mary R., *Theory of Know.
of Bonaventure*, 312
Daim, Wilfried, *Depth Psych. and
Salvation*, 91
Dalos, Patrick, *Critical Value of Concepts*, 56
Daniélou, Jean:
God and Ways of Knowing, 150
Lord of History, 264
D'Arcy, Eric, *Conscience and Its
Right to Freedom*, 177
D'Arcy, Martin:
Christian Morals, 177
Communism and Chris., 235
Meeting of Love and Knowledge,
116
Mind and Heart of Love, 117
Mirage and Truth, 151
No Absent God, 151
Of God and Man, 13
Pain of this World, 151
St. Augustine, 274

D'Arcy, Martin (*cont.*):
St. Thomas, 295
Sense of History, 264
Darwin's Vision and Chris. Perspectives, Ong, 104
Davitt, Thomas, *Nature of Law*, 177
Dawson, Christopher:
Crisis of Western Educ., 254
Dynamics of World History, 264
Judgment of Nations, 239
Day, Sebastian, *Intuitive Cognition*,
312
Deane, Herbert, *Political and Social
Ideas of Augustine*, 274
Decentralize for Liberty, Hewes, 228
Decline of Wisdom, Marcel, 327
De Coursey, Sr. Mary Edwin, *Theory
of Evil*, 117
Deferrari, Roy J.:
Complete Index of Summa, 5
Complete System of Cath. Educ. Is
Necessary, 254
Latin-Eng. Dictionary of Thomas,
5
Lexicon of Thomas, 5
Deferrari, Sr. Teresa Mary, *Problem
of Charity for Self*, 178
Degrees of Know., Maritain, 60
De Guchteneere, Raoul, *Judgment
on Birth Control*, 219
De Koninck, Charles, *Hollow Universe*, 56
Democracy and Marxism, Mayo, 237
Demonstration: A Disputed Work,
Thomas Aquinas, 290
Dempsey, Peter J., *Psych. for All*, 92
Demske, James M., *Intro. Metaph.*,
14
Deploige, Simon, *Conflict Between
Ethics and Sociology*, 178
Depth Psych. and Salvation, Daim,
91
De reductione artium ad theologian,
St. Bonaventure, 309
Desan, Wilfrid:
Planetary Man, 323
Tragic Finale, 323
Desire for God, Bastable, 173
Desire of God, O'Mahoney, 162
Development of Physical Theory,
Weisheipl, 82
Dialectic, Adler, 40

Dialectic of Morals, Adler, 173
Dialectical Materialism, Cornforth, 235
Dialectical Materialism, Wetter, 238
Dialectics, Glenn, 44
Dictionary of Schol. Phil., Wuellner, 7
Diggs, Bernard, *Love and Being,* 118
Dignity of Man, Staab, 108
Dignity of the Human Person, Cronan, 91
Dignity of Science, Weisheipl, 83
Directions in Contemporary Criticism, LaDriere, 247
Discipline Concepts in Education, Brown, 253
Discovery of God, Lubac, 159
Discursive Power, Klubertanz, 97
Disputed Questions on Christ's Knowledge, St. Bonaventure, 309
Distributive Justice, Ryan, 234
Divine Friendship, Wilms, 204
Divine Providence and the Problem of Evil, St. Augustine, 270
Divine Right of Kings, Figgis, 222
Division and Methods of the Sciences, Thomas Aquinas, 292
Doctrine of Being, Owens, 133
Does God Exist?, Mazzei, 161
Does God Matter for Me?, Martindale, 160
Dogmatic Principles of Soviet Phil., Bochenski, 235
Doherty, Richard, *Relation of Individual to Society,* 178
Domain of Being, Bittle, 114
Donahue, Lester, *Outline of Ethics,* 179
Donceel, Joseph:
    Natural Theol., 151
    Phil. Psych., 92
Dondeyne, Albert, *Cont. European Thought and Chris. Faith,* 152
    Faith and World, 152
Donovan, Mary, *Henological Argument,* 152
Doolan, Aegidius:
    Order and Law, 179
    Phil. for the Layman, 13
    Revival of Thom., 13
Dopp, Joseph, *Formal Logic,* 43

Dougherty, George, *Moral Basis of Social Order,* 179
Dougherty, Kenneth:
    Cosmology, 69
    General Ethics, 179
    Logic, 43
Douglas, Paul, *Ethics in Government,* 222
Drama of Atheist Humanism, Lubac, 159
Drennen, Donald, *Modern Intro. to Metaph.,* 118
Driscoll, John:
    Chris. Phil., 92
    God, 153
Drummond, William, *Social Justice,* 180
Dubarle, Dominique, *Scientific Humanism and Chris. Thought,* 13
Dubay, Thomas, *Phil. of State as Educator,* 255
Dubray, Charles, *Intro. Phil.,* 14
Duffey, Felix, *Psychiatry and Asceticism,* 210
Duffy, John, *Phil. of Poetry,* 246
Dulles, Avery, *Intro. Metaph.,* 14
Duns Scotus, Bettoni, 310
Duns Scotus, Harris, 314
Duns Scotus, Wolter, 318
Dupré, Louis:
    Contraception and Catholics, 219
    Kierkegaard as Theologian, 323
Dupuis, Adrian, *Phil. and Educ.,* 255
Dynamics of Morality, Menasce, 190
Dynamics of World History, Dawson, 264
Dynamic World Order, MacLean, 241

Early Thomistic School, Roensch, 303
Easby-Smith, Mildred, *Schol. Synthesis,* 14
Eastman, Max, *Marxism,* 235
Economics of Pesch, Mulcahy, 229
Educ. at the Crossroads, Maritain, 257
Educ. of Man, The, Gallagher, ed., 255
Educ. Psych., Kelly, 257
Efficient Causality, Meehan, 132
Effler, Roy R., *John Duns Scotus and "Omne quod movetur,"* 313

Elementary Chris. Metaph., Owens, 134

Elementary Handbook of Logic, Toohey, 51

Elements of Chris. Phil., Gilson, 296

Elements of Epist., Barron, 54

Elements of Ethics, Miltner, 191

Elements of Logic, Mercier, 48

Elements of Logic, Smith, 50

Elements of Psych., Barrett, 86

Emotions and Morals, O'Brien, 193

Encounter, Kwant, 126

End of the Modern World, Guardini, 265

End of Time, Pieper, 266

English, Michael, *Rebuilding Social Order*, 232

Epistemology, Coffey, 55

Epistemology, Regis, 62

Epistemology, Steenberghen, 64

Eppstein, John, *Cath. Tradition and Law of Nations*, 240

Eschmann, I. T., *"A Catalogue of St. Thomas' Works,"* 284

Essay in Chris. Phil., Trethowan, 35

Essay on Chris. Phil., Maritain, 24

Essay on Human Love, Guitton, 95

Essays in Chris. Phil., Rose, 33

Essays in Fabian Socialism, Shaw, 238

Essays in Modern Schol., Pegis, 29

Essays in Thom., Brennan, 10

Essence and Operation, Mullen, 132

Essentials in Formal Logic, Mahony, 48

Essentials of Theism, Hawkins, 156

Eternal Quest, O'Connor, 194

Ethics, Bourke, 173

Ethics, Brosnahan, 174

Ethics, Glenn, 182

Ethics, Hill, 185

Ethics, McAllister, 187

Ethics, Oesterle, 194

Ethics, Advertising, Quinn, 229

Ethics and Facts, Messner, 190

Ethics and Other Knowledge, 4

Ethics and the Materialist Conception of History, Kautsky, 236

Ethics and the Social Sciences, Ward, 227

Ethics for Modern Business, Bunting, 227

Ethics in Business, Garrett, 228

Ethics in Government, Douglas, 222

Ethics of Brain Surgery, Flood, 211

Ethics of Ectopic Operations, Bouscaren, 210

Ethics of Medical Homicide and Mutilation, O'Malley, 215

Ethics of Peace and War, Gigon, 240

Etienne Gilson Tribute, O'Neil, 28

Evidence and Its Function: Scotus, Vier, 317

Evil, Sharpe, 165

Evil and Suffering, Lavelle, 326

Evolution, Collin, 90

Examination of the First Principles, Sullivan, 141

Exercises in Logic, Riedl, 50

Existence and Analogy, Mascall, 131

Existence and Nature of God, Vol. XXVIII, *ACPA*, 4

Existence and the Existent, Maritain, 129

Existence of God, Pontifex, 163

Existential Background of Human Dignity, Marcel, 327

Existential Phenomenology, Luijpen, 127

Existential Psych., Caruso, 89

Existentialism, Harper, 324

Existentialism and Chris. Thought, Troisfontaines, 335

Existentialism and Religious Belief, Roberts, 333

Existentialism and Thom., Mihalich, 330

Existentialism from Within, Allen, 321

Existentialist Philosophies, Mounier, 330

Existentialist Revolt, Reinhardt, 332

Existentialists, Collins, 322

Exposition of ON GENERATION, Thomas Aquinas, 288

Exposition of ON THE HEAVENS, Thomas Aquinas, 288

Exposition of the METAPHYSICS OF ARISTOTLE, Thomas Aquinas, 288

Exposition of the PHYSICS OF ARISTOTLE, Thomas Aquinas, 289

Exposition of the POSTERIOR ANALYTICS, Thomas Aquinas, 290

Exposition of the METEOROLOGY, Thomas Aquinas, 289

Fackenheim, Emil, *Metaph. and Historicity*, 118
Fagothey, Austin, *Right and Reason*, 180
Failure of Technology, Jünger, 217
Faith and Reason, Roberts, 333
Faith and the World, Dondeyne, 152
Faith, Reason, and Modern Psychiatry, Braceland, 210
Faraon, Michael, J., *Metaph. and Psych. Principles of Love*, 119
Farrell, Walter:
  Companion to SUMMA, 14
  Natural Law, 180
Federn, Karl, *Materialist Conception of History*, 236
Fell, George, *Immortality of Human Soul*, 93
Ferree, William, *Act of Social Justice*, 180
Ferroli, Domenico, *Moral Science*, 181
Ficarra, Bernard J., *Newer Ethical Problems in Medicine*, 210
Field of Consciousness, Gurwitsch, 96
Figgis, John:
  Divine Right of Kings, 222
  Political Aspects of City of God, 274
Fink, C. T., *Handbook of Medical Ethics*, 213
Finney, Patrick, *Moral Problems in Hospital Practice*, 210
First Book in Ethics, Woods, 204
First Philosophy, Kreyche, 126
First Principles of Know., Rickaby, 62
Fischer, Jerome J., *Handbook of Logic*, 45
Fitzpatrick, Edward, *Phil. of Educ.*, 255
Fleming, Thomas, V., *Foundations of Phil.*, 15
Flood, Peter:
  Ethics of Brain Surgery, 210
  Medical Experimentation on Man, 212
  New Problems in Medical Ethics, 211

Flubacher, Joseph, *Concept of Ethics in History of Economics*, 228
Focus, Smythe, 7
Foerster, Friedrich W., *Marriage and Sex Problem*, 219
Footnotes for the Atom, Smith, 80
Forgotten Revelation, Morriss, 161
Formal Distinction of Scotus, Grajewski, 314
Formal Logic, Dopp, 43
Formal Logic, Maritain, 48
Formal Logic, Mourant, 49
Fortitude and Temperance, Pieper, 195
Forty Years After, Miller, 233
Foster, Kenelm, *Life of St. Thomas*, 295
Foundations of a Modern Guild System, Trehey, 234
Foundations of Justice, Newman, 192
Foundations of Phil., Fleming, 15
Foundations of Thom. Phil., Sertillanges, 304
Fountain of Justice, Wu, 204
Four Existentialist Theologians, Herberg, 325
Four Square, Rickaby, 197
Four Views on Time, Callahan, 273
Framework of a Chris. State, Cahill, 216, 221
Franciscan Phil., Sharp, 316
Francoeur, Robert, *World of Teilhard*, 324
Franz, Edward, *Thom. Doctrine of Possible Intel.*, 93
Free Will, Gruender, 95
Freedom and Providence, Pontifex, 164
Freedom, Grace and Destiny, Guardini, 120
Freedom in Modern World, Maritain, 129
Freedom of the Intell., Maritain, 24
Freedom of the Will, Sharpe, 108
Fremantle, Anne, *Age of Belief*, 296
French Existentialism, Kingston, 325
Friedrich, Lawrence W., *Nature of Physical Know.*, 70
From Aether to Cosmos, Bittle, 68
From an Abundant Spring, 15
From an Ivory Tower, Hausmann, 71

From Atomos to Atom, Melsen, 77
From Hegel to Marx, Hook, 236
From Luther to Hitler, McGovern, 223
From Plotinus to St. Thomas, Brode, 294
Fuchs, Oswald, *Psych. of Habit: Ockham*, 313
Fundamental Ethics, Poland, 197
Fund. Moral Attitudes, Hildebrand, 184
Fund. Questions of Phil., Brunner, 11
Fundamentals in the Phil. of God, Benedetto, 147
Fund. of Logic, Hartmann, 45
Fund. of Logic, Sullivan, 51
Future of Man, Teilhard de Chardin, 334

Gaffney, Mark A., *Psych. of Interior Senses*, 93
Gallagher, Donald A:
Achievement of J. and R. Maritain, 6
Educ. of Man, 255
Some Phil. on Educ., 256
Gallagher, Idella:
Achievement of J. and R. Maritain, 6
Educ. of Man, 255
Some Phil. on Educ., 256
Gallagher, Kenneth T.:
Phil. of Know., 56
Phil. of G. Marcel, 324
Gardeil, Henri D.:
Cosmology, 70
Psychology, 94
Gardiner, Harold, *Cath. Viewpoint on Censorship*, 222
Garrett, Thomas:
Ethics in Business, 228
Intro. Ethical Problems of Advertising, 228
Garrigou-Lagrange, Reginald:
Beatitude, 181
God, 153
One God, 153
Providence, 154
Reality, 15
Trinity and God Creator, 154
Garvey, Mary P., *St. Augustine*, 275

Gateway to Reality, Croonenburg, 12
Geach, P. T., *Three Philosophers*, 293
Geiger, James A., *Origin of the Soul*, 275
General and Special Ethics, Noonan, 193
General Ethics, Dougherty, 179
General Ethics, Sullivan, 200
General Metaph., Noonan, 133
General Metaph., Rickaby, 138
General Psych., Brennan, 87
General Science of Nature, Smith, 80
General Semantics and Cont. Thom., Gorman, 44
General Theory of Authority, Simon, 200
George, Henry, *Progress and Poverty*, 228
Gerhard, William A., *Infra-Rational Knowl.*, 181
Gerhart, Eugene C., *American Liberty and "Natural Law,"* 208
Gerrard, Thomas, *Marriage and Parenthood*, 219
Gerrity, Benignus:
Nature, Know. and God, 16
Relation between Theory of Matter and Know., 70
Gianelli, Arnold P., *Meaningful Logic*, 44
Gigon, Henri, *Ethics of Peace and War*, 240
Gilby, Thomas:
Barbara Celarent, 44
Between Community and Society, 217
Morals and Marriage, 219
Phoenix and Turtle, 57
Poetic Experience, 246
Political Thought of Thomas, 232
Gill, Eric, *Money and Morals*, 228
Gilson, Etienne:
Being and Some Phil., 119
Choir of Muses, 246
Chris. Phil. of Augustine, 275
Chris. Phil. of Thomas, 296
Chris. and Phil., 16
Elements of Chris. Phil., 296
God and Phil., 154
History of Chris. Phil. in Middle Ages, 297

Gilson, Etienne (cont):
  History of Phil. and Phil. Educ.,
    16
  Moral Values and Moral Life, 182
  Painting and Reality, 246
  Phil. and Theo., 17
  Phil. of Bonaventure, 313
  Reason and Revelation, 155
  St. Thomas and Phil., 297
  Spirit of Medieval Phil., 297
  Spirit of Thomism, 299
  Unity of Phil. Experience, 17
  Wisdom and Love, 120
Gleason, Robert W.:
  Counseling the Catholic, 212
  Search for God, 155
Glenn, Paul J.:
  Cosmology, 71
  Criteriology, 57
  Dialectics, 44
  Ethics, 182
  Intro. to Phil., 17
  Ontology, 120
  Psychology, 94
  Theodicy, 155
  Tour of SUMMA, 297
Glutz, Melvin A., Manner of Demon-
    strating, 71
God, Driscoll, 153
God, Garrigou-Lagrange, 153
God, Lattey, 158
God and His Attributes, Reys, 164
God and His Creatures, Bittle, 148
God and His Works, Thomas Aqui-
    nas, 286
God and Intelligence, Sheen, 165
God and Phil., Gilson, 154
God and the Atom, Knox, 241
God and the Unconscious, White,
    170
God and the Ways of Knowing, Da-
    niélou, 150
God and World Order, Ward, 169
God in Modern Phil., Collins, 150
God Infinite, Brosnan, 149
God Is Its Founder, Morrison, 220
God, Man and the Universe, Bivort
    de la Saudée, 263
God of Phil., Aveling, 146
God of Reason, Jolivet, 158
God of the Scientists, Chauvin, 149
God or Chaos, Kane, 158

God That Failed, Crossman, 235
Godin, Edgar, Hospital Ethics, 212
Gonella, Guido, World to Recon-
    struct, 240
Good, Frederick, Marriage, Morals
    and Medical Ethics, 212
Good in Existential Metaph., Sal-
    mon, 139
Good Society, Lippmann, 217
Goodness of Being, Smith, Sr., 140
Gorman, Margaret, General Seman-
    tics and Contemp. Thom., 44
Gornall, Thomas, Phil. of God, 155
Grabmann, Martin:
  Interior Life of St. Thomas, 298
  Intro. to Theol. SUMMA, 298
  Thomas Aquinas, 298
Grabowski, Stanislaus J.:
  All-Present God, 275
  Church, 276
Graham, George A., Morality in
    American Politics, 223
Grajewski, Maurice J., Formal Dis-
    tinction of Scotus, 314
Graven Images, Hildebrand and
    Jourdain, 184
Greatness of the Soul: The Teach-
    er, St. Augustine, 270
Greenwood, David, St. Augustine,
    276
Grenier, Henri, Thom. Phil., 18
Grindel, Carl W., Concept of Free-
    dom, 94
Gruender, Hubert:
  Free Will, 95
  Prob. of Psych., 95
  Psych. Without a Soul, 95
Gryst, Edward, Talk Sense, 18
Guardini, Romano:
  Conscience, 182
  End of Modern World, 264
  Freedom, Grace and Destiny, 120
  Power and Responsibility, 182
Guest, David, Textbook of Dialecti-
    cal Materialism, 236
Guide to THE CITY OF GOD, Vers-
    feld, 281
Guide to the Thought of Augustine,
    Portalie, 279
Guide to Thomas, Pieper, 302
Guilday, P., Cath. Phil. of History,
    263

Guitton, Jean:
Essay on Human Love, 95
Unity through Love, 156
Gurian, Waldemar:
Bolshevism, 236
Soviet Union, 236
Gustafson, Gustaf J., Theory of Natural Appetency, 96
Guzie, Tad W., Analogy of Learning, 96

Haas, Francis, Man and Society, 217
Hagmaier, George, Counseling the Catholic, 212
Haines, Charles, Revival of Natural Law Concepts, 208
Hamm, Victor, Language, Truth and Poetry, 247
Handbook of Chris. Social Ethics, Welty, 203
Handbook of Logic, Houde and Fischer, 45
Handbook of Medical Ethics, Larochelle and Fink, 213
Handren, Walter, No Longer Two, 219
Happiness and Contemplation, Pieper, 196
Harding, Arthur, Natural Law and Natural Rights, 208
Harding, Michael, Science of Metaph., 121
Harmon, Francis, Principles of Psych., 96
Harmony, in Cath. Univ., Linehan, 21
Harper, Ralph:
Existentialism, 324
Sleeping Beauty, 325
Harper, Thomas, Metaph. of the School, 121
Harris, Charles, Duns Scotus, 314
Hart, Charles:
Aspects of New Schol. Phil., 18
Thomistic Concept of Mental Faculty, 97
Thomistic Metaph., 121
Hartman, R., Profit Sharing Manual, 228
Hartmann, Sylvester:
Fund. of Logic, 45
Textbook of Logic, 45

Harvey, Rudolph, It Stands to Reason, 18
Hassett, Joseph, Phil. of Human Knowledge, 57
Hausmann, Bernard, From an Ivory Tower, 71
Hawkins, Denis:
Approach to Phil., 19
Being and Becoming, 122
Causality and Implication, 122
Chris. Ethics, 183
Criticism of Experience, 58
Crucial Prob. of Modern Phil., 19
Man and Morals, 183
Sketch of Medieval Phil., 299
Hayes, Edward, Moral Handbook of Nursing, 212
Hayes, James, American Phil. of Law, 209
Hayes, Paul, Moral Handbook of Nursing, 212
Healy, Edwin:
Marriage Guidance, 219
Medical Ethics, 212
Healy, Sr. Emma, St. Bonaventure's DE REDUCTIONE, 314
Heart of Man, Vann, 202
Henle, Robert:
Method in Metaph., 122
St. Thomas and Platonism, 299
Henological Argument, Donovan, 152
Henry, Francois, Phil. of Work, 230
Henry, Paul, St. Augustine on Personality, 276
Herberg, Will, Four Existentialist Theologians, 325
Hettinger, Franz, Natural Religion, 157
Hewes, Thomas, Decentralize for Liberty, 228
He Who Is, Mascall, 160
Higgins, Thomas, Man as Man, 183
Higher Law, McKinnon, 209
Hildebrand, Dietrich Von:
Christian Ethics, 184
Fundamental Moral Attitudes, 184
Graven Images, 184
In Defense of Purity, 219
Marriage, 219
True Morality, 185
What Is Phil.?, 19

Hill, Owen:
  Ethics, 185
  Psych. and Nat. Theol., 97
Historical Intro. to Ethics, Moore,
  191
Historical Materialism, Croce, 235
History and Philosophy of Science,
  Vol. XXXVIII, *ACPA,* 4
*History of Chris. Phil. in the Middle
  Ages,* Gilson, 297
History of Medieval Phil., Wulf,
  306
History of Phil. and Phil. Education,
  Gilson, 16
History of Psych., Brennan, 87
History of the Franciscan School,
  Böhner, 311
Hodgson, Peter, *Nuclear Physics,* 240
Hoenen, Peter:
  Phil. of Inorganic Compounds, 72
  Phil. Nature of Physical Bodies, 72
  Reality and Judgment, 58
Hollow Universe, De Koninck, 56
Holloway, Maurice:
  Being and God, 125
  Intro. to Nat. Theol., 157
Homo Viator, Marcel, 328
Hook, Sidney:
  From Hegel to Marx, 236
  Toward Understanding Karl Marx,
  236
Hope, Wingfield, *Life Together,* 220
Horrigan, Alfred, *Metaph. as Prin-
  ciple of Order,* 123
Hospital Ethics, Godin, 212
Houde, Roland:
  Handbook of Logic, 45
  Phil. of Knowledge, 58
  Readings in Logic, 46
Hovre, Franz De:
  Cath. and Educ., 256
  Phil. and Educ., 256
How to Reason, Bodkin, 41
*How To Think About War and
  Peace,* Adler, 139
Hughes, Mary, *Intelligibility of Uni-
  verse,* 123
Hughes, Philip, *Pope's New Order,*
  232
*Human Person and the World of
  Values,* Schwarz, 199
Human Possibilities, Kiley, 20

Human Rights, 208
Human Wisdom of St. Thomas, Pie-
  per, 302
Humanism and Theol., Jaeger, 157
Hunt, R.:
  Marxism, 236
  *Theory and Practice of Commu-
  nism,* 236
Husslein, Joseph, *Chris. Social Mani-
  festo,* 232
Hutchins, Robert, *St. Thomas and
  World State,* 241
Hyde, Douglas:
  Answer to Communism, 236
  I Believed, 236

I Believed, Hyde, 236
Idea Men of Today, Smith, 34
*Idea of God in the Phil. of Augus-
  tine,* Tolley, 281
Image of God, Sullivan, 109
Image of His Maker, Brennan, 87
Immortality, Mainage, 100
Immortality of the Human Soul,
  Fell, 93
Imprudence, O'Neil, 195
In Defense of Purity, Hildebrand,
  219
Inagaki, B., *Schol. Bibliog. in Japan,*
  6
*Infra-Rational Knowledge and the
  Intel.,* Gerhard, 181
In Search of the Unknown God,
  Zundel, 170
Insight, Lonergan, 59
Integrating Mind, Lynch, 21
Intellectual Virtues, Brennan, 89
Intellectualism of St. Thomas, Rous-
  selot, 63
Intelligibility of the Universe,
  Hughes, 123
Interior Life of St. Thomas, Grab-
  mann, 298
International Union of Social Stud-
  ies, *Code of International Eth-
  ics,* 241
*Intro. into Some Ethical Prob. of
  Modern American Advertising,*
  Garrett, 228
Intro. to Logic, Bachuber, 40
Intro. to Metaph., Miltner, 132
Intro. to Metaph., Vaske, 142

Intro. to Nat. Theol., Holloway, 157
Intro. to Phil., Glenn, 17
Intro. to Phil., Raeymaeker, 31
Intro. to Phil., Rieth, 106
Intro. to Phil., Ryan, 33
Intro. to Phil., Sullivan, 35
Intro. to Dialectical Materialism, Conze, 235
Intro. to St. Thomas, Pegis, 284
Intro. to Schol. Phil., Wulf, 306
Intro. to the Metaph. of St. Thomas Aquinas, Anderson, 114
Intro. to the Phil. of Animate Nature, Koren, 98
Intro. to the Phil. of Being, Klubertanz, 125
Intro. to the Phil. of Natural and Math. Sciences, Sullivan, 82
Intro. to the Phil. of Nature, Kocourek, 73
Intro. to the Phil. of Nature, Koren, 289
Intro. to the Phil. of St. Augustine, Mourant, 271
Intro. to the Science of Metaph., Koren, 126
Intro. to the Study of Human Conduct, Wolfe, 261
Intro. to the Theol. SUMMA *of St. Thomas*, Grabmann, 298
Intro. to the Works of Bonaventure, Bougerol, 312
Introductory Phil., Dubray, 14
Introductory Metaph., Dulles, Demske, and O'Connell, 14
Intuitive Cognition, Day, 312
Inward Morning, Bugbee, 322
Irreversible Decision, Batchelder, 239
Is There a Chris. Phil.?, Nedoncelle, 27
It Stands to Reason, Harvey, 18
Itinerarium mentis in Deum, Bonaventure, 309

Jaeger, Werner, *Humanism and Theol.*, 157
Jaffa, Harry, *Thomism and Aristotelianism*, 185
Jarrett, Bede, *Social Theories*, 241
Johann, Robert, *Meaning of Love*, 123

John Duns Scotus:
    Duns Scotus: Phil. Writings, 310
    De Principio, 310
John Duns Scotus, Saint Maurice, 316
John Duns Scotus and the Principle, Effler, 313
John of St. Thomas:
    Material Logic, 59
    Outlines of Formal Logic, 46
Johnson, Brian, *Catholic Nurse*, 213
Johnston, Herbert:
    Business Ethics, 229
    Phil. of Educ., 256
Jolivet, Régis:
    God of Reason, 158
    Man and Metaph., 124
Joseph, Horace, *Labor Theory of Value*, 236
Jourdain, Alice, *Graven Images*, 184
Journet, Charles, *Meaning of Evil*, 124
Joyce, George:
    Christian Marriage, 220
    Principles of Logic, 46
    Principles of Nat. Theol., 158
Judgment of the Nations, Dawson, 239
Judgment on Birth Control, De Guchteneere, 219
Jünger, Friedrich, *Failure of Technology*, 217
Junkersfeld, Mary J., *Aristotelian-Thom. Concept of Chance*, 72
Justice, Vol. XXXVI, *ACPA*, 4
Justice, Pieper, 196
Justice for All, Masse, 217

Kahn, Herman, *On Thermonuclear War*, 241
Kane, Robert, *God or Chaos*, 158
Kane, William H.:
    Approach to Phil., 19
    Science in Synthesis, 72
Kane, William T., *Some Princ. of Educ.*, 257
Karl Marx and the Close of His System, Bohm-Bawerk, 235
Karl Marx's Capital, Lindsay, 236
Karl Marx's Interpretation of History, Bober, 235

Kautsky, Karl, *Ethics and Materialist Conception of History*, 236
Kavanaugh, James, *Manual of Social Ethics*, 186
Keane, Henry, *Primer of Moral Phil.*, 186
Keeler, Leo, *Prob. of Error*, 59
Kelly, Ellen, *Moral Handbook of Nursing*, 212
Kelly, Gerald, *Medico-Moral Problems*, 213
Kelly, Otis, *Marriage Morals and Medical Ethics*, 212
Kelly, William, *Educ. Psych.*, 257
Kelsen, Hans, ed., *What Is Justice?*, 208
Kelso, Louis, *Capitalist Manifesto*, 229
Kendzierski, Lottie, *Phil. of Being*, 140
Kennedy, Daniel, *St. Thomas and Medieval Phil.*, 299
Kenny, John, *Principles of Medical Ethics*, 213
Kevane, Eugene, *Augustine the Educator*, 257
Key to the Study of St. Thomas, Olgiati, 27
Keystones and Theories of Phil., Bruckmann, 10
Kierkegaard as Theologian, Dupré, 323
Kiley, W. Paul, *Human Possibilities*, 20
Killeen, Sylvester M., *Philosophy of Labor*, 232
Kingston, Frederick Temple, *French Existentialism*, 325
Klocker, Harry R., *Thom. and Mod. Thought*, 20
Klubertanz, George P.:
    Being and God, 125
    Chris. Wisdom, 22
    Discursive Power, 97
    Intro. to Phil. of Being, 125
    Phil. of Human Nature, 98
    St. Thomas on Analogy, 125
Knowableness of God, Schumacher, 165
Knowledge, Weigel and Madden, 66
Knowledge and Expression, Vol. XXIX, *ACPA*, 4

Knowledge and Object, Talbot, 64
Knox, Ronald A., *God and Atom*, 241
Kockelmans, Joseph A., *Phenomenology and Physical Science*, 73
Kocourek, Roman A., ed., *Intro. to Phil. of Nature*, 73
Kopp, Joseph, *Teilhard de Chardin*, 325
Koren, Henry J.:
    Intro. to Phil. of Animate Nature, 98
    Intro. to Phil. of Nature, 73
    Intro. to Science of Metaph., 126
    Readings in Phil. of Nature, 74
Kreilkamp, Karl, *Metaph. Foundations of Thom. Jurisprudence*, 208
Kreyche, Robert J.:
    First Philosophy, 126
    Logic for Undergrad., 47
Kwant, Remy C.:
    Encounter, 126
    Philosophy of Labor, 232

Labor Theory of Value, Joseph, 236
LaDrière, James C., *Directions in Contemporary Criticism*, 247
Laer, Pierre H. Van:
    Philosophico-Scientific Problems, 74
    Phil. of Science, 74
Langan, Thomas, *Meaning of Heidegger*, 326
Langmead Casserley, J., *Bent World*, 216
Language, Truth and Poetry, Hamm, 247
Larochelle, Stanislas A., *Handbook of Medical Ethics*, 213
Latin-Eng. Dictionary of St. Thomas, Deferrari, 5
Latin Treatises on Comets, Thomas Aquinas, 289
Lattey, Cuthbert, ed.:
    God, 158
    St. Thomas, 21
Lauer, Quentin, *Triumph of Subjectivity*, 326
Lavelle, Louis, *Evil and Suffering*, 326

Lawlor, Monica, *Personal Responsibility*, 186
Laws of Thought, Poland, 49
LeBuffe, Francis P., *American Phil. of Law*, 209
Lechner, Robert, *Aesthetic Experience*, 247
Leclercq, Jacques:
    Christ and Modern Conscience, 186
    Marriage and Family, 220
Leen, Edward, *What Is Educ.?*, 257
Leeuw, Gerardus Van der, *Sacred and Profane Beauty*, 247
Leff, Gordon, *Medieval Thought from Augustine to Ockham*, 276
Lehane, Joseph, *Morality of Eugenical Sterilization*, 214
Leibell, Jane F., ed., *Readings in Ethics*, 187
Leisure, the Basis of Culture, Pieper, 31
Lessons in Logic, Turner, 51
Lessons in Schol. Phil., Shallo, 34
LeTroquer, René, *What Is Man?*, 98
Letter of Saint Thomas Aquinas, "De occultis operationibus naturae," 291
"Letter of St. Thomas to Brother John: 'De modo studendi,' " White, 291
Letters, St. Augustine, 270
Letters from a Traveller, Teilhard de Chardin, 334
Lexicon of St. Thomas, Deferrari, 5
Liberal Arts, Conway and Ashley, 12
Liberty, Cox, 176
Life and Spirit of Thomas Aquinas, Petitot, 302
Life, Death, and the Law, St. John-Stevas, 215
Life of St. Thomas, Foster, 295
Life Together, Hope, 220
Life's Final Goal, Schuyler, 198
Lindsay, Alexander, *Karl Marx's Capital*, 236
Linehan, James A.:
    Harmony in Cath. Univ., 21
    Rational Nature of Man, 99
Lippmann, Walter, *Good Society*, 217
Little, Arthur:
    Nature of Art, 248

Little, Arthur (*cont.*):
    Phil. Without Tears, 21
    Platonic Heritage of Thom., 300
    Logic, Clarke, 42
    Logic, Crumley, 43
    Logic, Dougherty, 43
    Logic, Oesterle, 49
    Logic, Walsh, 52
Logic and Epist., Cotter, 43
Logic for All, Bodkin, 41
Logic for Undergrad., Kreyche, 47
Logic of Analogy, McInerny, 47
Logic of Ockham, Moody, 315
Logic of Science, Smith, 64
Lonergan, Bernard J., *Insight*, 59
Lord, Daniel, *Armchair Phil.*, 21
Lord of History, Daniélou, 264
Love and Being, Diggs, 118
Lubac, Henri de:
    Discovery of God, 159
    Drama of Atheist Humanism, 159
Luijpen, William A., *Existential Phenomenology*, 127
Lunn, Arnold, *Science of World Revolution*, 237
Lure of Wisdom, Collins, 116
Lynch, William F., *Integrating Mind*, 21
Lyttkens, Hampus, *Analogy between God and World*, 127

McAllister, Joseph B., *Ethics*, 187
McCall, Raymond J., *Basic Logic*, 47
McCall, Robert E., *Reality of Substance*, 128
McCormick, John F.:
    Being, 128
    Natural Theol., 159
    St. Thomas, 22
McCoy, Charles N., *Structure of Political Thought*, 223
McDonald, William J., *Social Value of Property*, 229
McDougall, Eleanor, *St. Augustine*, 277
McFadden, Charles:
    Medical Ethics, 214
    Philosophy of Communism, 237
McGannon, J. Barry, *Chris. Wisdom*, 22
McGillivray, George J., ed., *Moral Principles and Practice*, 187

McGlynn, James V., *Modern Ethical Theories*, 188
McGovern, William, *From Luther to Hitler*, 223
McGucken, William, *Cath. Way in Educ.*, 258
McInerny, Ralph, *Logic of Analogy*, 47
McKenny, Charles, *Moral Problems in Social Work*, 217
McKeough, Michael J., *Meaning of "Rationes Seminales,"* 277
McKinnon, Harold, *Higher Law*, 209
McLaughlin, Joseph A., *Outline and Manual of Logic*, 47
McLean, Donald:
  Dynamic World Order, 241
  Morality of Strike, 233
McLean, George F., ed.:
  Phil. and Integration of Cont. Cath. Educ., 258
  Phil. in a Technological Culture, 188
  Teaching Thom. Today, 22
McMahon, George J., *Order of Procedure in Phil. of Nature*, 75
McMorrow, George J.:
  Metaph. Study on Individual and Person, 128
  Preface to Cath. Phil., 23
McMullin, Ernan, ed., *Concept of Matter*, 75
MacMurray, John, *Philosophy of Communism*, 237
McNabb, Vincent J., *Cath. Church and Phil.*, 23
MacPartland, John, *March toward Matter*, 99
McWilliams, James A.:
  Cosmology, 75
  Phil. for Millions, 23
  Physics and Philosophy, 289
  Progress in Phil., 23
Madden, Arthur G.:
  Knowledge, 66
  Religion and Knowledge of God, 170
Magner, James, *Art of Happy Marriage*, 220
Maher, Michael, *Psychology*, 99
Mahony, Michael J., *Essentials in Formal Logic*, 48

Main Problems of Phil., Robles, 32
Mainage, Theodore, *Immortality*, 100
Major Logic, Varvello, 65
Makers of the Modern Mind, Neill, 27
Man Against Mass Society, Marcel, 328
Man and His Nature, Royce, 106
Man and Metaph., Jolivet, 124
Man and Morals, Bittle, 173
Man and Morals, Hawkins, 183
Man and Society, Haas, 217
Man and the State, Maritain, 223
Man as Man, Higgins, 183
Man from Rocca Sicca, Coffey, 294
Man the Lonely, Straelen, 333
Manner of Demonstrating, Glutz, 71
Man's Approach to God, Maritain, 160
Man's Know. of Reality, Wilhelmsen, 66
Man's Last End, Buckley, 175
Man's Physical and Spiritual Nature, Collingwood, 90
Man's Thirst for Good, Sullivan, 201
Manual of Modern Schol. Phil., Mercier, 25
Manual of Neo-Schol. Phil., Baschab, 9
Manual of Phil., Munier, 26
Manual of Social Ethics, Kavanaugh, 186
Marcel, Gabriel:
  Being and Having, 327
  Creative Fidelity, 327
  Decline of Wisdom, 327
  Existential Background of Human Dignity, 327
  Homo Viator, 328
  Man Against Mass Society, 328
  Metaphysical Journal, 329
  Mystery of Being, 328
  Phil. of Existentialism, 329
March toward Matter, MacPartland, 99
Marcuse, Herbert, *Reason and Revolution*, 237
Margenau, Henry, *Thomas and Physics 1958*, 76
Marique, Pierre, *Phil. of Chris. Educ.*, 258

Maritain, Jacques:
Approaches to God, 160
Art and Poetry, 248
Art and Scholasticism, 248
Creative Intuition, 249
Degrees of Know., 60
Educ. at Crossroads, 259
Essay on Chris. Phil., 24
Existence and the Existent, 129
Formal Logic, 48
Freedom in Modern World, 129
Freedom of the Intel., 24
Frontiers of Poetry, 248
Intro. to Phil., 24
Man and State, 223
Man's Approach to God, 160
Moral Philosophy, 188
On Phil. of History, 264
On Use of Phil., 25
Person and Common Good, 189
Phil. of Nature, 76
Preface to Metaph., 130
Range of Reason, 60
Responsibility of Artist, 249
Rights of Man, 189
St. Thomas Aquinas, 300
St. Thomas and Prob. of Evil, 130
Scholasticism and Politics, 223
Science and Wisdom, 25
Sin of the Angel, 130
Social and Political Writings of J.
Maritain, 224
Some Reflections on Culture, 264
True Humanism, 189
Maritain, Jacques and Raissa, Situation of Poetry, 249
Markus, Robert A., Chris. Faith and Greek Phil., 9, 146
Marling, Joseph, Order of Nature, 131
Marriage, Hildebrand, 219
Marriage and Parenthood, Gerrard, 219
Marriage and Rhythm, Thomas, 220
Marriage and the Family, Clemens, 219
Marriage and the Family, Leclercq, 220
Marriage and the Family, Mihanovich, Schnepp, and Thomas, 220

Marriage and the Family, Schmiedeler, 220
Marriage and the Sex Problem, Foerster, 219
Marriage Guidance, Healy, 219
Marriage, Morals and Medical Ethics, Good and Kelly, 212
Marrou, Henri:
Meaning of History, 266
St. Augustine, 277
Marshall, John, Medicine and Morals, 214
Martin, William O.:
Metaph. and Ideology, 131
Order and Integ. of Know., 25
Martindale, Cyril C., Does God Matter?, 160
Marxism, Eastman, 235
Marxism, Hunt, 236
Mascall, Eric L.:
Existence and Analogy, 131
He Who Is, 160
Masse, Benjamin, Justice for All, 219
Material Logic, John of St. Thomas, 59
Materialist Conception of History, Federn, 236
Mauriac, François, Communism and Christians, 237
Maves, Paul B., Church and Mental Health, 214
Mayo, Henry B., Democracy and Marxism, 237
Maziarz, Edward A., Phil. of Math., 76
Mazzei, Alfred M., Does God Exist?, 161
Meaning of Evil, Journet, 124
Meaning of Existence, Pontifex and Trethowan, 135
Meaning of Heidegger, Langan, 326
Meaning of History, Marrou, 266
Meaning of Love, Johann, 123
Meaning of Man, Mouroux, 102
Meaning of Marxism, Cole, 235
Meaning of Persons, Tournier, 142
Meaning of the "Rationes Seminales" in St. Augustine, McKeough, 277
Meaningful Logic, Gianelli, 44
Mechanism and Vitalism, Schubert-Soldern, 107

Medical Ethics, Healy, 212
Medical Ethics, McFadden, 214
Medical Experimentation on Man,
  Flood, 212
Medicine and Morals, Marshall 214
Medico-Moral Problems, Kelly, 213
Medieval Philosophy, Copleston, 295
*Medieval Thought from Augustine
  to Ockham*, Leff, 276
Meehan, Francis X., *Efficient Causal-
  ity*, 132
Meer, Frederick Van Der, *Augustine*,
  277
Meeting of Love and Know., D'Arcy,
  116
Melania Grace, Sr., *Books for Cath.
  Colleges*, 6
Melsen, Andrew G. Van:
  From Atomos to Atom, 77
  Phil. of Nature, 77
  Science and Technology, 77
Menasce, Giovanni De, *Dynamics of
  Morality*, 190
Menges, Mathew C., *Concept of Uni-
  vocity: Ockham*, 315
Mercier, Désiré F.:
  Elements of Logic, 48
  Manual of Modern Schol. Phil., 25
  Origins of Cont. Psych., 100
  *Relation of Experimental Psych.
  to Phil.*, 100
Merrill, Harwood, *Responsibilities of
  Business Leadership*, 229
Messner, Johannes:
  Ethics and Facts, 190
  Social Ethics, 190
*Metaphysical and Psych. Principles
  of Love*, Faraon, 119
*Metaph. Foundations of Thom. Juris-
  prudence*, Krielkamp, 208
Metaph. Journal, Marcel, 329
*Metaph. Study on the Individual
  and the Person*, McMorrow, 128
Metaphysics, Peters, 135
Metaphysics, Varvello, 142
Metaph. and Historicity, Fackenheim,
  118
Metaph. and Ideology, Martin, 131
Metaph. and Man, Collins, 11
Metaph. and the Existence of God,
  O'Brien, 162
Metaph. as a Principle of Order,
  Horrigan, 123

Metaph. of Love, Wilhelmsen, 144
Metaph. of St. Thomas, Reith, 137
Metaph. of the School, Harper, 121
Method in Metaph., Henle, 122
Meyer, Hans, *Phil. of St. Thomas*,
  300
Michel, Virgil, *Christian Social Re-
  construction*, 218
Middle Ages and Phil., Pegis, 29
Mihalich, Joseph C., *Existentialism
  and Thom.*, 330
Mihanovich, Clement, *Marriage and
  Family*, 220
Milieu Divin, Teilhard de Chardin,
  334
Miller, Barry, *Range of Intellect*,
  101
Miller, Raymond, *Forty Years After*,
  233
Miltner, Charles C.:
  Elements of Ethics, 191
  Intro. to Metaph., 132
Mind, Pyne, 105
Mind and Heart of Love, D'Arcy,
  117
Minor Logic, Varvello, 52
Mirage and Truth, D'Arcy, 151
Miron, Cyril H., *Problem of Altru-
  ism*, 191
Mirror of Phil., Versfeld, 36
Misiak, Henry K.:
  Catholics in Psych., 101
  Phil. Roots of Scientific Psych., 101
Mitchell, Robert A., *Phil. of Human
  Know.*, 57
Modeling of Mind, Sayre and Cros-
  sen, 107
Modern Ethical Theories, McGlynn
  and Toner, 188
Modern God, Weigel, 169
Modern Intro. to Metaph., Drennen,
  118
*Modern Science and the Truths Be-
  yond*, Moreux, 26
Modern Thom. Philosophy, Phillips,
  30
Modern War and Basic Ethics, Ryan,
  242
Monahan, William B., *Psych. of St.
  Thomas*, 101
Monan, James, *Phil. of Human
  Knowledge*, 57
Money and Morals, Gill, 228

Montgomery, W., *St. Augustine*, 278
Moody, Ernest A.:
  Logic of Ockham, 315
  Truth and Consequences in Medieval Logic, 48
Moore, Edward, *Case Against Birth Control*, 220
Moore, Thomas V.:
  Historical Intro. to Ethics, 191
  Principles of Ethics, 191
Moral Aspects of Sterilization, Ryan, 215
Moral Basis of Social Order, Dougherty, 179
Moral Handbook of Nursing, Hayes, Hayes, and Kelly, 212
Moral Phil., Maritain, 188
Moral Phil., Rickaby, 197
Moral Principles and Medical Practice, Coppens, 211
Moral Principles and Practice, McGillivray, 187
Moral Problems in Hospital Practice, Finney and O'Brien, 211
Moral Problems in Social Work, McKenny, 217
Moral Science, Ferroli, 181
Moral Universe, Sheen, 199
Moral Values and the Moral Life, Gilson, 182
Morality and Business, Wirtenberger, 230
Morality and Modern Warfare, Nagle, 242
Morality and War, Vann, 243
Morality in American Politics, Graham, 223
Morality of Eugenical Sterilization, Lehane, 214
Morality of Mercy Killing, Sullivan, 216
Morality of Organic Transplantation, Cunningham, 211
Morality of the Strike, McLean, 233
Morals and Independence, Coventry, 176
Morals and Man, Vann, 202
Morals and Marriage, Gilby, 221
Morals and Missiles, Thompson, 243
Morals in Medicine, O'Donnell, 215
Morals in Politics, Connell, 222
Moreux, Theophile, *Modern Science and Truths Beyond*, 26

Morris, Hilaire, *Phil. for Beginners*, 26
Morrison, Bakewell, *Think and Live*, 26
Morrison, Robert, *God Is Its Founder*, 220
Morriss, Frank, *Forgotten Revelation*, 162
Mounier, Emmanuel:
  Be Not Afraid, 330
  Character of Man, 330
  Existentialist Philosophies, 330
  Personalism, 331
  Personalist Manifesto, 331
  Spoil of the Violent, 331
Mourant, John A.:
  Formal Logic, 49
  Intro. to Phil. of Augustine, 271
Mouroux, Jean, *Meaning of Man*, 102
Mulcahy, Richard, *Economics of H. Pesch*, 229
Mullally, Joseph, *Phil. of Knowledge*, 58
Mullane, Donald T., *Aristotelianism in Thomas*, 301
Mullen, Mary D., *Essence and Operation*, 132
Munier, André, *Manual of Phil.*, 26
Munier, Joseph D., *Some Approximations to Pius X's* INDUSTRIES AND PROFESSIONS, 233
Murphy, Edward F., *St. Thomas' Political Doctrine*, 224
Murray, John C., *We Hold These Truths*, 224
Murray, Michael V.:
  Problems in Conduct, 192
  Problems in Ethics, 192
Murray, Thomas E., *Nuclear Policy for War and Peace*, 242
Must It Be Communism?, Osgniach, 218
Mystery of Being, Marcel, 328
Mystical Opuscula, St. Bonaventure, 309

Nagle, William J., *Morality and Modern Warfare*, 242
National Patriotism in Papal Teaching, Wright, 243
Nationalism and Internationalism, Sturzo, 243

Natural Desire for God, O'Connor, 194

Natural Law, Farrell, 180

Natural Law, Passerin d'Entrèves, 195

Natural Law, Rommen, 198

Natural Law and International Relations, Vol. XXIV, *ACPA,* 4

Natural Law and Modern Society, Cogley, 221

Natural Law and Natural Rights, Harding, 208

Natural Law Reader, Brown, 175

Natural Religion, Hettinger, 157

Natural Rights, Ritchie, 209

Natural Rights and History, Strauss, 209

Natural Species, Cotter, 91

Natural Theol., Anderson, 146

Natural Theol., Boedder, 148

Natural Theol., Donceel, 151

Natural Theol., McCormick, 159

Natural Theol., Smith, 167

Nature and Functions of Authority, Simon, 200

Nature and Grace, Thomas Aquinas, 286

Nature and Origins of Scientism, Wellmuth, 83

Nature and Unity of Metaph., Buckley, 114

Nature, Knowledge and God, Gerrity, 16

Nature of Art, Little, 248

Nature of Demonstrative Proof, Bennett, 40

Nature of Law, Davitt, 177

Nature of Man, Vol. XXV, *ACPA,* 4

Nature of Physical Know., Friedrich, 70

Nature of the Practical Intellect, Naus, 192

Naughton, James, *Pius XII on World Problems,* 233

Naus, John E., *Nature of Practical Intellect,* 192

Nédoncelle, Maurice, *Is There a Chris. Phil.?,* 27

Neill, Thomas:
Communism, 237
Makers of Modern Mind, 27
Religion and Culture, 161

Nell-Breuning, Oswald Von, *Re-organization of Social Economy,* 233

Neurosis in the Light of Rational Psych., Terruwe, 110

New Men for New Times, Avalos, 253

New Problems in Medical Ethics, Flood, 211

New Things and Old in St. Thomas, O'Neill, 284

Newer Ethical Problems in Medicine, Ficarra, 211

Newman, Jeremiah:
Foundations of Justice, 192
Studies in Political Morality, 225

Nicholl, Donald, *Recent Thought,* 27

No Absent God, D'Arcy, 151

No Longer Two, Handren, 219

Nogar, Raymond J.:
Science in Synthesis, 72
Wisdom of Evolution, 103

Noonan, John P.:
General and Special Ethics, 193
General Metaph., 133

Nordberg, Robert, *Phil. and Educ.,* 255

Notes on Epistemology, Cunningham, 56

Notion of Time and Place: Ockham, Shapiro, 316

Nuclear Physics In Peace and War, Hodgson, 240

Nuclear Policy for War and Peace, Murray, 242

Nuclear Weapons, Stein, 242

Nuttin, Joseph, *Psychoanalysis and Personality,* 103

Nys, Désiré, *Cosmology,* 78

O'Brien, John A., *Sex-Love-Marriage,* 220

O'Brien, Kevin J., *Proximate Aim of Educ.,* 259

O'Brien, Mary C.:
Antecedents of Being, 133
Christian Social Principles, 193

O'Brien, Patrick:
Emotions and Morals, 193
Moral Problems in Hospital Practice, 210

O'Brien, Thomas C., *Metaphysics and Existence of God,* 162

Ockham, Böhner, 311
Ockham, Tornay, 317
O'Connell, Robert J., *Intro. Metaph.*, 14
O'Connor, Daniel A., *Cath. Social Doctrine*, 194
O'Connor, William, *Concept of Human Soul*, 278
O'Connor, William R.:
  Eternal Quest, 194
  Natural Desire for God, 194
Odenwald, Robert, *Psychiatry and Cath.*, 216
O'Donnell, Clement M., *Psychology of Bonaventure and Thomas*, 315
O'Donnell, Thomas, *Morals in Medicine*, 215
Oesterle, John A.:
  Ethics, 194
  Logic, 49
Of God and His Creatures, Thomas Aquinas, 285
Of God and Man, D'Arcy, 13
O'Grady, Daniel C.:
  Cosmology, 78
  Intro. to Metaph., 132
O'Hanlon, J. P. E., *Hospital Ethics*, 212
O'Hara, Sr. Kevin, *Persons and Personality*, 111
O'Leary, Conrad, *Substantial Composition of Man: Bonaventure*, 103
Olgiati, Francesco, *Key to Study of Thomas*, 27
O'Mahony, James E.:
  Chris. Phil., 28
  Desire of God, 162
  Reform or Revolution, 28
O'Malley, Austin, *Ethics of Medical Homicide and Mutilation*, 215
O'Meara, John:
  Charter of Christendom, 278
  Young Augustine, 279
O'Meara, Thomas A., *Paul Tillich in Cath. Thought*, 332
On Being and Essence, Thomas Aquinas, 290
On Charity, Thomas Aquinas, 287
On Combining of the Elements, Thomas Aquinas, 291
On Man, Thomas Aquinas, 286

On Searching into God, Thomas Aquinas, 292
On Spiritual Creatures, Thomas Aquinas, 287
On the Movement of the Heart, Thomas Aquinas, 291
On the Phil. of History, Maritain, 265
On the Power of God, Thomas Aquinas, 287
On the Truth of the Catholic Faith, Thomas Aquinas, 285
On the Use of Phil., Maritain, 25
On the Virtues in General, Thomas Aquinas, 287
On Thermonuclear War, Kahn, 241
One God, Garrigou-Lagrange, 153
O'Neil, Charles J.:
  Etienne Gilson Tribute, 28
  Imprudence, 195
O'Neill, H., *New Things and Old in St. Thomas*, 284
O'Neill, John, *Cosmology*, 78
O'Neill, Reginald:
  Readings in Epist., 61
  Theories of Knowledge, 61
Ong, Walter J., *Darwin's Vision and Chris. Perspectives*, 104
Ontology, Coffey, 115
Ontology, Glenn, 120
Ontology, Steenberghen, 141
O'Rahilly, A., *Notes on St. Thomas on Credit*, 290
Order and Integ. of Know., Martin, 25
Order and Law, Doolan, 179
Order of Nature, Marling, 131
Order of Procedure in the Phil. of Nature, McMahon, 75
Origin of Russian Communism, Berdyaev, 234
Origin of the Soul, Geiger, 275
Origins of Chris. Phil., Tresmontant, 168
Origins of Contemp. Psych., Mercier, 100
Origins of Man, Corte, 91
Osgniach, Augustine J.:
  Analysis of Objects, 133
  Must It Be Communism?, 218
Outline and Manual of Logic, McLaughlin, 47

Outline of Ethics, Donahue, 179
Outlines of Formal Logic, John of
    St. Thomas, 46
Owens, Joseph:
    Doctrine of Being, 133
    Elementary Chris. Metaph., 134
    *St. Thomas and Future of Meta-
    ph.*, 134

Pain of This World, D'Arcy, 151
Painting and Reality, Gilson, 246
*Papal Pronouncements on the Politi-
    cal Order*, Powers, 225
Papini, Giovanni, *St. Augustine*, 279
Passerin d'Entrèves, Allessandro:
    *Aquinas: Selected Political Writ-
    ings*, 225
    Natural Law, 195
Patterson, Robert, *Conception of
    God*, 162
Paul Tillich in Cath. Thought,
    O'Meara and Weisser, 332
Pegis, Anton:
    Basic Writings of St. Thomas, 284
    Chris. Phil. and Intel. Freedom, 28
    Essays in Modern Schol., 29
    Gilson Reader, 29
    Intro. to St. Thomas, 284
    Middle Ages and Phil., 29
    Origins of Thom. Notion of Man,
    104
    St. Thomas and Greeks, 301
    St. Thomas and Phil., 301
    St. Thomas and Problem of Soul,
    104
Pegues, Thomas, *Catechism of Sum-
    ma*, 302
Peifer, John, *Concept in Thomism*,
    105
Perennial Order, Versfeld, 36
Perrier, Joseph, *Revival of Schol.
    Phil.*, 30
Person and the Common Good, Ma-
    ritain, 189
Personal Responsibility, Lawlor, 186
Personalism, Mounier, 331
Personalist Manifesto, Mounier, 331
Persons and Personality, Walters,
    111
Peters, J., *Present Situation of Phil.*,
    30
Peters, John, *Metaphysics*, 135

Peterson, Gilbert, *Books for Cath.
    Colleges*, 6
Petitot, Henri, *Life and Spirit of St.
    Thomas*, 302
Phantasm, Coady, 90
Phelan, Gerald B.:
    St. Thomas and Analogy, 135
    *Some Illustrations of Thomas' De-
    velopment of Wisdom of Au-
    gustine*, 302
Wisdom of Anselm, 163
Phenomenology and Physical Science,
    Kockelmans, 73
*Phenomenology of the Human Sci-
    ences*, Strasser, 109
Phenomenon of Man, Teilhard de
    Chardin, 334
Phillips, Richard, *Modern Thom.
    Phil.*, 30
*Philosophical Basis for Individual
    Differences*, Slavin, 108
Phil. Nature of Physical Bodies, Hoe-
    nen, 72
Phil. Physics, Smith, 81
Phil. Psych., Anable, 85
Phil. Psych., Donceel, 92
Phil. Roots of Scientific Psych., Mis-
    iak, 101
Phil. Studies, Ryan, 33
Philosophico-Scientific Problems,
    Laer, 74
Philosophy, Bochenski, 9
Philosophy and Civilization, Wulf,
    306
Phil. and Educ., Dupuis and Nord-
    berg, 255
Phil. and Educ., Hovre, 256
Phil. and Finality, Vol. XXIII, *ACPA*,
    4
Phil. and Linguistic Analysis, Char-
    lesworth, 54
Phil. and Order, Vol. XVII, *ACPA*, 4
Phil. and Psychiatry, Vol. XXXV,
    ACPA, 4
Phil. and Reconstruction, Vol. XIX,
    ACPA, 4
Phil. and the Arts, Vol. XXXIX,
    ACPA, 4
Phil. and the Experimental Sciences,
    Vol. XXVI, *ACPA*, 4
*Phil. and the Integration of Cont.
    Cath. Educ.*, McLean, 258

Phil. and the Modern Mind, Canfield, 11
Phil. and the SUMMA, Wheeler, 305
Phil. and Theol., Gilson, 17
Phil. and Unity, Vol. XXVII, *ACPA*, 4
Phil. for Beginners, Morris, 26
Phil. for the Layman, Doolan, 13
Phil. for the Millions, McWilliams, 23
Phil. Frontiers of Physics, Smith, 80
Phil. in a Pluralistic Society, Vol. XXXVII, *ACPA*, 4
Phil. in a Technological Culture, McLean, 188
Phil. in the Making, Bremond, 10
Phil. of Being, Vol. XXI, *ACPA*, 4
Phil. of Being, Raeymaeker, 136
Phil. of Being, Renard, 137
Phil. of Being, Smith, 140
Phil. of Biology, Smith, 108
Phil. of Bonaventure, Gilson, 313
Phil. of Christ. Educ., Marique, 258
Phil. of Communism, McFadden, 237
Phil. of Communism, MacMurray, 237
Phil. of Decadentism, Bobbio, 321
Phil. of Democracy, Vol. XX, *ACPA*, 4
Phil. of Democratic Government, Simon, 226
Phil. of Education, Vol. XIII, *ACPA*, 4
Phil. of Educ., Fitzpatrick, 255
Phil. of Educ., Johnston, 256
Phil. of Educ., Shields, 260
Phil. of Educ., Ward, 261
Phil. of Evil, Siwek, 140
Phil. of Existentialism, Marcel, 329
Phil. of Form, Watkin, 144
Phil. of G. Marcel, Gallagher, 324
Phil. of God, Gornall, 155
Phil. of God, Renard, 164
Phil. of Human Know., Hassett, Mitchell, and Monan, 57
Phil. of Human Nature, Klubertanz, 98
Phil. of Inorganic Compounds, Hoenen, 72
Phil. of Knowledge, Gallagher, 56
Phil. of Know., Houde and Mullally, 58

Phil. of Labor, Killeen, 232
Phil. of Labor, Kwant, 232
Phil. of Labor, Tannenbaum, 234
Phil. of Man, Renard, 105
Phil. of Math., Maziarz, 76
Phil. of Morality, Renard, 197
Phil. of Nature, Collingwood, 68
Phil. of Nature, Maritain, 76
Phil. of Nature, Melsen, 77
Phil. of Physics, Smith, 81
Phil. of Poetry, Duffy, 246
Phil. of Religion, Vol. X, *ACPA*, 4
Phil. of Religion, Sheen, 166
Phil. of St. Thomas, Meyer, 300
Phil. of Science, Laer, 74
Phil. of Science, Sheen, 79
Phil. of Science, Smith, 81
Phil. of Society, Vol. IX, *ACPA*, 4
Phil. of the Sciences, Vol. XI, *ACPA*, 4
Phil. of the State, Vol. XV, *ACPA*, 4
Phil. of the State as Educator, Dubay, 255
Phil. of Value, Ward, 143
Phil. of Work, Borne and Henry, 230
Phil. without Tears, Little, 21
Phoenix and Turtle, Gilby, 57
Physics and Philosophy, McWilliams, 289
Pieper, Josef:
  Belief and Faith, 163
  End of Time, 266
  Fortitude and Temperance, 195
  Guide to Thomas, 302
  Happiness and Contemplation, 196
  Human Wisdom of Thomas, 302
  Justice, 196
  Leisure, 31
  Prudence, 196
  Scholasticism, 303
  Silence of Thomas, 303
Pius XII on World Problems, Naughton, 233
Pivotal Prob. Educ., Cunningham, 254
Plamenatz, John, *What Is Communism?*, 237
Planetary Man, Desan, 323
Plater, Charles, *Primer of Peace and War*, 242
Platonic Heritage of Thomism, Little, 300

Plotinus and the Ethics of Augustine, Switalski, 280
Pocket Aquinas, 280
Poetic Experience, Gilby, 246
Poets and Mystics, Watkin, 250
Poland, William:
    Fundamental Ethics, 197
    Laws of Thought, 49
Political and Social Ideas of Augustine, Deane, 274
Political Aspects of St. Augustine's CITY OF GOD, Figgis, 274
Political Ideas of St. Thomas, Bigongiari, 221
Political Phil., Vol. VII, *ACPA,* 4
Political Thought of Thomas, Gilby, 222
Pontifex, Mark:
    Existence of God, 163
    Freedom and Providence, 164
    Meaning of Existence, 135
Pope, Hugh, *Augustine,* 279
Pope Pius XII and Cath. Educ., Yzermans, 261
Pope's New Order, Hughes, 232
Pope's Plan for Social Reconstruction, The, Bruehl, 231
Portalie, Eugene, *Guide to Thought of Augustine,* 279
Possony, Stefan, *A Century of Conflict,* 237
Power and Responsibility, Guardini, 182
Powers, Francis, *Papal Pronouncements on Political Order,* 225
Preface to Cath. Phil., McMorrow, 23
Preface to Happiness, Smith and Ryan, 200
Preface to Metaph., Maritain, 130
Prentice, Robert, *Psych. of Love: Bonaventure,* 315
Present-day Thinkers, Zybura, 37
Present Situation of Phil., Peters, 30
Primacy of Metaph., Casey, 115
Primer of Moral Phil., Keane, 186
Primer of Peace and War, Plater, 242
Principles and Problems of Ethics, Wood, 204
Principles for Peace, 242
Principles of Education, Conway, 253
Principles of Ethics, Moore, 191
Principles of Logic, Joyce, 46

Principles of Medical Ethics, Kenny, 213
Principles of Nat. Theol., Joyce, 158
Principles of Nature, Thomas Aquinas, 291
Principles of Psych., Harmon, 96
Problem of Altruism, Miron, 191
Problem of Charity for Self, Deferrari, 178
Prob. of Error, Keeler, 59
Problem of Evil, Zimmermann, 205
Problem of Free Choice, St. Augustine, 270
Problem of Liberty, Vol. XVI, *ACPA,* 4
Problem of One or Plural Substantial Forms, Campbell, 89
Problems for Thomists, Adler, 85
Problems in Conduct, Murray, 192
Problems in Ethics, Murray, 192
Problems of Psychology, Gruender, 95
Professional Secrecy, Regan, 215
Profit Sharing, Thompson, 230
Profit Sharing Manual, Hartman, 228
Progress and Poverty, George, 228
Progress in Phil., McWilliams, 23
Progressive Schol., Bruni, 10
Prolegomena to Ethics, Brossnahan, 174
Prospect for Metaph., Ramsey, 137
Prospects of Phil., Rolbiecki, 32
Providence, Garrigou-Lagrange, 154
Providence and Predestination, Thomas Aquinas, 287
Proximate Aim of Educ., O'Brien, 259
Prudence, Pieper, 196
Przywara, Erich, *Augustine Synthesis,* 280
Psychiatry and Asceticism, Duffey, 211
Psychiatry and Cath., Van der Veldt and Odenwald, 216
Psychoanalysis and Personality, Nuttin, 103
Psychology, Gardeil, 94
Psychology, Glenn, 94
Psychology, Maher, 99
Psych. and Nat. Theol., Hill, 97
Psych. for All, Dempsey, 92
Psych. of Habit: Ockham, Fuchs, 313

Psych. of Love: Bonaventure, Prentice, 315
Psych. of St. Bonaventure and Thomas, O'Donnell, 315
Psych. of St. Thomas, Monahan, 101
Psych. of the Interior Senses, Gaffney, 93
Psych. Without a Soul, Gruender, 95
Pyne, John, *Mind*, 105

Quest of Certainty, Cass, 115
Quest of Reality, Walshe, 36
Quinn, Francis, *Ethics, Advertising and Responsibility*, 229

Rabbitte, Edwin, *Cosmology*, 79
Rabut, Olivier, *Teilhard de Chardin*, 332
Raeymaeker, Louis de:
Intro. to Phil., 31
Phil. of Being, 136
Truth and Freedom, 136
Ramsey, Ian, *Prospects for Metaphysics*, 137
Ramsey, Paul, *War and Christian Conscience*, 242
Range of Intellect, Miller, 101
Range of Reason, Maritain, 60
Rational Nature of Man, Linehan, 99
Raven, Charles, *Teilhard de Chardin*, 332
Readings in Epist., O'Neill, 61
Readings in Ethics, Leibell, 187
Readings in Logic, Houde, 46
Readings in Metaph., Rosenberg, 138
Readings in Nat. Theol., Baisnee, 147
Readings in the Phil. of Education, Carron and Cavanaugh, 253
Readings in the Phil. of Nature, Koren, 74
Realism and Nominalism, Veatch, 52
Realism and the Background of Phenomenology, Chisholm, 322
Realistic Phil., Reinhardt, 31
Reality, Garrigou-Lagrange, 15
Reality and Judgment, Hoenen, 58
Reality and the Mind, Bittle, 54
Reality of Substance, McCall, 128
Reason and Revelation, Gilson, 155
Reason and Revolution, Marcuse, 237
Rebuilding the Social Order, English and Wade, 232
Recent Thought, Nicholl, 27

Redden, John, *Cath. Phil. of Educ.*, 259
Redemption of Thinking, Steiner, 304
Reform or Revolution, O'Mahony, 28
Regan, Robert, *Professional Secrecy*, 215
Régis, Louis:
Epistemology, 62
St. Thomas and Epist., 62
Reinhardt, Kurt:
Existentialist Revolt, 332
Realistic Phil., 31
Reith, Herman, *Metaph. of St. Thomas*, 137
Relation Between the Theory of Matter and Know., Gerrity, 70
Relation of Experimental Psych. to Phil., Mercier, 100
Relation of the Individual to Society, Doherty, 178
Religion and Art, Weiss, 251
Religion and Culture, Neill, 161
Religion and the Know. of God, Weigel and Madden, 170
Religion Without God, Sheen, 166
Renard, Henri:
Phil. of Being, 137
Phil. of God, 164
Phil. of Man, 105
Phil. of Morality, 197
Renoirte, Fernand, *Cosmology*, 79
Reorganization of Social Economy, Nell-Breuning, 233
Responsibilities of Business Leadership, Merrill, 229
Responsibility of the Artist, Maritain, 249
Restoration of Property, Belloc, 227
Revival of Natural Law Concepts, Haines, 208
Revival of Schol. Phil., Perrier, 30
Revival of Thom., Doolan, 13
Reynolds, Sr. Mary Regis, *Cath. Bookman's Guide*, 6
Reys, Arthur, *God and His Attributes*, 164
Rickaby, John:
First Principles of Know., 62
General Metaph., 138
Rickaby, Joseph:
Four Square, 197

Rickaby, Joseph (*cont.*):
  Moral Phil., 197
  St. *Augustine's* CITY OF GOD, 280
  Scholasticism, 32
  Studies on God, 164
Riedl, John, *Exercises in Logic*, 50
Riet, Georges Van, *Thom. Epis.*, 63
Rieth, Herman, *Intro. to Phil. Psych.*,
  106
Right and Reason, Fagothey, 180
Rights of Man, Maritain, 189
Rintelen, J. Von, *Beyond Existential-
  ism*, 333
Ritchie, David, *Natural Rights*, 209
Roberts, David, *Existentialism and
  Religious Belief*, 333
Roberts, James, *Faith and Reason*,
  333
Robles, Oswaldi, *Main Problems of
  Phil.*, 32
Roensch, Frederick, *Early Thom.
  School*, 303
Rolbiecki, John, *Prospects of Phil.*,
  32
Role of Assent, Tyrrell, 65
*Role of Demonstration in Moral
  Theol.*, Wallace, 203
*Role of Phil. in the Cath. Liberal
  College*, Vol. XXX, ACPA, 4
Role of the Chris. Phil., Vol. XXXII,
  ACPA, 4
Role of the "sensus communis,"
  Ryan, 106
Rommen, Heinrich:
  Natural Law, 198
  State in Catholic Thought, 226
Rose, Mary, *Essays in Chris. Phil.*, 33
Rosenberg, Jean, *Readings in Meta-
  ph.*, 138
Ross, John:
  Christian Ethics, 198
  Cooperative Plenty, 230
Rother, Aloysius:
  Beauty, 250
  Being, 138
  Certitude, 63
  Truth and Error, 63
Rousselot, Pierre, *Intel. of St. Thom-
  as*, 63
Royce, James, *Man and His Nature*,
  106
Rueve, Stephen, *Think and Live*, 26

Ruffini, Ernesto, *Theory of Evolu-
  tion*, 106
Russell, John, *Science and Metaph.*,
  138
Ryan, Edmund, *Role of "sensus com-
  munis,"* 106
Ryan, Francis, *Cath. Phil. of Educ.*,
  259
Ryan, James, *Intro. to Phil.*, 33
Ryan, John A.:
  Better Economic Order, 234
  Cath. Principles of Politics, 226
  Distributive Justice, 234
  Moral Aspects of Sterilization, 215
Ryan, John K.:
  *Basic Principles and Problems of
  Phil.*, 33
  Modern War and Basic Ethics, 242
  Phil. Studies, 33
  *Studies in Phil. and History of
  Phil.*, 34
Ryan, Louis, *Preface to Happiness*,
  200

Sacred and Profane Beauty, Leeuw,
  247
St. Augustine, Adam, 271
St. Augustine, Bonner, 272
St. Augustine, D'Arcy, 274
St. Augustine, Garvey, 275
St. Augustine, Greenwood, 276
St. Augustine, McDougall, 277
St. Augustine, Montgomery, 278
St. Augustine, Papini, 279
St. Augustine, Pope, 279
St. Augustine, Vega, 281
St. Augustine and His Influence, Mar-
  rou, 277
St. Augustine on Personality, Henry,
  276
St. Augustine's CITY OF GOD, Rick-
  aby, 280
St. Augustine's Phil. of Beauty, Chap-
  man, 273
St. Bonaventure, Bettoni, 311
St. Bonaventure's DE REDUCTIONE,
  Healy, 314
St. John-Stevas, Norman, *Life, Death,
  and Law*, 215
Saint-Maurice, Béraud de, *John Duns
  Scotus*, 316
St. Thomas, Chesterton, 294

St. Thomas, Conway, 294
St. Thomas, D'Arcy, 295
St. Thomas, Lattey, 20
St. Thomas, McCormick, 22
St. Thomas, Maritain, 300
St. Thomas, Sertillanges, 304
St. Thomas, Vann, 305
St. Thomas, Walz, 305
St. Thomas and Analogy, Phelan, 135
St. Thomas and Epist., Regis, 62
St. Thomas and Phil., Pegis, 301
St. Thomas and Platonism, Henle, 299
St. Thomas and the Existence of God, Bryar, 149
St. Thomas and the Future of Metaph., Owens, 134
St. Thomas and the Gentiles, Adler, 293
St. Thomas and the Greek Moralists, Bourke, 174
St. Thomas and the Greeks, Pegis, 301
St. Thomas and the Problem of Evil, Maritain, 130
St. Thomas and the Problem of the Soul, Pegis, 104
St. Thomas and the World State, Hutchins, 241
St. Thomas Aquinas and Medieval Phil., Kennedy, 299
St. Thomas Aquinas and Phil., Gilson and Pegis, 297
St. Thomas Aquinas on Aristotle's LOVE AND FRIENDSHIP, Thomas Aquinas, 288
St. Thomas Aquinas ON KINGSHIP, Thomas Aquinas, 292
St. Thomas Aquinas: Philosophical Texts, Gilby, 285
St. Thomas Aquinas: Theological Texts, Gilby, 285
St. Thomas on Analogy, Klubertanz, 125
St. Thomas on the Object of Geometry, Smith, 81
St. Thomas' Political Doctrine, Murphy, 224
Salmon, Elizabeth, *Good in Existential Metaph.*, 139
Sayre, Kenneth, *Modeling of Mind*, 107
Scharlemann, Robert, *Thomas and John Gerhard*, 304

Scheu, Sr. Marina, *Categories of Being*, 139
Schmiedeler, Edgar:
Marriage and Family, 220
Sterilization in the United States, 215
Schnepp, Bro. Gerald, *Marriage and Family*, 220
Scholastic Bibliog. in Japan, Inagaki, 6
Schol. Synthesis, Easby-Smith, 14
Scholasticism, Pieper, 303
Scholasticism, Rickaby, 32
Scholasticism, Staunton, 34
Scholasticism and Politics, Maritain, 223
School Examined, Smith, 260
Schubert-Soldern, Rainer, *Mechanism and Vitalism*, 107
Schumacher, Magnus, *Knowableness of God*, 165
Schumpeter, Joseph, *Capitalism, Socialism, and Democracy*, 238
Schuyler, Henry, *Life's Final Goal*, 198
Schwarz, Balduin, *Human Person and World of Values*, 199
Science and Metaph., Russell, 138
Science and Technology, Melsen, 77
Science and Wisdom, Maritain, 25
Science in Synthesis, Kane, Corcoran, Ashley, and Nogar, 72
Science of Correct Thinking, Bittle, 41
Science of Ethics, Cronin, 176
Science of Logic, Coffey, 42
Science of Metaph., Harding, 121
Science of World Revolution, Lunn, 237
Science, Religion and Chris., Balthasar, 147
Science Versus Phil., Connolly, 12
Scientific Art of Logic, Simmons, 50
Scientific Humanism and Chris. Thought, Dubarle, 13
Scientific Methodology: Theodoric, Wallace, 82
Scott, James, *Cath. Conception of International Law*, 242
Scrutiny of Marxism, Cameron, 235
Search for God, Gleason, 155
Search for Values, Coleburt, 116

Self-determination, Zavalloni, 111

Selsam, Howard, *Socialism and Ethics,* 238

Sense of History, D'Arcy, 264

Sertillanges, Antonin:
Foundations of Thom. Phil., 304
St. Thomas, 304

Servile State, Belloc, 227

Sex-Love-Marriage, O'Brien, 220

Shallo, M., *Lessons in Schol. Phil.,* 34

Shapiro, Herman, *Notion of Time and Place: Ockham,* 316

Sharp, Dorothy, *Franciscan Phil.,* 316

Sharpe, Alfred:
Evil, 165
Freedom of Will, 108

Shaw, George, *Essays in Fabian Socialism,* 238

Sheed, Francis, *Society and Sanity,* 199

Sheed, Frank, *Communism and Man,* 238

Sheen, Fulton:
Communism and Conscience of the West, 238
God and Intelligence, 165
Moral Universe, 199
Phil. of Religion, 166
Phil. of Science, 79
Religion Without God, 166

Shields, Thomas, *Phil. of Educ.,* 260

Shircel, Cyril, *Univocity of Being: Scotus,* 316

Short History of Western Phil. in the Middle Ages, Curtis, 295

Significance of Beauty in Nature and Art, Cory, 245

Silence of St. Thomas, Pieper, 303

Sillem, Edward, *Ways of Thinking About God,* 166

Simmons, Edward, *Scientific Art of Logic,* 50

Simon, Yves:
General Theory of Authority, 200
Nature and Functions of Authority, 200
Phil. of Democratic Government, 226

Sin of the Angel, Maritain, 130

Situation of Poetry, Maritain, 249

Siwek, Paul, *Phil. of Evil,* 140

Six Existentialist Thinkers, Blackham, 321

Sketch of Medieval Phil., Hawkins, 299

Slavin, Robert, *Phil. Basis for Individual Differences,* 108

Sleeping Beauty, Harper, 325

Smith, Elwood, *Preface to Happiness,* 200

Smith, Sr. Enid, *Goodness of Being,* 140

Smith, Gerard:
Natural Theology, 167
Phil. of Being, 140
Truth that Frees, 141

Smith, Vincent:
Elements of Logic, 50
Footnotes for Atom, 80
General Science of Nature, 80
Idea Men of Today, 34
Logic of Science, 64
Philosophical Frontiers of Physics, 80
Phil. Physics, 81
Philosophy of Biology, 108
Phil. of Physics, 81
Phil. of Science, 81
St. Thomas on Object of Geometry, 81
School Examined, 260

Smith, William:
Spotlight on Labor Unions, 234
Spotlight on Social Order, 234

Smythe, Donald, *Focus,* 7

Social and Political Writings of Maritain, Maritain, 224

Social Ethics, Messner, 190

Social Justice, Drummond, 180

Social Principles and Economic Life, Cronin, 231

Social Theories of the Middle Ages, Jarrett, 241

Social Thought of John XXIII, Calvez, 216

Social Value of Property, McDonald, 229

Socialism, Sweezy, 238

Socialism, Von Mises, 238

Socialism and Ethics, Selsam, 238

Society and Sanity, Sheed, 199
Some Approximations to Pius X's "Industries and Professions," Munier, 233
Some Illustrations of Thomas' Development of the Wisdom of Augustine, Phelan, 302
Some Philosophers on Educ., Gallagher, 256
Some Principles of Educ., Kane, 257
Some Reflections on Culture and Liberty, Maritain, 265
Somerville, John, Soviet Philosophy, 238
Sorokin, Pitirim, Crisis of Our Age, 218
Soul, Thomas Aquinas, 286
Soul in Metaph. and Empirical Psych., Strasser, 109
Soviet Phil., Somerville, 238
Soviet Union, Gurian, 236
Space and Spirit, Whittaker, 170
Spargo, Emma, Category of Aesthetic: Bonaventure, 317
Special Ethics, Sullivan, 201
Speculative Phil., Collins, 12
Spirit of Medieval Phil., Gilson, 297
Spirit of Thomism, Gilson, 299
Spiritual Doctrine of St. Augustine, Barrachina, 271
Spoil of the Violent, Mounier, 331
Spotlight on Labor Unions, Smith, 234
Spotlight on Social Order, Smith, 234
Springs of Morality, Todd, 202
Staab, Giles, Dignity of Man, 108
State in Catholic Thought, Rommen, 226
Status of Man, Van Eyken, 111
Staunton, John, Scholasticism, 34
Steenberghen, Fernand Van:
Epistemology, 64
Ontology, 141
Stein, Walter, Nuclear Weapons, 242
Steiner, Rudolf, Redemption of Thinking, 304
Sterilization in the United States, Schmiedeler, 215
Story of Political Phil., Catlin, 221
Strachey, John, Theory and Practice of Socialism, 238

Straelen, Henricus Van, Man the Lonely, 333
Strasser, Stephen:
Phen. of Human Sciences, 109
Soul in Metaph. and Empirical Psych., 109
Stratmann, Franziskus:
Church and War, 242
War and Christianity Today, 242
Strauss, Leo, Natural Rights and History, 209
Structure of Political Thought, McCoy, 223
Studies in Phil. and the History of Phil., Ryan, 34
Studies in Political Morality, Newman, 225
Studies on God, Rickaby, 164
Studt, Virginia:
Catholics in Psych., 101
Phil. Roots of Scientific Psych., 101
Stufler, Johann, Why God Created, 167
Sturzo, Luigi, Nationalism and Internationalism, 243
Substantial Composition of Man: Bonaventure, O'Leary, 103
Sullivan, Daniel:
Fund. of Logic, 51
Intro. to Phil., 35
Sullivan, Sr. Helen, Intro. to Phil. of Natural and Math. Sciences, 81
Sullivan, James, Examination of First Principles, 141
Sullivan, John, Image of God, 109
Sullivan, Joseph F.:
General Ethics, 200
Special Ethics, 201
Sullivan, Joseph V., Morality of Mercy Killing, 216
Sullivan, Robert, Man's Thirst for Good, 201
Summa Contra Gentiles, Thomas Aquinas, 285
Summa Theologiae, Thomas Aquinas, 285, 286
Summary of Schol. Principles, Wuellner, 7
Sweezy, Paul, Socialism, 238
Switalski, Bruno, Plotinus and Ethics of Augustine, 280

Symposium on Evolution, Boelen, 87
System of Thomas, Wulf, 307

Talbot, Edward, *Know. and Object,* 64
Talk Sense, Gryst, 18
Philosophy of Labor, Tannenbaum, 234
Teacher-The Mind, The, Thomas Aquinas, 287
Teaching and Morality, Wade, 260
Teaching Thom. Today, McLean, 22
Teilhard de Chardin, Pierre:
  Future of Man, 334
  Letters from a Traveller, 334
  Milieu Divin, 334
  Phenomenon of Man, 334
Teilhard de Chardin, Kopp, 325
Teilhard de Chardin, Rabut, 332
Teilhard de Chardin, Raven, 332
Terruwe, Anna, *Neurosis in Light of Rational Psych.,* 110
Textbook of Dialectical Materialism, Guest, 236
Textbook of Logic, Hartmann, 45
Theodicy, Glenn, 155
Theol. of Wisdom, Conley, 150
Theories of Know., O'Neill, 61
Theories of Know., Walker, 65
Theory and Practice of Communism, Hunt, 236
Theory and Practice of Socialism, Strachey, 238
Theory of Demonstration: Ockham, Weberling, 318
Theory of Esthetics, Callahan, 245
Theory of Evil, De Coursey, 117
Theory of Evolution, Ruffini, 106
Theory of Know.: Bonaventure, Dady, 312
Theory of Natural Appetency, Gustafson, 96
Thibon, Gustave, *What God Has Joined Together,* 220
Think and Live, Morrison and Rueve, 26
This Creature, Man, Barrett, 86
This Nation Under God, Costanzo, 253
This Way Happiness, Bruehl, 175
Thomas and the Physics of 1958, Margenau, 76

Thomas Aquinas, works in English, see 284-292
Thomas Aquinas, Grabmann, 298
Thomas Aquinas and John Gerhard, Scharlemann, 304
Thomas Aquinas: Selected Writings, D'Arcy, 285
Thomas, John:
  Marriage and Family, 220
  Marriage and Rhythm, 220
Thomism and Aristotelianism, Jaffa, 185
Thomism and Mod. Thought, Klocker, 20
Thomistic Bibliog., Bourke, 5
Thom. Concept of Mental Faculty, Hart, 97
Thom. Doctrine of the Possible Intel., Franz, 93
Thom. Epistemology, Riet, 63
Thom. Metaph., Hart, 121
Thom. Phil., Grenier, 18
Thom. Psych., Brennan, 87
Thomistic Texts: First Lectures of All Expositions, Conway, 287
Thomistic Theory of the Passions, Baker, 86
Thompson, Charles, *Morals and Missiles,* 243
Thompson, Kenneth, *Profit Sharing,* 230
Three Philosophers, Anscombe and Geach, 293
Time and Idea, Caponigri, 263
Todd, John, *Springs of Morality,* 202
Tolley, William, *Idea of God in Phil. of Augustine,* 281
Toner, Jerome, *Closed Shop,* 234
Toner, Jules, *Modern Ethical Theories,* 188
Toohey, John, *Elementary Handbook of Logic,* 51
Tornay, Stephen, *Ockham,* 317
Tour of the SUMMA, Glenn, 297
Tournier, Paul, *Meaning of Persons,* 142
Toward Know. of God, Tresmontant, 168
Toward the Understanding of Karl Marx, Hook, 236
TRACTATUS DE PRAEDESTINATIONE ET DE PRAESCIENTIA, Böhner, 312

Tragic Finale, Desan, 323
Transcendentals: Scotus, Wolter, 318
Treatise on God, Thomas Aquinas, 286
Treatise on Happiness, Thomas Aquinas, 286
Treatise on Law, Thomas Aquinas, 286
Treatise on Man, Thomas Aquinas, 286
Treatise on Separate Substances, Thomas Aquinas, 292
Trehey, Harold, *Foundations of Modern Guild System*, 234
Tresmontant, Claude:
  Origins of Chris. Phil., 168
  Toward Know. of God, 168
Trethowan, Illtyd:
  Basis of Belief, 168
  Certainty, Phil. and Theol., 169
  Essay in Chris. Phil., 35
  Meaning of Existence, 135
Trinity, Augustine, 270
Trinity and God the Creator, Garrigou-Lagrange, 154
Trinity and The Unicity of the Intellect, Thomas Aquinas, 292
Triple Way, Bonaventure, 309
Triumph of Subjectivity, Lauer, 326
Troisfontaines, Roger, *Existentialism and Chris. Thought*, 335
True Humanism, Maritain, 189
True Morality, Hildebrand, 185
Truth, Thomas Aquinas, 287
Truth and Consequences in Medieval Logic, Moody, 48
Truth and Error, Rother, 63
Truth and Falsity, Thomas Aquinas, 286
Truth and Freedom, Raymaeker, 136
Truth in the Contemporary Crisis, Vol. XVIII, *ACPA*, 4
Truth that Frees, Smith, 141
Turner, William, *Lessons in Logic*, 51
Tyrrell, Francis M., *Role of Assent*, 65

Unity of Phil. Experience, Gilson, 17
Unity through Love, Guitton, 156
Univocity of the Concept of Being: Scotus, Shircel, 316

Values and Reality, Ward, 143
Van der Veldt, James, *Psychiatry and Cath.*, 116
Van Eyken, Albert, *Status of Man*, 111
Vann, Gerald:
  Awake in Heaven, 111
  Heart of Man, 202
  Morality and War, 243
  Morals and Man, 202
  St. Thomas, 305
Varvello, Francesco:
  Major Logic, 65
  Metaphysics, 142
  Minor Logic, 52
Vaske, Martin, *Intro. to Metaph.*, 142
Veatch, Henry, *Realism and Nominalism*, 52
Vega, Angel, *St. Augustine*, 281
Versfeld, Martin:
  Guide to THE CITY OF GOD, 281
  Mirror of Phil., 36
  Perennial Order, 36
Vier, Peter, *Evidence and Its Function: Scotus*, 317
Vio, Tommaso (Cajetan) de, *Analogy of Names*, 143
Von Mises, Ludwig, *Socialism*, 238

Wade, Francis, *Teaching and Morality*, 260
Wade, William, *Rebuilding Social Order*, 232
Walker, Leslie, *Theories of Knowledge*, 65
Wallace, William:
  Role of Demonstration in Moral Theol., 203
  Scientific Methodology: Theodoric, 82
Walsh, Joseph, *Logic*, 52
Walshe, Thomas, *Quest of Reality*, 36
Walters, Sr. Annette, *Persons and Personality*, 111
Walz, Angelus, *St. Thomas*, 305
War and Christianity Today, Stratmann, 242
War and the Christian Conscience, Ramsey, 242
Warbasse, James, *Cooperative Democracy*, 230

Ward, Leo:
  Chris. Ethics, 203
  Ethics and Social Sciences, 227
  God and World Order, 169
  Phil. of Educ., 261
  Phil. of Value, 143
  Values and Reality, 143
Watkin, Edward:
  Phil. of Form, 144
  Poets and Mystics, 250
Ways of Thinking About God, Sillem, 166
We Hold These Truths, Murray, 224
Webering, Damascene, Theory of Demonstration: Ockham, 318
Weigel, Gustave:
  Knowledge, 66
  Modern God, 169
  Religion and the Knowledge of God, 170
Weisheipl, James:
  Development of Physical Theory, 82
  Dignity of Science, 83
Weiss, Paul, Religion and Art, 251
Weisser, Celestin, Paul Tillich in Cath. Thought, 332
Wellmuth, John, Nature and Origins of Scientism, 83
Welty, Eberhard, Handbook of Chris. Social Ethics, 203
Wetter, Gustav, Dialectical Materialism, 238
What God Has Joined Together, Thibon, 220
What Is Communism?, Plamenatz, 237
What Is Corporative Organization?, Ares, 230
What Is Educ.?, Leen, 257
What Is Justice?, Kelsen, 208
What Is Life?, Biot, 86
What Is Man?, LeTroquer, 78
What Is Phil.?, Hildebrand, 19
What Man Has Made of Man, Adler, 85
What Modern Catholics Think About Birth Control, Birmingham, 218
What's Wrong With the World, Chesterton, 228

Wheeler, Mother Mary, Phil. and SUMMA, 305
White, Victor, God and Unconscious, 170
Whittaker, Edmund, Space and Spirit, 170
Whole Man, Bittle, 87
Why God Created the World, Stufler, 167
Wild, John, Challenge of Existentialism, 335
Wilhelmsen, Frederick:
  Man's Knowledge of Reality, 66
  Metaph. of Love, 144
Will in Western Thought, Bourke, 87
William of Ockham, Ockham: Phil. Writings, 310
Wilms, Jerome, Divine Friendship, 204
Wirtenberger, Henri, Morality and Business, 230
Wisdom and Love, Gilson, 120
Wisdom of Evolution, Nogar, 103
Wisdom of St. Anselm, Phelan, 163
Woelfel, Br. Lasalle, Business and Chris. Virtues, 230
Wolfe, John, Intro. to Study of Human Conduct, 261
Wolter, Allan:
  Duns Scotus, 318
  Transcendentals: Scotus, 318
Wood, Robert, Principles and Problems of Ethics, 204
Woods, Henry, First Book in Ethics, 204
Works of Aurelius Augustinus, Augustine, 270
World of Teilhard, Francoeur, 324
World to Reconstruct, Gonella, 240
Wright, John, National Patriotism in Papal Teaching, 243
Wu, John, Fountain of Justice, 204
Wuellner, Bernard:
  Chris. Phil. of Life, 36
  Dictionary of Schol. Phil., 7
  Summary of Schol. Principles, 7
Wulf, Maurice de:
  Art and Beauty, 251
  History of Medieval Phil., 306
  Intro. to Schol. Phil., 306
  System of Thomas, 307

Young Augustine, O'Meara, 279

Yzermans, Vincent, *Pope Pius XII and Cath. Educ.*, 261

Zavalloni, Roberto, *Self-determination*, 111

Zimmermann, Otto, *Problem of Evil*, 205

Zundel, Maurice, *In Search of Unknown God*, 170

Zybura, John, *Present-day Thinkers*, 37